T0338211

The Wellbeing of Nations

The Wellbeing of Nations

Meaning, Motive and Measurement

Paul Allin

and

David J. Hand

Department of Mathematics, Imperial College, London, UK

WILEY

Library of Congress Cataloging-in-Publication Data applied for

A catalogue record for this book is available from the British Library.

ISBN: 978-1-118-48957-4

Set in 10/12pt Times by Aptara Inc., New Delhi, India.
Printed and bound in Malaysia by Vivar Printing Sdn Bhd

1   2014

Contents

List of tables and figures

Tables

Figures

Preface

In searching for a title for this book we quickly settled on 'The Wellbeing of Nations' with more than a nod to Adam Smith's great work, 'The Wealth of Nations'. Would that our book becomes as well known and as long lasting as his! We do feel we are in the same territory, especially as some initiatives to measure national wellbeing and progress talk about the 'true wealth' of nations. It seems to us that looking at stocks and capitals – not just financial wealth but also human, social and natural capital – could in the longer run provide a substantial bedrock on which to build measures of national wellbeing, sustainable development and progress.

However, our much more modest aim in writing this book is to record the considerable interest around the world in measuring wellbeing and progress in ways that go beyond purely economic measures, and the headline measure of GDP in particular. Many initiatives and new measures are being produced at local, national and international levels. Many are well established. We do detect a build up of interest and, perhaps, some convergence of established approaches such as quality of life measures, sustainable development and human development indicators. However, rather than just documenting these initiatives – an almost impossible task given the range and dynamicism of this area – we set out to reflect on all of this and, in the words of our subtitle, to consider the meaning of national wellbeing and the motive for measuring it, as well as how to measure it.

In our exploration of wider measures of wellbeing and progress, we have benefited from talking to and listening to many people including Martine Durand, Marco Mira d'Ercole (with thanks for many helpful comments on a draft) and Tim Clode at OECD; Peter Harper, Deputy Australian Statistician; Marleen De Smedt at Eurostat; Charles Seaford and colleagues in the New Economics Foundation Centre for Well-being; Jil Matheson, Glenn Everett, Stephen Hicks and colleagues in the Office for National Statistics (ONS) Measuring National Wellbeing Programme; Paul Anand, Paul Dolan, David Halpern, Peter Helm, Daniel Kahneman, Lord Richard Layard, Ewen McKinnon, Lord Gus O'Donnell, Andrew Oswald, Don Sellwood and all members of the ONS's Technical Advisory Group; Danny Dorling at Oxford University; Jonathan Portes and Alex Bryson of the National Institute for Economic and Social Research; Ian Bache at Sheffield University and Karen Scott, Wellbeing and Resilience Champion at the Newcastle University Institute for Social Renewal.

Our assessment of the rise of environmental awareness in Chapter 2 draws on Dieter Roelstraete's description of the birth of Land and Environmental Art (2010, p. 39). Thanks to Lewis Evans for advice on progress from a philosophical point of view; Chris Farrell for insights into what technology and innovation do for quality of life; Chris Drew for observations on the strengths and weaknesses of the system of national accounts; Anthony S. Mann of the Committee on National Statistics for updates on US work on self-reported wellbeing; Tommaso Rondinella of Istat for updating us on 'Equitable and Sustainable Wellbeing' in Italy; Peter Goldblatt of the University College London Institute of Health Equity for keeping in touch on the Marmot Review work in this area; Jorunn Sem Fure for responding to our questions about Telemark Museums; Graham Eele and Rachael Beaven for their overview of the international statistical system, particularly with an international development focus, and for information about statistical capacity building; Neil Jackson of the UK Department for International Development for information about the expected international timetable and process for agreeing on what should replace the current set of Millennium Development Goals, when the deadline for those goals is reached in 2015; Alan Smith for opening our eyes to data visualisation and to Debbie Jupe, Richard Davies and their colleagues at Wiley for support, encouragement and advice. We thank our wives, Karen and Shelley, for looking after our wellbeing, tolerating our preoccupation with the book and helping us shape our understanding of this topic through their ideas and actions.

Paul Allin, Newport, United Kingdom
David J. Hand, London, United Kingdom

Reference

Roelstraete D. (2010). *Richard Long: A Line Made by Walking*, Afterall Books, London.

1

What is national wellbeing and why measure it?

> not all the calculators of the National Debt can tell me the capacity for good or evil, for love or hatred, for patriotism or discontent ... at any single moment in the soul of one of these its quiet servants.
>
> Charles Dickens, *Hard Times*

This book is about social progress: its definition and its measurement. In particular, it is concerned with the overall wellbeing or quality of life of the people in a nation at a point in time, how this has changed (i.e. 'progress') and whether it is sustainable. In exploring this topic, the book seeks to address three primary questions:

What is national wellbeing?
Why should national wellbeing be measured?
How should national wellbeing be measured?

Underlying those three primary questions lie others, including:

What is individual wellbeing?
What is wrong or inadequate with existing measures of progress?
How do we *measure* national wellbeing, rather than just describe the state of the nation when we measure specific aspects of wellbeing?
How do the current and future states of the environment, including stocks of natural resources, fit into our understanding of wellbeing?

All of these questions are interwoven. For example, the definition of wellbeing and its method of measurement are two sides of the same coin, and the meaning of *national* wellbeing depends both on what is meant by *individual* wellbeing and on how one *aggregates* individual

The Wellbeing of Nations: Meaning, Motive and Measurement, First Edition. Paul Allin and David J. Hand.
© 2014 John Wiley & Sons, Ltd. Published 2014 by John Wiley & Sons, Ltd.

values to produce a national value, as well as whether there are aspects of national wellbeing which are distinct from individual wellbeing, which should somehow be included as part of the definition.

Formally, perhaps we should take the opening three questions in the order given above: start by defining the concept, then give the motivation for measuring it and then describe how to measure it. That, however, would make for rather dry reading. It would rely on the forbearance of the reader, who would have to plough through the definition before getting to the reason for reading the book and then to how it was to be done. Better, we think, to begin with the motivation, so that the pressing need for the ideas and tools described in the book serve to drive the reader on. Once the motivation has been established – once we can see the need for such an exercise – then we can dig down into precisely what it means and how we might go about it.

For this reason, we begin in the next section with the motivation: what is wrong with current approaches, current tools and current strategies for gauging the state of society and whether it is advancing or regressing. We then move on to discuss the nature and aspects of individual wellbeing and how to measure the wellbeing of individuals, before embedding this in the larger context of national wellbeing. The measurement of national wellbeing certainly involves aggregating the wellbeing of the individuals in the nation, but it also involves other aspects, such as higher level societal properties which are not evident at the level of individuals as well as other factors which may influence wellbeing and permit improved measures. As the UK Office for National Statistics report *Measuring National Well-being: Life in the UK, 2012* put it (Self *et al.*, 2012, p. 3 and see Chapter 7 below): 'The well-being of the nation is influenced by a broad range of factors including economic performance, quality of life, the state of the environment, sustainability, equality as well as individual well-being.'

It may be that the individuals within a population appear to be fine, while the larger picture shows something rather different (we are reminded of the parable of the turkeys, congratulating themselves on how wonderful life is, as Christmas approaches). Conversely, and as does appear to be reflected in some of the measures, aspects of individual wellbeing may not show things in so positive a light as do some aspects of national wellbeing. For example, individual anxiety about crime may increase even while measures of actual crime rates are decreasing; likewise, increased longevity might be taken as a sign of national wellbeing, even while the ailments associated with advancing age may lead to lower individual wellbeing scores. Such discrepancies, when they occur, need to be explored and explained. (And, for the last particular example, this is one reason why Self *et al.*, 2012, look at 'healthy life expectancy' rather than simply 'life expectancy'.)

Before delving into the details, however, some introductory comments are appropriate.

First, the measurement of wellbeing is a big subject. This book is very much our perspective on it: other authors will doubtlessly have different views of what is important, and will place their emphasis on different topics.

Second, and related to the first point, the book will not seek to provide an exhaustive list of relevant measures. Apart from the sheer size of such a task, it is probably impossible, simply because the area is a dynamic one, experiencing growth and change. Any list we produced would be outdated by the time this book was published. We limit ourselves to taking stock of current developments and drawing in depth on some of them.

This dynamic growth is a consequence of a third characteristic of the area: it is currently the focus of a huge amount of research attention. On the one hand, this means that governments and other actors are exploring how best to apply such ideas in policy formulation, while on the other hand it also means that the very concepts themselves, along with how to measure them, are mutable and are still being refined and polished. Some people suspect that this refinement will take a long time, pointing out that the system of national economic accounts has been refined over decades. Waiting for the refinement to be completed (if it ever is) would appear to be out of the question.

Fourth, this book is primarily about *measuring* wellbeing. It is not about the policy implications of the results, although we do recognise that policy uses of any new measure need to be taken into account in designing and delivering it. Likewise, it is only in part about what influences wellbeing – the fact that, for example, marital status can have an effect – though inevitably there is some discussion of such matters: causes and effects may be indicators of the extent of wellbeing and thus might be used to improve measures of wellbeing, via regression or calibration models.

The history of measurement in general is one of gradual encroachment, as concept after concept succumbed to the advance of quantification. But it has been a slow and painful advance. Almost every step forward in measurement technology has faced opposition from those who thought attempts to measure or quantify some attribute were impossible or meaningless:

> Such pretensions to nicety in experiments of this nature are truly laughable! They will be telling us some day of the WEIGHT of the MOON, even to drams, scruples, and grains - nay, to the very fraction of a grain! - I wish there were infallible experiments to ascertain the quantum of brains each man possesses, and every man's integrity and candour: - This is a desideratum of science which is most of all wanted. (Harrington, 1804, p. 217)

The history of attempts to measure wellbeing can be traced back as far as one likes. Writing 130 years ago Edgeworth remarked 'hedonism may still be in the state of heat or electricity before they became exact sciences' (Edgeworth, 1881, p. 98). It is perhaps an indication of the difficulty of 'hedonimetry', as Edgeworth calls it, that it is only relatively recently that sound underpinning models and theories for measuring wellbeing have been developed.

Measuring wellbeing is also characterised by its multidisciplinary nature. Psychologists, sociologists, economists, statisticians, medical researchers, ecologists and others all have something to say about how it should be done. In part this is because they have different potential uses for such a measurement in mind, but in large part it is because the issue is fundamentally multidisciplinary. Wellbeing may be a characteristic of an individual, but it is at least partly a reflection of social interactions and is influenced by external forces.

1.1 Motivation: Why measure wellbeing?

United Nations Resolution 65/309 says:

> '*The General Assembly ...*

> 1. *Invites* Member States to pursue the elaboration of additional measures that better capture the importance of the pursuit of happiness and well-being in development with a view to guiding their public policies;

2. *Invites* those Member States that have taken initiatives to develop new indicators, and other initiatives, to share information thereon with the Secretary-General as a contribution to the United Nations development agenda, including the Millennium Development Goals;

3. *Welcomes* the offer of Bhutan to convene, during the sixty-sixth session of the General Assembly, a panel discussion on the theme of happiness and well-being;

4. *Invites* the Secretary-General to seek the views of Member States and relevant regional and international organizations on the pursuit of happiness and well-being and to communicate such views to the General Assembly at its sixty-seventh session for further consideration'.

The UK Office for National Statistics report *Measuring National Well-being: Life in the UK, 2012* (Self *et al.*, 2012, p. 3) said:

'In particular, having a more complete picture of national well-being will lead to:

- better understanding of policy impacts on well-being;

- better allocation of scarce resources via more informed policy evaluation and development;

- comparisons between how different sub-groups of the population are doing, across a range of topics;

- more informed decisions on where to live, which career to choose, based on well-being information for that area/organisation;

- assessments of the performance of government;

- comparisons between the UK with other countries'.

Implicit in these two extracts is the fact that a (perhaps the) key role of a government is to ensure the wellbeing of those it governs. That in itself probably provides sufficient answer to the question posed in this section's heading.

Only if one can measure wellbeing can one tell if the government is succeeding and, even more, if progress is being made. Furthermore, government policies ought, above all, to be evidence based, and usually that evidence will be quantitative, so that *measures* of wellbeing are critical. Such measures, when developed for groups, at more than the individual level, will allow one to monitor change (are things getting better or worse?), to compare groups (do the sexes have different degrees of wellbeing? Do different ethnic or social groups progress differentially?) and generally to investigate the impact of policies (have changes to education systems enhanced overall quality of life?). There are then other general questions which require answers. For example, what explains the frequently observed U-shaped distribution of wellbeing (with greater wellbeing being observed in younger and older age groups)? What explains the weakness of the correlation between income and wellbeing over time? Why in many countries are aggregate levels of happiness much the same as they were at the end of the Second World War, despite the dramatic growth in income per capita since then? And so on.

From the time of the Second World War to the present, economic measures, typically in the form of national economic accounts, have taken the primary place in monitoring progress. Measures such as gross domestic product (GDP) and gross national product (GNP) are headline indicators. But economic indicators focus on just one aspect of life. They do not touch on health, for example (other than through the cost of health service provision). There is concern in some quarters that standard measures of economic performance and progress are not really suited to the policy decisions which they are being used to inform. In 2009, the economists Joseph Stiglitz, Amartya Sen and Jean-Paul Fitoussi, wrote in the preface of their report on measuring societal wellbeing, commissioned by Nicholas Sarkozy, the then French President:

> We see the world through lenses not only shaped by our ideologies and ideas but also shaped by the statistics we use to measure what is going on, the latter being frequently linked to the former. GDP per capita is the commonly used metric: governments are pleased when they can report that GDP per capita has arisen [sic], say, by 5%. But other numbers can tell a very different picture. In Russia, declining life expectancy suggests there are underlying problems, even if GDP per capita is rising. So, too, in the United States, most individuals saw a decline in income, adjusted for inflation, from 1999 through 2008 - even though GDP per capita was going up - providing a markedly different picture of performance. Such a disparity may arise when income inequality increases at the same time that income increases. (Stiglitz *et al.*, 2010, p. xix).

There are other similar examples: Egypt showed a per capita GDP increase from $4760 to $6370 between 2005 and 2010, and yet the proportion of survey respondents classified as 'thriving' declined from 29% to 12% (OECD, 2013, p. 27).

An example of the disconnect between crude economic indicators such as GDP and more general measures of wellbeing is given in the United Kingdom by current intensive debate about whether a third runway should be built at Heathrow. From a narrow economic perspective the answer is clearly yes. The United Kingdom is suffering, relative to other European countries, from its limited capacity for long-haul flights to other parts of the world, especially the Far East. But from the perspective of the wellbeing of people in West London and surrounding villages living under the flight paths of 1300 wide-bodied jets taking off and landing every day, economic measures only scrape the surface of what is meant by wellbeing. Likewise, they fail to tap into the environmental impacts of increased air travel.

So GDP misses central aspects of what people regard as important. GDP was not designed to be an overall measure of wellbeing, so it is not surprising that it is now judged inadequate in that respect. More generally, as we shall see, perhaps *economic* measures themselves are inadequate or insufficient. After all, contentment, happiness, quality of life etc. are influenced by more than mere financial wealth or income. The richest person, suffering constant pain from an incurable disease, may well not rate their wellbeing as very high. Likewise, exhaustion of natural resources may lead to a short-term benefit, but it will mean the consequent enhanced quality of life will not be sustainable.

Furthermore, some things which increase economic activity, and hence GDP, are best regarded as decreasing wellbeing. A famous comment made by Robert Kennedy (which we will quote in Chapter 2) illustrates this, referring to such things as jails, napalm and nuclear warheads as contributing to GNP but hardly enhancing national wellbeing. Sitting in traffic jams consumes fuel and hence adds to GDP, but is hardly beneficial to society.

Another reason for the divorce of measures such as GDP from the wellbeing of any one person is that the former are necessarily *aggregate* measures. Any measure at the national scale must be an aggregate measure, but it is not, a priori, clear that the same concepts or ideas should apply at the national level as at the individual level. To take a trivial analogy: we can talk about the variance or the skewness of a set of values (as, e.g. wealth distributions are typically skewed, with long right tails), but we cannot talk about the variance or skewness of individual values. This example, of skew wealth distributions, is particularly relevant to wellbeing, as there is evidence that *inequalities* in the distribution of resources across a population have a negative impact on perceived wellbeing. Compelling evidence for this is adduced by Richard Wilkinson and Kate Pickett in their book *The Spirit Level* (Wilkinson and Pickett, 2010). As Stiglitz *et al.* (2010, p. xi) remark: 'One of the reasons that most people may perceive themselves as being worse off even though average GDP is increasing is *because they are indeed worse off*' (their italics). In general, it is entirely possible for the majority of people to experience a decrease in some variable while the average still increases.

In fact, even in the context of straightforward economic indicators, GDP has peculiarities as a measure of a country's 'economic wellbeing'. It excludes revenue earned from overseas production but paid to a country's residents, and it includes income paid to non-residents. It also ignores internal household work, such as childcare, and, at a more fundamental level, a level which is increasingly being recognised as of fundamental importance, GDP takes no account of sustainability: are finite natural resources being consumed, so that current 'economic progress' is being achieved at the cost of a future loss?

Most important of all, however, is the straightforward limited scope of GDP, in that it focuses on economic measures and fails to tap aspects which are regarded just as central to wellbeing, such as security, health, social networks, freedom to pursue what interests one, leisure time and so on.

Crime will decrease wellbeing overall in society. This is apparent even in such measures as GDP, where fraud has a negative impact. For example, the collapse of the Kabul Bank in Afghanistan as a result of fraud cost the country 5% of its GDP (BBC, 2012). But keeping such gross examples aside, GDP completely fails to tap into other aspects of crime which arguably have a much more direct adverse effect on individual wellbeing. So-called 'quality-of-life' crimes, including low-level things such as broken windows, littering and vandalism have a tiny economic impact but a large wellbeing impact. As we stress throughout the book, different aspects of wellbeing are interlinked in a complex way, so that minor quality-of-life crimes may have a larger impact through the subliminal messages they send about the extent to which people (including the authorities) care.

Chapter 6 discusses the shortcomings of GDP in more detail, but the fact is that GDP was never intended to be used as a global indicator of *wellbeing*. Its dominant role as an indicator of economic progress gives a very one-sided view of a multifaceted concept. This is a point to which we will repeatedly return, especially when we consider whether it is in fact possible to measure wellbeing by a single index, or whether something more is needed – a 'dashboard' of indicators, perhaps.

Having said all the above, GDP does have some attractive properties. We should learn from this when we try to develop more appropriate measures of wellbeing. For example, GDP adopts a monetary numéraire, translating *everything* into financial units. This means one can balance different attributes against each other. We shall say more about this when we discuss *conjoint measurement* in Section 1.7.

The report by Stiglitz *et al.* (Stiglitz *et al.*, 2010) makes five recommendations relating to GDP to improve its relevance as a measure of living standards.

Recommendation 1: When evaluating material wellbeing, look at income and consumption rather than production.

Recommendation 2: Emphasise the household perspective.

Recommendation 3: Consider income and consumption jointly with wealth.

Recommendation 4: Give more prominence to the distribution of income, consumption and wealth.

Recommendation 5: Broaden income measures to non-market activities.

These recommendations will be discussed in detail in Chapter 6, but here we merely remark that recommendations 1 and 3, and to a certain extent 4, might be regarded as a manifestation of the Micawber philosophy (Dickens, 1850): 'Annual income twenty pounds, annual expenditure nineteen pounds and six, result happiness. Annual income twenty pounds, annual expenditure twenty pounds ought and six, result misery'. (This refers to Great Britain's pre-decimalisation currency, in which there were 240 pence in a pound.) Recommendation 2 is concerned with the distinction between the (almost) individual level rather than the aggregate national level and recommendation 5, with the fact that economic measures are not everything. With the exception of 5, these recommendations still refer only to economic performance. Wellbeing goes beyond that.

The Stiglitz report goes on to cover aspects beyond the economic, making a further seven recommendations.

Recommendation 6: Quality of life depends on people's objective conditions and capabilities. Steps should be taken to improve measures of people's health, education, personal activities and environmental conditions. In particular, substantial effort should be devoted to developing and implementing robust, reliable measures of social connections, political voice, and insecurity that can be shown to predict life satisfaction.

Recommendation 7: Quality-of-life indicators in all the dimensions covered should assess inequalities in a comprehensive way.

Recommendation 8: Surveys should be designed to assess the links between various quality-of-life domains for each person, and this information should be used when designing policies in various fields.

Recommendation 9: Statistical offices should provide the information needed to aggregate across quality-of-life dimensions, allowing the construction of different indexes.

Recommendation 10: Measures of both objective and subjective well-being provide key information about people's quality of life. Statistical offices should incorporate questions to capture people's life evaluations, hedonic experiences and priorities in their own survey.

Recommendation 11: Sustainability assessment requires a well-identified dashboard of indicators. The distinctive feature of the components of this dashboard should be that they are interpretable as variations of some underlying 'stocks'. A monetary index of sustainability has its place in such a dashboard but, under the current state of the art, it should remain essentially focused on economic aspects of sustainability.

Recommendation 12: The environmental aspects of sustainability deserve a separate fol-lowup based on a well-chosen set of physical indicators. In particular there is a need for a clear indicator of our proximity to dangerous levels of environmental damage (such as associated with climate change or the depletion of fishing stocks.)

Recommendation 6 needs to be read in conjunction with a list of seven aspects of life presented by Stiglitz *et al.* as the key dimensions to be taken into account, ideally simultaneously, in measuring quality of life. Six of the seven dimensions are actually mentioned in the recommendation: they all need improved measures. One of these, the environment, is linked to sustainability, the subject of Recommendations 11 and 12, because it is meant to address future conditions as well as the present condition of the environment. The other dimension of quality of life, material living standards, covers income, consumption and wealth, which are also the subjects of Recommendations 1–5. So, while there is no precise definition of wellbeing here, the recommendations do cover economic performance, quality of life, the environment and sustainability. We will discuss the recommendations in detail in Chapters 4 and 6.

Finally, as a last illustration, the Belgian Federal Planning Bureau (2005) describes three areas of capital that can be used and developed.

1. *Human capital: comprising the standard of living (material well-being), health (both mental and physical) and knowledge/capacities (what individuals know and are able to do).*

2. *Environmental capital: including both natural resources (water, air, land and mineral resources) and the biosphere with all its biological diversity.*

3. *Economic capital: subdivided in physical and technological capital (equipments, build-ings, infrastructure, and intangible assets including software and technology patents) and net financial assets.*

Only one of these three is primarily about economics.

1.2   What is individual wellbeing?

Wellbeing has been the subject of a very considerable amount of research, stretching back decades, especially within the psychological and medical communities, and has been defined in various ways. For example:

Wellbeing ... comprises objective descriptors and subjective evaluations of physi-cal, material, social and emotional wellbeing, together with the extent of personal development and purposeful activity, all weighted by a set of values. (Felce and Perry, 1995)

Well-being is a complex construct that concerns optimal experience and func-tioning (Ryan and Deci, 2001).

Well-being can be understood as how people *feel* and how they *function*, both on a personal and a social level, and how they *evaluate* their lives as a whole (Michaelson *et al.*, 2012).

Other, closely related terms are also used, including such things as an individual's 'quality of life' and 'life satisfaction'. Indeed, Easterlin (2003) opens his discussion paper on 'building a better theory of well-being' by saying 'I take the terms wellbeing, utility, happiness, life satisfaction and welfare to be interchangeable'.

Fayers and Machin (2000, p. 3) comment:

It is clear that QoL [Quality of Life] means different things to different people, and takes on different meanings according to the area of application. To a town planner, for example, it might represent access to green space and other facilities. In the context of clinical trials we are rarely interested in QoL in such a broad sense, but are concerned only with evaluating those aspects that are affected by disease or treatment for disease. This may sometimes be extended to include indirect consequences of disease such as unemployment or financial difficulties.

The word 'happiness' also often crops up. It appears, for example, in the extract from the UN General Assembly resolution quoted at the start of Section 1.1 – though note that it is invariably in the context of the phrase 'happiness and well-being' rather than in isolation. This suggests that happiness is different from wellbeing. However, any differences are often lost in popular media accounts, which frequently characterise the measurement of wellbeing as the measurement of happiness. The New Economics Foundation report, *Measuring Well-being: A Guide for Practitioners* (Michaelson *et al.*, 2012, p. 6), has this to say about happiness (based on a well-established understanding of wellbeing in psychological terms):

It is worth pointing out that well-being is not exactly the same as happiness. **Happiness** often refers to how people are feeling moment-to-moment and does not always tell us about how they evaluate their lives *as a whole* (although it can do), or about how they *function* in the world. **Well-being is a much broader concept** than moment-to-moment happiness: it includes happiness but also other things such as *how satisfied people are with their lives as a whole*, and things such as *autonomy* (having a sense of control over your life), *purpose* (having a sense of purpose in life).

Wellbeing and quality of life are different from 'standard of living', which is taken to refer primarily to economic aspects – income, wealth and general material conditions such as quality of accommodation, access to health care and so on. It is clear from this that quality of life and wellbeing are broader concepts, since they also cover such things as social life, the environment and cultural activities and also subjective happiness.

Things are then further complicated by the existence of specialised variants, such as Activities of Daily Living scales, Health Related Quality of Life (HRQoL) and others. Activity of Daily Living scales measure the extent to which people can perform personal activities and normal self-care functions. They cover such things as dressing, bathing and personal hygiene, feeding oneself, organising things at home and so on. One might argue that a high state of wellbeing would be reflected by a high score in such areas. HQoL scales often cover similar things, though they may be relative to what the patient might expect, given their condition. That last point leads to a potential complication in wellbeing measures in general: the response to a question such as 'overall, how satisfied are you with your life?' might well be qualified (perhaps not explicitly) by 'under the circumstances (of your condition) . . . '.

None of the above should be surprising. Wellbeing is an intrinsically complex and multi-dimensional concept, with different parties naturally having interests in different aspects, so to expect a single universally agreed definition would be to expect too much. But it can lead to problems. Fayers and Machin (Fayers and Machin, 2000, pp. 3–4) say that 'In the absence of any agreed formal definition of quality of life, most investigators circumvent the issues by describing what *they* mean by quality of life and then letting the items (questions) in their questionnaire speak for themselves'. As we discuss in Section 1.4 and Chapter 4, defining the concept in terms of its measurement procedure is fine. What is less fine, however, is producing a superficial definition which fails to meet the basic criteria of a measurement or indicator. These issues are discussed in Section 1.5. More generally, if one does have multiple descriptors, each addressing some aspect of wellbeing, then in some circumstances one can sidestep summarising them into a single number, instead of reporting a profile: painting a picture rather than a single score.

Wellbeing, especially in the psychological sense of flourishing, is in some sense the opposite of clinical conditions such as depression. There has been a huge amount of work on measuring depression – see, for example, Dunn *et al.*, 1993; Santor *et al.*, 2006. The latter notes that 'since 1918, more than 280 measures of depressive severity have been developed and published'. It is perhaps interesting that relatively little of the work on wellbeing makes explicit reference to the work on depression, despite the complementary relationship between the two. For example, Table 1 of Santor *et al.*, 2006, lists symptom domains covered by various depression scales. This list includes sleep, irritability, anxiety, hopelessness, suicidal tendency, concentration, energy/fatigue, worthlessness, agitation, withdrawal, no interest in others and so on, all of which researchers in wellbeing will recognise. More generally, Kahneman *et al.* (2003, preface) note that, in the context of hedonic psychology – the psychology of 'pleasurable and unpleasurable states of consciousness' – 'another characteristic of past research is the remarkable accentuation of the negative. Textbooks that do not mention pleasure or well-being at all devote many pages to the clinical phenomena of anxiety and depression'.

A high level informal definition of wellbeing might be that it is 'what matters to people', and indeed the phrase 'What matters to you?' was adopted as the strapline for the study on wellbeing policy in the United Kingdom and the measuring national wellbeing programme of the UK Office for National Statistics (see Chapter 7). This informal definition drives home the fact that wellbeing is something to be hoped for, aspired to and aimed at.

Section 1.5 discusses the basic principles of measurement. We shall see that measurement procedures have two aspects – sometimes termed their *representational* and *pragmatic* aspects. Representational aspects are those concerned with preserving the relationships between the objects under study, when mapping from the system being measured to a numerical representation. Pragmatic aspects are those concerned with deciding what characteristics are relevant, and how they should be captured within the measurement index (the 'items' in the terminology of Fayers and Machin, though pragmatic aspects go much further than the mere choice of questions in a questionnaire).

Wellbeing measures typically have a large pragmatic component, and so to a large extent their definition and measurement procedure are one and the same; the specification of the way wellbeing is measured is also a definition of what is meant by wellbeing. The large pragmatic component inevitably means that not everyone will agree on a definition – perhaps because they have different intended uses for the indicator in mind or because they have different philosophical bases for what they mean by measurement. For example, even if you and I agree that having a supportive social network and being healthy are key contributors to wellbeing, we might disagree on the relative weight to be assigned to them in our overall index.

In summary, in general we should expect there to be multiple measures of wellbeing: different measures, that is, different *definitions* of wellbeing, will be suitable for different purposes – just as different measures of inflation are appropriate according to whether one is seeking a macroeconomic indicator or a cost of living indicator.

1.3   Aspects of individual wellbeing

We have stressed that individual wellbeing has multiple aspects. The potential constituents of individual wellbeing can be classified in various ways. In this section we shall look at some useful distinctions. We shall discuss how the constituents might be combined to yield an overall measure in the next section.

McAllister (2005) classified constituents into five types. 'Most researchers agree about the domains that make up wellbeing: physical wellbeing; material wellbeing; social wellbeing; development and activity; emotional wellbeing. The elements can be paraphrased as physical health, income and wealth, relationships, meaningful work and leisure, personal stability and (lack of) depression. Mental health is increasingly seen as fundamental to overall health and wellbeing. These elements are sometimes viewed as "drivers" of wellbeing.'

In contrast, the Organisation for Economic Co-operation and Development (OECD) study *How's Life: Measuring Well-Being* (OECD, 2011a) and the OECD *Compendium of Well-being Indicators* (OECD, 2011b) identified two pillars of wellbeing. The first was *material living conditions*, covering such things as income and wealth, jobs and earnings and housing. The second was *quality of life*, covering such things as health, work/life balance, education, civic engagement, social connections, environmental quality, personal security and subjective wellbeing. Then, in addition to these two, they added *sustainability*, necessary if current levels of wellbeing are to be maintained over time. Data availability and other issues meant this last one was not discussed in detail in the *How's Life* report, although in other work the OECD does report on sustainable development and green growth indicators and how these might be used within the broader picture of national wellbeing (e.g. Strange and Bayley, 2008). It is this broader picture of national wellbeing in which we are particularly interested, seeing future and current wellbeing as integral to 'how a country is doing'.

We see immediately from this that the OECD definition does not treat quality of life as synonymous with wellbeing, but rather as a subcomponent of it. Since subjective wellbeing is regarded as a component of quality of life, at first glance it might look as if a rather circular definition results, but in fact overall wellbeing includes other, objective aspects, noted above.

A less high-level classification of the constituents of wellbeing, focussing more on the quality of life aspects, is into cognitive and affective components, with the affective component being further partitioned into positive and negative aspects. This is a quite common distinction. Thus, for example, the *Commission on the Measurement of Economic Performance and Social Progress* (see Stiglitz *et al.*, 2010) asserted that 'subjective well-being (encompasses) three different aspects: cognitive evaluations of one's life, positive emotions (joy, pride) and negative ones (pain, anger, worry)'. Particular, measures, (e.g. the Positive and Negative Affect Schedule, Watson *et al.*, 1988) focus on specific aspects.

And digging down yet further, the New Economics Foundation guide to measuring wellbeing (Michaelson *et al.*, 2012), focuses very much on subjective wellbeing, and identifies three aspects for practitioners to consider:

– how people feel, covering emotions such as happiness and anxiety;
– how people function, covering such things as 'sense of competence' and 'sense of being connected to those around them';
– how people evaluate their lives, covering such things as satisfaction with life, and comparison with the best possible life.

We can see from the above that how wellbeing is defined – and hence how it is measured – depends very much on the level at which it is approached. A high-level perspective will include things such as the freedom to express political opinion. A low-level perspective might focus very much on subjective wellbeing. There also is a clear link to the notions of exogenous and endogenous variables in economics, with the former being external things which influence wellbeing, and the latter internal aspects of wellbeing. In the next section we draw a related distinction between 'influences on' and 'consequences of' when constructing measures of wellbeing. This is a distinction which has not been widely recognised, but could have an important impact on the quality of the measurement system which results. Traditionally, in wellbeing measurement, all related variables have been treated in the same way.

An important distinction underlying notions of wellbeing is that between *hedonic* and *eudemonic* wellbeing. Rather than being alternatives, however, they might properly be regarded as complementary aspects of a larger whole.

The hedonic perspective might be seen as the 'naive' perspective, and is certainly the viewpoint that popular media often take. This perspective regards wellbeing as a degree of happiness. In contrast, the eudemonic perspective might be characterised as regarding wellbeing as a fulfilled potential and meaning in one's life.

Notions of hedonic wellbeing can be traced back to the ancient Greeks, in a balance of pleasure against displeasure. Utilitarianists such as John Stuart Mill and Jeremy Bentham held that the proper aim of actions should be to maximise 'utility', defined in terms of positive happiness and negative suffering. For example, Bentham's *An Introduction to the Principles of Morals and Legislation* begins

> Nature has placed mankind under the governance of two sovereign masters, pain and pleasure. It is for them alone to point out what we ought to do . . . By the principle of utility is meant that principle which approves or disapproves of every action whatsoever according to the tendency it appears to have to augment or diminish the happiness of the party whose interest is in question: or, what is the same thing in other words to promote or to oppose that happiness. I say of every action whatsoever, and therefore not only of every action of a private individual, but of every measure of government. (Bentham, 2009)

Nobel Laureate Daniel Kahneman and his co-editors, in their book *Well-being: The Foundations of Hedonic Psychology*, defined 'the new field of hedonic psychology' as being about 'what makes experiences and life pleasant and unpleasant' (Kahneman *et al.*, 2003). The perspective is very much a subjective one.

Like hedonic wellbeing, notions of eudemonic wellbeing can be traced back at least as far as the ancient Greeks, with, for example, Aristotle characterising simple (hedonic) happiness as suitable only for beasts. In contrast, eudemonic wellbeing arises when one's life is most in accordance with one's beliefs and attitudes, when there is personal development and a sense of achievement or fulfilment. Descriptions such as 'positive functioning', 'fully functioning', 'personal growth', 'meaningfulness', 'acting with integrity' and so on are often associated with eudemonic happiness.

As we mentioned in Section 1.1, a key motivation underlying the recent interest and work on measuring wellbeing is the intention to use such measures as indicators of the effectiveness of public policies. This will only be possible if wellbeing can be influenced and changed by such policies. That raises a number of issues.

The obvious one is whether wellbeing is a psychological trait or state. A trait is fairly constant over time, whereas a state is something which depends on circumstances and experiences. Happiness, for example, will probably usually be regarded as a state. If wellbeing is a trait, then, while measuring it might be of scientific interest, it would be of limited value for policy decisions. In contrast, if wellbeing is a state that could be influenced by external events and experiences, then it clearly does have policy implications. The distinction is tied to the notion of homeostasis.

A homeostatic system is one which, when perturbed by shocks, tends to revert to its original condition – an equilibrium state, one might say. If a state of wellbeing (whether low or high wellbeing) is such a homeostatic equilibrium, then measurements of it would not be expected to change much over time (at least not in the aggregate), so that again wellbeing would be of purely scientific interest, rather than policy interest. Indeed, a classic study of lottery winners and accident victims suggested that this homeostatic notion might be true, with the happiness of both groups later returning to their pre-incident levels (although this result has recently been criticised by Helliwell, CSLS, 2011). This phenomenon has also been termed *the hedonic treadmill* (Brickman and Campbell, 1971).

We must also ask ourselves whether different people are likely to have different basic degrees of wellbeing. For example, it does not seem unreasonable to suppose that someone predisposed to depression will have a lower degree of wellbeing than others. In a meta-analysis, DeNeve and Cooper (1998) found that subjective wellbeing and various personality traits were correlated, with (perhaps unsurprisingly) extraversion and agreeableness being positively correlated and neuroticism negatively correlated.

Then, even if measured wellbeing does (or can) change over time, we need to be sure we can identify the cause of the change, and determine that it is not merely due to measurement characteristics or other kinds of change. The Flynn effect illustrates the dangers. This is the phenomenon, discovered by James R. Flynn, that IQ scores have increased from generation to generation over the past century (Flynn, 2012). One explanation is that successive generations are becoming more intelligent, and not in a minor way – the changes have been described as massive and for some populations are much larger than one standard deviation of the IQ distribution. But this seems unlikely on other grounds – the evidence of history shows that our great grandparents were not idiots. A far more convincing explanation is that people are becoming more skilled at the kinds of abstract reasoning which IQ tests typically measure. Any observed changes in measured wellbeing would not be attributable to the same cause (increased skill in abstract reasoning), but we need to be confident that they do not have some cause other than the policy change we may be investigating.

This sort of phenomenon is related to issues of cultural difference. Apart from measuring the impact of public policies, one of the ways that wellbeing measures will be used is to compare groups. Nationally, these will be social, ethnic, gender, age and other groups within a country, but the measures will also be used internationally to compare nations. The difficulty is, as countless cross-cultural comparisons have found in the past, that such comparative statements are fraught with problems. At the very simplest level, translations of questionnaires can change the meaning, and we know, even at the most basic of levels, that question wording can have a huge impact on responses. Moreover, as Christopher (1999) has pointed out, definitions of wellbeing are necessarily culture dependent. The problem of identifying equivalent constructs across different cultures may well defy effective solutions.

Another way of classifying aspects of wellbeing is into 'objective' and 'subjective' aspects. An objective aspect will be something external to the individual but which is thought to have an impact on their wellbeing or be indicative of their state of wellbeing. A subjective aspect will be (for example) a simple self-reported state of someone's wellbeing. Note, however, that it is not the self-reporting which makes the indicator subjective, but rather the fact that it is reporting on an internal (subjective) aspect of their condition.

Yet another classification is into those which represent some kind of predictability, choice or control and those which do not. For example, if one feels one has made one's own choice about education, daily personal activities, use of leisure time, political voice and so on, then one is likely to feel more at ease with oneself than if one feels these choices were imposed upon one. Being told what to do all the time is not conducive to psychological wellbeing. The notion that one is able to control and influence things, rather than being subject to the whims of fate, is something which will recur in our consideration of wellbeing. The feeling of being unable to control things may be one reason why unemployment is generally associated with poor wellbeing beyond the extent to be expected as a consequence of loss of income.

Likewise, one can distinguish between aspects which represent security and those which do not. For example, feelings about health, crime, a safe place to live, good nutrition, strong social networks and so on will all impact the degree of wellbeing.

Various objective measures have been identified as central to wellbeing. They include the following.

- *Education*: An educated workforce is necessary for a modern technological society, and so education and economic progress are related. But more than this, we have already mentioned the importance of choice and control, and education gives people greater choice and control. Education breeds opportunity. A higher level of education is also associated with better health, lower unemployment and greater social engagement, though clearly the causal links may not be straightforward. On the other hand, there are subtleties. For example, there is the complication that perhaps education can promote inequality. It might lead to a greater dispersion in income over a population. Such things are discussed below, in the light of evidence that societies which have higher degrees of inequality may have lower aggregate measures of wellbeing (Verme, 2011). This illustrates the importance of measuring the shapes of distributions, not merely their means or medians. Alternatively, increased education might lead to increased dissatisfaction if appropriate jobs are not available.

Human capital measurement, as quoted from the Belgian Federal Planning Bureau document at the end of Section 1.2, invariably focuses on the labour market benefits of education and training. This has the result that someone unemployed or retired has no human capital. Of course, there is a wider concept of human capital, defined in terms of contributions to society and to one's own fulfilment and wellbeing.

– *Personal activities*: Again, having the freedom to pursue one's own interests represents an aspect of choice and control, and so is likely to promote wellbeing.

– *Political voice and governance*: Stiglitz *et al.* (2010, p. 78) stress 'political voice [as] an integral dimension of the quality of life'. Once again, this is closely related to notions of control, rather than being subject to the (potentially arbitrary and unpredictable) whims of someone else. It permits individuals to feel they have a say, at a fundamental level, in how their lives proceed. This opens up important cross-cultural and cross-national issues: if political voice is to be included as a contributory factor in a wellbeing measure, how should countries with different political structures be compared? These ideas are also closely related to trust in public institutions, showing why responsible and accountable regulatory authorities are so important.

– *Security*: This is almost too obvious to need mentioning, but a feeling of safety – from crime, war, accidents, economic crises and so on – is conducive to higher degrees of wellbeing. Security is, of course, also related to health – the feeling that one is safe from disease or illness. As far as crime is concerned, we must distinguish between the actual level of crime and the perceived level of crime. For example, 'when people have a perception of crime as a problem in an area, the experience of crime or worrying about crime does not offer much additional purchase in understanding their quality of life' (Christmann and Rogerson, 2004). Indeed, anxiety about crime can go up while true crime rates go down. Economic security and the anxieties which can arise from it, are particularly pertinent at present, in the straitened economic conditions consequent on the banking crisis. This includes things like financial insecurity, employment insecurity (unemployment, as we have noted, impacts wellbeing to an extent beyond the obvious financial hit), as well as long-term insecurity as people fear what may await them in retirement.

– *Social networks*: Strong social support networks induce benefits at several levels. At the basic level, there is a correlation between strength of social network and quality of life, and there is considerable evidence that social support is associated with better health and wellbeing in general. Of course, there may be issues of causal direction. At a higher level, clearly a larger social support network means that one is more likely to be in employment, and possibly have a higher level of education. The positive impact of being married (at least, for men) is one aspect of this and, in general having an intimate partner confers some protection from the potentially detrimental consequences of adverse life events. All these things are correlated.

– *Environmental conditions*: Immediate environmental conditions have an impact on our everyday quality of life. The contrast between living next to a busy motorway and a tinkling stream illustrates this. But there is also a larger impact on health through pollution or on cost of living due to droughts impacting food prices, for example. Moreover, unsustainable costs or resource consumption incur a debt to the future. It means that future quality of life will be proportionately lower. This is why more recent thinking includes sustainability having an impact on wellbeing. One can see particular difficulties here, because of the timescales involved, and the need to determine likely impacts in the future.

- *Material living standards*: This is the aspect which has received most attention in the past, so perhaps it is unnecessary to say much about it here. We will return to it below.
- *Health*: In Chapter 2 we quote the World Health Organisation definition of health, as contained in its constitution: 'Health is a state of complete physical, mental and social well-being and not merely the absence of disease or infirmity'. Again we have something of the circular in the definitions: Measures of wellbeing often include health as an aspect, but the WHO definition of health includes wellbeing. Despite this, health clearly has a central impact on wellbeing.

We have already mentioned that all these various aspects are correlated. Blunt description fails to capture the subtle causal relationships, and indeed to tease these out would be a vast project. But it also fails to identify the fact that there are probably synergistic relationships. Being both unemployed and ill is likely to have a greater impact than the mere 'sum' of the parts. At the least this means that one cannot simply combine the results of instruments measuring the distinct aspects of wellbeing, but have to look at things from a holistic perspective: both the measures and their interactions need to be studied.

1.4   How to measure individual wellbeing?

1.4.1   Basics of measurement

In a detailed discussion of the foundations of measurement, Hand (2004, p. 23) pointed out that we view the world through the spectacles of measurement. Modern technology, modern civilisation, is built on quantitative characterisation of the objects and attributes about us. It is such quantitative characterisations which ensure that our bridges do not fall down, our food distribution networks function, transport systems get us to work and our television, telephone and other communications systems do what they were intended to. It is such quantitative characterisation which enables us to measure how well we are doing, and to set targets and assess our achievements against them. But such quantitative characterisations have not always come easily.

We noted in Section 1.2 that all measurement can be thought of as a mix of two aspects, the representational and the pragmatic. Representational measurement is concerned with the mapping from the system of objects and the relationships between them to a corresponding numerical representation. A simple example would be placing two rocks on the two pans of a weighing scale and assigning a larger number to the rock which forced its pan down. By this means we could assign a set of numbers to the rocks which represented their weight, in the sense that larger numbers were associated with heavier rocks. Then, going further, we could place two rocks together on one pan, and find a third rock which just balanced this pair of rocks. It is then possible to assign numbers to the rocks such that the sum of the two numbers assigned to the pair on the same pan equalled the number assigned to the other rock. These numbers have the properties of our usual measure of weight. Indeed, we could take a particular rock and let the number assigned to it be unity, and then all the other rocks would have weight defined in terms of it. In standard usage, such a procedure determines the unit of measurement, with 'unity' corresponding to 1 oz or 1 kg and so on.

Representational measurement, as illustrated by our rocks example, is all very well, but clearly something more is needed when we attempt to measure wellbeing. This 'something else' is the pragmatic aspect of measurement. The representational aspect of measurement constrains the numbers we can use to represent the magnitudes of attributes of objects by requiring the relationships between these numbers to be the same as the relationships between the objects (e.g. the number assigned to represent the weight of one rock is greater than that assigned to represent the weight of another if the first rock 'is heavier than' than the second, i.e. the first rock tips the scale). The pragmatic aspect of measurement also places constraints on the numbers we can use, but these constraints are chosen for reasons of convenience, practicality or to encapsulate our intended meaning of the attribute in question. In measuring wellbeing, for example, as the preceding sections will have made abundantly clear, different researchers regard different properties as being part of the overall concept of wellbeing. To assign a number to the wellbeing of an individual, we first have to decide which of these properties we regard as relevant, and then we have to decide how to combine these properties. As Hand (2004, p. 13) puts it: '[Pragmatic constraints] *crystallize* the numerical assignment, so that we know exactly what we are talking about.'

There are a number of consequences of this. Different researchers may well have different views on what is relevant or important. The various sets of relevant characteristics listed in the previous section illustrate some different perspectives. It is reassuring, however, that the various sets have much in common. The main difference appears to be the scope of the lists.

Different researchers will also have different views on how to combine the various characteristics which are parts of wellbeing. Should one use a weighted sum – a sum of the values of the characteristics, with each one weighted according to its perceived importance? If so, what weights are appropriate? Is some more elaborate combination method appropriate? Since different choices can be made, different researchers will have different definitions, as well as different ways of measuring wellbeing. This is fine: unlike 'weight', 'wellbeing' is a complex concept, and we should expect different definitions, meanings and measurement procedures to emerge as we dig down into exactly what we mean by it and as we tap into and emphasise different aspects of it. But we should not lose sight of the concomitant obligation that when one talks of wellbeing one must be explicit about precisely what definition one is using.

Domains such as wellbeing, which have a very substantial pragmatic component, present tougher measurement challenges than largely representational domains, such as weight. But the differences are perhaps not so great as some believe. As Quetelet put it in the mid-nineteenth century: 'Although we are here in a new field, where facts cannot be estimated mechanically, as in the physical sciences, the difference, nevertheless, is not to be held so great as it may appear at first sight. Even the physical sciences sometimes rest on facts which are not identically the same, as deaths and births should be, and which may lead to appreciations and conclusions more or less great. With the use even of an instrument, when one wishes to discover a temperature, a magnetic declination or the force and direction of a wind, does one really find the quantities which are sought? When one measures an individual, is the real height positively discovered? Errors, greater or lesser, may be committed, and observation alone can recognise the limits within which they range. Has the consideration of the average life of man been rejected, because that average rests upon numbers which vary, without doubt, within limits as extended as can be conceived?' (Quetelet, 1842, p. ix).

And, one might add, measurement error aside, individual heights are not well defined: they change over the course of a day, under the inexorable force of gravity squashing the cartilages and organs of the human body.

In all measurement, whether representational or pragmatic, one must be sure one is measuring the right thing. Now, 'right', out of context, is meaningless. This means that, before we can decide how to measure an attribute, we need to decide what is the purpose of our measurement. And then we need to match our measurement procedure to that purpose. Someone on a slimming diet basing their success on their height or the length of their hair would not make much progress.

Measurement procedures which are heavily pragmatic are typically found in very complex areas, and usually the social or behavioural sciences, but not solely: Baggott (2004, p. 320) gives an example from quantum mechanics. He says 'Remember that we have no way of knowing the "actual" signs of the phase factors because this is information that is not revealed in experiments. However, we can adopt a phase convention which, if we stick to it rigorously, will always give results that are both internally consistent and consistent with experiment'. But in the social and behavioural areas in particular, one needs to tread carefully to ensure that one really is measuring what one wants to measure, and also that the measuring procedures have desirable characteristics. The next two subsections look at just some of these issues.

To conclude this subsection, we should comment on gold standards in measurement, and the role they might play in measuring wellbeing. A gold standard is the true value of the attribute being studied, and sometimes situations arise where it is possible or perhaps possible in principle, to measure this true value directly. For example, in studies of osteoporosis, we might regard radiography as leading to the true extent of bone deterioration (the gold standard). But for reasons of cost we might prefer to adopt a questionnaire based on items concerning age, diet, exercise, etc., which we know to give scores correlated with the radiographic result, and which are much quicker and cheaper to determine, as well as being non-invasive. Or, as another example, we might wish to know something about the true state of a disease so that we can treat it, in situations where the true state can be discovered only at a post mortem examination. Here we might again try to develop a screening instrument which is highly correlated with the true disease status.

Unfortunately wellbeing admits of no such gold standard. Indeed, as we have seen, the very complexity of the concept means that there are multiple interpretations of what is meant by 'wellbeing'. Even such straightforward approaches as simply asking people questions like 'are you satisfied with your life?' arguably touch on only certain aspects of wellbeing.

However, even though no gold standard exists, there are indicators which one might expect to be highly correlated with wellbeing. When this is the case, advantage can be taken of this expected relationship to test and refine potential definitions. For example, at the aggregate level, where we are trying to determine the wellbeing of a population, we might reasonably expect suicide rate to be negatively correlated with wellbeing. If it is not, it suggests either that our measure of wellbeing is missing something or that we have misunderstood something about the potential relationship between these two variables. Either way it will lead to exploration and improvement of understanding and the measures.

1.4.2   What is measured matters

In Section 1.2, we noted that one informal definition of wellbeing was 'what matters'. But this can be inverted, so that what is measured may be taken to be what matters – purely because the solid numbers assigned to it give it a spurious sense of accuracy, validity and reality. Many authors have cautioned against this mistake.

For example, there is the McNamara Fallacy. Charles Handy (Handy, 1995) describes it thus: 'The first step is to measure what can be easily measured. This is OK as far as it goes. The second step is to disregard that which cannot be easily measured or to give it an arbitrary quantitative value. This is artificial and misleading. The third step is to presume that what cannot be measured easily really is not important. This is blindness. The fourth step is to say that what cannot easily be measured really does not exist. This is suicide'. Handy summarises this as 'What does not get counted does not count'.

Chambers (1997) put a similar message more poetically:

> *Economists have come to feel*
> *What can't be measured isn't real*
> *The truth is always an amount*
> *Count numbers, only numbers count.*

Enrico Giovannini, then the OECD Chief Statistician, has put a more positive spin on this: 'by measuring progress, we foster progress'. While sympathetic to the intent, we feel that may be a claim too far, at least if it is interpreted as requiring measurement and only acting on the results of that measurement.

Goodhart's law is a related phenomenon – see Hand (2007). This says that 'any observed statistical regularity will tend to collapse once pressure is placed upon it for control purposes' (Goodhart, 1984). It basically means that an indicator adopted as a measure of effectiveness of policy gradually loses its usefulness as people and organisations work towards the target. For example, on the subject of health indicators, McDowell and Newell (1996, p. 11) say 'Social reforms are based on the information that is available to us, so the selection and publication of indicators of health both reflect and guide social and political goals. Hence the very choice of indicators tends to affect the health of the population; publication of an indicator focuses attention on that problem, such as infant mortality, and the resulting interventions (if successful) will tend to reduce the prevalence of the problem, in turn reducing the value of the indicator as a marker of current health problems'. The measures themselves contain the seeds of their own irrelevance.

Goodhart's law can be taken even further in the variant sometimes known as Campbell's law: 'The more any quantitative social indicator is used for social decision-making, the more subject it will be to corruption pressures and the more apt it will be to distort and corrupt the social processes it is intended to monitor'. In some cases this can even take the form of explicit manipulation of the data. For example, *The Telegraph* of 28th February 2003 reported that 'the Commission for Health Improvement rebuked bosses at West Yorkshire ambulance service for reporting better than average performance ... According to the watchdog, West Yorkshire Metropolitan Ambulance Service NHS Trust (WYMAS) downgraded some category A calls, if the ambulance crew arrived at the scene and decided the call was not, in hindsight, serious enough to warrant a category A response ... The watchdog also found a substantial time lag between the time a call was received and the time the trust started the clock to time its response' (Telegraph, 2003).

This example also illustrates one of the intrinsic difficulties with social and behavioural measurement systems used for social policy development, namely that such measurements may have (at least!) two rather distinct but typically intertwined purposes. The first purpose is simply to gauge performance. Areas of strength and weakness can be identified, so that effort and resources can be focused on those domains where improvement is necessary. This purpose is essentially internal. But the second purpose is to *report* performance – perhaps to compare with a stated target, or to provide input to a league table. This usage is essentially external.

A straightforward example of this dichotomy is that of school tests. For the first purpose, a test will show how individual students are doing, where difficulties are arising with the taught material, and on whom the teacher needs to focus attention. For the second purpose, a test will show what level the students have reached, so that, for example, employers know that the graduates have reached a requisite level of knowledge. From the perspective of a student, it would be advantageous if they admitted to doing poorly on those aspects of the test where they were weak when the test was being used for the first purpose, but concealed this when it was being used for the second.

One way to reduce the potential for 'gaming', or working towards the target, is to use multiple indicators, in what is sometimes called a 'dashboard'. The different components of wellbeing discussed in Section 1.3 could all be reported separately, so that a performance profile results. This clearly gives a better picture of what is going on, but at the cost of increased complexity. Furthermore, in many situations a single performance measure will be needed (e.g. the media, especially with their insatiable appetite for league tables, will doubtless require one). We shall return to this point below.

A second strategy for tackling such problems is to change the target indicator in unpredictable ways periodically. This may be a good strategy for the first purpose above, but it creates difficulties for the second purpose, because consistent time series cannot be constructed. It has been suggested that deliberately leaving some flexibility or ambiguity in definitions – of wellbeing, for example – can serve the same purpose of making gaming more difficult. But it could equally have the opposite effect as different users refine the measures to their particular advantage.

There are many further complicating issues. As we have seen, most researchers regard health as an intrinsic part of wellbeing. But health care provision is not static and, in particular, health care technology progresses over time. This could have various consequences which could work in either direction: the overall health of a population might improve over time or the expectations within a population might exceed practical results, inducing dissatisfaction. Certainly, more medical investigations and procedures become possible as things progress, but at an increased cost. This is one of the dilemmas with which health care systems, worldwide, are currently battling. Likewise, medical screening can serve to identify potentially fatal diseases at an earlier stage (so increasing the apparent survival rate merely because the disease has been identified earlier), but this can come at a very substantial cost in terms of large numbers of medical procedures carried out on the false positives or those with benign conditions (and all medical procedures carry some risk).

It is well known that blood pressure can become elevated by the tension of having a nurse or doctor take one's blood pressure. This illustrates a basic problem: How can we measure something if the very act of measurement distorts the thing we want to measure? The same effect is manifest elsewhere. In particular, the subjects of a study can respond positively to the mere fact of being studied (the attention they receive, for example), so that their scores are better than they should be. This phenomenon, called the Hawthorne Effect, is described in detail in Hand (2007). Wellbeing studies are potentially particularly vulnerable to this sort of effect: Paul Dolan has reminded us that Schkade and Kahneman's (1998) observation, that 'Nothing in life is quite as important as you think it is while you are thinking about it', clearly applies in the measurement of subjective wellbeing (Dolan and Powdthavee, 2012).

1.5   Properties of measurements

We referred to 'measurement error' in Section 1.4. This represents the discrepancy between the observed measurement and the underlying 'true' value. Clearly this is a difficult concept when, as with measuring wellbeing, the very concept of an underlying 'true' value is troublesome. More generally, we will be interested in a range of aspects of a measurement, including such things as the following.

- *Data availability*: Can the elements which are combined to yield a wellbeing score themselves be measured? We saw, for example, that sustainability was regarded as an important pillar of wellbeing by the OECD in its *How's Life* study, but that problems of data availability meant that it was not discussed in detail in that report.
- *Timeliness*: If a wellbeing measure is to be used to monitor change over time, for example, in an exploration of the effect of policy changes, then clearly it is important to be able to collect the data and derive the wellbeing score on a timescale which makes it possible to detect the relevant changes.
- *Sensitivity*: It is critical that the wellbeing score should be sufficiently sensitive to changes of a size which matter in its component factors. In contrast, the fluctuations arising from changes which do not matter should have a limited impact in terms of changes to the wellbeing score. At the two opposite extremes we have a score which fluctuates dramatically from day to day and a score which barely changes over time. Something in between is needed.
- *Data quality*: There are many aspects to this. Examples include floor and ceiling effects (in which minimum and maximum values to the measurement scale lead to bunching near those values), incomplete data (if a wellbeing questionnaire includes questions which are likely to elicit many missing values, such as 'what is your spouse's income?', then it will be problematic) and distortions arising from poorly worded questions. At an aggregate level, an important aspect of data quality is sample selection bias.

Such issues are related to the characteristics of measurement scales known as *validity* and *reliability*.

1.5.1   Validity

Validity indicates the extent to which the test measures what you want it to measure: How close the measured values are to the underlying 'truth'. So validity is about 'meaning'.

The concept of validity has been the subject of a very considerable amount of attention, especially in the behavioural and social sciences. This has led to the exploration of different kinds of validity, including the following.

- *Content validity*: Does the measuring instrument properly capture the entirety of the concept in question. For example, if the instrument consists of a number of questions, the responses to which are combined to yield an overall score, does the collection of questions cover the full range of aspects of the concept?
- *Criterion validity*: This is an indication of how well a measure correlates with some gold standard. It will be used when a proposed new measure is quicker, cheaper, or more timely (e.g. a diagnostic test vs. a posthumous dissection) than the existing gold

standard measure, and is only relevant when there *is* a gold standard, so that it is seldom relevant in measuring wellbeing. However, even if a gold standard is not available, there may be other external characteristics with which one might expect it to be correlated, such as suicide rate, in the context of national wellbeing.

– *Construct validity*: When there is no gold standard, one strategy is to relate multiple measures of the same phenomenon, to see if they are correlated and indeed if these correlations fit in with theoretical expectations.

– *Face validity*: If a test looks as if it should measure the attribute one is aiming to measure, then it is said to possess face validity; one might say that 'at face value' it measures what one wants to measure. Looking as if it measures what one wants to measure is not the same as being *proved* to measure what one wants to measure, of course, so in a sense face validity is a complement to content validity.

1.5.2   Reliability

Reliability measures how close the measured values are to each other – how consistent are the results. If one repeatedly measures the same thing when there has been no opportunity for the underlying characteristic to change, how much variability is there in the scores? This is hypothetical: If one actually measured the same thing in quick succession, people are likely to remember their previous response, so that an overestimate of the reliability of the measurement procedure would result. Some more sophisticated way to measure reliability needs to be devised. Various strategies have been explored to tackle this, including such things as parallel forms approaches (in which different questions aim at the same concept).

More details of the concepts of validity and reliability can be found in Hand (2004).

1.6   Objective or subjective?

We mentioned several objective aspects of wellbeing in Section 1.3, including education, ability to perform daily activities, political voice, security, extent of social network and environmental conditions. But one might argue that the *subjective* aspects are the key to measuring wellbeing. After all, we want to know how satisfied and content people are, and who better to judge someone's state than the person oneself? This raises rather subtle questions. For example, as we mentioned earlier, in the United Kingdom (and indeed elsewhere) the crime rate has dropped in recent years, but fear about it has gone up. It is a subtle question whether objective or subjective measures, as a component of wellbeing, are more appropriate in this context.

At their most basic level, subjective measures can be based on a single question (e.g. 'Taking all things together, would you say you are: very happy, quite happy, not very happy or not at all happy?', van Hoorn, 2007). However, both experience and psychological measurement theory shows that better estimates can be found by identifying and measuring different component aspects, and also by combining multiple measures of the same thing.

Regarding the first of these points, we have already noted that subjective wellbeing may be regarded as being composed of a cognitive component of life evaluation, and an affective component, including both positive and negative aspects, capturing feelings at the time. Some researchers also include an explicitly eudemonic component describing sense of engagement or purpose. Given these various aspects, we are then back to the issue of how to combine them to yield an overall measure, discussed further below.

Subjective wellbeing, even more than objective measures, is susceptible to difficulties in making cross-national and cross-cultural comparisons. The term 'cultural bias' has sometimes been used to describe the differences between measured values which are the consequence of measurement instruments rather than underlying reality. Inadequacy of measuring instrument is one thing, but another is simply the way in which people *report* their personal experiences, regardless of what those experiences are. Despite these difficulties, there are various surveys which include subjective wellbeing measures and attempt to make them comparable across different countries, such as the *Gallup World Poll* and the *World Values Survey*.

Perhaps the defining feature of subjective measures of wellbeing is that they are, well, *subjective*. There is no ground truth against which we can compare the subjective rating. Nonetheless, the fact that subjective measures do reflect some sort of reality is indicated by correlations between such measures and objective measures or outcomes: for example, one might expect that people who rate themselves as dissatisfied with their jobs tend to leave them at a greater rate than others who claim to be satisfied. There are also various feedback mechanisms. An optimist, feeling positive about their chances of winning a lottery, might buy a ticket. A pessimist, 'knowing' they will not win, will not buy a ticket. Hardly surprising, then, that a study might show a correlation between an optimism/pessimism scale and the probability of winning a lottery. Michaelson *et al.* (2012, p. 6) have something to say about this: 'Whilst well-being covers more than happy feelings, recent research suggests that positive feelings like happiness can actually lead to better well-being overall. This is because positive feelings broaden people's potential responses to challenging situations and build their personal resources and capabilities. We should think of feeling happy not only as a goal in itself, but also as a way of increasing people's potential for doing well'.

Broadly, speaking, measurement of subjective wellbeing has been approached in two different ways. One way seeks immediate reports as things happen in normal surroundings (and not, for example, in psychology laboratories); the advantage of this is that it has pragmatic validity – it is how people evaluate their own experience as it occurs (see, for example, Scollon *et al.*, 2003), and is not subject to retrospective perceptual and memory distortion. The other approach is a retrospective one, in which respondents keep a diary of the day before, evaluating how they felt at each hour or event during the day (e.g. Kahneman *et al.*, 2004). All retrospective methods are at risk of memory bias.

It is perhaps worth commenting that subjective measures of wellbeing are potentially intrusive, and as with all intrusive survey questions, responses may be susceptible to various kinds of distortion. This is tied in with ethical issues. It is incumbent on statistical agencies to have a clear purpose for collecting data, not only because of the public cost of collecting the data, but also because of the intrusiveness involved.

1.7 Combining multiple aspects

As we have stressed, wellbeing is not a simple representational measurement concept, like length or weight, which readily admits to being mapped to a unidimensional numeric variable, but is a confluence of various aspects. This means that, rather than trying to represent wellbeing by a single indicator or index, it might be better to use a multivariate profile – a 'dashboard', as we said above. Such profiles cannot have too many component indicators or they are useless: one would not know where to start if presented with a profile of some hundreds of measures. (An obvious trap to avoid, one might think, but its obviousness has not prevented various public bodies falling into this trap when devising profiles of key performance indicators.)

One strategy for easing things is to use a hierarchy of indicators, with a few (or even just one) headline indicators, and a range of secondary indicators associated with each of the headline indicators.

All this is very well, but it is probably inevitable that at some stage the various components of the profile will be combined to yield a single measure. With single scalar measures it is much more straightforward to make comparisons – over time, culture, policies, etc. It is important that this summarisation be done in a principled and informed manner by the designers of the measurement scale than in a simple *ad hoc* approach by people not versed in the subtleties of measurement technology.

There are, broadly speaking, two philosophically different perspectives on how to combine multiple indicators to give a single overall score. These two perspectives have gone under various names. For example, Feinstein (1987) calls them *psychometric* and *clinimetric*.

Fayers and Hand (2000, p. 241) explain the difference between the two perspectives: 'The objective of the psychometric approaches ... might be characterised as *attempting to measure a single attribute using multiple items*. In contrast, clinimetric methods *attempt to summarise multiple attributes with a single index*'. (our italics)

A prime illustration of the psychometric perspective is factor analysis. This is perhaps hardly surprising, since factor analysis was initially developed by and for the psychological and psychometric communities. Factor analysis postulates the existence of an underlying 'factor' or characteristic, which cannot be measured directly, hence also called a 'latent' or hidden factor. 'Intelligence' is a classic example. In fact, factor analysis typically generalises this structure to postulate the existence of several underlying factors which cannot be measured directly, but for the purposes of this exposition it is sufficient to assume just one.

Observable variables (in the case of intelligence these might be scores on different tests – numerical reasoning, verbal reasoning, etc.) are correlated with the unobservable latent factor. In fact, in the standard factor analysis model, a subject's score on any one of these observable variables is the sum of that subject's value of the underlying latent factor and a 'specific' part due to the particular variable being observed. Covariances between the observable variables are explained by virtue of the fact that they have the latent variable in common. Statistical methods, applied to the covariance matrix between the observed variables, allow one to separate out the contributions from the latent variable and the specific variables. In particular, by such means one can estimate a subject's score on the latent variable, even though it cannot be observed directly.

A key thing about factor analysis is that it is based on a postulated *model*. It says 'the observed covariance matrix arises because there is this underlying structure'. And then seeks to estimate the details of the structure from the observed matrix. This is clearly very much in the psychometric mould, as described above; it seeks to measure a *single* unobservable attribute using the observed values of *multiple* items which are related to the unobservable attribute by the assumed model structure. (Of course, if the assumed model structure is wrong, then things can go awry, but a discussion of that is beyond the scope of this book.)

This situation appears rather different from the case of wellbeing and quality of life. Not everyone agrees that there is some underlying characteristic – wellbeing – with observed attributes (such as subjective contentment, adequate income, strong social connections, low fear of crime, a warm place to live, etc.) arising largely because of this underlying factor. Such an assumption seems rather odd – the observable attributes clearly lack any intrinsic homogeneity. Rather it is thought that there are a number of *completely distinct* characteristics which together can be taken as an indicator of wellbeing. This is the clinimetric perspective, in which the aim is 'to summarise multiple attributes with a single index'.

Of this aim of combining completely distinct attributes, Fayers and Hand (2002) say '... a single index loses the intrinsic differences between the attributes and it also sacrifices any possibility of allowing for an interaction ... Instead the researchers aim their strategies at choosing and suitably emphasizing the most important attributes to be included in the index ... In fact, of course, we are choosing how to *define* the concept being measured by our choice of variables and the way of combining them ... Clinimetric scales are different from psychometric scales because, in the former, the items to be included are chosen according to what we want the scale to do, whereas in the latter they are chosen because they are thought to be related to an underlying concept which defies explicit measurement'.

The choice of characteristics to be included in a clinimetric index, along with the method by which they are to be combined, is very much a pragmatic one – in the technical sense defined in Section 1.4. It is a deliberate choice, to reflect one's aim, not a choice in any way determined by empirical relationships (such as an observed covariance matrix). A classic example of a clinimetric scale is the Apgar score for the state of health of newborn infants. This combines the very distinct items of body colour, heart rate, respiration, reflex response and muscle tone.

The word 'clinimetric' sits a little uncomfortably with the topic of this book, since wellbeing is not intended to have any clinical implications. We have therefore decided to stick to the word 'pragmatic' to describe the approach to constructing a measurement scale based on an explicit combination of the components regarded as relevant. This term is also being adopted by others (e.g. Paruolo *et al.*, 2013).

This abstract (clinimetric and pragmatic) structure is the approach adopted in almost all strategies for constructing wellbeing measures. But one can go further in various ways.

One extension is to combine psychometric and pragmatic approaches. This has been done in a rather elegant model described in the New Economics Foundation report *Measuring Our Progress* (NEF, 2011, p. 13). At its base is a fundamentally psychometric model, linking two aspects of wellbeing (good feelings, such as happiness, joy, contentment and satisfaction; and good functioning, such as autonomy, competence, safety and social contacts) to external conditions and personal resources in a causal model. But these two aspects then have to be combined to yield an overall measure of wellbeing, and the relative balance taken between good feelings and good functioning must be a pragmatic decision.

Another extension is to adopt a form of *conjoint* measurement. Conjoint measurement derives additive relationships between different components purely from ordinal scales. One can regard it as essentially seeking to balance the various contributory components so that a unit change in one component has an equal effect to a unit change in another. In essence it finds contours, in the space spanned by the constituent components, so that all profiles lying on the same contour have the same degree of the characteristic to be measured (wellbeing, in our case). This approach has occasionally been applied in the wellbeing context (e.g. EPICURUS, 2006) and in related areas (e.g. Bridges *et al.*, 2008).

The characteristics thought relevant to wellbeing can be thought of as of three types. First, there are characteristics which are regarded as fundamental aspects of wellbeing. Subjective states might mostly be regarded as of this type. Second there are those which are thought to affect or influence wellbeing. For example, one might regard income, education and skills as things which influence wellbeing: we might expect low income and lack of education and skills to lead to lower wellbeing. And third, there are those which are regarded as being affected by or influenced by wellbeing. A sense of competence, and hence satisfaction with life, might be regarded as something which is a consequence of or an indicator of wellbeing.

It is not always clear whether a particular item is best regarded as an influence on, a consequence of or simply an aspect of wellbeing. Sometimes it is more than one, since feedback loops can occur. For example, a simple explanation of the fact that marital status is positively related to wellbeing amongst men might be that the support it provides is beneficial, so that marital status affects wellbeing. In the other hand, it is entirely possible that positive wellbeing induces a more optimistic and outgoing outlook which in turn is more likely to lead to strong personal relationships. In contrast, something like gender (women tend to have higher subjective wellbeing scores than men) can clearly work in only one direction: enhanced wellbeing cannot cause a gender change (we realise, as we write this that there are occasional exceptions, in which lack of wellbeing arising from gender dysphoria leads to a gender change operation; but these are very rare, and certainly occur in insufficient numbers to have a material effect on measures of national wellbeing!). And, likewise, the U-shaped relationship between age and wellbeing already mentioned can work in only one direction: enhanced wellbeing does not lead to one's age decreasing or increasing.

Quality of life models of this kind, involving an explicit recognition that there is more than one kind of characteristic (in fact two kinds – those which influence wellbeing and those which are consequences of wellbeing) are explored in detail in Fayers and Hand (2002). Characteristics which are influenced by wellbeing might well be summarised usefully by a factor form of model, but those which influence it can, at least in principle, be completely unrelated. The overall result can be thought of as a combination of, or a generalisation of, both factor models and regression models. The same sort of structure, applied in a different context, but one which has similar characteristics, is described in Hand and Crowder (2005). Sometimes such models are called *multiple indicator, multiple cause* (MIMIC) models.

1.8   What is national wellbeing?

Interpreting the wellbeing of a population in a very broad sense, one can discern a continuum of progress in developing measures, from simple mortality rates, via crude economic measures, to the current interpretation in terms of quality of life and beyond; again recall the World Health Organisation's definition of health as being 'a state of complete physical, mental and social well-being and not merely the absence of disease or infirmity' (WHO, 1946). It is interesting to recall that when this definition was introduced it was criticised by some as immeasurable. It is a mark of how far measurement technology has come that this criticism no longer holds any force.

So far we have been discussing what is meant by individual wellbeing, and how to measure it. We have seen that this is difficult enough. But measuring, and even defining, national wellbeing opens up further layers of difficulty. National wellbeing is, at least certainly in part, some kind of aggregate or average of individual wellbeing, which raises the question of how that aggregation or averaging should be effected. This is discussed in the next section. However, as we noted earlier, national wellbeing is more than merely a summary of the individual wellbeing of the members of a population. There are also additional higher level issues which should be taken into account when measuring things at the national level. For example, use of non-renewable resources, while having little impact on individual short-term day-to-day experience, may be accumulating difficulties for the nation's future wellbeing. Perhaps this suggests that a concept of national wellbeing should avoid the short-term nature which is an inevitable part of individual wellbeing by integrating or averaging over time. This explains why sustainability plays a part in many discussions.

Chapter 2 gives a history of measuring national wellbeing. The history is a long one, inevitably, if one regards a government's prime aim as being to promote national wellbeing. Familiar examples we give there include the United States Declaration of Independence of 1776, with its reference to 'the pursuit of happiness', and Sir John Sinclair's Statistical Account of Scotland of 1791, an 'inquiry into the state of a country for the purpose of ascertaining the quantum of happiness enjoyed by its inhabitants and the means of its future improvement'. That last is precisely the concern of the current interest in national wellbeing – it took only two centuries to get there.

Two more recent examples of measures which combine characteristics at different levels are the *Human Development Index* (see Chapter 2) and the *Happy Planet Index*. The definition of the *Human Development Index* has changed over time, but broadly speaking it is the geometric mean of three basic dimensions: (i) life expectancy at birth; (ii) education; (iii) and an income index. The *Happy Planet Index* (see link in Appendix), introduced by the New Economics Foundation in 2006, is defined as a combination of a subjective measure of life satisfaction, life expectancy at birth, and a measure of individual demand on the Earth's ecosystems (so-called 'ecological footprint').

Chapter 6 discusses in detail the different levels which need to be combined, covering national economic accounts (for which aggregate measures already exist), extension of the national accounts to cover such things as time spent on voluntary work and the distribution of income within and across households, specific social conditions such as environmental conditions and aggregates of individual wellbeing and life satisfaction. Note that since one use of a national wellbeing measure will be to compare different countries, measures such as GDP that depend on the size of the population will need to be standardised – giving, for example, GDP per capita.

1.9   And how to measure *national* wellbeing?

We see from the above that, to produce a measure of *national* wellbeing, we have to *aggregate* the measures of individual people into an overall measure for the population, and then combine the resulting aggregate(s) with other higher level populations aspects.

Methods of aggregating or averaging individual values, to yield an overall population summary, have long been used in other areas. One domain is that of health statistics, evaluated at the population level by aggregating from the individual level. Perhaps the best known example is that of mortality statistics (dating back at least as far as John Graunt's *Natural and Political Observations Made upon the Bills of Mortality*, in 1662 (Graunt, 1662)), but there are also population measures of morbidity. Indeed the discipline of *epidemiology* is defined as the study of patterns of diseases in populations, and there are many classic examples, including William Farr's collection of data relating to cholera in the nineteenth century. The strong link between public health and population wellbeing is illustrated by the following extract from *The Spirit Level* (Wilkinson and Pickett, 2010, p. 277).

> It is now almost universally accepted amongst scholars and practitioners of pub-
> lic health that the most important determinants of health are social and eco-
> nomic circumstances. Geoffrey Rose, who was one of the most highly influential
> and respected epidemiologists of the second half of the twentieth century, said,

'medicine and politics cannot and should not be kept apart'. Our growing understanding of human health and wellbeing are so deeply affected by social structure
inevitably pushes science into politics.

In principle, aggregation is straightforward: individual level scores are determined using a
survey, and then one simply calculates the proportion who respond positively to some question
(e.g. 'overall, are you satisfied with your life nowadays?') or derives an appropriate average,
such as an arithmetic mean (e.g. from the question 'overall, how happy did you feel yesterday,
on a scale from 1 to 10?') or quantile values (e.g. what percentage of people had a score of
three or lower on the previous question?).

Adolphe Quetelet, working in the nineteenth century, was a founder of the notion of
extracting an 'average' or aggregate view of the individuals making up a population. He
wrote: 'It is of primary importance to keep out of view man as he exists in an insulated,
separate or in an individual state, and to regard him only as a fraction of the species. In thus
setting aside his individual nature, we get quit of all which is accidental, and the individual
peculiarities, which exercise scarcely any influence over the mass, become effaced of their
own accord, allowing the observed to seize the general results' (Quetelet, 1842, p. 5). Quetelet
thus stressed the need to strip away the individual-specific variation, to reveal the larger scale
underlying property. It is this, in essence, which the measurement of *national* wellbeing seeks
to do.

Quetelet was very much aware of the advantages which derived from aggregation. For
example, (Quetelet, 1842, p. 6): 'It would appear, then, that moral phenomena, when observed
on a great scale, are found to resemble physical phenomena; and we thus arrive, in inquiries
of this kind, at the fundamental principle, that *the greater the number of individuals observed,
the more do individual peculiarities, whether physical or moral, become effaced, and leave in
a prominent point of view the general facts, by virtue of which society exists and is preserved'.*
(His italics)

The first part of Quetelet's *A Treatise on Man and the Development of his Faculties*
(Quetelet, 1842) is concerned with population growth, birth rates and death rates, and the
second part is concerned with physical characteristics such as height, weight and strength.
The third part is entitled 'Development of the moral and intellectual qualities of man', and is
predominantly concerned with attributes such as memory, imagination, judgement, insanity,
temperance, courage, genius, prudence and propensity for evil, including crime. He could so
easily have extended this to wellbeing! Again he stresses the advantages of working with a
mass of people (p. 73): 'It appears to me that it will always be impossible to estimate the
absolute degree of courage, etc, of any one particular individual: for what must be adopted
as unity? – shall we be able to observe this individual long enough, and with sufficient
closeness, to have a record of all his actions, whereby to estimate the value of the courageous
ones; and will these actions be numerous enough to deduce any satisfactory conclusion from
them? Who will guarantee that the dispositions of this individual may not be altered during
the course of the observations? When we operate on a great number of individuals, these
difficulties almost entirely disappear, especially if we only want to determine the ratios, and
not the absolute values'. If anywhere, it would be this part of Quetelet's book which dealt with
wellbeing and happiness. But such a discussion does not figure there. The nearest Quetelet
gets is a discussion of suicide rates.

There are subtleties in what we have called the 'aggregation' from the individual level to
population level. One, in particular, has already been mentioned. This is the fact that there

seems to be a relationship between inequality and national wellbeing (Wilkinson and Pickett, 2010). Inequality, of wealth for example, is not a property of an individual, and a simple average of the wealth of the individuals in a population will not reveal such inequality. At the least one needs to look at measures of dispersion, and for properties such as wealth, which cannot take negative values and which tend to be very positively skewed; measures of skewness are also needed. For a skew distribution with a long positive tail, the majority of values will be less than the average, when 'average' is taken to be the arithmetic mean (so leading to the old joke about most people earning less than the average), with a very long tail of exceptionally large values being balanced by a large number of very small values. This would seem to be a natural driver of envy. Perceptions are probably aggravated by the constant media comment on large salaries and wealth, even to the extent that newspapers regularly report the value of the house owned by a story's protagonist. The fact is that wellbeing is influenced by relative perceptions. The saying 'It is not enough to succeed; it is also necessary that others must fail' or variants of it, has been variously attributed to a wide range of authors.

Inequality can manifest at various levels. One is the distributional level of wealth or income, but others appear in the form of gender or ethnic disparities leading to exclusion from education (and the enhancement of wellbeing that brings), jobs and even health care. The question of inequality and the various ways in which it can arise mean that measures of national wellbeing have to be sufficiently fine grained that subgroup analysis can be undertaken. A small simple random survey of an entire population may be insufficient to tease out important sources of poor wellbeing.

When surveys are being used to collect wellbeing data, and when the intention is to aggregate the wellbeing of the individual members of a population, it is perhaps unnecessary to note that great care must be taken over the data collection. The measured individuals must be representative of the population in some sense. Perhaps more than most areas, wellbeing is susceptible to distortions of various kinds arising from poor data collection strategies.

Our discussion on aggregating low-level values to yield a (component of) a national measure of wellbeing has focused on individuals as the elements. But some aspects aggregate other elements. Air quality, noise levels and even global temperature are examples. They can be measured at specific points, but precisely how to determine an overall 'average' requires some careful thought, not least because if one chose different points one could get very different values.

Examples of higher level population characteristics, not generally associated with values describing individuals, are high-level economic indicators, public value and sustainability. High-level economic indicators, of the kind currently measured, such as GDP and GNP, are based on the system of national accounts. Despite their imperfections as measures of wellbeing, they are important aspects of it. Compiling the national accounts involves much data collection including from individual businesses and households. The resulting aggregates, though, refer only to the economy as a whole (or to whole sectors of the economy). We do not talk about the GDP of an individual business. While we can measure household or individual debt, we also need to look at the national debt in terms of the amount that the government owes, from the securities and bonds it has issued or the amounts it has borrowed from international organisations for example. Paradoxically, much of a government's income has to be drawn from individuals and businesses through taxation, so that government debt is indirectly the debt of individuals and businesses.

When looking at public value, the essence is that something has value to the public at large. A public park, for example, enhances wellbeing, but it is part of the national fabric and cannot be attributed to individuals. Public value is deemed to be intrinsic to things like parks: they are valued by the public whether or not they use them. However, we will see in Chapter 6 that cost-benefit analyses of public policy decisions might draw on how they affect individual wellbeing.

Sustainability, in a number of arenas, tells us whether our present way of life can be maintained. It is therefore necessarily a high-level assessment, but it is also something that can only be fully assessed in retrospect. We will look more closely at sustainable development in Chapter 2, but to summarise the point here, sustainable development is often defined as development that 'meets the needs of the present without compromising the ability of future generations to meet their needs' (World Commission on Environment and Development, 1987). Such foresight is asking a lot of current measurement systems.

There have been many attempts to quantify sustainability: Chapter 3, of Stiglitz *et al.* (2010) includes a review, and as they say 'This abundance of measures is a serious drawback insofar as different synthetic indicators convey widely divergent messages. This leads to a great deal of confusion among statisticians and policymakers'. They argue that sustainability is complementary to current wellbeing or economic performance and 'must be examined separately', going so far as to say that attempting to combine these two aspects into a single indicator leads to confusion. As a result, they recommend a dashboard of indicators.

1.10   Structure of the book

We began this chapter by presenting three fundamental questions: what is national wellbeing, why should it be measured, and how should it be measured? Chapter 1 has thus set the scene for what follows. Since national wellbeing is clearly built on individual wellbeing, we described what we mean by individual wellbeing, we looked briefly at its component aspects and then outlined notions of how to measure it, including some basic measurement theory. This introductory discussion included examination of objective and subjective aspects, and also how the various different aspects should be combined to yield a single overall measure (given the inevitable need for a single measure even where a dashboard containing several measures is presented). We also argue that the wellbeing of individuals is but one aspect of *national* wellbeing. A nation, as a whole, must address issues at a population level, consider the future, and generally take note of aspects which may not impact individuals, at least at the time of measurement.

Chapter 2 sets our development in context by giving a history of the concept of national wellbeing and its measurement. The concept certainly has a long history, with the economic aspects of national wellbeing going back at least as far as the 1600s. But, as we repeatedly stress in this book, echoing one of the key drivers behind the global initiatives to measure national wellbeing, economics is but one aspect of wellbeing. The ideas covered in this chapter span philosophies of government, utilitarianism, the United Nation's System of National Accounts, quality of life, the rise of psychological measures of wellbeing, the capabilities approach, issues of sustainability and others.

From the history, we move in Chapter 3 to examine more recent developments. The report by Stiglitz, Sen and Fitoussi, produced by a commission established by the then president of France, Nicholas Sarkozy, has been seminal, as have the detailed developments by the OECD. We also discuss concurrent initiatives, especially to replace the Millennium Development Goals, in which measures of wellbeing and progress are also core.

Because individual wellbeing is so central to national wellbeing (some would say individual wellbeing is the entirety of national wellbeing). Chapter 4 is devoted to how individual wellbeing can be measured. The very notion of measuring wellbeing sometimes encounters lay scepticism. But this is in ignorance of profound developments which have been made in recent decades, both in terms of the theory of measurement, and in terms of its practical implementation. The fact is that degrees of subjective feeling can be quantified, and indeed, can be quantified accurately. These measures build on a huge amount of work on measuring psychophysical responses, opinions and attitudes, as well as subjective phenomena such as pain and depression.

Chapter 5 steps up a level, from the individual to the nation, examining what measures of national wellbeing and progress might be used for: it is in their very nature that different measures, and different measurement procedures, will be needed if the results are to be used for different purposes, just as a price index for macroeconomic purposes may not be suitable for use as a measure of inflation pressure on households.

Chapter 6 then looks at the details of how to construct a suitable measure of national wellbeing. The economic aspects (with the ubiquitous GDP leading the charge) are but one aspect of national wellbeing, and they need extending – in order to capture economic aspects properly, but, more importantly, more widely to capture non-economic social, cultural and environmental aspects. The chapter also examines ideas, methods and tools from around the world.

Measuring national wellbeing is of global interest, with a large number of initiatives being undertaken. To complement the broad brush approach elsewhere in the book, and to give the flavour of the depth of investigations being carried out, Chapter 7 provides a case study: that of the United Kingdom. The chapter describes the historical development of the measuring national wellbeing initiative in the United Kingdom, and outlines where it has got to.

Finally, in Chapter 8, we look back at where we have got to, and look ahead to the future. We note the potential that new data capture and analytic technologies have for the measurement of wellbeing. And we note that, to go beyond economic measures of wellbeing and progress will not be straightforward; we describe it as requiring a paradigm shift. Although the signs are promising, it is clear that, if all this effort is to do any good, the measures must start to be used. Words are all very well, but the measures must be integrated into government policy decisions, with businesses and households also making decisions that similarly go beyond the purely economic.

We conclude the book with an appendix of sources. Perhaps one of the most striking things about the entire area is the amount of work being undertaken. It really is a global movement. And it is a dynamic movement: we were aware that new developments were being made even as we were writing. Despite that, it is clear that ideas are converging: we expect the material covered in this volume to continue to hold true, as national wellbeing measures are crystallised.

References

Baggott J. (2004). *Beyond Measure: Modern Physics, Philosophy and the Meaning of Quantum Theory*. Oxford University Press, Oxford.

BBC. (2012). Kabul Bank: Afghan Politicians 'interfered with enquiry'. http://www.bbc.co.uk/news/world-asia-20523217 (accessed 15 March 2013).

Belgian Federal Planning Bureau. (2005). *Transdisciplinarity and the Governance of Sustainable Development*. Belgian Federal Planning Bureau, Task Force Sustainable Development.

Bentham J. (2009). *An Introduction to the Principles of Morals and Legislation*. Dover Publications Inc.

Brickman P. and Campbell D.T. (1971). Hedonic relativism and planning the good society. In: M.H. Apley (ed.) *Adaptation 0-Level Theory: A Symposium*. Academic Press, New York. pp. 287–302.

Bridges J., Haber B., Marshall D. *et al.* (2008). A Checklist for Conjoint Analysis Applications in Health: Report of the ISPOR Conjoint Analysis Good Research Practices Task Force. http://www.ispor.org/taskforces/documents/A_CHECKLIST_FOR_CONJOINT_ANALYSIS_APPLICATIONS_IN_HEALTH.pdf (accessed 25 April 2014).

Chambers R. (1997). *Whose Reality Counts? Putting the First Last*. Intermediate Technology, London.

Christmann K. and Rogerson M. (2004). *Crime, Fear of Crime and Quality of Life Identifying and Responding to Problems*. Research Report 25, New Deal for Communities: The National Evaluation, Sheffield Hallam University.

Christopher J.C. (1999). Situating psychological wellbeing: exploring the cultural roots of its theory and research. *Journal of Counseling and Development*, **77**, 141–152.

CSLS. (2011). Happiness as a Goal for Public Policy: Ready for Primetime? A Synthesis of the CSLS-ICP Conference on Happiness and Public Policy, CSLS Research Note 2011-1. http://www.csls.ca/notes/Note2011-1.pdf (accessed 4 July 2013).

DeNeve K.M. and Cooper H. (1998). The happy personality: a meta-analysis of personality traits and subjective well-being. *Psychological Bulletin*, **124**, 197–229.

Dickens C. (1850). The Personal History, Adventures, Experience and Observation of David Copperfield the Younger of Blunderstone Rookery (Which He Never Meant to Publish on Any Account).

Dolan P. and Powdthavee N. (2012). Thinking about it: a note on attention and well-being losses from unemployment. *Applied Economics Letters*, **19**(4), 325–332. doi:10.1080/13504851.2011.5770008

Dunn G., Sham P.C. and Hand D.J. (1993). Statistics and the nature of depression. *Journal of the Royal Statistical Society, Series A*, **156**, 63–87. (Reprinted in Psychological Medicine, **23**, 871–889).

Easterlin R.A. (2003). Building a better theory of well-being. Discussion Paper No. 742, Institute for the Study of Labour, Bonn.

Edgeworth F.Y. (1881). *Mathematical Psychics: An Essay on the Application of Mathematics to the Moral Sciences*. C. Kegan Paul and Co, London.

EPICURUS. (2006). Societal and Economic Effects on Quality of Life and Well-being: Preference Identification and Priority Setting in Response to Changes in Labour Market Status: Final Report, HPSE-CT-2002-00143. European Commission, Directorate General for Research, Brussels.

Fayers P.M. and Hand D.J. (2002). Causal variables, indicator variables, and measurement scales, with discussion. *Journal of the Royal Statistical Society, Series A*, **165**, 233–261.

Fayers P.M. and Machin D. (2000). *Quality of Life: Assessment, Analysis and Interpretation*. Wiley, Chichester.

Feinstein A.R. (1987). *Clinimetrics*. Yale University Press, New Haven, Connecticut.

Felce D. and Perry J. (1995). Quality of life: its definition and measurement. *Research in Developmental Disabilities*, **16**, 51–74.

Flynn J.R. (2012). *Are We Getting Smarter: Rising IQ in The Twenty-First Century*. Cambridge University Press, Cambridge.

Goodhart, C.A.E. (1984). *Monetary Theory and Practice*. Macmillan, Basingstoke.

Graunt. (1662). Natural and political OBSERVATIONS mentioned in a following INDEX, and made upon the Bills of Mortality. http://www.edstephan.org/Graunt/bills.html (accessed 21 December 2013).

Hand D.J. (2004). *Measurement Theory and Practice: The World Through Quantification*. Wiley, Chichester.

Hand D.J. (2007). *Information Generation: How Data Rule Our World*. One World Publications.

Hand D.J. and Crowder M.J. (2005). Measuring customer quality in retail banking. *Statistical Modelling*, **5**, 145–158.

Handy C. (1995). *The Empty Raincoat: Making Sense of the Future*. Arrow, London.

Harrington R. (1804). *The Death-Warrant of the French Theory of Chemistry*. Longman, London.

Kahneman D., Diener W. and Schwarz N. (eds) (2003) *Well-Being: The Foundations of Hedonic Psychology*. Russell-Sage Foundation, New York.

Kahneman D., Krueger A.B., Schkade D., Schwarz N. and Stone A. (2004). Toward national well-being accounts. *American Economic Review*, Papers and Proceedings, **94**, 429–434.

McAllister F. (2005). *Wellbeing Concepts and Challenges*. Sustainable Development Research Network.

McDowell I. and Newell C. (1996). *Measuring Health: A Guide to Rating Scales and Questionnaires* (2nd ed.). Oxford University Press, Oxford.

Michaelson J., Mahony S. and Schifferes J. (2012). *Measuring Well-being: A Guide for Practitioners*. New Economics Foundation, London.

NEF. (2011). Measuring Our Progress: The Power of Well-Being. http://dnwssx4l7gl7s.cloudfront.net/nefoundation/default/page/-/files/Measuring_our_Progress.pdf (accessed 2 August 2013).

OECD. (2011a). *How's Life: Measuring Well-Being*. OECD Publishing.

OECD. (2011b). *Compendium of OECD Well-Being Indicators*. OECD Publishing.

OECD. (2013). *OECD Guidelines on Measuring Subjective Well-Being*. OECD Publishing.

Paruolo P., Saisana M. and Saltelli A. (2013). Ratings and rankings: voodoo or science? *Journal of the Royal Statistical Society, Series A*, **176**, 609–634.

Quetelet M.A. (1842). *A Treatise on Man and the Development of His Faculties*. Burt Franklin, New York.

Ryan R.M. and Deci E.L. (2001). On happiness and human potentials: a review of research on hedonic and eudemonic well-being. *Annual Review of Psychology*, **52**, 141–166.

Santor D.A., Gregus M. and Welch A. (2006). Eight decades of measurement in depression. *Measurement*, **4**, 135–155.

Schkade D. and Kahneman D. (1998). Does living in California make people happy? A focusing illusion in judgments of life satisfaction. *Psychological Science*, **9**, 340–346.

Self A., Thomas J. and Randall C. (2012). *Measuring National Well-being: Life in the UK, 2012*. Office for National Statistics.

Stiglitz J.E., Sen S. and Fitoussi J-P. (2010). *Mismeasuring Our Lives: Why GDP doesn't Add Up*. The New Press, New York.

Strange T. and Bayley A. (2008). *Sustainable Development: Linking Economy, Society, Environment*. OECD.

Telegraph (2003). Ambulance service 'lied over response rates'. http://www.telegraph.co.uk/news/1423338/Ambulance-service-lied-over-response-rates.html (accessed 26 December 2012).

van Hoorn A. (2007). A short introduction to subjective well-being: its measurement, correlates and policy uses. International Conference on Is Happiness Measurable and What Do Those Measures Mean for Policy? University of Rome 'Tor Vergata', 2–3; April, 2007.

Verme P. (2011). Life satisfaction and income inequality. *Review of Income and Wealth*, **57**, 111–127.

Watson D., Clark L.A. and Tellegen A. (1988). Development and validation of brief measures of positive and negative affect: the PANAS Scales. *Journal of Personality and Social Psychology*, **54**, 1063–1070.

WHO. (1946). Preamble to the Constitution of the World Health Organization as adopted by the International Health Conference, New York, 19–22; June, 1946; signed on 22 July 1946 by the representatives of 61 States (Official Records of the World Health Organization, no. 2, p. 100) and entered into force on 7 April 1948.

Wilkinson R. and Pickett K. (2010). *The Spirit Level: Why Equality is Better for Everyone*. Penguin Books, London.

World Commission on Environment and Development. (1987). *Our Common Future*, Oxford University Press, Oxford.

Scollon C.N., Kim-Prieto C., and Diener E. (2003). Experience sampling: Promises and pitfalls, strengths and weaknesses. *Journal of Happiness Studies*, **4**, 5–34.

2

A short history of national wellbeing and its measurement

> Too much and too long, we seem to have surrendered community excellence and community values in the mere accumulation of material things.
>
> Robert Kennedy (1968)

At the heart of this book is the issue of the adequacy of current measures of economic performance. There are questions about how the current measures are defined, and in particular the transactions that are included or excluded in coming to the headline measure of a country's Gross Domestic Product (GDP). There are also much broader concerns about how well the GDP figures measure the wellbeing of society, both at a point in time and as measures of economic, environmental and social sustainability.

When we ask someone 'How are you?' we are usually aware that they are likely to take different things into account in replying. We know from qualitative research that many different things matter to people in the United Kingdom. There are some common themes: health, good connections with family and friends, job satisfaction and economic security, present and future conditions of the environment and education and training (ONS, 2011, p. 6). The reply to our greeting from someone in the United Kingdom is therefore likely to be influenced mostly by their health and those of people around them, by their work or by their job prospects. Different things may matter to people in other countries. There may also be cultural differences in how open, or not, people are in responding to such questions.

This book is essentially about asking the same question but in terms of a country as a whole. It seems that to answer an apparently simple question – 'how is the country doing these days?'; there are three broad areas we might want to assess. What inevitably comes first is to ask how the economy is performing. In answering that, we would want, for example, to see who benefits, not just the overall size of the economy. Second, what about people and the way of life? What do we make of the quality of life, not just of course for economic players (entrepreneurs, landlords, employees) but for everyone in society? Third, what are

The Wellbeing of Nations: Meaning, Motive and Measurement, First Edition. Paul Allin and David J. Hand.
© 2014 John Wiley & Sons, Ltd. Published 2014 by John Wiley & Sons, Ltd.

we doing to the planet? What natural resources are being used up and what is happening to air and water quality and to climate change? In our mind, therefore, the issue is not just about wellbeing in the present time: integral to that is the question of whether or not our current way of life is sustainable over time.

The concept and the measurement of a country's national economic accounts can be traced back at least to the mid-1600s. The widespread and systematic measurement, publication and use of national accounts only took off in the middle of the twentieth century. It has often been noted that the national accounts were designed for specific purposes, to assess economic conditions and to plan, deliver and monitor economic policy. GDP was never meant necessarily to be a measure of national or societal wellbeing. Social and environmental reporting also both have a venerable history, though, somehow, never quite achieving the status of barometers of society that is accorded to the national accounts and GDP in particular.

In this chapter we focus on how the idea of what we now call national or societal wellbeing has developed over time. In particular, we are keen to explore whether or not there is something that is tangible as national wellbeing, broader than the health of a nation's economy, because we usually need to define something before we can measure it. We will see that there are many other candidates beyond the formal national economic accounts, put forward by social scientists, environmentalists and official statisticians either explicitly as additional measures of wellbeing or which we can now see as fitting well with the idea of national wellbeing. These measures have largely been developed from the middle of the twentieth century. They include the measurement of social capital, the compilation of environmental accounts and sustainable development indicators, as well as measures of subjective wellbeing. We will explore all of these in greater depth in following chapters, but the point here is that there are substantial foundations on which to build new measures of national wellbeing, although the originators of such developments may or may not have had the concept of national wellbeing in mind. Indeed, it is always worth bearing in mind that each development is essentially a product of a particular time and place: the ideas, culture and institutions in which they were germinated may not hold in later times or different places.

This chapter is far from a complete history. Whole books have been written on the history of happiness and wellbeing (e.g. McMahon, 2006). We will be giving a highly selective presentation. The current desire for better measures of national wellbeing and progress is characterised as 'GDP and beyond'. So, we will look at the history of GDP and we will also identify measures that have been proposed as alternatives or supplements to GDP over the years. We will introduce a number of different approaches and set them in the context of how people have talked about the good society or the wellbeing of the nation. We will explore recent developments in Chapter 3, before exploring candidate measures, and the process of selecting them, in subsequent chapters.

There have, over time, been many ideas and developments on which we can build a better understanding of national wellbeing and how to measure it. We start with some philosophy.

2.1   The good society and philosophies of the role of government, from ancient times

At many times during the history of Western thought we can trace discourse and debate on what is society, what makes a good society, and on the role of government in achieving a good society for the wellbeing of citizens. The idea of progress is perhaps less apparent, though we will find many clues and traces of progress towards the ideal society, and indeed the notion of progress as a purpose to human life. We write this knowing that our knowledge and understanding of Arabic, Chinese and other societies is considerably weaker than that of Western societies. This is not meant in any way to restrict the development of wider measures of wellbeing and progress. Indeed, we write this book believing that there is 'a new global movement' under way and we look forward to learning more about developments from around the world at future OECD forums and in other ways. We are reassured that the 'Istanbul Declaration', which we will meet later, was signed by 'representatives of the European Commission, the Organisation for Economic Cooperation and Development, the Organisation of the Islamic Conference, the United Nations, the United Nations Development Programme and the World Bank'.

We want to use the past as a means of examining the present. However, this is always problematic and may be particularly so in the case of tracking national wellbeing and progress. As Nurnberg (2012) has noted, in the context of reviewing two successful historical novels, 'temporal distance does complicate things'. Nurnberg quotes and acknowledges Ian McEwen's point that 'it would not be possible to read and enjoy literature from a time remote from our own, or from a culture that was profoundly different from our own, unless we shared some common emotional ground, some deep reservoir of assumptions, with the writer ... what we have in common with each other is just as extraordinary as all our exotic differences'. In Nurnberg's view, though, the balance is with Henry James's concern that the distance is too great, that 'it would be unrealistic to believe we could imagine the thoughts and emotions of people from an age so different from our own'. Runciman (2010, p. 119) nevertheless takes this to a higher level, suggesting that 'concern about the potential for conflict and disorder which is inherent in all known human societies is timeless'.

With that in mind, there are then many possible starting points. To take just one, let us go back to Plato, who lived in the ancient Greek city-state of Athens between 427 and 347 BC. In 386 BC Plato founded the Academy as a school for statesmen and he taught there for the rest of his life. One of the products of Plato's early years in the Academy is what has been translated and published as the book *The Republic*. As the translator H.D.P. Lee points out, the title is misleading to the modern reader – 'Plato, in fact, was writing about society or the state, and this is what his title means' (Lee, 1955, p. 26). Or, perhaps more precisely, as Runciman (2010, p. 123) has noted, Plato's Republic is an example of '*optative* sociology'. Plato was describing a good or ideal society which, if it ever *were* to come about, would result in the world being a much better place.

The Republic starts with a moral question: Why should I be good? (Lee, 1955, p. 28). Plato draws on discussions with other philosophers. In particular his teacher Socrates had replied that, as summarised by Lee, 'the problem is too difficult to solve in the individual; he must look at it "in larger letters" in society'. So, as Lee continues, there is in three parts of The Republic 'the first sketch of an ideal society'. This covers social organisation, education and the way of life of leaders and others in society.

Much of *The Republic* describes what was regarded as the civilised society of Plato's time and then challenges why this was unhealthy, setting out reforms needed to address the imperfections of society. One passage particularly relevant to our study of progress and wellbeing concludes that the pursuit of unlimited material possessions in ancient Greece had the inevitable and dire consequence of war. Plato saw acquisitiveness as the origin of most evil, individual or social (Lee, 1955, p. 108). Plato returns to the individual in Part V of this work, seeking to show, in Lee's summary, 'by an analysis of the elements in the human mind, that its well-being, full development and happiness are to be secured by doing right and not by doing wrong' (Lee, 1955, p. 29).

Aristotle (384–322 BC) was a pupil of Plato and his approach to ethics is that individuals should take steps to be good and to do good, not just understand what a good society would look like. In Aristotle's philosophy, to function optimally as a human is to aim for eudemonia, usually translated as happiness or wellbeing. Layard calls eudemonia 'the object of life ... a type of happiness associated with virtuous conduct and philosophic reflection' (2006, p. 22). In order to achieve eudemonia requires a good character – areté, usually described as moral or ethical virtue or excellence. Jaeger explains areté as 'a power, an ability to do something. Strength and health are the areté of the body; cleverness and insight the areté of the mind' (taken from Werner Jaeger's *Paideia*, quoted in each edition of the arts journal Areté, www.aretemagazine.com).

Aristotle thought of wellbeing in distinctly humanistic terms, in particular excellence in the exercise of the virtues as opposed to, say, being rich and owning lots of slaves. He also sharply distinguished wellbeing from any subjective psychological state. So, despite frequent references back to Aristotle in the 'happiness' literature, happiness is a dangerous translation of his concept of eudemonia. According to Aristotle, that your life is going well is a matter of what you are doing, rather than how you feel. The ancient philosophers were concerned with what life was for, and what it might be. We do not search their texts for advice on how to measure wellbeing and progress! It was not until the twentieth century, as we shall see in Chapter 4, that happiness and personal wellbeing came to be measured by social scientists.

Anderson looks over the history of the notion of growth and progress, rather than the good society, and writes that the concept of progress 'can be traced back through many different routes to many different origins. Amongst these is the Jewish and Christian sense that human history has a particular meaning and purpose, a beginning and an end. This sense of history moving in a particular direction finds echoes and expressions in many of the major movements of thought in Western civilisation, including Marxism, Darwinism and growth-oriented economics, though in each case it is qualified and modified in a particular way' (Anderson, 1991, p. 42).

Having mentioned two religions, we must record that for people of many faiths or religions, their wellbeing and progress is directed towards, and assessed or measured, in those terms alone. The destination for people committed to biblical Christian beliefs is the Kingdom of Heaven. We will see later that measures of participation in religious activities might be included in measures of the wellbeing of a nation, reflecting, for example, the extent of affiliation to the values shared within a society, which also acts as a marker for the significance of religion in people's lives (e.g. Newport *et al.*, 2012). However, for many people, it is their faith that is their driving force.

As the then Archbishop of Canterbury, Rowan Williams, explained in his 2011 Easter sermon, authentic happiness 'isn't a matter of theory: it simply happens that way'. Christian joy 'is offered to the world not to guarantee a permanently happy society in the sense of a society free from tension, pain or disappointment, but to affirm that whatever happens in the unpredictable world ... we are able to live honestly and courageously with the challenges constantly thrown at us' (Williams, 2011). This is not to say that people of faith do not care about national wellbeing and progress. There are many examples of church action on poverty, for example.

It is tempting to explore how formulations of a good society and progress played out through the rise fall of many societies, nations and empires. Looking at the history of any nation will no doubt reveal similar examples to that of Hywel Dda (Hywel the Good) in Wales. He is now credited with convening the first sort of parliament in Wales, in AD 930, and with producing a legal code with the basic principle of protecting the weak (Sager, 2002, p. 232). To do justice to this history would demand we scrutinise scarce and fragmentary records and recognise how interpretation of accumulated evidence might change over time. (e.g. discoveries of hoards of intricate and finely crafted gold jewellery have challenged the characterisation of a period of English history commonly called the Dark Ages).

We will therefore skip over many years of human development and progress, not only to maintain brevity but because the Age of Enlightenment, which lasted between roughly 1650 and 1800, sought to establish societies based on reason, including by rediscovering and building on the ideas of ancient Greece. In particular, the perspective that the achievement of happiness is the aim of life was taken up in the Enlightenment in the ethical position called utilitarianism. This is concerned with actions that give rise to the maximum happiness in society. It provides a more recent, but still distant, time period in which to look for the foundations of societal wellbeing and progress. It also, of course, reminds us that there are many shades of meaning to 'happiness'. Happiness as an aim of life generally means something more than simply the gaining of momentary pleasure.

2.2   Utilitarianism

In 1725, around the middle of the Age of Enlightenment and some two thousand years after Plato, Francis Hutcheson offered a test and justification for action. Hutcheson (1725/2002, p. 515) proposed that the best action results in 'the greatest happiness for the greatest numbers'. This expression of the ethical theory of utilitarianism, which is actually an ancient concept, was developed by Jeremy Bentham, to whom it is often now attributed. Bentham (2009, p. 1) described the principle of utility as determining the extent to which an action appears to increase or reduce the happiness of those affected by the action and he made it clear that the principle should apply not only to private individuals but 'to every measure of government'. There have been, and continue to be, many extensions to, and debates about, utilitarianism – see Scarre (1996) for a late twentieth century survey of the history and condition of utilitarian ethics.

Utilitarianism is sometimes described as our 'common sense', which we apply to all sorts of decisions. However, the danger with common sense is that it is sometimes neither sensible, nor commonly agreed on! We do need some measurements to help us. As we are concerned with the measurement of wellbeing we will look briefly at how early proponents of utilitarianism considered measurement.

Hutcheson not only set out the goal of delivering the greatest happiness for the greatest numbers, he also thought about what is involved in measuring this. That is, he got as far as identifying the quantities that would need to be measured. Alongside the quote above, Hutcheson refers to the quantity of the happiness that a given action would generate. This is presumably for each person affected because he also identifies the total number of people who would enjoy happiness in that case, and he envisages multiplying the two together (a 'compound ratio' in the language of the time) to give the overall 'moral quantity' of an action (its virtue, or if the action brings displeasure, its misery). There is also a hint that the total outcome could include some weighting, towards particular types of people, because he talks about 'the dignity, or moral importance of persons, [which] may compensate numbers'.

Although Hutcheson in effect sets out a formula for determining the happiness generated by a given action, he does not advise his readers on how to measure each component and hence how to compute the result. He is more concerned with the mathematics of happiness, presumably with the aim of ascertaining how to maximise it, than with the practicalities of measuring happiness. Hutcheson removed his algorithms from later editions of his book 'because they appeared useless, and were disagreeable to some readers'.

Bentham (2009, Chapter IV) presented a 'hedonic calculus', involving valuing a pleasure or pain and considering the extent of or the number of people affected by the action. Unlike Hutcheson, Bentham stood by his calculus, arguing that people were able to form a clear view of their own interest, and that the calculus would be needed by those framing public policy and legislation. In particular, Bentham (1798) saw education as the key to reform: 'The proper end of education is no other than the proper end of life'. Education was the key to the achievement of the greatest happiness of the greatest number. This might also suggest that we do not need to measure the outcome if we are sure of the means to achieving that, an idea further explored in Chapter 4, where we note the distinction between causes, effects and correlates of an individual's wellbeing and how they might each be used to measure or improve the measurement of wellbeing.

Later debate about utilitarianism has included whether or not the consequences of action are knowable at the time the action needs to be taken. If they are not knowable then they cannot be measured. If they are knowable it is not always obvious that they can be measured with the precision needed to make a decision. Although it seems rational to explore the consequences of an action before acting, we might also consider whether undertaking the additional analysis – being seen to be considering certain actions – might itself influence the outcome. This is a form of the 'observer' effect in measurement. In principle the observer effect could be minimised by improving the subtlety of the method of measurement, but this also indicates the potential complexity of measurement.

There were many other books written during the Age of Enlightenment about the growth and nature of society and how it should function. However, there generally appears to be little in this literature about how actually to measure pleasure or happiness, especially how to measure the happiness or otherwise of everyone in society likely to be affected by a proposed action. The algorithms and calculus highlighted above are a way of calculating the utility of a course of action but rely on an assessment or evaluation of several variables that are needed as inputs. At best, those seeking to use this approach at the time it was proposed, and for a century or more afterwards, have had to feed in their personal evaluation of these variables; there were no censuses or surveys to capture the information more objectively (although we can look back to find contemporary examples using the notion of samples in other fields; for example, the notion of taking a sample of coins to check the purity of the minting process).

The age of rationality produced a fine theory. It might be the case that an individual following utilitarianism principles and algorithms would have a viable framework for making personal decisions. However, it would be many years before practical tools and measures were available in order to be able to implement the theory as a basis for government action.

It is generally accepted that one legacy of the Age of Enlightenment is the idea of human advances in medicine, technology and intellectual activities. As Ince and Cox (2012) point out, the foundation for these changes is the scientific method and they claim that 'The story of the past hundred years is one of unparalleled human advances ... a hundred years of unabated progress'. They are talking of scientific progress, which they argue remains desirable and necessary. This presents an interesting counterpoint to the views we will report later in this and the next chapter, which present a paradox of unabated progress.

There are schools of thought that see utilitarianism as counter-intuitive. This has led to what they present as a more liberal, individualistic framework for political theory. Under this approach, public policies must be to create an overarching framework of personal freedom so that individuals and groups can freely pursue their wellbeing. For authors such as Philip Booth, government should 'focus on creating the framework in which persons can pursue happiness', rather than promoting our happiness or maximising our happiness (Booth, 2012, p. 31). This raises interesting measurement issues. How do we measure the freedom to pursue happiness, and how government has facilitated this, rather than the outcome of happiness itself? (Assuming of course that we value such measurement as a way of assessing the performance of government).

We could go much further down the road of philosophy in seeking to understand societal wellbeing and progress, though regrettably we do not have the space here to do so. Among many interesting, relevant and challenging concepts, for example, is the idea of a pluralism of values. Isaiah Berlin approached this from the belief that the point of life is life itself. This leads to a multitude of different values for the things each of us care about, and which make a good life. If these are irreducibly various, with no common measure, then this is a serious threat to utilitarianism and to later approaches based on comparing the costs and benefits of any proposed action (Cherniss and Hardy, 2010, Section 4.1).

As a final point in this section (though far from our final word on the subject of the individual 'versus' society) we note that societal wellbeing and progress appear rooted in individual wellbeing when approached through philosophy. For example, Crisp notes that philosophers use the word wellbeing to mean something broader than the health of a person, which is often how wellbeing is popularly used, but still rooted in the individual. Wellbeing 'amounts to the notion of how well a person's life is going for that person' (Crisp, 2013, Section 1). An individual's wellbeing might be influenced by the wellbeing of others, say the wellbeing of a child affecting the wellbeing of their parent. However, philosophy seems to point to the wellbeing of a society as being formed from the wellbeing of each individual within it. Likewise on progress, Meek Lange points out that 'Philosophical proponents of progress assert that the human condition has improved over the course of history and will continue to improve … To argue successfully that human well-being is increasing over the long term, theorists of progress must offer an interpretation of well-being compatible with that claim. They are committed either to interpret human well-being as a single value, or as a set of incommensurable values that are empirically connected' (Meek Lange, 2011, Section 1).

2.3   The American constitution

Difficulties we might now identify in implementing the political values of the Age of Enlightenment did not affect their significance in what were then revolutionary times. The political values are particularly captured in the constitutional documents of societies that they gave rise to, including the United States Declaration of Independence:

> We hold these truths to be self-evident, that all men are created equal, that they are endowed by their Creator with certain unalienable rights, that among these are Life, Liberty and the pursuit of Happiness (United States Declaration of Independence, July 4, 1776).

The reference to the pursuit of happiness by the founding fathers of the United States of America has been taken as evidence that one of the aims of government is the wellbeing and happiness of citizens. Indeed, when contributing to an earlier book on wellbeing (Allin, 2014, p. 409), we quoted Garry Wills (2002, p. 164) that 'When Jefferson spoke of pursuing happiness, he had nothing vague or private in mind. He meant a public happiness which is measurable; which is, indeed, the test and justification of any government'.

We have now seen that Hamowy (1979, pp. 519–521) had previously reviewed the first publication of Wills' book and questioned his conclusion. Hamowy examined relevant source material and concluded that 'the right to pursue happiness stands logically prior to the establishment of government, and the function of government is clearly to secure this right, not to see that most people attain the state they pursue'. This foreshadowed Booth's point in Section 2.2. In these terms, public happiness would not itself be a test of government. Nevertheless, we do not go as far as Johns and Ormerod (2007, p. 74), who conclude that the widespread use of 'happiness evidence' would not be conducive to good governance. We aim to show in this book that a range of objective and subjective measures of wellbeing are available for use by governments and others.

The British national anthem, God Save the King/Queen, was in use by 1745, ahead of the US Declaration, and includes the wish by citizens for their monarch to be 'victorious, happy and glorious'. When Queen Elizabeth II took the throne in 1952 she promised to always work 'to advance the happiness and prosperity' of her people. It is interesting how the long-standing idea of happiness was by then coupled with the idea of advancement, which we will see fits well with the contemporary economic model.

Bok (2010, p. 4) notes that 'the idea of happiness as a goal for public policy reached its high watermark in the eighteenth century' and lists a number of political theorists who advanced this. He reminds us that the pursuit of happiness was included not only in the United States Declaration of Independence but also in the constitutions of more than half of the states, and that the French Constitution of June 24, 1793 declared 'Le but de la société est le bonheur commun', which can be translated into 'the purpose (or goal) of society is the common good (or general happiness)'.

Whether or not Jefferson and others meant a public or general happiness which is measureable, it is far from clear how scientifically or objectively this could have been measured across society at that time. Perhaps measuring the pursuit of happiness might have seemed more achievable? Drawing on the Greek philosophical appraisal of a good, happy society discussed earlier, the things to measure might conceivably include, for example, the proportion of a population gaining particular levels of educational qualifications, because education was seen as a step towards the good society. The health of the nation was already starting to be a concern and, after the passage of another 100 years or so, this and other aspects of wellbeing were starting to be measured.

2.4   Official statistics – statistics about the state and about the state of society

There is no evidence that the signing of the United States Declaration of Independence was shortly followed by the creation of a statistics office to collect facts and figures on the state of society. However, across a number of countries and at different times, the new profession of statistician was emerging and the science of statistics was taking shape. It is generally accepted that the root of the word 'statistics' is the Latin word for 'the state' and that the word statistics came to be used during the Age of Enlightenment to mean the analysis of data about the state, although in works produced in English this was initially referred to as political arithmetic. Sir John Sinclair's *Statistical Account of Scotland*, first published in 1791, appears to be the first work in English to use the word statistics (Ball, 2005, p. 65) as well as referring to 'the quantum of happiness', as we noted in Chapter 1.

Soon many learned papers, reports and tomes were published with systematic collections of demographic and economic data about nation states, and starting to compare the position between states. The Charter of the Royal Statistical Society, dating from 1887, records that the Society was to 'collect, arrange, digest and publish facts illustrating the conditions and prospects of society in its material, social and moral relations'. As Dorling has noted, 'The Royal Charter was granted at a time of deep economic distress, but also at a time when new ways of alleviating that distress were being devised. The first recording of the word "unemployment" dates to the following year. In recognizing unemployment, rather than pauperism, those who counted the unemployed were making a statement. The unemployed lacked jobs; paupers were just poor. Statisticians have always had a great influence on moral debates' (Dorling, 2013a). At least some of the statisticians of the Victorian period were financiers and business people who were used to dealing with numbers in making entrepreneurial decisions. They brought this approach with them when they looked beyond their banks and factories and become involved in social reform.

The data that were used were initially from administrative systems. For example, the registers of individual births, deaths and marriages maintained in parishes or by local councils were summarised to give the numbers of each of these vital events each year, and analysed by the personal characteristics, such as age, sex, occupation, where these had been recorded. Economic data were principally derived from the records held to administer taxation, other sources of government revenue and government expenditure.

We will return later to highlight statistics relevant to the measurement of national wellbeing. The broad sweep of official statistics might best be summed up as seeking to describe society as well as to count the aspects of it that are needed for effective government. Such descriptions are intended not just for government but for everyone to see. As Dudley Seers (1983, p. 130) saw it, 'We cannot, with our own eyes and ears, perceive more than a minute sample of human affairs, even in our own country – and a very unrandom sample at that. So we rely on statistics in order to build and maintain our own model of the world. The data that are available mould our perceptions'. Paraphrasing George Box, we should be looking for a useful model, bearing in mind that all models are wrong.

Although we are concerned in this book with measurement, we acknowledge that there are qualitative descriptions of society as well as quantitative data, measures and reports. Politicians and policymakers draw on both qualitative and quantitative sources. Qualitative work can also inform the development of quantitative measures and both can draw on surveys and observation. Author George Orwell lived as a down-and-out in Paris and London before writing his account of that life (Orwell, 1933/1975). Some 60 years later, photographer Nick Danziger followed in Orwell's footsteps for 4 weeks before embarking on a much lengthier series of journeys around 15 parts of the United Kingdom. There are few statistics in his subsequent book and those that are quoted jump out, such as an estate in South Wales where 93% of the population were unemployed. Danziger expresses some concerns about prying into people's lives but decides to tell their stories and take pictures as a way of giving snapshots of many aspects of British life as well as describe a Britain 'of increased polarization where both ends of the spectrum of material wealth lead to spiritual deprivation' (Danziger, 1996, p. 8). Visual artists can also be acute observers as well. Stanley Donwood was recently described as 'angry at injustice, damning of our environmental irresponsibility, positively raging about social inequality' (Severs, 2013).

2.5   National accounts and GDP

We are thinking about the meaning of national wellbeing and the motive for measuring it in every section in this chapter. However, it is only from this section onwards that we will get to examine some tangible measurement approaches and to start thinking about measurement issues. National accounts are central to any country's set of official statistics. They tell us a lot about the total economic activity that took place within a given period and they tell the story of the overall standard of living of a country, though we will see that they need to be supplemented with much more information before we reach a better understanding of what the standard of living means and how the standard of living varies across the population. We should also be aware of the challenges in compiling a set of national accounts to capture the many transactions, often of a complex nature, within a specified boundary and time period.

There is a long history of national accounting. Grice (2011) reports that Vanoli's history of national accounting starts in 1665 with the work of William Petty, with subsequent contributions by eminent economists such as Turgot, Adam Smith, Lavoisier and Marx. Most developments in national accounts took part during the twentieth century.

Sir William Petty (1623–1687) came to prominence serving Oliver Cromwell and the Commonwealth in Ireland. Petty developed efficient methods to survey land that was to be confiscated and given to Cromwell's soldiers. Petty went on to become a polymath, making significant contributions to economics, science (he was one of the founders of the Royal Society) and philosophy as well as being an inventor and businessman. His theories on economics and his methods of political arithmetic are now seen as his particular strengths.

It was while setting out proposals for taxation that Petty first estimated the overall wealth of the Kingdom of England, in around 1685. Petty clearly saw the need for reliable quantitative information as the basis for decision-making in government. Fox (2007, p. 4) has noted that Petty made the case for what we would now call a national statistics office (Petty proposed an office headed by an 'Accountant General of the People') to collect demographic statistics, data on trade, tax and prices, and to maintain a land registry. That would have enabled him to calculate gross national product and income with some precision. He was ahead of his time in calling for a government statistical service but, using taxation and other data that were available, and making a number of assumptions and interpolations, Petty produced his own estimate of total wealth. As Fox says, 'To some extent the precise accuracy of the figures was less important to Petty as a political economist than the lessons they taught about the health and wealth of a city or nation. He was interested in what it was that made societies prosper and in recommending the means by which that prosperity might be increased' (2007, p. 7). National accounting can indeed be seen to be born here, at least in recognising key aggregates and in making first, if approximate, assessments of their magnitude.

Adam Smith (1723–1790) was born one hundred years after William Petty. He published 'An Inquiry into the Nature and Causes of the Wealth of Nations' in 1776, the year of the American declaration of independence, with several subsequent revised and extended editions. It has been translated into at least 14 other languages. Invariably described as a masterpiece and the foundation of modern economic thought, and usually simply called '*The Wealth of Nations*', it in particular explains the rise of, and the principles behind, modern capitalism. As Reich observes in his introduction to a modern edition (see Smith, 1776/2000, p. xv), Smith was writing as 'a moral philosopher, intent on explaining why people and societies function the way they do, and also how they *should* function'. Reich notes that, to Smith, the wealth of a nation 'wasn't determined by the size of its monarch's treasure or the amount of gold and silver in its vaults, nor by the spiritual worthiness of its people in the eyes of the Church. A nation's wealth was to be judged by the total value of all the goods its people produced for all its people to consume' (Reich, 2000, pp. xv–xvi). Here is the essence of the national economic accounts as they came to be devised, standardised and produced. Smith explores all of the components subsequently needed to compile national accounts, such as wages, rent, profits, stock and capital and public expenditure.

Smith also set down foundations for defining the economy that is to be measured in compiling national accounts. The wealth of a nation, in his terms, is generated by 'productive' work. This ignores many other activities, including those carried out as household tasks or as a volunteer, because they are deemed to be without economic value and hence not part of the economy that they may nevertheless support. Smith's view that the wealth of a nation is measured by the productivity and living standards of its people was certainly ground-breaking and far-reaching. On the other hand, his perception of the quality of life and wellbeing was more limited than that of modern times and has perhaps over-constrained the wide view.

This is not to be churlish. *The Wealth of Nations* is, as Reich summarises, widely and properly read as being 'resolutely about human beings – their capacities and incentives to be productive, their overall well-being, and the connection between productivity and well-being'. Smith states that a nation's wealth grows because of 'the skill, dexterity, and judgement with which its labour is generally applied'. He also explains how people we would now call entrepreneurs, business owners or employers – he cites the butcher, the brewer or the baker – automatically contribute to the wellbeing of others through pursuing their own self-interest. Smith uses the metaphor of an 'invisible hand' of an unfettered market with open competition between producers each seeking to promote their own self-interest and buyers each seeking the best deal for themselves. Reich notes this is 'perhaps the most famous, or infamous bodily metaphor of social science': famous as the long-standing justification of capitalism; infamous in some eyes because open market competition may not always be viable, acceptable or allowed to operate, and because self-interest does not immediately square with classical ideals of doing right and being good (all quotes from Reich, 2000, pp. xvii–xviii).

The Wealth of Nations is effectively a paean to economic growth. Goods and services are produced to be consumed. Smith defines a progressive state as one that is 'advancing to the further acquisition, rather than when it has acquired its full complement of riches'. It is this progressive state that is 'in reality the cheerful and the hearty state to all the different orders of the society' (Smith, 1776/2000, p. 93). Campbell and Skinner, in a commentary in the same modern edition, note that Smith's model of capital accumulation 'may be seen as a self-generating process' (Smith, 1776/2000, p. 1148), that is it inherently produces economic growth, with two provisos: first, that sufficient income is saved, not consumed; second, economic growth depends on the relative productivity and mix of different branches of industry. Smith also writes about progress, which he calls the 'progress of opulence' and by which he means the ways in which economic advancement and the accumulation of wealth have been and can be achieved in different nations (Smith, 1776/2000, pp. 407–453).

Reich points out that Smith was concerned about the consequences of factory work for the character of working people and that Smith was not fond of the rich when their 'chief enjoyment of riches consists in the parade of riches', proposing a progressive income tax (Reich, 2000, pp. xix/xx). Reich highlights Smith's 'revolutionary notion … that the wealth of a nation is measured not by its accumulated riches but by the productivity and living standards of all its people' (Reich, 2000, p. xx).

Looked at through modern eyes, Smith does not appear to have given much consideration to the impact that economic growth may have on the environment. He certainly includes land, mines and fisheries as essentials for productive agriculture, manufacture and trade and he recognises that the economy requires continual supplies. However, it is not clear that Smith considered if there will be limits to economic growth from finite environmental resources.

As Anderson notes, 'all the major figures of nineteenth-century political economy – Malthus, Ricardo, Mill and Marx' built on, or argued against, Smith and, like him, discussed the economy in the context of society and ethics. Ricardo and Marx were concerned with the distribution of income and wealth across different classes of society. Malthus was concerned with the limits which the natural world might place on economic growth and population growth (Anderson, 1991, p. 43). This foreshadows twentieth-century concerns on the 'triple bottom line' of the economy, society and the environment, and the possibility of sustainable growth.

As Daniel Tammet (2012) has concluded, 'Great thinkers of the 17th, 18th and 19th centuries passed down to us the notion of civilisation moving in a single – and desirable – direction … Time, risk and mortality are now told in numbers and quantified, since incremental progress relies on accurate measurement'. He was writing at the time of the 2012 Olympic and Paralympic Games. The Latin motto for the modern Olympic Games, proposed in 1894, is 'Citius, Altius, Fortius': How are we to judge that modern Olympians are performing faster, higher or stronger than previously without accurate and trusted measurements of all their performances? But while these measurements of achievement are necessary, Tammet reminds us that they are not sufficient to describe the 'human drama and infinite variety' of the event. So, while one outcome of the Age of Enlightenment is the burgeoning panoply of measurement, there are some important and huge topics – the progress of a country, for example – for which we have yet to set up and use measurement systems. And where we do have indicative measures, we should not forget that they do not tell the whole story.

By the beginning of the twentieth century the essence of national accounts were understood, at least by those who needed to grapple with the nation's finances, in accounting terms. They are a set of accounts not for an individual business but for all of the productive activity in the country as a whole. Actually there is a degree of circularity in this definition, because the productive activity measured in the national accounts is that within a production boundary which is itself defined in the accounts. Unlike the scope of an individual business, the production boundary calls for national accountants to assess whether things are inside or outside the boundary, and so counted or not. (We will explore this further in Chapter 6). With that proviso, the national accounts are then developed around a basic national accounting identity. Within a given period of time, national income must equal output from productive assets as defined, and both must equal national expenditure, on current consumption or on capital goods that will generate further output, in later periods.

We should also log the often-overlooked point that the national accounts are an aggregate model of the economy (as defined) as a whole. While the accounts are also available for broad sectors of activity, the main focus of the accounts is to learn what is happening to the aggregate economy. The national accounts are a model; they are not the actual economy. They do need to mirror what is happening in the real world, but we are looking at an image, not at the real thing. The image can and does get revised, as estimates are revisited in the light of later and more robust data. And we always need to remember that the image is of something called the economy, not of society or the environment as a whole.

As Anderson notes, 'one of the strengths which "economic growth" has as an idea is that it can be measured statistically' (1991, Introduction). This is a high bar against which other measures of wellbeing and progress seem to have to compete and, to change the sporting analogy, this is a race in which economic measures were first out of the starting blocks as measures of progress, and have a considerable lead. On the other hand, as Jonathan Schlefer (2012, p. 25) has noted of neoclassical economic models, when economic growth is incorporated in any economic theory or forecast, it becomes part of an economic model in which assumptions need to be made.

Grice (2011) comments that around 1930 there was acceleration in the development, refinement and standardisation of the concepts of economic growth into an integrated system of national accounts. Leaders included Clark and Kuznets in the United States and Richard Stone in the United Kingdom. The UN website (see Appendix) traces the origin of a formal system of national accounts to the 1947 report of the Sub-Committee on National Income Statistics of the League of Nations Committee of Statistical Experts under the leadership of Richard Stone. At its first session in 1947, the United Nations Statistical Commission (UNSC) emphasized the need for international statistical standards for the compilation and updating of comparable statistics in support of a large array of policy needs. By 1953 the first international standards for national accounts were published as the United Nations System of National Accounts and Supporting Tables (usually abbreviated as 'SNA').

Market economies and economic interactions in the world have evolved, resulting in updated versions of the SNA in 1968, 1993 and 2008. Each version of the SNA was adopted by the UNSC as the international standard for compilation of national accounts statistics and for the international reporting of comparable national accounting data. The SNA is published jointly by the United Nations, the Commission of the European Communities, the International Monetary Fund, the Organisation for Economic Co-operation and Development and the World Bank. Handbooks provide guidance on implementation (see Appendix). The UN Statistics Division facilitates the implementation programme for the 2008 SNA and supporting statistics through regional and interregional workshops and seminars, and through a limited number of individual country technical assistance missions.

While the SNA is a global standard, there are also customised versions in different parts of the world. The United Nation works in collaboration with regional commissions and regional agencies. For example, at the time of writing, the version of the SNA used across the European Union is the 1995 European System of National and Regional Accounts (abbreviated to 'ESA 95'). This incorporates the 1993 SNA and is described as a major improvement on the previous version, which dates from 1979. Progress had been achieved in the harmonisation of methodology and in the precision and accuracy of the concepts, definitions, classifications and accounting rules which have to be applied in order to arrive at a consistent, reliable and comparable quantitative description of the economies of the member states of the European Union. The European Commission explains the need for ESA and the statistics produced according to it as follows: 'To achieve the objectives set by the Treaty on European Union, and more specifically Economic and Monetary Union, we need high-quality statistical instruments which provide the Community institutions, governments and economic and social operators with a set of harmonised and reliable statistics on which to base their decisions' (see Appendix).

National statistical offices across Europe are gearing up to move to an updated version, 'ESA2010'. This reflects changes in national economies and is consistent with the worldwide System of National Accounts 2008 (SNA2008). (It is also consistent with the IMF Balance of Payments International Investment Position Manual, 'BPM6'). EU Member States are required to use ESA2010 for their statistical returns to Eurostat from September 2014.

An interesting point arises when a country's national accounts estimates are revised as a result of adopting a later version of the SNA, or just by using improved estimation techniques. If the estimate of GDP for a given year is markedly increased – and there are examples of revisions of 10% as well as of revisions of under 1% – then is this a larger economy than previously, or strictly just a larger estimate of the same economy? We mention this because media reports can give the impression that the economy has grown in such cases, or indeed that it has shrunk if the estimate is lower than previously published.

National accounts are an integrated description of all economic activity within the economic territory of a country (including activity involving both domestic/resident units and external units resident in other countries). They are meant to be comprehensive, fully integrated and internally consistent set of accounts. Accounts can also be produced for regions, sub-regions and local areas of the country. The Office for National Statistics, which produces the UK national accounts, captures the essence of them as follows: 'The national accounts are drawn together using data from many, many different sources. These different sources not only help to ensure that the national accounts are comprehensive: they provide different perspectives on the economy, for example sales by retailers and purchases by households. By comparing and contrasting these different sources, the national accounts produce a single picture of the economy which is consistent, coherent and fully integrated' (from ONS website, see Appendix).

Many of the most well-known economic statistics are produced within the national accounts, including, GDP, the household saving ratio, public sector net borrowing, the balance of trade and household consumption. More fully, there are core accounts for the economy overall and for sectors within it, on production, consumption, the generation, distribution and redistribution of income, capital investment and the financing of these activities and transactions. So-called 'satellite accounts' cover activities linked to the economy, but which are treated separately, most notably the environmental accounts and household production.

It is interesting that Grice (2011) records as a watershed in the production of national accounts in the United Kingdom, the publication in 1941 of '*An Analysis of the Sources of War Finance and Estimate of the National Income and Expenditure in 1938 and 1940*'. Here, at the start of a World War, was a very pertinent need for an accurate and actionable set of accounts of the state of the nation's economy and public finances. By the time of the 2008 SNA, the United Nation makes it clear that national accounts have a number of purposes. Grice (2011) draws attention to two key purposes. The first is macroeconomic management, to give governments, Treasury and Central Bank officials' information covering different types of economic activities and the different sectors of the economy. This purpose supports the building of economic models to design and test policy options, and to forecast how the economy as a whole might change over time. The second purpose is as a measure of national welfare. Or rather, as the SNA manual observes, 'Welfare is a wide-ranging concept with many different facets. Some of these may be captured reasonably well by one or more of the key aggregates' (see Appendix for link to SNA material). In the view of a number of influential economists and others, who we will meet in the next chapter, this now seems something of an understatement.

Fioramonti has reviewed the development of GDP, what he calls 'the best-known "number" in the contemporary world and an extremely powerful political tool' (2013, p. 9). He tracks in some detail how the developers of the system of national accounts defined and presented key aggregate measures and how these measures have been misinterpreted over time. One of many striking examples reported by Fioramonti is that, while Simon Kuznets defined national income produced from 'the efforts of the individuals who comprise a nation', he understood this product was only a measurement of market transactions, rather than a comprehensive assessment of the overall activity in the nation. Fioramonti reviews the gamut of criticisms of GDP and how the debate has widened over time, including questioning the long-term effects of economic growth.

Even with the caveat that the national accounts cover market transactions only, this is far from an easy task. For all sorts of reasons, transactions within the market economy vary in how visible they are. Despite pledges of confidentiality by the compilers of national accounts, to avoid individual transactions being revealed, and despite the use of statutory powers to collect data in some cases, there are inevitable transactions that are not included in the national accounts, either because they are hidden or are merely missed. The way in which business is conducted appears to be constantly changing (e.g. think of internet transactions), partly driven by a desire to find a competitive edge, and regulatory and statistical agencies have to work hard to keep up with the market. This is a particular problem when the value of such hard-to-find transactions is changing in different ways from the picture shown by the recorded transactions. There has been much analysis of such activity in post-mortems of the banking, financial and economic crises of recent years (e.g. Peston, 2012; Martin, 2013).

From one perspective, the system of national accounts is just a set of statistical tables. However, it does seem clear that the underlying ethos of the national accounts and GDP is of economic growth. So, while GDP in a period is measured as an absolute monetary amount, it is assessed by comparing it with earlier periods. A positive change signifies economic growth while negative change for two or more successive periods is described as an economic recession. The recession ends when there is an increase in GDP, even though the level of GDP may not have returned to the level seen prior to the start of the recession.

In other statistical contexts we may set out a neutral, null hypothesis, such as that there is neither growth nor decline, and then test this. Looking at the economy we might want to assess change taking into account price changes and population growth, by comparing GDP per head in real terms. But the statistical presentation of the GDP figures each quarter, and certainly the way they are reported, is against an expectation of growth. Can statistical systems be blind to how change in the numbers is defined and interpreted, or should we be realistic that GDP and the national accounts are measures of economic growth?

The national accounts do capture what have been some quite dramatic changes in material living standards. Susannah Walker has noted that: 'At the end of the 1950s, Britain was a very different country from that of ten years previously. While some of this was due to developments like the arrival of teenagers, television advertising and hire purchase, the biggest single change was better standards of living' (Walker, 2013, p. 52). Within the national accounts there is a headline indicator measuring household disposable income per head that we can use to see what has been happening to living standards overall, over that time and more recently. The series is derived by dividing the total household disposable income calculated in the accounts by the total population number each year. The fact that income distributions are invariably

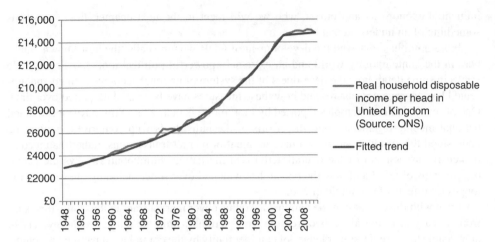

Figure 2.1   The post-war rise in real household disposable income in the United Kingdom (expressed in 2009 prices).

skewed means the result is not a good measure of 'average' disposable income, but it can be used to show how disposable income has varied over time.

Figure 2.1 shows real household disposable income per head ('real' meaning that the effect of price inflation has been removed) between 1948 and 2011. We have also plotted a line between the value in 1948 and that in 2011 as if there had been three periods, each with a constant annual growth rate. The first period is of an annual growth rate of 2.7%, between 1948 and 1981. The second period shows a higher annual growth rate, of 3.3%, between 1981 and 2003. Finally, to reach the end point we have used an annual growth of only 0.2% between 2003 and 2011. As a first approximation our 'trend line' fits the actual figures closely, apart from in a few years of economic turbulence (e.g. our line is not really the trend between 2003 and 2011, but simply shows what annual growth rate would have taken the 2003 value to that in 2011). The chart suggests that living standards in the United Kingdom rose steadily not only during the 1950s but continuing into the start of the twenty-first century, before levelling off during the latest economic and financial crises. We can also see that an increase of only 0.5 percentage points in the annual growth rate in 1981–2003, compared with 1948–1981, accounts for the noticeable higher increase in disposable income per head in the 1980s and 1990s.

Figure 2.1 also invites us to think what might happen in the future. With all the caveats about how it shows at best some kind of average, for one measure of economic wellbeing, it is still tempting to anticipate that living standards will resume an upward trend. Whether or not this is the case, we trust that this book is making the case for looking at more than one measure of wellbeing and progress, both to understand more fully what economic wellbeing is (and how it is distributed) and to paint a wider picture of wellbeing and progress.

Before we leave this look at the national economic accounts, we should reflect on whether or not we now have a clear definition and understanding of the 'economic wellbeing' of a country. This phrase is much used, both in the media and more formally. For example, there is legislation in the United Kingdom to regulate, and to allow for, the investigatory powers of the state, including surveillance and the activities of intelligence services. At several places in the legislation, actions are justified by one or more of a number of reasons, including 'for the purpose of safeguarding the economic well-being of the United Kingdom' (e.g. RIPA, 2000, Section 5 (3) (c)). The phrase is not defined, explained or interpreted in this legislation, however. Nor have we been able to find a satisfactory, detailed explanation – that is, one that does not define economic wellbeing other than by defining it as what is measured by the national economic accounts, which were themselves designed with a particular view of economic wellbeing in mind.

Economic wellbeing is also used in policy discussions about groups of people in the population, for example, young people. The economic wellbeing of young people is defined in a UK policy document 'Every Child Matters' as 'not being prevented by economic disadvantage from achieving their full potential in life'. As the National Youth Agency (Jones, n.d., p. 3) comments on this phrase, it is a negative definition, rather than a positive definition given for other aspects of the policy, which 'indicates that it is harder to identify the positive impact of economic wellbeing than to identify the risks associated with its absence'. It is also difficult, if not impossible, to measure: How can we evaluate the life potential of someone who may not even yet be in the labour market?

Despite the existence of GDP as a measure of economic welfare or wellbeing, the concept and general understanding of economic wellbeing seems to refer in some vague way to living standards, or to the ability of the economy to function in order to provide employment, incomes and returns on investments. Even more difficult to pin down is when politicians talk of the 'national economic interest'. They are unlikely to be talking purely in terms of what a course of action might do precisely for GDP, but this is invariably how economic wellbeing is assessed.

2.6   More to life than GDP

It should be apparent by now that the national economic accounts are not, and were not designed to be, a record of the economic advancement and social progress of all people. The breadth of modern life is indicated by the scope of the United Nations, the international organization founded in 1945 after the Second World War, with countries committed to maintaining international peace and security, developing friendly relations among nations and promoting social progress, better living standards and human rights. The purposes of the United Nations, as captured in the current Charter for its 193 Member States, include solving 'international problems of an economic, social, cultural, or humanitarian character' (United Nations, 1945, Chapter 1).

In Britain the building of a post-war welfare state was based on proposals for universal welfare provision, covering education, health care and other social services, by William Beveridge. He drew on Beatrice Webb's contribution to the Royal Commission on the Poor Laws and Relief of Distress 1905–1909, presented in the form of a Minority Report, which was about what the good society should look like. As Knight reflected later, for the 30 years following the end of the Second World War, 'the state took prime responsibility for poverty by committing itself to full employment as a goal of economic policy and to a secure population as a goal of social policy ... [and it seemed it] would banish poverty forever' (Knight, 2011, p. 12). However, research in the 1960s rediscovered poverty even in earlier studies which had suggested that it had disappeared. Debate raged over the effectiveness of public services and whether or not they were perpetuating the kinds of conditions they were meant to eliminate.

In the United States an aspiring presidential candidate was also concerned by the impoverished conditions in many parts of his country. Robert Kennedy associated this with what he saw as the priority given to economic conditions. In a speech in 1968 he referred to gross national product (GNP), another headline measure of the national economic accounts, rather than to GDP but the point is made equally powerfully:

> Too much and too long, we seem to have surrendered community excellence and community values in the mere accumulation of material things. Our gross national product [...] – if we should judge America by that – counts air pollution and cigarette advertising, and ambulances to clear our highways of carnage. It counts special locks for our doors and jails for those who break them. It counts the destruction of our redwoods and the loss of our natural wonder in chaotic sprawl. It counts napalm and the cost of a nuclear warhead, and armoured cars for police who fight riots in our streets. It counts Whitman's rifle and Speck's knife, and the television programs which glorify violence in order to sell toys to our children.
>
> Yet the gross national product does not allow for the health of our children, the quality of their education or the joy of their play. It does not include the beauty of our poetry or the strength of our marriages, the intelligence of our public debate or the integrity of our public officials. It measures neither our wit nor our courage, neither our wisdom nor our learning, neither our compassion nor our devotion to our country, it measures everything in short, except that which makes life worthwhile. And it can tell us everything about America except that why we are proud that we are Americans. (Kennedy, 1968)

While Kennedy identifies many stark examples of activities that many of us would agree are damaging, where to draw the line? Following Hurricane Sandy, the New York Times (2012) published an article noting that disaster is good for some businesses. It reported that sales of emergency supplies, storm shelters and generators are all driven by preparations for, or the aftermath of, disasters.

If we are not just to judge a country by its GNP or GDP, then Kennedy set a huge challenge for statisticians. To produce broader measures would mean taking stock of many intangible, difficult to define and probably impossible to measure (the beauty of our poetry?). As we will see, more prosaic approaches have been devised to go beyond GDP, although these generally have yet to achieve GDPs prominence and use in managing economies and running countries. This is at the heart of the issue: even if economic growth is the goal then should GDP be the leading indicator of wellbeing and progress, or can we decouple the driver of economic growth from measures of other outcomes, not only in the economy but also in society and the environment?

Why the specific measure of GDP has such prominence is not immediately obvious, given the developments to the national accounts and related measures that have occurred alongside the regular publication of GDP statistics. There has been widespread discussion and publication of wider economic and social measures, much of it stimulated through the conferences and publications of the International Association of Research in Income and Wealth (IARIW – website address in Appendix). The IARIW was founded in September 1947, in conjunction with a meeting of the International Statistical Institute. Its organizers were individuals who were actively engaged in national income accounting research or who, in their official or academic positions, had been instrumental in developing the important techniques in national income and national budgeting that had been implemented in a number of countries during the Second World War and the immediate post-war period.

The interests of the IARIW are clearly wider than the compilation of national accounts and the GDP headline statistics. They include the furthering of research on national and economic and social accounting, including the development of concepts and definitions for the measurement and analysis of income and wealth, and the development and further integration of systems of economic and social statistics. As we will see with other developments later, this was perhaps a case of the producers of statistics extending the range of statistical measures on offer. It is less clear that the potential users of official statistics – governments, business, the media and citizens – understood these developments and gave them the same amount of attention as they gave to the core accounts and headline GDP results.

We will look at these measures in Chapter 6, simply noting here that they embrace the use of different measures within the national accounts as defined, expansion through 'satellite accounts' and the derivation of new measures such as social accounting matrices and the index of sustainable economic welfare. As mentioned in Section 2.5, the System of National Accounts, the international standard overseen by the United Nations Statistical Office, has evolved, both in its core constructs and through adopting at least some of the wider measures, such as satellite accounts for non-paid production in households.

There have also been many expressions of alternative thinking, of counter cultures to the goal of economic growth. Robert M. Pirsig's 1974 book *Zen and the Art of Motorcycle Maintenance* is sub-titled 'An Inquiry into Values' and, in its own way, set out to seek and define the good life. The author does not accept the view that there has been no real progress, in spite of mass warfare, pollution and the factory system, since prehistoric times. He concludes: 'From that agony of bare existence to modern life can be soberly described only as upward progress, and the sole agent for this progress is quite clearly reason itself' (Pirsig, 1974/1999, p. 128). However, Pirsig also offers a 'more serious alternative to (the American dream) material success. It's not so much an alternative as an expansion of the meaning of "success" to something larger than just getting a good job and staying out of trouble. And also something larger than mere freedom' (Pirsig, 1974/1999, p. 415).

2.7   Social indicator movement and measuring quality of life

In some ways a parallel development to the production of national economic accounts has been the social indicator movement, concerned in particular with measuring quality of life as well as giving more detail on material standards of living and how these are distributed. One central question facing governments in the second half of the twentieth century was how to use the dividends of economic success, in particular to raise social standards. There are now hundreds if not thousands of different social indicators, each aiming to regularly monitor particular aspects of the living conditions and wellbeing of the population and how this is changing over time. This is a huge resource and provides a bank of information that anyone can look into. The compilers of indicator sets may bring individual indicators together into an index, a term that covers broad collections of series as well as the more usual statistical meaning, of a single summary number.

This approach tends to skirt round a precise and common definition of quality of life, in the same way that we found there is no concise and single definition of economic wellbeing. As

Bache (2013) has noted, the terms 'wellbeing' and 'quality of life' have specific meanings in some academic disciplines and literatures, while in others they do not. The OECD recognizes that quality of life 'is a broad term covering those aspects of overall well-being that are not captured only by material conditions' (OECD, 2013d, p. 148). Thus we have quality of life defined as the difference between two other concepts, overall wellbeing and material living standards. Despite this, compilations of social indicators have generally covered broadly the same ground in describing quality of life. They have included areas or domains such as material living standards (income, consumption and wealth); health; education; personal activities including work; political voice and governance; social connections and relationships; environment (present and future conditions); insecurity, of an economic as well as a physical nature. (This particular list of the domains of quality of life is taken from the Stiglitz, Sen and Fitoussi report of 2009 that we will look at in the next chapter.)

Over 40 years ago the official statistical compendium Social Trends was launched in the United Kingdom with an understanding that '*economic progress must be measured, in part at least, in terms of social benefits*' and the fact that '*it is just as important to have good statistics on various aspects of social policy (than it is economic statistics)*' (Nissel, 1970). It is a collection of statistical series, tables, text and analysis: a resource that has been much valued, like many similar publications in other countries, as a social report. However, it does not provide an overall assessment of how the quality of life in the United Kingdom is changing, and it was never intended to. The eminent social statistician Claus Moser was director of the UK Central Statistical Office at the time and he wrote 'It is unlikely that anyone will be able meaningfully to measure a single concept of the quality of life in the same way that we measure, for example, changes in the gross national product; and I personally doubt whether it would even be a desirable aim' (Moser, 2000). Rather, the aim was to illustrate broader aspects of society and quality of life, alongside economic data.

Social Trends was one child of the social indicator movement, along with the Netherlands life situation reports and the French 'Donnés Sociales (La société française)', presented in recent years as 'France, portrait social'. Over the years nearly all European countries, and many other countries, have started the publication of comprehensive and regular social reports. Examples of countries that have started more recently include Poland, Spain and Switzerland. GESIS, the Leibniz Institute for the Social Sciences is one of the key hubs of current research into social indicators and publication of social data. As the GESIS website notes, 'Regular social reporting is by far the most important and most successful application of social indicators and quality of life research' (see Appendix for links to all these reports).

In addition to overall social reporting, the social indicator movement continues to research the construction of social indicators and to hone their use in welfare research, measuring quality of life and social inequality, and in ensuring sound cross-national comparisons. The contribution of such work particularly on the distribution of income, wealth and quality of life is considerable. The core national accounts are aggregate measures, so derived averages, such as per capita statistics, tell us nothing about the underlying distribution. It is only with social indicators such as Gini coefficients of income that we can begin to understand distributions and inequalities. Dorling (2013a), for example, has tracked inequalities in Britain since 1910. Writers, such as Mount (2012), have analysed how it is not just wealth or income that has become more unevenly distributed, it is that political and social power is also increasingly concentrated in the hands of a small proportion of society. Sen and Drèze (2013) identify deeply entrenched inequality, among many social indicators that they draw on, as at the heart of India's slow development. There has long been political interest in the extent to which taxation and welfare benefits can reduce inequalities in income, with associated technical developments in measurement, such as the use of 'equivalence scales' to improve comparability by taking proper account of the effect of differences in household size on household income and material wellbeing.

More recently the spotlight has turned on 'predistribution', or seeking a more equal distribution of economic power and rewards before taxes are collected and welfare benefits paid out, which are long established as ways of redistributing income (e.g. Hacker, 2011). In a critique of this concept, Kenworthy (2013) runs through nine ways in which predistribution can occur, such as through education, jobs in manufacturing and the provision of public goods and services, all of which would require statistical data to plan policy, monitor implementation and evaluate effectiveness. In some cases, such as public goods, services and spaces, and how free time is used, any increase in living standards 'doesn't show up in income statistics, but it's real, nonetheless' (Kenworthy, 2013, 115). Any government going down this route will presumably want to have some reliable evidence to show that it is working, adding to the need to improved statistics about quality of life.

Indicators are often used to produce league tables of 'everything from economic competitiveness to social health to happiness', as a leader article in *The Economist* recently observed (in its 2 February 2013 edition). Despite the work of GESIS and others, including the indefatigable John Hall (see Appendix for website), in researching and measuring quality of life and developing and promoting social indicators, there is no social indicator equivalent of GDP and the national accounts. One factor may be the sheer number of indicators. Almost every collection of indicators functions primarily as a databank. They are resources to draw on, for detailed comparisons over time or between locations, rather than to assess changes in wellbeing and progress.

For example, the World Bank's World Development Indicator databank draws from a wider set of indicators, selecting 331 indicators arranged in 10 topics (from education to the public sector, when topics are listed alphabetically) for over 200 economies. Its purpose is to present 'the most current and accurate global development data available' (see Appendix). It is still unclear how to summarise social indicators and how to assess how things are changing over time. Perhaps this is a false goal, although there does seem to be a need for simple, clear summaries of how a country is doing, beyond its economic activity. We recall reading a review of *Social Trends* (we think in *The Financial Times*) a few years ago, along the lines of 'a good read, but what does it all add up to?'

We should also be aware that statistics are sometimes contested. Statistics and indicators should be published for the public good. This means they should be thoroughly reviewed and tested during their development, so that published indicators are trusted and can be seen to be trusted. We are therefore slightly concerned when particular sets of measures continue to be challenged, as may be happening over the World Bank's 'Doing Business' indicators (see Appendix for website). These indicators aim to provide objective measures of business regulations for local firms in 185 economies and selected cities at the subnational level. The World Bank has published their internal audit of the measures (Independent Evaluation Group, 2008). However, there still seems to be some lingering concerns in the international development community over, for example, partiality of the indicators. A letter in *The Economist* (8 June 2013) raised a number of issues, including that the cost to business of regulatory policy, as measured in these indicators, ignores the social benefit of having some taxation and some regulation of the labour market and the environment.

One clear demonstration of the power of indicators is when they are used in presentations that communicate well. As Royal Statistical Society President John Pullinger has said, the challenge is to bring together relevant statistics and present them well 'to get them into people's thinking' (Pullinger, 2013). This needs data (numbers), charts with messages and well-written commentary, because many people communicate with words, not with pictures. Building on a long tradition of statistical graphics, such as the work of Tufte (e.g. Tufte, 1990), on-line diagrams, charts and maps are becoming increasingly useful at revealing patterns in the underlying data. For example, there are long-established indicator sets measuring aspects of poverty, including indices of multiple deprivation, but it is only recently that UK poverty 'black spots' have been mapped. The version published in 2013, showing the picture in 2012, contains markedly fewer words and more charts than earlier versions (see Appendix for website).

Social indicators form the basis of new measures of national wellbeing and progress, as we will see in Chapter 6 and in the Appendix, with developments such as Scotland Performs and Measures of Australia's Progress. Social indicator sets also continue to be mined in great quantities in the production of research and official reports, as can be seen, for example, in discussion of a recent report from a Commission on Living Standards (e.g. Wintour, 2012).

2.8   Health and wellbeing

Turning now to the health of people living in a country, we can see that there are many, well-developed systems of statistics that are used to assess the health of a nation. We can start with mortality rates. Calculating the annual number of deaths per 1000 people in a country starts to tell us something about the health, or not, of that area, especially when compared with elsewhere. It strictly, of course, tells us only about the retrospective state of health of the people who died during a given year, reflecting their life experience up to that time, rather than the current state of health of everyone alive in that year. We can also look at the infant mortality rate, the annual number of deaths of children younger than 1 year per 1000 live births, and other age-specific mortality rates to build up a profile of the lengths of life for people in the country.

Measures such as average life expectancies, child and maternal mortality rates might be seen as outcome measures by which to assess health-care systems, with the caveat that they can only record what has been happening to date. They represent the transition point from what has happened to what might happen from then on. Nevertheless, we can see some major progress in wellbeing. For example, according to World Bank figures (see Appendix for link to their databank), in the 51 years from 1960 to 2011 life expectancy at birth for females in the United Kingdom rose from just over 74 years to nearly 83 years, an increase of 11% even during the second half of the twentieth century, when conditions were relatively stable. In China over the same period, life expectancy at birth for females increased steadily from 45 to 76 years, to reach the level that the United Kingdom had been in the late 1970s and showing an overall increase of nearly 70%. (Virtually the same percentage increase was recorded in India).

Detailed statistics can then be maintained on the illnesses and diseases prevalent within populations (morbidity), as well as their causes of death (mortality), including according to an International Classification of Diseases (ICD, see Appendix), used in epidemiology, health management and for clinical purposes. The ICD is maintained by the World Health

Organisation (WHO, an arm of the United Nations set up in 1945) and used and updated across the health sector with the same rigour as national accounts support the UN's System of National Accounts. The ICD dates back to the 1850s and was first known as the International List of Causes of Death. Health analyses using data organised in this way help identify risk factors behind chronic diseases, and how these change over time.

Since at least the middle of the twentieth century, there has been a move to stress the positive dimension of health and wellbeing, rather than disease, illness and death. Health is a resource for everyday life, not the object of living. It is a positive concept emphasizing social and personal resources as well as physical capabilities. The WHOs definition of health, as given at the start of its constitution, is that 'Health is a state of complete physical, mental and social well-being and not merely the absence of disease or infirmity' (WHO, 1946). Mental health is similarly defined, as a state of wellbeing in which every individual realises his or her own potential, can cope with the normal stresses of life, can work productively and fruitfully, and is able to make a contribution to her or his community.

Medical researchers investigating new treatments and doctors prescribing specific courses of action are looking for measurable outcomes, such as improved health status and wellbeing sustained over a significant period. One measurement development related to this is that, in addition to calculating average life expectancies for the population, national statistical offices are increasingly measuring 'healthy' and 'disability-free' life expectancies. While life expectancy provides an estimate of average expected lifespan, healthy life expectancy divides total life expectancy into years spent in good or 'not good' health. Similarly, disability-free life expectancy divides life expectancy into years lived with and without a chronic illness or disability. Life expectancy is usually taken from life tables. Measures of health, disability and chronic illness are needed to estimate the health expectancies and these may require household surveys if data are not routinely available in this form from health-care administration systems.

Over the last decade or more, it seems that public authorities, private companies and charities have been increasingly concerned with our wellbeing, not just with our health. It is not always clear whether wellbeing is seen as the goal, or as a factor shaping quality of life, happiness and fulfilment, spirituality, job satisfaction, organisational effectiveness and productivity. Beyond the individual, wellbeing is linked with the environment, social inclusion and social justice. There are differences between countries in how such concepts are accepted. A parallel can be seen in the extent of the adoption of positive thinking and motivational psychology in different parts of the world.

There are examples of the focus on wellbeing all around us. A local council's health, social care and wellbeing strategy 2011–2014 (the latest of a series introduced in 2003) is advertised in banners along the city street: 'Healthy body ... Healthy mind ... Healthy Newport' (Newport, 2013). The Forestry Commission has published a research review concluding that 'There is strong evidence suggesting that green spaces have a beneficial impact on mental well-being and cognitive function through both physical access and usage, as well as access to views' (Forest Research, n.d.). Anyone with a taste for chocolate may be relieved to know that it is 'good for the mind, body and spirit' (Dyer, 2006). Gyms have become health clubs, fitness and wellbeing centres. Exercise machines in the health club that one of us uses carry the following message loop.

Wellness the new lifestyle
Wellness means living longer

Wellness means physical and mental balance

Wellness means more vitality over the years

Wellbeing also emerged more clearly as an aim of government. Developments in the UK government are included in Chapter 7, including noting the emergence of a 'common understanding' of what wellbeing means in a policy context. There are many considerations of wellbeing in policy (see Allin, 2014, for a review with a focus on wellbeing at work policy). However, as we show in the case of the United Kingdom, while there is a commitment to wellbeing, and a substantial measurement programme, the political narrative is centred on economic growth.

It is interesting that the UN General Assembly's 2011 resolution on happiness, wellbeing and development quoted in Chapter 1 does not explicitly mention health. We take this as read to mean that health statistics will nevertheless form an important source on which to draw in measuring national wellbeing and progress, not least because health statistics are already included in development goals and measures.

2.9   Rise of measurement of psychological wellbeing (life satisfaction, happiness, worthwhile lives)

Psychiatrist Oliver James points out that the Human Genome Project is 'rapidly proving that genes play little part in causing mental illness: the huge differences in prevalence between different countries strongly suggest politico-economic and cultural factors are vital'. As an individual's wellbeing might in some way be considered the counterpart to mental illness, this gives us a clue as to the importance of measuring wellbeing and the factors surrounding it. Indeed, James continued, 'There is now also overwhelming evidence that our electro-chemical thermostatic settings result from care during the first six years of our lives and from prenatal factors, putting us more or less at risk. This vulnerability is exacerbated in later life by high economic inequality, excessive materialism and excessive stress on individuality at the expense of collectivism. We need a total rethink of what our society is for – is it the profits of a tiny few or the wellbeing of the majority? The status quo is not only ecologically unsustainable but emotionally too' (James, 2013).

When psychologists talk about happiness, as Dan Jones has observed, 'they usually use the term to mean our overall and long-term subjective well-being and life satisfaction' (Jones, 2010). This harks back to Aristotle and eudemonia which, as we noted in Section 2.1, refers to a deeper level of happiness associated with a flourishing and contented life. It contrasts with the everyday usage of happiness, which is akin to pleasure or joy, something we experience in the moment as a result of enjoyable activities. Poets and song writers have captured many if not all of the things that make us feel happy at any one time. Besides pleasure, there are of course many different positive emotions, such as awe, pride and gratitude that might also contribute to our general mood at that time.

The word 'subjective' in Jones's description of happiness in the fuller, psychological sense is important. It usually refers to the wellbeing of a person being considered (i.e. the subject) and that this is their own assessment of their wellbeing. Over at least four decades, happiness in the broad sense has been 'probed' (in Jones's word) from subjects in systematic ways, with questionnaires that ask them to rate how much they agree or disagree with each of a list of statements (e.g. 'If I could live my life over, I would change almost nothing'). A fuller definition of 'subjective' phenomena appeared in a 1981 report for the US National Research Council, which we quote at length:

> Subjective phenomena are those that, in principle, can be directly known, if at all, only by persons themselves, although a person's intimate associates or a skilled observer may be able to surmise from indirect evidence what is going on 'inside'. Objective phenomena are those that can be known by evidence that is, in principle, directly accessible to an external observer. Often that evidence is actually a matter of record, although the relevant records may not be easily sampled for the population of interest.
>
> Thus, if an individual is asked to name a favourite author, to state whether the draft system is fair, to indicate how many children she wants to have, to identify an area in which she or he is afraid to walk at night, or to say whether he or she has ever wished to belong to the opposite sex, the information sought is subjective. But if an individual is asked whether he has served in the Armed Forces, how many children she has ever borne, how far she or he lives from the place of work, or to state his or her sex, the information is objective, even though its measurement may rely solely on the respondent serving as an informant rather than on records or reports of observers (Turner and Martin, 1981, p. 2).

The report notes, as we did earlier in this chapter, that the Declaration of Independence affirms the pursuit of happiness as one of the rights of citizens of the United States. The report concludes that 'One way to inquire how well we are doing in maintaining that heritage is to investigate the state and trend of "happiness". Moreover, in order to interpret social indicators based on objective data, subjective data are also needed to disclose the goals that people may have in mind: for example, how much pollution is "too much"?' (Turner and Martin, 1981, p. 4).

The report was prepared by a panel of survey practitioners and academics. It came after some 10 years or so of increasing amounts of survey work and research into happiness, satisfaction and perceived quality of life, building on surveys into other subjective matters, such as political opinion polls and surveys of consumer wants, that had been established after the Second World War. The report is strongly supportive of the value of subjective surveys. However, it also contains a number of wide-ranging recommendations for the social science community, commissioners and users of surveys (including the public). These were all with the aim of creating an improved climate for the conduct of polls and surveys, as well as to upgrade survey practice and to advance the state of the art of survey measurement and the scientific use of survey data. This is not the place to review in detail the progress made to implement their 18 recommendations, though clearly much has been done to bring polls and surveys into the evidence base for policy and public debate, and ensure they are well constructed and well used.

In 1971, John Hall and Mark Abrams had run a pilot survey of the quality of life in Britain, funded by the then Social Science Research Council. The survey asked a sample of adults to rate their current satisfaction levels (on 0–10 ladder scales) with various life and policy domains (housing, district, job, family life, friendships, leisure, health, children's education, police and courts, welfare services). Respondents were also asked open-ended questions on what would need to change to make them more or less satisfied. Analytical material was also collected (using the Srole–Christie Anomy scale and Crowne–Marlowe Social Desirability scale) as well as standard demographics. This appears to be one of the earliest measures of subjective wellbeing (see John Hall's website, details in the Appendix).

A centre at the University of Pennsylvania provides information about 17 positive psychology questionnaires that researchers can use (see Appendix). The earliest of these, dating from 1985, is Ed Diener's Satisfaction with Life Scale, developed to assess satisfaction with people's lives as a whole. It is a short exercise, taking only a few minutes to complete. It does not assess satisfaction with specific life domains, such as health or finances, but assumes that subjects will integrate and weigh these domains and any other factors in whatever way they choose, in coming to their overall rating.

The development of measures of psychological wellbeing has been part of a wider awareness of how psychology can be applied to improve the lives of individual people and communities beyond relieving suffering. The Pennsylvania centre includes scales based on the work of Martin Seligman, who is often presented in the media as the 'inventor' of positive psychology, a major figure in the understanding of happiness and wellbeing and how to achieve them in childhood and as adults. There is a large and growing literature drawing on positive psychology (e.g. Layard, 2006 and Seligman, 2011) and developments in measurement beyond North America. Huppert and So have operationalised the concept of flourishing, predominantly with questions on the European Social Survey. A person can be said to be flourishing if they experience 'life going well. [Flourishing] is a combination of feeling good and functioning effectively' (Huppert and So, 2013). Flourishing is one of a range of ways of conceptualising wellbeing by focusing on the opposite end of the spectrum to common mental disorders like depression and anxiety. We will see later that, in measuring wellbeing overall, we need to consider the complete distribution of wellbeing.

Other major initiatives in academic centres beyond the United States include the Warwick–Edinburgh Mental Well-being Scale (WEMWBS, see Appendix), which was developed at those universities to meet growing demand for instruments to monitor mental wellbeing at a population level and evaluate mental health promotion initiatives. WEMWBS was developed and validated as a new scale, comprised only of positively worded items relating to different aspects of positive mental health. It is used for example in Scotland's annual health survey and for one of Scotland's national indicators (see Appendix). Also, the World Health Organisation Quality of Life Group has defined quality of life as 'an individual's perceptions of their position in life, in the context of the culture and value systems in which they live and in relation to their goals, expectations, standards and concerns' (Skevington, 2002). The group developed quality of life assessment instruments specifically valid for cross-cultural research.

We can call all of these subjective wellbeing instruments. As well as use in clinical situations and in research, they have also been taken up by commercial organisations, Gallup especially, working in collaboration with academics. Gallup's World Poll aims to measure 'What the World is Thinking' (see Appendix), with hundreds of questions asked in some 160 countries. One of the indexes used to present World Poll results is a Well-Being Index, using items in which respondents have rated their current and past quality of life. Gallup also produces a *Positive Experience Index*, scored for each country as the proportion of respondents saying 'yes' to all six questions about their positive feelings during the previous day.

As we will see in Chapter 4, there are many technical, philosophical and operational issues to consider in measuring subjective wellbeing. One consideration might be that such questions could be seen as probing instruments but, unlike a doctor's efforts to diagnose a situation, asking a survey respondent to assess their own wellbeing may be asking them to consider something that they would not otherwise have done. There are many different sets of questions used to collect subjective wellbeing, some intended to be used individually in a clinical situation, or only designed for small-scale surveys. There may be a fundamental issue in that, like wealth and personal morality, happiness levels are 'experienced as largely relative to those of your close peers' (McNaughton, 2007, p. 30), so that measuring subjective wellbeing might need to be undertaken in ways that capture such comparisons.

We will also see that there are several different types of approach. There is therefore now a first attempt, undertaken by the OECD, to provide international guidelines on collecting, publishing and analysing subjective wellbeing data. The OECD guidelines also summarise possible uses of subjective wellbeing data – 'complementing existing measures of well-being; better understanding the drivers of subjective well-being; subjective well-being as an input for other analyses, particularly cost-benefit analysis' (OECD, 2013d, p. 181). While some of these potential uses are quite general, we will see in Chapter 6 that subjective wellbeing data are starting to be used in quite specific ways, for example, to estimate the value to people of non-market goods and services within cost-benefit analyses of policy options.

Our own assessment is that measuring subjective wellbeing is still an emerging science. We are not convinced that we should be relying on the measurement of subjective wellbeing as the overall measure of national wellbeing and progress. We are much more comfortable with the way forward proposed by the Stiglitz, Sen and Fitoussi Commission, which we explore in Chapter 6, that includes subjective wellbeing measures as one of a number of different dimensions of national wellbeing. We should therefore be able to make progress with measuring progress whilst the measurement of subjective wellbeing is further researched and standardised. We do not go as far as Nussbaum (2012), who concludes: 'In short, the appeal to subjective well-being, as currently used in the psychological literature, is not utterly useless, but at present, it is so riddled with conceptual confusion and normative *naïveté* that we had better pause and sort things out before going any further'.

2.10   The Easterlin paradox

Up to now we have presented the history of the measurement of progress as if it was made up of largely self-contained developments. Here is one way in which the development of GDP, as a measure of economic wellbeing, and of individual subjective wellbeing came together. One of the points is support of radical reform to the theory behind public economics is that, as Layard summarised it, 'despite massive increases in purchasing power, people in the West are no happier than they were fifty years ago' (Layard, 2006a).

As Fender *et al.* (2011, p. 2) have noted, this is about the link between GDP and wellbeing, which has become the subject of increasing research and discussion. An influential paper by Easterlin (1974) first identified the paradox that bears his name. This says that, after a certain level of national income has been reached, average national measures of subjective wellbeing do not appear to increase, despite further increases in per capita income. Easterlin noted that there is a positive relationship between GDP and reported levels of happiness over time when both are growing from a low base in a country. However, the strength of the relationship between income and reported levels of happiness declines markedly as per capita income rises. In many advanced economies, average reported subjective wellbeing scores have remained more or less unchanged.

Many studies have followed Easterlin in examining the relationship between national income and measures of subjective wellbeing. Sacks *et al.* (2010) presented an alternative interpretation of income and life satisfaction data. They argued that absolute income plays an important role in influencing wellbeing and that those countries experiencing more rapid economic growth also tend to experience more rapid growth in life satisfaction. There are other aspects to consider, including the more prosaic point that life evaluation measures are effectively bounded (e.g. on a 0–10 scale) while GDP is unbounded, with no upper limit on its value. Deaton (2013, p. 20) notes that working with percentage differences between national income (GDP per head), rather than with absolute amounts, removes the paradox: equal percentage differences in average income tend to produce equal absolute shifts in average life evaluation, across the spectrum of poor and rich countries. The debate continues. We draw from the paradox that relying on GDP alone is not sufficient in determining societal wellbeing and progress. It also alerts us to think about how the goods and services we use in our everyday lives change over time and between generations. Part of the paradox may be because we quickly become attuned to 'better' goods and services, so our satisfaction with them, and with life more generally, stays broadly the same.

2.11   Taking note of the change in the quality of the goods and services we use

Nick Ashley-Cooper's great-grandfather died in 1961, aged 91. Reflecting recently on this, Nick observed that his great-grandfather's generation had been through two world wars, the invention of the motor car and aeroplane, and the beginning of space exploration. He might have added many other goods and services, such as telephones, broadcasting and mass tourism. Peston (2012, p. 79) has reported how in many parts of the developing world, the arrival of the mobile Internet is opening up 'a world of information and knowledge on a scale that is difficult for us in the West to comprehend: it would be like opening a door to hundreds of years of accumulated knowledge in the space of a few short years'. Each of these goods and services continues to evolve and to offer even more functions and options.

Not all progress has been so beneficial. The Nick we met in the previous paragraph is an English aristocrat, known more formally as the 12th Earl of Shaftesbury, inheriting a house that was built in 1650–1651, right at the start of the Age of Enlightenment. His great-grandfather had not been able to maintain the house, an era was drawing to a close and for many the rural aristocracy life changed irrevocably (Beddow, 2012). While most of us live in far less-grand surroundings, we may still recognise two intriguing and potentially contradictory aspects of progress: that progress is both complex and that we can adapt to things that we thought we had to have to satisfy our needs – recall the discussion of homeostatic systems in Chapter 1. This may be one of the factors at play in the Easterlin paradox.

It would be interesting to know if it is an inherent human characteristic always to want more. Some artists have suggested this may be so. Jenny Holzer, for example, made a number of works based on the idea that we might need protecting from what we want, as opposed to what we might need. (One of these was a neon 'advertising' display in Times Square, New York in 1985.) With a background in consumer research, Chris Farrell has drawn to our attention a number of television programmes that put modern families in a reconstruction of earlier times (see Appendix for his Technology Matters website). These invariably demonstrate that later generations may not be wholly satisfied with what was considered the best available by earlier generations. Horn (2011) made a similar observation during his study of an aspect of youth culture: 'Recollections from those who visited these cafes [where juke-box music could be heard] in their youth, however, reveal vivid memories of glamour decor and cosmopolitan atmospheres that, with hindsight, only appeared to be sophisticated because of limited expectations'.

It is not just that goods and services get more sophisticated. We also need to be aware that the producers of goods and services may be pursuing particular business strategies. They may, for example, seek to move purchasers 'up the ladder' to premium (i.e. expensive) items or brands, or establish value (i.e. cheap) brands to draw people in. There is something here about supply creating its own demand. Mix in pricing strategies that might be in play across the price range and it becomes very difficult to understand how economic growth, measured simply as the rate of growth in economic output or consumption between two time periods, can be taken as a measure of real progress, rather than as a measure of change within the predominant economic system.

We might also touch here on what since the 1950s has been called 'planned' or 'built-in' obsolescence in consumer products, the choice of phrase depending on one's point of view. The positive take on this is that selling product with more limited durability provides opportunities to continuously improve and to create new styles and variations. Producers say this increases competitiveness and earnings. Not all consumers welcome this, though, when faced with product failure and breakdowns of household appliances. They note with regret that things do not last as long as previously.

The message here is that it is important to understand and to properly capture quality changes. It is sometimes asserted that slowdowns in GDP growth are overstated because, as Deaton puts it, 'the statisticians miss a lot of quality of improvements, especially for services, which represent an increasing share of national output' (Deaton, 2013, p. 327). One of the reasons for the slow pace of statistical developments in this area is that 'the statisticians' want to be sure that all aspects of quality change are taken into account, including any potentially less beneficial effects such as a reduction in social interaction, before we can agree with Deaton that 'The information revolution and its associated devices do more for wellbeing than we can measure' (Deaton, 2013).

We may have realised that defining and measuring wellbeing and progress was never going to be easy. Issues such as those just raised here mean that we will need a clear understanding of the concepts of wellbeing and progress, and a robust framework to help with measuring them. This framework will need to identify cause and effect, or resources, outputs and outcomes. There may be inter-relations between a number of outcomes, rather than a single goal. The specific issue of quality change already affects economic measures and the national accounts. There will be lessons to learn from this in measuring wellbeing and progress more widely. Before we do so, there are more approaches to national wellbeing and progress to consider.

2.12   Capability approach to quality of life (Sen) and the human development index

Amartya Sen's 'capability approach' to quality of life has been much discussed, studied and applied in development policy and practice. (Professor Sen was also a member of the Stiglitz, Sen and Fitoussi Commission which we will meet more fully in Chapter 3). According to Alkire *et al.* (2008, p. 2) the capability approach to measuring, understanding and delivering quality of life is based on two distinct but related concepts: capability and functioning. The authors report that functionings are what Sen calls 'the various things a person may value being and doing'. There is no agreed or definitive list of core or basic functionings because different things and sets will be relevant to different population groups and in different settings. The kinds of things that could feature in an individual's list of functionings include being adequately nourished (or eating well, if one is more of a gourmet), being in good health, avoiding treatable illness, being happy, having self-respect, and taking part in family life or the life of the community.

Sen's view of a person's capability, according to Alkire *et al.* (2008), is that it 'represents the various combinations of functionings (beings and doings) that a person can achieve'. It reflects one's freedoms and real opportunities. Sen used these two concepts to analyse many issues, including the quality of life, egalitarian justice and poverty, to ensure that the analysis was informed by more than monetary resources, income or 'utility' (even where this is understood as happiness or desire satisfaction).

Anand *et al.* (2011) note that, in addition to functionings and capabilities, Sen identifies happiness as part of an alternative approach to welfare economics. In this formulation, functionings (the set of things that a person is or does) depends on access to resources and happiness depends on functionings. Capabilities are defined as the set of all functionings that a person could choose, given their resources.

Noble gives the example of a person leaving school in a small rural community with only one option, to work on their parent's farm, as having a much reduced capability set than someone who leaves school with achievable options of carrying on into further education, going to work for a company or starting their own business. Whether or not the rural school-leaver is happy to work on that farm, she suggests that Sen would argue that that their lack of real options, compared to others, is a form of poverty, a lack of capability (Noble, 2010, p. 16).

Measuring functionings and capabilities can be problematic. Noble explores this in presenting a case study of subjective wellbeing in Ukraine in which she settles on a questionnaire survey, drawn from the literature, plus in-depth interviews (Noble, 2010, pp. 68–88).

On the other hand, Sen's analysis using the capability approach also underpins a simple and widely used measure to assess a country's development over time, and to compare between countries, the Human Development Index (HDI). This summary measure is included in the series of Human Development Reports, launched in 1990 with the declared goal of putting people at the centre of development, going beyond income to assess people's long-term wellbeing. The central message of the first report was 'that while growth in national production (GDP) is absolutely necessary to meet all essential human objectives, what is important is to study how this growth translates – or fails to translate – into human development in various societies. Some societies have achieved high levels of human development at modest levels of per capita income. Other societies have failed to translate their comparatively high income levels and rapid economic growth into commensurate levels of human development' (United Nations Development Programme, 1990, p. iii). Publication of the report was expected to share practical insights into 'a much better link between economic growth and human development, which is by no means automatic' (United Nations Development Programme, 1990, p. iii).

The HDI was a new way of measuring development by combining indicators of life expectancy, educational attainment and income into a composite human development index, the HDI. The HDI is maintained and published by the UN, and as they explain on their website, 'The breakthrough for the HDI was the creation of a single statistic which was to serve as a frame of reference for both social and economic development. The HDI sets a minimum and a maximum for each dimension, called goalposts, and then shows where each country stands in relation to these goalposts, expressed as a value between 0 and 1'. Just four indicators, covering the three dimensions, are combined to form the HDI (for more details, see the UNDP website, link in Appendix).

During the course of preparing this chapter we realised that many of the things we have identified as potentially contributing to a fuller understanding of national wellbeing and progress have their own academic disciplines and professional associations. There is a massive community concerned with human development studies. For example, one family within this community is the Human Development and Capability Association (see Appendix), which promotes research from many disciplines on problems related to impoverishment, justice and wellbeing. HDCA members live in over 70 countries. In taking forward the measurement of national wellbeing and progress, it will be beneficial for national statistical offices and international organisations to form strong links with all such communities, to draw on their research and experience and to involve them in the process of forming relevant, useful and trusted measures.

2.13   Social capital and public value

Part of the debate about defining and measuring national wellbeing is over whether we are concerned with stocks or with flows. Flows are essentially the aggregation of all transactions taking place within a specified period, say a calendar quarter or a year. Stocks represent the total amount of something that we own, or can draw on, at a given point in time. Economists also refer to this as capital, meaning not just financial worth but any asset that can be drawn on. The point of this, in capitalist economics, is to draw on this capital to produce more wealth or capital. Access to capital therefore gives an advantage to the owner. A more technical point is that it is only one's net worth that can be drawn on, not all or one's gross wealth. Any outstanding liabilities need to be deducted from gross wealth to identify the assets or capital available for use.

There are generally accepted to be six main forms of capital:

- Financial capital is made up of money and paper assets, including money in a bank or invested in stocks and shares.

- Physical capital is made up of produced goods that contribute to the production of other goods and services, such as the machinery and equipment used in manufacturing, buildings and houses (which provide the service of shelter).

- Other tangible assets are the things that nature provides that are needed for production, such as land, water and minerals and raw material that are extracted from the earth.

- Intangible assets include intellectual property (captured in legal form as copyright, patents, trademarks) and more general attributes of a company, such as know-how and reputation.

- Human capital is usually defined as the stock of skills and knowledge accumulated by a worker. This definition means that someone not in the labour force has no human capital; so the definition is sometimes extended to cover all skills and expertise that humans acquire over the life course, not just those things that are valued for their potential to generate income.

- Social capital, variously defined such as 'social networks and the norms and expectations that govern their character' (Halpern, 2005, p. 4).

The first five of these forms of capital have been, or are being, developed within established economics and business practices. They are familiar to national accountants, even if they are not yet all formally part of the system of national accounts, so we will discuss them further in Chapter 6. There is also the concept of cultural capital. This has a literature of its own, but for the sake of our argument we can consider this as an essential part of human capital, broadly defined rather than narrowly measured in terms of labour market productive capacity. (We realise that this does not do justice to the theories and many applications of cultural capital; see, for example, Martin and Szelényi, 2000, p. 278).

Social capital has a separate pedigree, coming from social research. It is seldom measured by national statistical offices. A clue to this is the difficulty in defining social capital. The rationale is simple enough: that societies are not just a group of separate individuals, but that people are connected with other people by relationships, structures and shared understandings of how to behave. While Adam Smith and others recognised this, it was not until the second decade of the twentieth century that the term 'social capital' was used and defined by L.J. Hanifan as 'those tangible assets [that] count for most in the daily lives of people: namely goodwill, fellowship, sympathy, and social intercourse among the individuals and families who make up a social unit' (Halpern, 2005, p. 6). Halpern (Halpern, 2005, p. 6) also notes that by 1995 Robert Putnam had summarised social capital as referring to 'social connections and the attendant norms and trusts', which the World Bank broadened 4 years later to 'not just the sum of the institutions [that] underpin a society – it is the glue that holds them together'.

Social capital features in the development of measures of national wellbeing because, in Halpern's words, it 'captures the political Zeitgeist of our time: it has a hard-nosed economic feel while restating the importance of the social … social capital gives a name to something that many came to feel was missing' (Halpern, 2005, p. 1) in the neo-liberalism approach adopted in several large economies, in place of a version of capitalism. It also appears from academic research that at least some aspects of social capital can be measured, with the result that relationships between the nature, and effectiveness, of social networks and outcomes, such as economic growth, health and crime, are starting to be understood. Yaojun Li has recently reviewed the measurement of social capital, exploring how it is conceptualised and how at least some aspects of social capital can be captured using social surveys. Li concludes that 'the problem of socio-economic inequality' is at the root of disparities in the distribution of social capital (Li, 2010, p. 174). It looks as if social capital should be seen and measured as part of national wellbeing.

Social capital has, however, also been seen as problematic because of a tension between different kinds of social capital. Bonding capital is seen within close-knit groups or organisations (we are not necessarily talking just about the Mafia; this would extend to a social club that restricts admission to 'people like us'). Bridging capital is the kind of social capital that allows for different groups to get along together. Some research also identifies 'linking' social capital. This describes connections with people in positions of power and is characterised by relations between those within a hierarchy where there are differing levels of power. It is different from bonding and bridging in that it is concerned with relations between people who are not on a more equal footing.

The challenge in measuring social capital is therefore to include the measurement of different kinds of social capital. In the United Kingdom, the Office for National Statistics ran a 'social capital project' reporting in 2005 on different ways of measuring social capital (see Appendix for website link). Survey questions were developed and used in several household surveys around that time. Social capital has not, however, been measured on a regular basis in UK official surveys but it has been identified, with other capitals, as being relevant to the measurement of societal wellbeing (e.g. Allin, 2008).

While social capital has been researched for over 20 years, it has recently seen a revival within the emerging idea of the 'connected society' as the model for the relation between individual citizens and the nation as a whole. In a connected society, the focus is not on achieving the 'oneness' or homogeneity or total integration of society, but on achieving its wholeness. Danielle Allen, for example, sees an effective connected society as one which respects bonding social ties while seeking to maximise active – in the sense of alive and engaged – bridging social ties. Social capital is used to gain jobs, wellbeing and happiness at the individual or private level, as well as the public goods of 'generalised trust, mutual support, cooperation and institutional effectiveness' (Allen, 2012).

The study of sociology more generally is based on the view that humans are necessarily social beings. We are not purely individuals, but we have a complex of actual and potential relationships with other people and hence with society. There is more. We also have relationships with the economy, as employees, business owners, investors, consumers, and with the natural environment. Such ideas came out of the 'conscious-expansion' and Mother Earth movements of the 1960s and 1970s are still worthy of consideration as one underpinning for the concept of national wellbeing as reflecting the state of society, the economy and the environment.

Social or public value is another concept that could be seen as another form of social capital gaining use in public policy. We briefly mentioned this at the end of Chapter 1, when discussing the need to look at things belonging to a society, rather than at individual attributes, and we will return to this in Chapter 6. Here we will just note, in our brief history of national wellbeing, that wider public policy goals are now recognised in legislation, specifically the Public Services (Social Value) Act, which is 'to require public authorities [in England and, to some extent, those in Wales] to have regard to economic, social and environmental well-being in connection with public services contracts' (UK Parliament, 2012). The legislation does not define 'wellbeing' but official guidance notes that 'In these tight economic times it is particularly important that maximum value in public spending is achieved. However currently some commissioners [of public service contracts] miss opportunities to secure both the best price and meet the wider social, economic and environmental needs of the community'. (Local Government Lawyer, 2013).

The concept and measurement of public value both specifically in operational decisions and more generally as a component of national wellbeing opens up further interesting, and as yet unanswered, questions. For example, is there an intrinsic value to the arts and cultural institutions in a country or city, separate from the value of the wellbeing gained by people experiencing arts and cultural events at those institutions?

2.14   Limits to growth and sustainable development indicators

Some people and communities have always lived closely attuned to nature and in ways that depend on an understanding and stewardship of the earth's natural resources. From a scientific point of view, Friederichs identifies Haeckel as introducing the concept of ecology in 1866 and defining it 3 years later as 'the entire science of the relations of the organism to the surrounding exterior world, to which relations we can count in the broader sense all the conditions of existence' (Friederichs, 1958).

However, for many others, we might recall Philip Larkin's opening words of his poem Annus Mirabilis, in which he recounts sexual intercourse beginning in the year 1963, because public awareness of environmental issues also seems to have begun around then. *Silent Spring* was probably the first book (Carson, 1962) addressed to the wider public on the environmental impact of what people were starting to talk about as an ecstasy of production and consumer fever. (And, to recall Larkin again, this may have been rather on the late side). This might be seen as the start of an environmental movement, or rather an increasing range of interest groups, activities, academic research and media reporting, all focussed on aspects of the state of the natural environment.

Major oil spills from tankers in the late 1960s, together with poisoning caused by the industrial discharge of mercury into the rivers and coastal waters of an area of Japan, cruelly added to the tally of environmental impacts identified by Carson. Here were products intended (in one case literally) to fuel consumer demand that turned out to bring disbenefits as well, such as damage to the natural world and significant clear-up costs. What started out as relatively simple questions about the feasibility of indefinite growth, became starker as the cost of growth started to be recognised.

Public awareness was also triggered through the world's first Earth Day, 22 April 1970. The year 1972 saw more activity, with a United Nations conference on environment, the Club of Rome report on 'Limits to Growth' (Meadows *et al.*, 1972), and a special issue of the Ecologist Magazine 'A Blueprint for Survival' (Science News of the Week, 1972). A key assertion in all of these was that the industrial way of life, with its ethos of expansion, had a major defect, which is that it is not sustainable. They predicted the effects of unchecked economic and population growth against finite natural resources, in some cases foreseeing societal and economic collapse. Other studies followed (notably Schumacher, 1973) questioning the supremacy of markets and market makers. Is it market inefficiency if firms fail, or is the problem having too many suppliers offering what they want people to want, rather than what people need? There were other views, of course; that such predictions failed to take account of human ingenuity in finding new solutions to resource limitations, or that population growth is more complex than that represented in the models.

Computer models such as that underpinning the Club of Rome report drew on available data and it soon became apparent that these data were also valuable in their own right. As with social indicators, there was a movement to bring environmental indicators and data to the attention of policymakers and the public. Characterised as the development of 'new economics', Anderson (1991, p. 13) summarises this as aiming 'to bring into economic debate the environmental and human factors so often left out by mainstream economic theory'. If the debate was to be conducted on economic territory – and there continues to be a lively debate about economic growth and its impact or not on climate and on the natural environment – then this had to be undertaken using statistical data of the same quality as that traditionally used by economists. New sources of energy would need to be counted in statistics of energy use, for example. If energy use was going to be more efficient then this efficiency needed to be measured. Over time statistical developments have taken place along three broad strands: sustainable development indicators, green growth indicators and natural resource accounting.

2.14.1 Sustainable development indicators

While there was some initial feeling that recognising limits to growth was unhelpful and bound to lead to no growth, support for the new economics began to emerge, especially following publication of the 'Brundtland' Report (World Commission on Environment and Development, 1987), commissioned by the United Nations. This set out the concept of sustainable development: development that contributes to the welfare and wellbeing of the current generation, without compromising the potential of future generations for a better quality of life. This draws on an ancient ideal. An English translation of part of the Athenian ephebic oath is a pledge that, during your lifetime, you will leave your country 'greater and better' (see extract at Lycurgus, 1962). This has been taken into modern statements of how to live one's life. The architect Richard Rogers, for example, quotes this oath as that he 'shall leave this city not less but more beautiful than I found it' (Royal Academy of Arts, 2013).

There are clearly a number of challenges in assessing whether development is sustainable. Among these is that it will only be known in the future if future generations enjoy a quality of life that is at least as good as ours. Nevertheless, there was much work to produce measures – sustainable development indicators – that could be used to help steer current development.

In an early paper looking towards sustainable development indicators, Opschoor and Reijnders (1991) set out 'a first attempt ... to arrive at a system of indicators of the condition of the environment in terms of its capacity to sustain economic activity'. This approach recognises the practical issue that, to be useful at a point in time, indicators can only draw on information available at that point. We can at best make a current assessment of the impact our current way of life will have on the quality of life of future generations. Azapagic (2004) has discussed this in the context of the mining and minerals industry, which 'faces some of the most difficult sustainability challenges of any industrial sector'. Azapagic notes that 'To secure its continued "social licence" to operate, the industry must respond to these challenges by engaging its many different stakeholders and addressing their sustainability concerns. The industry must also be able to measure and assess its sustainability performance and to demonstrate continuous improvements over long term'. This leads to a need to develop a framework for sustainable development indicators for this industry. These would ideally include sector-specific indictors but set in a broader, common approach to measuring sustainable development.

Opschoor and Reijnders (1991, p. 1) envisaged sustainability indicators more generally will 'reflect the reproducibility of the way a given society utilizes its environment. Hence, they differ from classical environmental indicators: they do not simply reflect environmental conditions or the pressures on the environment, but they indicate to what degree certain pressures or environmental impacts the earth can deal with in a long-term perspective, without being affected in its basic structures and processes'. This formulation of sustainable development reflects the way in which the economy and the environment are each affected by the other. Indicators are to be designed to help assess performance against 'a desirable condition or goal' (Opschoor and Reijnders, 1991, p. 1).

Sets of sustainable development indicators invariably cover more than the environment. They tend to address whether development is sustainable from an economic, environmental and social point of view. Candice Stevens, in an OECD Statistics Brief, summarises various frameworks that have been adopted by countries and international organisation to measure development against these three dimensions of welfare. Measures included in the OECDs own core set of sustainable development indicators cover environmental assets, economic assets and human capital. They are organised into resource indicators (are we maintaining our asset base?) and outcome indicators (are we satisfying current needs?). Other frameworks, with Sweden given as the example, also explicitly recognise implications of current activities for future generations (Stevens, 2005).

Some economists have interpreted the basic idea of sustainability in economic terms, that future generations should be entitled to at least the same level of economic opportunities as the present generation. There are a number of different ways of approaching this. Whether or not they really broaden the concept of economic wellbeing to include social and environmental wellbeing is not always clear, even where environmental assets have monetary values placed on them. Pearce and Barbier (2000, p. 100) reviewed the state of environmental and ecological economics around the turn of the millennium, concluding that there is a new commitment to the environment, to valuing it and acting to solve environmental problems. However, that does not mean that everyone acts in line with this commitment, or even supports it. When economic times get tough, we have seen much political talk of a sustainable recovery, where that means sustaining economic growth and avoiding future downturns, for example, through a more balanced economy, rather than sustainability according to the Brundtland way of thinking.

It is important to phrase with some precision the questions that we look to sustainable development measures to answer. If not, there is a danger of not getting beyond the rhetoric of politicians, for whom the environment and sustainability may not be precisely formulated and measurable concepts. Looked at from the starting point of economic growth, Helm (2012), for example, has discussed key questions like: How to secure energy supply in a world where emerging economies are increasing their demand, developed countries are hardly reducing their demand, and national reserves of accessible oil and gas are declining? How to implement a sustainable energy system quickly enough to make a difference to climate change? How to do this while ensuring continuity and affordability of supply? Each question requires much research and analysis, not just headline measures. The role of headline measures is to present a clear, comparable and useful overview, as the context for more detailed analysis.

By 2010 the United Kingdom's set of sustainable development indicators (SDIs) contained 68 indicators, a number of which had several dimensions. At the time of writing they are under review but we will look further at them in the context of work in the United Kingdom on measuring wellbeing and progress, in Chapter 7. Two points are worth making here. First, the indicators are intended to measure and report progress towards the government's commitment to sustainable development. The coalition UK Government set out that commitment in a 'mainstreaming' vision, stating that: 'This means making the necessary decisions now to realise our vision of stimulating economic growth and tackling the deficit, maximising wellbeing in society and protecting our environment, without negatively impacting on the ability of future generations to do the same. This Government believes in going beyond the short term with eyes fixed firmly on a long term horizon shift in relation to our economy, our society and the environment' (Department for Environment Food & Rural Affairs, 2012, p. 3).

Second, how do the UK SDIs, published by a government department, fit with a programme developing new measures of national wellbeing at the UK Office for National Statistics? The government response to the consultation on new sustainable development indicators says that they 'are intended to provide an overview of national progress on key issues that are important economically, socially and environmentally in the long term. They are intended to complement the National Wellbeing Measures published by the Office for National Statistics' (Department for Environment Food & Rural Affairs, 2013, p. 1). The proposal appears to be to cast SDIs as indicators of intergenerational wellbeing which will complement and sit alongside the national (current) wellbeing measures under a banner of measuring progress. This is an interesting alignment, though it may need to recognise that some people include an eye to the future when assessing their current wellbeing.

Karen Scott has reviewed the potential conflict more generally between improving wellbeing and sustainability as two central public policy goals of government. There is much common ground, especially through the focus each policy area has on broadly the same set of indicators. However, Scott (2012, p. 169) is not convinced that there is a potential win-win, single scenario of wellbeing and sustainability, arguing instead for clearer conceptual frameworks for policy makers regarding different wellbeing constructs, which would facilitate more transparent discussions. Scott uses discourse analysis to highlight tensions on one hand between various constructs of wellbeing and sustainable development, and on the other between current individual and societal notions of wellbeing. She advocates an approach based on recognising and valuing conflicting views where notions of participation and power are central to discussions. We will see in the next chapter that international organisations previously working on environmental or developmental agendas appear to be working more on the common ground of sustainable development, but that there are what Melamed *et al.* (2012) describe as different politics and different economics underpinning the original agendas.

The Welsh Government is an example of a national administration that has put sustainable development at the heart of everything it does. It has a broad definition of sustainable development, which it describes as 'an emphasis on social, economic and environmental wellbeing for people and communities, embodying our values of fairness and social justice. We must also look to the longer term in the decisions we make now, to the lives of our children's children as well as current generations' (Welsh Government, 2012, p. 1). Keeping in touch with international best practice, the government has also drafted a Sustainable Development Bill, including proposing a new independent sustainable development organisation to strengthen the governance framework for sustainability in Wales. The government would retain responsibility for sustainable development indicators, which are still evolving, while giving the new body responsibility for 'recommending and monitoring key indicators of progress' (Welsh Government, 2012, p. 13). As well as making annual reports to ministers, to be presented to the national assembly of Wales, the new body would 'produce from time to time, but not less frequently than once every five years, a report and progress on sustainable development in Wales' (Welsh Government, 2012, p. 17).

In developing the concept of sustainability in measures of national progress, we need to be alert to how the word is used in many different ways. Rachel Stancliffe, director of the UK Centre for Sustainable Healthcare, is clear that the crucial aspect of sustainability in terms of what she means is long-term sustainability for the environment: 'Carbon is a real resource and we're running out of carbon. Looking at a triple bottom line: financial, social and carbon. In terms of sustainable health care, we would go back to sustainable development, which is development that provides the outcomes you want now but also provides them for the next generation and into the future – not just for the next five years, which is the political timeframe' (quoted in *New Statesman*, 11–17 January 2013).

However, there are other definitions and uses of the word 'sustainable'. It is sometimes used by architects to describe something that is well built, that will be long lasting. The UK Engineering and Physical Sciences Research Council (EPSRC) takes a broader definition of sustainability when looking at the infrastructure systems essential to society, in order to ensure a healthy, productive and sustainable society that is able to support economic growth.

To the EPSRC, being sustainable is about doing things which use less environmental and economic resources and are low carbon and affordable. Another approach is 'good growth', which uses qualitative and quantitative research to identify the most important issues for the public and businesses in economic policy, and which has been applied to British regions and to cities (PwC and Demos, 2012, p. 8). Dixon (2011) argues for more 'social sustainability' as well as debating the state of the environment.

Following the economic and financial crises around 2010, another aspect of sustainability has become important. Countries with a high level of public debt, compared with their annual GDP, are described as unsustainable; higher economic growth is needed to generate more income for the government from individual and corporate taxation. This seems to take us back to only looking at the economics, rather than taking a broad consideration of sustainability. We see a number of media reports in which 'sustainable' is used to describe 'sustained' economic growth (and indeed the OECD refers often to sustained growth, albeit environmentally aware, in its latest economic survey of the United Kingdom, OECD 2013c). We do wonder what politicians mean when they look for 'sustainable recovery' to the economic and financial crisis. We also need to be careful to distinguish between a current policy that is intended to be sustainable (or sustained) and an assessment looking back over whether progress during a period met the criteria to be marked as sustainable. Such assessments need to be made in time to make changes, should the verdict turn out that we are not on a sustainable path, of course.

2.14.2   Green growth indicators

Alongside sustainable development there is also 'green growth'. To the OECD, green growth means 'fostering economic growth and development while ensuring that natural assets continue to provide the resources and environmental services on which our well-being relies. To do this, it must catalyse investment and innovation which will underpin sustained growth and give rise to new economic opportunities' (OECD, 2011, p. 9). While this is about an interaction of economic and environmental issues, it is debateable that green growth was once a more narrowly focussed concept than sustainable development. At least initially, 'green growth' appeared to be restricted to describe activities, such as renewable energy supply, that were in themselves sustainable. Including some generic socio-economic and growth indicators for context, the emerging set of green growth indicators now appears to be based on a measurement framework presenting an overall picture of economic growth, the greening of growth and the state of the environment (OECD, 2011a, p. 12). The OECD Green Growth Strategy was presented at the May 2011 OECD Ministerial Council meeting. Ministers welcomed the Strategy and encouraged the OECD to continue work on indicators for green growth in line with its indicators report.

The Global Green Growth Institute (GGGI) has a more bullish approach to green growth. It also focuses on establishing this in developing and emerging countries. The GGGI was established as a new international organisation in June 2012, at the UN Rio+20 Conference. It sees green growth as a new model of strong economic and environmental performance that simultaneously targets key aspects of economic performance, such as poverty reduction, job creation and social inclusion, and those of environmental sustainability, such as mitigation of climate change and biodiversity loss and security of access to clean energy and water. The GGGIs vision is that the world (not just developing and emerging countries) makes a paradigm shift to green growth. While there is some good practice to share and to build on, the GGGI notes on its website, under a heading 'Theory of Change', that 'there is not yet a convincing economic theory and policy agenda to explain the fundamentals of green growth and guide its pursuit' (see Appendix for website link).

2.14.3   Natural resource accounting

Natural resource and ecosystem accounting form the third strand of statistical developments relevant to understanding the relationship between the economy and the environment. The conceptual model for environmental accounts adopted by national statistical offices such as that in the United Kingdom, and the international statistical community, is the United Nations' System of Economic and Environmental Accounts (SEEA), a satellite system of the System of National Accounts (SNA) that we looked at in Section 2.5. Although there is some understandable feeling that satellite accounts are peripheral to the core national accounts, the positive take on this is that accounts produced under this standard bring environmental and economic information together within a common framework. This allows for consistent analysis of how environmental resources are used in economic activities, impacts of the economy on the environment, say in the form of pollution and the efficiency of the use of environmental resources within the economy.

SEEA is at an earlier stage of development than the main system of national accounts. One of the stated areas for development in SEEA is experimental accounts for ecosystems. The starting point is that the SEEA measurement framework includes environmental assets, defined as: 'individual assets that comprise the environment. The scope comprises those types of individual components that may provide resources for use on economic activity. Generally the resources may be harvested, extracted or otherwise moved for direct use in economic production, consumption or accumulation. The scope includes land and other areas of a country that provide space for undertaking economic activity' (see Appendix for website link).

Environmental assets are classified into timber resources, mineral and energy resources, land, soil resources, aquatic resources, water resources and other biological resources. It will be seen from this that there is a danger of slipping into the assumption that the environment is primarily there for humans to use in their economic activity. Perhaps to counter this, in 2000 the then Secretary General of the United Nations, Kofi Annan, called for a Millennium Ecosystem Assessment (MEA) (e.g. Millennium Ecosystem Assessment Board, 2005, p. 1). The objective of the MEA was to assess the consequences of ecosystem change for human wellbeing and the scientific basis for action needed to enhance the conservation and sustainable use of those systems and their contribution to human wellbeing. It was, in short, focusing on the ecology of the planet, not on natural resources as an input to economic activity.

The MEA defines an ecosystem as 'A dynamic complex of plant, animal and micro-organism communities and their non-living environment interacting as a functional unit' and classifies ecosystems by type, such as inland water, rivers and other wetlands (e.g. MEA Board, 2005, p. 6). Rather than simply seeing ecosystems as resources, the MEA presents four categories of services that can be associated with ecosystems, by humans or by natural forces. These contribute to human wellbeing in various ways:

- Provisioning services – products such as food (e.g. crops, meat and dairy products, fish and honey), water, fibrous materials (e.g. timber and wool) and fuel;

- Regulatory services – activities such as water purification, climate regulation, noise and air pollution reduction and flood hazard reduction, all of which bring benefits;

- Cultural services – non-material benefits, for example, through cultural heritage, recreation (visits to national parks) or aesthetic experience. Accessible green spaces provide recreation and enhance health and social cohesion;

- Supporting services – production of all other ecosystem services, for example, soil formation, pollination and nutrient cycling.

The SEEA experimental ecosystem accounts now under development will aim to finalize the classification of ecosystem services, set out definitions and measurement for ecosystem accounting units and establish methods for recording and valuing stocks and flows relating to ecosystems and ecosystem services.

In general the aim of asset accounting in the SEEA is to measure the quantity, quality and value of environmental assets and to record and explain the changes in those assets over time. The first stage is to measure physical stocks and to assess whether the stock is increasing or decreasing, and how the quality has been changing. In terms of sustainability, this is with a view particularly to doing whatever is necessary to keep each resource above some critical threshold. (In a classic example of apples and pears, the SEEA suggests that physical asset accounts are separately compiled for specific types of assets rather than for combination of different assets, because each asset will usually be recorded in different units and hence aggregation across assets in physical terms is not possible).

The SEEA also allows for monetary accounts when, in certain circumstances, physical environmental assets are converted into a monetary equivalent. (For national accounts, one implicit assumption in this is of substitutability between different types of capital when monetary accounts are added together). Considerable caution is needed as such an approach has several potential limitations due to the absence of markets on which valuations of assets could be based. Even when there are market values, there is no guarantee that they adequately reflect how the different assets matter for future wellbeing. The monetary approach requires imputations and modelling. SEEA therefore starts with a modest approach, focusing the monetary aggregation on items for which reasonable valuation techniques exist, such as certain natural resources that are traded in the market.

A number of countries are assessing their national ecosystem. Much of the above description of natural resource and ecosystems accounting was informed by a paper setting out developments in the United Kingdom (Khan, 2011). Governments in the United Kingdom are supporting these developments because the natural world, its biodiversity and its ecosystems are critically important to our wellbeing and economic prosperity, but are consistently undervalued in conventional economic analyses and decision-making (Watson and Albon, 2011, p. 5). An increasing number of such national and international studies suggest that current patterns and practices of economic activity are depleting and degrading available environmental assets more quickly than they can regenerate themselves. To address these concerns, it is essential that the contribution of the natural environment to society's overall wellbeing is considered alongside its contribution to economic growth.

As we noted in Section 2.5, over the last 60 years macroeconomic policy has largely been based on information flowing from the System of National Accounts (SNA) framework. The SNA was introduced as an international standard for measuring economic activity and therefore focused exclusively upon measuring economic growth and in particular production in markets for which prices are available (plus government output for which market prices are not available). One view is that, with hindsight, the SNA was introduced when there was no need for better treatment of natural resources and the environment, as resources were considered abundant and environment as an inexhaustible sink. Since then, however, the world population and the world economy have grown tremendously, which has put a stress on the natural environment. As a result, there is a danger that we are running down our natural capital stock without fully understanding the value of what we are losing.

Sir David Attenborough is one of a number of people who see things more simply and more starkly. In a lecture on people and planet, he said: 'The fundamental truth that Malthus proclaimed [in 1798] remains the truth. There cannot be more people on this earth than can be fed. Many people would like to deny that this is so. They would like to believe in that oxymoron "sustainable growth". Kenneth Boulding, President Kennedy's environmental advisor 45 years ago said something about this. "Anyone who believes in indefinite growth in anything physical, on a physically finite planet", he said, "is either mad – or an economist"' (Attenborough, 2011).

Unfortunately in the rough and tumble of political life, such rationality and insistence on evidence are not always followed. During Italian elections of early 2013, there was more than a hint that pro-environment policies may well appeal to the popular vote but many seemed to argue that such policies could end up dragging Europe back into a debt crisis (e.g. Kington, 2013). It is not clear what model of economic, social and environmental factors this is based on.

2.15 Commentary

We have sought to show in this brief review of a long history that there are many different ideas, approaches and measurements that appear relevant to national wellbeing. The current interest in defining, measuring and using national wellbeing is drawing on a number of diverse and well-established areas. On the one hand, it is reassuring that there is a rich base to start from. On the other hand, this feels like starting without a clear and generally agreed definition of what it is that we mean by national wellbeing and progress.

In particular, we have seen an interweaving of individual wellbeing and national or societal wellbeing. The ancient Greek philosophers seemed to be able to distinguish between the individual and society as a whole. They were essentially reflecting on the good life and how individuals and societies could progress towards that. Ideas that were rekindled in the Age of Enlightenment might at first be taken to focus on individual wellbeing or happiness, promoting societal wellbeing through seeking to allow everyone to reach their full potential.

However, the Age of Enlightenment also gave rise to the aim of progress through economic growth, measured through the national accounts and often reduced to the single measures of GDP. Social scientists, epidemiologists, environmentalists and official statisticians have presented a huge range of other indicators, covering individual, social and environmental conditions.

We conclude that there is a tension between whether the unit of analysis for national wellbeing and progress is the individual or society. We are not questioning the need for close study of individual human nature. Herzberg (1966), for example, studied how humans are compelled by the laws of nature to have a need for personal growth, as well as material and emotional needs. Nor are we uneasy with more abstract concepts of society, such as that workplaces can be seen as organised groups of individuals. However, we are not yet clear whether measures of national wellbeing and progress should be constructed primarily by aggregating across individual measures, or by measurements taken at the societal level. If we want to assert any moral purpose for the way in which a society is organised and governed – be it ensuring freedom, making money, living harmoniously with each other and with nature – are we always sure how we are assessing how society is doing against whatever goals we choose?

There is a strong moral case for starting any assessment of national wellbeing by valuing people as individuals. We look at measuring individual wellbeing in Chapter 4, including exploring dimensions of wellbeing at the individual level. There is also a strong tradition of social welfare measurement, research and policy, which sees social welfare are the wellbeing of the entire society. It is not the same as standard of living but is more concerned with the quality of life overall and for social groups, such as children and families or older adults, and in terms of factors such as labour market participation, provision of social services, crime, drug abuse, as well as religious and spiritual aspects of life. In many cases this is also now extending to consider the quality of the built and natural environment, going beyond housing, and their impact on quality of human life. There are many sets of social welfare statistics, for example, the aggregate expenditure on providing services under various policy headings, number of beneficiaries and outcomes. These are often used not only in specific policy contexts but are also quoted to show the way we are as a nation. (We do not, by the way, go along with Lynn and Vanhanen (2002, p. 195) in ascribing a permanent part of the differences in the wealth of nations to differences in IQ, because we believe they have overstated what IQ tests measure and made too many assumptions in their data sources and in their statistical analysis).

Part of the complexity is that we cannot study and understand individual wellbeing without looking at society. There has long been interest in inequalities, as measured by how individual incomes, wealth and health, for example, are distributed. Harrison *et al.* (2013) have demonstrated how many decisions taken by individuals and in the formation of public policy may reflect, among other things, individual preferences towards the wellbeing of others. Similarly, status-seeking behaviour is observed in many settings. Individuals continually compare themselves to others. Economists have formally captured this idea through the concept of relative utility (e.g. Mujcic and Frijters, 2013).

Considering all of this, we come down on the side of measuring national (or regional, or local) wellbeing in terms of the society in that place (country, region or local area). This has the advantage of providing the same unit of analysis for current wellbeing and for sustainability, though we acknowledge that there are other, equally valid approaches. Much of what is being done to measure wellbeing around the world focuses on the wellbeing of the individual, while a more nuanced approach to sustainability might be to focus on the sustainability of the economic, social and environmental systems on which we all depend, as Marco Mira D'Ercole has helpfully reminded us (personal communication, December 2013).

There have been many analyses of the condition of Britain, including during the depression in the 1930s and in the 1950s, when the country enjoyed 'full' employment and rising prosperity (but still rediscovering poverty). In a recent essay on the condition of Britain, Labour Members of Parliament Jon Cruddas and Liam Byrne (2013) started from 'the lived experience of people in Britain today', rather than an abstract political study. Their aim was 'primarily to shape a new centre-left understanding of British society ... a profound and demanding challenge for politics, questioning whether it is possible to build and maintain a good society in austere times ... remind the centre-left of its concern for moral worth as well as material worth'. They quote Robert Kennedy, as we did in Section 2.6, and not only imply that broader measures are needed, but also state their 'belief in the importance of people playing an active part in solving their problems, alongside others, not living in isolation or dependency'. But before trying to help 'sort things out', there is a need to understand things better, to take the temperature of society and the condition of a nation state. This is about bridging the gap between the country as it is and the country, its citizens would like to be.

We take it as given that a country will be better governed if politicians of all parties have a better, shared understanding of what the electorate thinks and why. How to achieve this is one of the underlying themes of this book. We will see in Chapter 5, for example, that this is not just about producing better statistics but also ensuring that they meet the needs of modern society.

In the next chapter we turn to contemporary developments, where the history of the measurement of national wellbeing and progress is still being made.

References

Alkire S., Qizilhash M. and Comim F. (2008). Introduction. In: F. Comin, M. Qizilhash and S. Alkire (eds) *The Capability Approach: Concepts, Measures and Applications*. Cambridge University Press, Cambridge. pp. 1–25.

Allen D. (2012). What is a connected society? *Institute for Public Policy Research Review (Juncture)*. **19**(3), 209–210.

Allin P. (2008). From measuring social capital to measuring societal well-being: some early thoughts from the United Kingdom. In: *Measuring Capital – Beyond the Traditional Measures*. Proceedings of the Seminar Session of the 2007 Conference of European Statisticians, UNECE and Statistics Netherlands, United Nations, New York. pp. 137–141.

Allin P. (2014). Measuring wellbeing in modern societies. In: P.Y. Chen and C.L. Cooper (eds) *Work and Wellbeing: Wellbeing: A Complete Reference Guide*, vol. III. John Wiley & Sons, Chichester. pp. 409–463.

Anand P., Durand M. and Heckman J. (2011). Editorial: The measurement of progress – some achievements and challenges. *Journal of the Royal Statistical Society, Series A*, **174**(4), 851–855.

Anderson V. (1991). *Alternative Economic Indicators*. Routledge, London.

Attenborough D. (2011). *People and Planet: RSA President's Lecture 2011*. http://www.thersa.org/__ data/assets/pdf_file/0004/390307/Sir-David-Attenborough-speech-text-Planet-and-Population-10. 03.2011.pdf (accessed 3 August 2013).

Azapagic A. (2004). Developing a framework for sustainable development indicators for the mining and minerals industry. *Journal of Cleaner Production*, **12**(6), 639–662. http://www. sciencedirect.com/science/article/pii/S0959652603000751 (accessed 1 August 2013).

Bache I. (2013). Measuring quality of life for public policy: an idea whose time has come? Agenda-setting dynamics in the European Union. *Journal of European Public Policy*, **20**(1), 21–38.

Ball P. (2005). *Critical Mass: How One Thing Leads to Another*. Arrow Books/Random House, London.

Beddow T. (2012). Shaftesbury's Avenue. *The World of Interiors*, August 2012, 38–44.

Bentham J. (1798). *Pauper Management Improved*. UCL Bentham Project papers, http://www. benthampapers.ucl.ac.uk (accessed 24 July 2013).

Bentham J. (2009). *An Introduction to the Principles of Morals and Legislation*. Dover Publications Inc.

Bok D. (2010). *The Politics of Happiness: What Government can Learn from the New Research on Well-Being*. Princeton University Press, Princeton.

Booth P. (ed) (2012). '. . . and the Pursuit of Happiness: Wellbeing and the Role of Government'. The Institute for Economic Affairs, London.

Carson R. (1962). *Silent Spring*. Houghton Mifflin, Boston.

Cherniss J. and Hardy H. (2010). Isaiah Berlin. In: Edward N. Zalta (ed) *The Stanford Encyclopedia of Philosophy*. Stanford University http://plato.stanford.edu/archives/fall2010/entries/berlin/ (accessed 24 July 2013).

Crisp R. (2013). Well-Being. In: Edward N. Zalta (ed) *The Stanford Encyclopedia of Philosophy*. Stanford University http://plato.stanford.edu/archives/sum2013/entries/well-being/ (accessed 24 July 2013).

Cruddas J. and Byrne L. (2013). The condition of Britain. *Public Policy Research*, **19**(4), 217–225.

Danziger N. (1996). *Danziger's Britain: A Journey to the Edge*. HarperCollins, London.

Deaton A. (2013). *The Great Escape: Health, Wealth, and the Origins of Inequality*. Princeton University Press, Princeton.

Department for Environment Food & Rural Affairs. (2012). *Informal Consultation on Sustainable Development Indicators*. https://www.gov.uk/government/uploads/system/uploads/attachment_data/file/82559/sus-dev-indicators-consult-doc.pdf (accessed 1 August 2013).

Department for Environment Food & Rural Affairs. (2013). *Consultation on new Sustainable Development Indicators: Government response*. https://www.gov.uk/government/uploads/system/uploads/attachment_data/file/209589/sd-indicators-consult-gov-response-20130628.pdf (accessed 1 August 2013).

Dixon T. (2011). *Putting the 'S-word' Back into Sustainability*. The Berkeley Group, Cobham.

Dorling D. (2013a). Fairness and the changing fortunes of people in Britain. *Journal of the Royal Statistical Society Series A*, **176**(1), 97–128.

Dyer K.A. (2006). Chocolate: good for the mind, body & spirit. *Medical Wellness Archives*, **3**(1), 13–15. http://www.medicalwellnessassociation.com/articles/chocolate_benefits.htm (accessed 29 July 2013).

Easterlin R.A. (1974). Does economic growth improve the human lot? In: P.A. David and M.W. Reder (eds) *Nations and Households in Economic Growth: Essays in Honor of Moses Abramovitz*. Academic Press, New York, pp. 116–139.

Fender V., Haynes J. and Jones R. (2011). *Measuring Economic Well-being*. Office for National Statistics. http://www.ons.gov.uk/ons/guide-method/user-guidance/well-being/publications/previous-publications/index.html (accessed 29 July 2013).

Fioramonti L. (2013). *Gross Domestic Problem: The Politics behind the World's Most Powerful Number*. Zed Books, London.

Forest Research. (n.d.). *Psychological Health and Mental Well-being*. http://www.forestry.gov.uk/pdf/urgp_evidence_note_008_Psychological_health_and_mental_well_being.pdf/$FILE/urgp_evidence_note_008_Psychological_health_and_mental_well_being.pdf (accessed 29 July 2013).

Fox A. (2007). *Sir William Petty, Ireland, and the Making of a Political Economist, 1653–1687*. http://www.shc.ed.ac.uk/Profiles/documents/fox1.pdf (accessed 25 July 2013).

Friederichs K. (1958). A definition of ecology and some thoughts about basic concepts. *Ecology*, **39**(1), 154–159.

Grice J. (2011). National accounts, wellbeing, and the performance of government. *Oxford Review of Economic Policy*, **27**(4), 620–633.

Hacker J.S. (2011). *The Institutional Foundations of Middle-Class Democracy*. http://www.policy-network.net/pno_detail.aspx?ID=3998&title=The+institutional+foundations+of+middle-class+democracy (accessed 3 July 2013).

Halpern D. (2005). *Social Capital*. Polity Press, Cambridge.

Hamowy R. (1979). Jefferson and the Scottish Enlightenment: a critique of Garry Wills's inventing America: Jefferson's declaration of independence. *The William and Mary Quarterly*, 3rd series, **36**(4), 503–523.

Harrison G.W., Lau M.I, Rutström E. and Tarazona-Gómez M. (2013). Preferences over social risk. *Oxford Economic Papers*, **65** 25–46.

Helm D. (2012). *The Carbon Crunch: How We're Getting Climate Change Wrong – and How to Fix It*. Yale University Press, New Haven.

Herzberg F. (1966). *Work and the Nature of Man*. World Publishing, Cleveland.

Horn A. (2011). Juke boxes, coffee bars and Americanisation in the North West, 1945–60. *Manchester Region History Review*, **22**, 85–100.

Huppert F.A. and So T.T. (2013). Flourishing across Europe: application of a new conceptual framework for defining well-being. *Social Indicators Research*, **110**, 837–861.

Hutcheson F. (1725/2002). The original of our ideas of beauty and virtue. In: J.B. Schneewind (ed) *Moral Philosophy from Montaigne to Kant*. Cambridge University Press, Cambridge.

Ince R. and Cox B. (2012). Politicians must not elevate mere opinion over science. *New Statesman*, 21 December 2012–3 January 2013 edition, 22–23.

Independent Evaluation Group. (2008)'*Doing Business:An Independent Evaluation Taking the Measure of the World Bank-IFC Doing Business Indicators*'. http://siteresources.worldbank.org/EXTDOIBUS/Resources/db_evaluation.pdf (accessed 25 April 2014)/

James O. (2013). *Should Workplaces Have On-Site Psychiatrists?* http://www.guardian.co.uk/commentisfree/2013/feb/16/should-workplaces-have-on-site-psychiatrists (accessed 29 July 2013).

Johns H. and Ormerod P. (2007). *Happiness, Economics and Public Policy*. The Institute of Economic Affairs, London.

Jones D. (2010). *How to be Happy (but not too much)*. New Scientist, 28 Sept 2010. http://www.newscientist.com/article/mg20727791.000-how-to-be-happy-but-not-too-much.html (accessed 1 October 2010).

Jones G. (n.d.) *Economic Wellbeing: The implications for youth work of Every Child Matters*. The National Youth Agency: Research Programme Series Book 6. http://nya.org.uk/dynamic_files/research/Economic%20Wellbeing.pdf (accessed 27 June 2013).

Kennedy R.F. (1968). University of Kansas Address, 18 March 1968. http://www.youtube.com/watch?v=z7-G3PC_868 (quote starts at 16.22 minutes) (accessed 26 July 2013).

Kenworthy L. (2013). What's wrong with predistribution. *Institute for Public Policy Research Review (Juncture)*, **20**(2), 111–117.

Khan J. (2011). *Towards a sustainable environment: UK natural capital and ecosystem economic accounting*. Office for National Statistics. http://www.ons.gov.uk/ons/rel/environmental/uk-environmental-accounts/2011—blue-book-update/artnaturalcapital.html#tab-Measurement-of-natural-capital (accessed 3 August 2013).

Kington T. (2013). News dispatch from Rome. *The Observer*, 24 February 2013. p. 2.

Knight B. (2011). Introduction. In: B. Knight (ed) *A Minority View: What Beatrice Webb Would Say Now*. Webb Memorial Trust series on poverty, vol. 1. Alliance Publishing Trust, London, pp. 9–20.

Layard R. (2006). *Happiness: Lessons from a New Science*. Penguin Books, London.

Lee H.D.P. (translator). (1955). *Plato, The Republic*. Penguin Books, Harmondsworth.

Li Y. (2010). Measuring social capital: formal and informal activism, its socio-demographic determinants and socio-political impacts. In: M. Bulmer, J. Gibbs and L. Hyman (eds) *Social Measurement through Social Surveys: An Applied Approach*. Ashgate Publishing Limited, Farnham, pp. 173–194.

Local Government Lawyer. (2013). *Cabinet Office Issues Advice on Public Services (Social Value) Act 2012*. http://www.localgovernmentlawyer.co.uk/index.php?option=com_content&view=article&id=12764%3Acabinet-office-issues-advice-on-public-services-social-value-act-2012&catid=53&Itemid=21 (accessed 31 July 2013).

Lycurgus. (1962). Extract from *Against Leocrates*. http://www.perseus.tufts.edu/hopper/text?doc= Perseus%3Atext%3A1999.01.0152%3Aspeech%3D1%3Asection%3D77 (accessed 31 July 2013).

Lynn R. and Vanhanen T. (2002). *IQ and the Wealth of Nations*. Praeger Publishers, Westport.

Martin B. and Szelényi I. (2000). Beyond cultural capital: towards a theory of symbolic domination. In: D. Robbins (ed) *Pierre Bourdieu*, vol. I. Sage Publications, London. pp. 278–301.

Martin F. (2013). *Money: the Unauthorised Biography*. The Bodley Head, London.

McMahon D. (2006). *The Pursuit of Happiness: A History from the Greeks to the Present*. Allen Lane/Penguin, London.

McNaughton P. (2007). *Perspective and Other Optical Illusions*. Wooden Books, Glastonbury.

Meadows D.H., Meadows D.L., Randers J. and Behrens W.W. (1972). *The Limits to Growth*. Universe Books, New York.

Meek Lange M. (2011). Progress. In: Edward N. Zalta (ed) *The Stanford Encyclopedia of Philosophy*. http://plato.stanford.edu/archives/spr2011/entries/progress/ (accessed 24 July 2013).

Melamed C., Scott A. and Mitchell T. (2012). *Separated at Birth, Reunited in Rio? A Roadmap to Bring Environment and Development Back Together*. Overseas Development Institute. http://www. odi.org.uk/publications/6513-environment-sustainable-development-post-2015.

Millennium Ecosystem Assessment Board. (2005). *Living Beyond Our Means: Natural Assets and Human Well-being Statement from the Board*. UN Environmental Programme, New York. http://www.unep.org/maweb/documents/document.429.aspx.pdf (accessed 3 August 2013).

Moser C. (2000). *Foreword in Social Trends 30*. Office for National Statistics, London.

Mount F. (2012). *The New Few: Or a Very British Oligarchy*. Simon & Schuster, London.

Mujcic R. and Frijters P. (2013). Economic choices and status: measuring preferences for income rank. *Oxford Economic Papers*, **65**, 47–73.

Newport. (2013). *Health, Social Care & Wellbeing Strategy 2011–14*. http://onenewportlsb.newport. gov.uk/oneNewport/index.cfm/content/healthy (accessed 29 July 2013).

Newport F., Witters D. and Agrawal S. (2012). *In U.S., Very Religious Have Higher Wellbeing Across All Faiths, Gallup® Wellbeing*. http://www.gallup.com/poll/152732/Religious-Higher-Wellbeing-Across-Faiths.aspx?utm_source=alert&utm_medium=email&utm_campaign=syndication&utm_ content=morelink&utm_term=Wellbeing (accessed 24 July 2013).

New York Times. (2012). *Hurricane Sandy and the Disaster-Preparedness Economy*. http://www. nytimes.com/2012/11/11/business/hurricane-sandy-and-the-disaster-preparedness-economy.html? pagewanted=all&_r=0 (accessed 26 July 2013).

Nissel M. (1970). Editorial. In: M. Nissel (ed) *Social Trends*, vol. 1. Central Statistics Office, Her Majesty's Stationary Office, London.

Noble O. (2010). *Subjective Well-Being: A Ukrainian Case Study*. Lambert Academic Publishing, Saarbrücken.

Nurnberg A. (2012). Vigorous invention: Hilary Mantel's Cromwell and the historical novel. *Areté*, **38**, 111–123.

Nussbaum M.C. (2012). Who is the happy warrior? Philosophy, happiness research, and public policy. *International Review of Economics*, **59**(4), 335–361. http://www.springerlink.com/ content/m426713510376t24/fulltext.html?MUD=MP (accessed 29 July 2013).

OECD. (2011). *Towards Green Growth*. OECD Publishing, Paris. http://dx.doi:org/10.1787/ 9789264111318-en (accessed 3 August 2013).

OECD. (2011a). *Towards Green Growth: Monitoring Progress – OECD Indicators*. OECD Publishing, Paris. http://dx.doi: org/10.1787/9789264111356-en (accessed 3 August 2013).

OECD. (2013c). *OECD Economic Surveys: United Kingdom February 2013*. Organisation for Economic Co-operation and Development, Paris.

OECD. (2013d). *Guidelines on Measuring Subjective Well-being*. Organisation for Economic Co-operation and Development, Paris.

ONS. (2011). *Measuring what matters: National Statistician's reflections on the National Debate on Measuring National Well-being'*. UK Office for National Statistics. http://www.ons.gov.uk/ons/guide-method/user-guidance/well-being/publications/index.html (accessed 25 April 2014).

Opschoor H. and Reijnders L. (1991). Towards sustainable development indicators. In: O. Kuik and H. Verbruggen (eds) *In Search of Indicators of Sustainable Development*, Chapter 2. Kluwer Academic Publishers, Dordrecht. http://www.visionaryvalues.com/wiki/images/Towardsustain bedevvelopmentindicators_Opschor.pdf (accessed 31 July 2013).

Orwell G. (1933/1975). *Down and Out in Paris and London*. Penguin Books, Harmondsworth.

Pearce D. and Barbier E.B. (2000). *Blueprint for a Sustainable Economy*. Earthscan, London.

Peston R. (2012). *How Do We Fix This Mess? The Economic Price of Having it all, and the Route to Lasting Prosperity*. Hodder & Stoughton, London.

Pirsig R.M. (1974/1999) *Zen and the Art of Motorcycle Maintenance, 25th Anniversary Edition*. Vintage Books, London.

Pullinger J. (2013). *Statisticians Need to Have a Seat at Decision-making Tables*. http://www.statisticsviews.com/details/feature/4364371/Statisticians-need-to-have-a-seat-at-decision-making-tables-John-Pullinger-on-hi.html (accessed 31 July 2013).

PwC and Demos. (2012). *Good Growth for Cities: A report on Urban Economic Wellbeing*. http://www.pwc.com/gx/en/psrc/united-kingdom/good-growth-for-uk-cities.jhtml (accessed 1 August 2013).

Reich R. (2000). *Introduction* in Smith A. (1776/2000) *The Wealth of Nations*. The Modern Library, New York. pp. xv–xx.

RIPA. (2000). *Regulation of Investigatory Powers Act 2000*. http://www.legislation.gov.uk/ukpga/2000/23/contents (accessed 27 June 2013).

Royal Academy of Arts. (2013). *Richard Rogers RA, Inside Out, Gallery Guide*. Royal Academy of Arts, London.

Royal Statistical Society. (1887). *Charter*. http://www.rss.org.uk/uploadedfiles/documentlibrary/365.pdf (accessed 31 July 2013).

Runciman W.G. (2010). *Great books, Bad Arguments: Republic, Leviathan, and The Communist Manifesto*. Princeton University Press, Princeton.

Sacks D.W., Stevenson B. and Wolfers J. (2010). *Subjective Well-Being, Income, Economic Development and Growth*. National Bureau of Economic Research, working paper no. 16441. http://www.nber.org/papers/w16441 (accessed 29 July 2013).

Sager P. (2002). *Wales*. Pallas Athene, London.

Scarre G. (1996). *Utilitarianism (The Problems of Philosophy)*. Routledge, London.

Schlefer J. (2012). *The Assumptions Economists Make*. Belknap Press, Harvard.

Schumacher E.F. (1973). *Small is Beautiful: Economics as if People Mattered*. Harper & Row, New York.

Science News of the Week. (1972). Ecology, Survival and Society, *Science News* **101**(7), 100–101. www.jstor.org (accessed 27 May 2014).

Scott K. (2012). *Measuring Wellbeing: Towards Sustainability?* Routledge, Abingdon.

Seers D. (1983). *The Political Economy of Nationalism*. Oxford University Press, Oxford.

Seligman M.E.P. (2011). *Flourish: A New Understanding of Happiness and Well-being – and How to Achieve Them*. Nicholas Brealey Publishing, London.

Sen A. and Drèze J. (2013). *An Uncertain Glory: India and its Contradictions*. Allen Lane/Penguin, London.

Severs J. (2013). *Stanley Donwood: Hollywood Doom*. Chapter Gallery, Cardiff.

Skevington S.M. (2002). Advancing cross-cultural research on quality of life: observations drawn from the WHOQUOL development. *Quality of Life Research*, **11**, 135–144.

Smith A. (1776/2000). *The Wealth of Nations*. The Modern Library, New York.

Stevens C. (2005). *Measuring Sustainable Development*. Statistics brief no. 10. OECD, Paris. http://www.oecd.org/std/35407580.pdf (accessed 1 August 2013).

Tammet D. (2012). *Olympics: Are the Fastest and Strongest Reaching Their Mathematical Limits? The Observer.* 12 August 2012. http://www.guardian.co.uk/sport/2012/aug/12/olympic-records-time-numbers-mathematics (accessed 25 July 2013).

Tufte E.R. (1990). *Envisioning Information*. Graphics Press, Cheshire, Connecticut.

Turner C.F. and Martin E. (eds) (1981). *Surveys of Subjective Phenomena Summary Report*. National Academy Press, Washington DC. http://ia700202.us.archive.org/17/items/surveysof subject024185mbp/surveysofsubject024185mbp.pdf (accessed 29 July 2013).

UK Parliament. (2012). *Public Services (Social Value) Act*. http://www.legislation.gov.uk/ukpga/2012/3/introduction/enacted (accessed 31 July 2013).

United Nations. (1945). Charter *of the United Nations*. United Nations, New York. http://www.un.org/en/documents/charter/chapter1.shtml (accessed 26 July 2013).

United Nations Development Programme. (1990). *Human Development Report 1990*. Oxford University Press, Oxford. http://hdr.undp.org/en/reports/global/hdr1990/chapters/ (accessed 30 July 2013).

Walker S. (2013). *1950s Modern: British Style and Design*. Shire Publications, Oxford.

Watson R. and Albon S. (2011). *The UK National Ecosystem Assessment: Synthesis of the Key Findings*. UNEP-WCMC, Cambridge. Information Press, Oxford. http://uknea.unep-wcmc.org/Resources/tabid/82/Default.aspx (accessed 3 August 2013).

Welsh Government. (2012). *A Sustainable Wales: Better Choices for a Better Future*. Welsh Government, White Paper WG17030. http://wales.gov.uk/docs/desh/consultation/121203asusdevwhitepaperen.pdf (accessed 24 July 2013).

WHO. (1946). Preamble to the Constitution of the World Health Organization as adopted by the International Health Conference, New York, 19–22 June, 1946; signed on 22 July 1946 by the representatives of 61 States (Official Records of the World Health Organization, no. 2, p. 100) and entered into force on 7 April 1948.

Williams R. (2011). *Archbishop of Canterbury's 2011 Easter Sermon*. http://rowanwilliams. archbishopofcanterbury.org/articles.php/1926/archbishop-of-canterburys-2011-easter-sermon (accessed 24 July 2013).

Wills G. (2002). *Inventing America—Jefferson's Declaration of Independence*. Houghton Mifflin, New York.

Wintour P. (2012). *'Britain Stands at Equality Crossroads, According to Landmark Report'*. http://www.guardian.co.uk/business/2012/oct/30/economic-growth-commission-on-living-standards (accessed 29 July 2013).

World Commission on Environment and Development. (1987). *Our Common Future*. Oxford University Press, Oxford.

3

Recent developments: Towards economic, social and environmental accounts

> All progress is based upon a universal innate desire on the part of every organism
> to live beyond its income.
>
> Samuel Butler (1835–1902, from his Note-books, Life)

In this chapter, we review recent developments relating to the measurement of national wellbeing, and to the use of these measures in pursuing better lives, sustainable development and the eradication of poverty. It is a story of ongoing developments. While there appears to be greater interest in wider measures, and in using these measures, it is still early days in the consolidation of an agreed and widely used measurement system. There are not yet many countries where the prominence of national accounts, and the headline measure of GDP in particular, appears to have changed in political and public discourse. Bhutan is one example frequently quoted and we will look at that. The Government of the Republic of Colombia is also on record as pursuing peace and progress through 'economic development with social justice and in harmony with the environment ... social development with equality and well-being' (Scott, 2012).

We describe this chapter as moving towards a series of accounts because we detect a number of developments that aim to provide a set of information about wellbeing and progress, rather than a single number (GDP). Of course, GDP is but part of a system of national accounts, and we realise that the other developments do not yet have the full rigour of a set of financial accounts. But perhaps what is needed, at least initially, is more of an 'account' in the everyday sense of the word, describing the state of the economy, society and the environment in ways that can be used in government, business and by households.

A series of world forums on statistics, knowledge and policy, organised by the OECD, provides a way of tracking recent history in this area. It is, however, two separate reports

The Wellbeing of Nations: Meaning, Motive and Measurement, First Edition. Paul Allin and David J. Hand.
© 2014 John Wiley & Sons, Ltd. Published 2014 by John Wiley & Sons, Ltd.

that provide the political and intellectual influence and impetus towards developing and using wider measures than GDP, based on economic, social and environmental accounts.

The first of the scene-changing reports was the 2009 report from the Commission on the Measurement of Economic Performance and Social Progress (CMEPSP). The commission and the report are also known as 'Stiglitz, Sen and Fitoussi', after Professor Joseph E. Stiglitz, who chaired the commission, Professor Amartya Sen, the commission's advisor, and Professor Jean-Paul Fitoussi, its coordinator. A flavour of the commission's overall conclusion is in the main title of the report when published as a book: *Mismeasuring our lives* (Stiglitz *et al.*, 2010). It includes 12 recommendations for wider measures of national economic accounts, quality of life, sustainable development and the environment. The full report, including three chapters of 'substantial arguments' available only online (see Appendix for website), is a detailed and rigorous analysis of the limits of GDP as an indicator of economic performance and social progress.

We see the 2013 report 'A New Global Partnership', by a United Nations high-level panel, as a second, scene-changing report (United Nations, 2013). The panel was tasked with providing recommendations to eradicate poverty after the Millennium Development Goals (MDGs) expire in 2015. The panel proposed 12 illustrative (and measurable) universal goals and 54 illustrative national targets for the international community to rally around, to implement five big ideas to make the eradication of poverty a reality by 2030.

We understand that this is only one input to a complex United Nations process to implement post-2015 development goals. The process is still under way as we write and the outcome may well differ from the recommendations in this panel's report. There is also the danger of compartmentalisation, that this report is seen as only about poverty reduction and that measurement 'beyond GDP' is addressed elsewhere in the United Nations, as part of the 'Rio+20' process.

However, while poverty reduction is the obvious and much-needed focus of the high-level panel report, we believe that the report is also important in taking a wider look at wellbeing and progress for two reasons. First, the recommendations are addressed to every country, not just to those in which poverty is most widespread. This means it is more about the general wellbeing of nations, not only about improving the wellbeing of some sections of society. Secondly, the discourse and political interest around the report is about wellbeing and sustainable development, so again not just a narrow focus on how to reduce poverty. The panel's recommendations therefore should connect with international political debate about sustainable development and how well the 'roadmap' for sustainable development laid out in the Earth Summit at Rio de Janeiro in 1992 has, or has not, been followed (i.e. the 'Rio+20' process now also in play).

The OECD world forums

The aim of the OECD world forums, which started with a forum in Italy in 2004, is to discuss how best to measure and foster the progress of societies. The forums always attract some of the leading experts in this area, with speeches and presentations from heads of state, eminent statisticians and Nobel prize-winning economists.

The forum held in New Delhi, India, in 2012 (see Appendix for website), strengthened the connection between wellbeing, hitherto mainly being explored in developed economies, and the meaning of progress and development across the whole of the world. Eight years on from the first forum, discussion at the 2012 forum continued on the broad concept of what constitutes wellbeing, the factors that contribute to a good life and how public policy can play a part in it. Professor Joseph Stiglitz argued in his keynote speech, as the Stiglitz, Sen and Fitoussi report had done in 2009, that GDP was not enough to measure the success of a nation. 'Our preoccupation with GDP makes it difficult for politicians to back policies that are good for society and for the environment but which might not result in an increase in GDP', he said.

Delegates were also updated on the progress of initiatives taken since the 2009 world forum, when the OECD's Better Life Initiative was launched. Many national programmes measuring wellbeing and progress were identified, including the United Kingdom's Measuring National Well-being programme, launched in 2010 (we explore this in Chapter 7). The role of social research, elected assemblies and civil society was also debated. In the conference's concluding statement, the OECD repeated its commitment to promote better wellbeing measures globally as well as actively pursuing its outputs and initiatives. 'The drive towards better well-being measures will not be successful unless we show that these measures can lead to better policies', it said (OECD, 2012a). The next event has been scheduled for 2015.

At the beginning of Chapter 1, we quoted from a resolution adopted by the United Nations General Assembly in 2011. This noted that 'the pursuit of happiness is a fundamental human goal' to be considered within 'the promotion of the economic advancement and social progress of all peoples'. Development also needs to be sustainable. All of this points to the need to look in some broad way at what we mean by a good society and not just how we organize ourselves socially, but the results of all our economic and social actions and our stewardship of the natural world. It includes the role of government and public policies, but is also about how we as individuals, families and households live. This we suggest is national wellbeing in its fullest sense.

Others, however, see individual wellbeing as the new concept of progress. The World Economic Forum Global Agenda Council on Health and Well-being (World Economic Forum, 2012, p. 4) for example, talks about three main aspects of life which affect the wellbeing of each of us and 'to underline the point' uses headings 'me and my work', 'me and my family', and 'me and my community'. The authors do stress the 'feedback effect … Our well-being enables us to perform better at work and in our family life and our community' (World Economic Forum, 2012, p. 5) and they acknowledge that environmental assets need to be covered in the measurement framework needed to support wellbeing (World Economic Forum, 2012, p. 10). However, their primary interest seems to be in individual wellbeing.

Better measurement is not the final goal here. Better measurement is a means to better lives brought about through a paradigm shift in how governments work and are assessed, and in public policies, commercial practices and how we may live our lives. The General Assembly resolution of 2011 was followed by proclaiming each 20th of March as the International Day of Happiness (United Nations, 2012a). Both resolutions are a call for change, rather than a recognition that things have changed. The 2012 resolution includes encouragement through education and public awareness-raising activities.

3.1 Mismeasuring our lives: The report by the Commission on the Measurement of Economic Performance and Social Progress

The reason we are writing this book is to contribute to debates about the measurement of wellbeing, progress and sustainability, and to get these measures used in political and public life. We see the Commission on the Measurement of Economic Performance and Social Progress (CMEPSP) as a major influence on current developments in these areas. The commission had a short life – formed in 2008 and reporting in 2009 – but it left a huge legacy and worldwide impact. A book version of the report is called *Mismeasuring our lives: Why GDP doesn't add up* (Stiglitz *et al.*, 2010). This contains the executive summary and 'short narrative' chapters on the content of the report. The full report, available online, contains a further 200 pages of 'substantial arguments' (see Appendix for website).

As a prelude to our discussion of the commission and current developments more generally, we remind readers that we have already outlined a number of developments that were under way long before the commission was formed. Like Bache and Reardon (2013), we view current developments as the second wave of concern with wellbeing since the end of the Second World War. As Bache (2013) also notes, the first wave emerged in the context of postwar prosperity 'as the social costs of private affluence became evident. A "social indicators" movement emerged across a number of affluent states that resonated at the highest political levels in some countries, not least in the United States, where President Johnson famously spoke (in 1964) of the good society being "a place where men are more concerned with the quality of their goals than the quantity of their goods". However, while new surveys were developed, the movement ran out of steam as economic recession in the 1970s marginalised many of its claims'.

We might debate whether there was any running out of steam in the production of social indicators and social reports, or in the rise of sustainable development indicators. What seems beyond dispute, however, is that none of these wider statistical measures managed to challenge the neoclassical economic dominance and attention given to GDP in politics and in public policy.

The CMEPSP was established in February 2008 by Nicholas Sarkozy, the then President of France. The Commission's brief was to 'identify the limits of GDP as an indicator of economic performance and social progress, including the problems with its measurement; to consider what additional information might be required for the production of more relevant indicators of social progress; to assess the feasibility of alternative measurement tools and to discuss how to present the statistical information in an appropriate way' (Stiglitz *et al.*, 2010, p. 1).

The CMEPSP's report was formally a set of proposals on how to develop measures for France, but the background and reach of the commission suggest that it was always intended for a wider audience. Indeed, the French Government has been taking the report's conclusions to relevant international gatherings and has been encouraging international statistical organisations to modify their statistical systems in the light of the commission's recommendations (Stiglitz *et al.*, 2010, p. x). President Sarkozy wrote that the point is to avoid our future and the future of our children and grandchildren being 'riddled with financial, economic, social and environmental disasters'. We must 'change the way we live, consume and produce. We must change the criteria governing our social organizations and our public policies'. In short, 'We will not change our behaviour until we change the ways we measure our economic performance' (Stiglitz *et al.*, 2010, p. vii). He was clearly not just referring to France.

Sarkozy had asked Stiglitz, Sen and Fitoussi to set up a commission of the world's leading experts. There were 24 members of the commission in all. It was, in BBC social affairs editor Mark Easton's words, a 'stellar cast'. All members bar three came from academia, including a number of Nobel Prize winners. In the main, the academics were economists, albeit from a broad span of economic approaches. The commission described its composition as 'economists and social scientists … represent[ing] a broad range of specializations, from national accounting to the economics of climate change. The members have conducted [during their professional lives] research on social capital, happiness, and health and mental wellbeing' (Stiglitz *et al.*, 2010, p. 6). The three commission members from other organisations were: the then head of the UN Development Programme; the head of the French national statistics and economics institute INSEE and the chief statistician of the OECD. Commission members were mainly from the United States or France, in almost equal numbers, with three British members and one based in India.

Commission members had not only conducted earlier research in relevant areas but some had also already written about the limitations of GDP. For example, Joseph Stiglitz had set out why GDP 'is not the be-all and end-all of development', even though it is 'a handy measure of economic growth [and …] relatively easy to measure, it has become a fixation of economists' (Stiglitz, 2006, p. 45). He had stressed the importance of a vision of development which goes beyond GDP, noting that, for some, treating the environment with respect can be a matter of basic values or fairness to future generations (Stiglitz, 2006, p. 130). The importance of economic growth as a means – not an end – has similarly been one of the themes throughout Sen's writing, along with tackling deprivations such as ill health and illiteracy.

The commission gathered evidence through detailed sub-groups and a team of rapporteurs. The full report covers many different topics, broadly gathered to address three areas: towards better measures of economic performance in a complex economy, also described as classical GDP issues; measuring quality of life; and sustainable development and the environment. There are 12 high-level recommendations in the report, which we listed in Chapter 1 and which we repeat here in Table 3.1. We will explore these and some associated proposals further in Chapter 6. The point here is to recognise that nothing will happen as a result of the report unless countries and international organisations start to implement the recommendations and to adapt their economic, social and environmental policies and behaviour in the light of the data resulting from the new measures.

There is no doubt that the commission's recommendations have been welcomed and discussed around the world. They have given rise to a number of programmes of work in national statistical offices and international organisations. There was some media criticism, that, for example, the commission was set up to draw attention away from poor economic performance, or that the recommendations should be put on hold until better economic conditions prevail. Professor Stiglitz addressed this at an OECD conference 2 years on from when the report was published. He argued that there was such a positive reaction to the report because it 'opens up policies in the direction we want to go' (see Appendix for conference website link).

Professor Stiglitz set out how the economic and financial crisis has helped illuminate why GDP per capita growth alone is not sufficient as a measure of wellbeing and progress. He noted that growth had been based on debt which was not sustainable. The Stiglitz Commission report strongly proposes that we should take into account economic, social and political sustainability as well as environmental sustainability. Professor Stiglitz recalled that one of his predecessors on the US Council of Economic Advisors had captured the obvious truth about sustainability: that which is not sustainable will not be sustained.

Stiglitz also reminded his audience in Paris that prices do not always give good metrics. Rather than simply observing rising prices, governments should have realised there was an assets price bubble. Another message is that measures of how an economy and society are doing have to relate to what most people experience. US policy makers should have realised that most Americans were getting worse off despite the increase in the aggregate

Table 3.1   The Stiglitz, Sen and Fitoussi recommendations.

'Classical GDP issues'

1. When evaluating material wellbeing, look at income and consumption rather than production.
2. Emphasise the household perspective.
3. Consider income and consumption jointly with wealth.
4. Give more prominence to the distribution of income, consumption and wealth.
5. Broaden income measures to non-market activities.

Quality of life

6. Quality of life depends on people's objective conditions and capabilities. Steps should be taken to improve measures of people's health, education, personal activities and environmental conditions. In particular, substantial effort should be devoted to developing and implementing robust, reliable measures of social connections, political voice, and insecurity that can be shown to predict life satisfaction.
7. Quality-of-life indicators in all the dimensions covered should assess inequalities in a comprehensive way.
8. Surveys should be designed to assess the links between various quality-of-life domains for each person, and this information should be used when designing policies in various fields.
9. Statistical offices should provide the information needed to aggregate across quality-of-life dimensions, allowing the construction of different indexes.
10. Measures of both objective and subjective wellbeing provide key information about people's quality of life. Statistical offices should incorporate questions to capture people's life evaluations, hedonic experiences and priorities in their own survey.

Sustainable development and environment

11. Sustainability assessment requires a well-identified dashboard of indicators. The distinctive features of the components of this dashboard should be that they are interpretable as variations of some underlying 'stocks'. A monetary index of sustainability has its place in such a dashboard but, under the current state-of-the-art, it should remain essentially focussed on economic aspects of sustainability.
12. The environmental aspects of sustainability deserve a separate follow-up based on a well-chosen set of physical indicators. In particular, there is a need for a clear indicator of our proximity to dangerous levels of environmental damage (such as associated with climate change or the depletion of fishing stocks).

Source: Stiglitz *et al.*, 2010, pp. 11–21. Excerpt from *Mismeasuring Our Lives: Why GDP Doesn't Add Up* - Copyright © 2010 by The New Press. Reprinted by permission of The New Press. www.thenewpress.com

measure of GDP per head. This is because the distributions of incomes and of living standards are invariably skewed so that median points are well below the simple arithmetic mean of the distribution. Incomes were also increasing partly through people working longer hours: national accounts do not take into account value of leisure time.

Under the theme of measuring what matters, and continuing with the United States as his example, Professor Stiglitz recalled that there was survey data showing that most Americans were feeling greater insecurity about things such as their income, their health and the state of the economy but that those data were seen as outside of, and not relevant to, the measurement of GDP. An example would be that unemployment is wider than just being without paid work. Some 25 million American part-time workers would like a full-time job but cannot get one. Work is important part of our well-being. It has implications for human dignity, so full employment needs to be part of the political agenda. This also relates to sustainability. If a country has nearly half of its young people in long-term unemployment, as was the case in Spain, then the country is losing social capital.

As we noted earlier in this section, France has shown the lead, not only on adapting its official statistics in line with the Commission's recommendations (see Appendix for website link) but also by encouraging others to modify their statistical systems in accordance with the commission's recommendations. President Sarkozy pledged in his foreword to *Mismeasuring our lives* that 'France will put debate on this report's conclusions on the agenda of every international gathering and of every meeting and discussion concerned with the construction of a new global economic, social, and environmental order' (Stiglitz *et al.*, 2010, p. x).

The touchpaper was lit across the European Union through the efforts of a 'sponsorship group' co-chaired by France resulting in a 10-year work programme to develop European statistics adopted by the European Commission, to tackle the measurement issues identified in the European Commission's 2009 intention to go beyond GDP (see Appendix for website links to 'Beyond GDP' and work across the European Statistical System, the ESS). No doubt, this will reach beyond Europe through exposure in the OECD's global forums, along with developments in other parts of the world. We see that all of this is drawing on the many developments that we ran through in Chapter 2, such as extensions to the national accounts, more robust measures of various stocks or capitals (human, social and natural), distributional analyses and indicators and subjective wellbeing measures.

Changing behaviour is more problematic. France again gave a clear signal by saying it would 'put the study of this [i.e. the Stiglitz, Sen and Fitoussi] report on the curriculum of all the country's civil service training institutions' (Stiglitz *et al.*, 2010, p. x). The Commission itself regards its report as 'opening a discussion rather than closing it', called for 'a global debate around the issues and recommendations' raised in the report, and envisaged that national round tables would be established 'with the involvement of stakeholders, to identify and prioritize those indicators that carry to potential for a shared view of how social progress is happening and how it can be sustained over time' (Stiglitz *et al.*, 2010, p. 21–22).

Will the Stiglitz, Sen and Fitoussi report report be seen as triggering the paradigm shift in thinking about wellbeing and progress that they intend? Only time will tell. There are two obvious caveats to consider. First, the commission itself saw its work as 'unfinished business', anticipating further studies to understand what the new measures tell us. This might be taken by some as a reason not to press ahead, rather than to seek an evolution into territory 'beyond GDP'. The second caveat, clearly expected by the commission, is that the state of the traditional economy of a number of countries is not currently robust enough. The commission took the opposite view: action must be taken if the same mistakes are not to be made again in a dash for economic growth.

Clearly the point about unfinished business registered, for at the end of May 2013, the OECD announced that a high-level expert group is to be set up to continue the work of the CMEPSP (OECD, 2013). The group, which is attached to the OECD, will work until 2016 to review international projects on the measurement of wellbeing; connect measures and economic theory; commission analytical work on specific topics such as inequalities and sustainability and review achievements and identify gaps. The group's work will contribute to inform the OECD's own work in the area of measuring wellbeing and progress. The 'modus operandi' is the same as the original commission, bringing together an independent group of members of international standing with relevant experience in the measurement of wellbeing and progress. There is some overlap of membership and there are some new members.

3.2   Replacing the Millennium Development Goals

The Millennium Development Goals (MDGs) were essentially set by the 'North' – the countries providing foreign aid – for the 'South', the poorest countries in the world. Progress towards the MDGs is monitored using quantitative indicators that were defined through the United Nations process of expert committees and widespread consultation through UN organisations, national governments and civil society organisations. There is a handbook providing guidance on the definitions, rationale, concepts and sources of data for each of 54 indicators (on 48 topics) – from 'Proportion of population below $1 purchasing power parity (PPP) per day' through to 'Internet users per 100 population'.

As might be expected, the main criteria that guided the selection of indicators echoed the UN's fundamental principles for all official statistics (see Appendix for website link). According to the handbook, indicators should, for example, 'Provide relevant and robust measures of progress towards the targets of the Millennium Development Goals ... Be clear and straightforward to interpret and provide a basis for international comparison ... Be based to the greatest extent possible on international standards, recommendations and best practices'. However, two other of the five main criteria reflected obvious constraints, so that resources were not to be diverted for measurement purposes. The indicators were to be 'Broadly consistent with other global lists and avoid imposing an unnecessary burden on country teams, Governments and other partners' and 'Be constructed from well-established data sources, be quantifiable and be consistent to enable measurement over time' (United Nations Development Group, 2003, p. 1). This then appears to be another indicator set in the classic mould: compiled by experts from across many UN and other international organisations, drawing for very understandable reasons on existing measures, but lacking any underlying theory or coherence around the overall wellbeing and progress of countries.

The MDGs are set with a target date of 2015. We are writing this book while the process to agree successors to them is under way. The UN General Assembly resolution foreshadowing this, quoted in Chapter 1, talks of wellbeing. However, it appears (e.g. van der Hoeven, 2012) that some participants in the current discussions are calling for a 'new framework has to be based on a global social contract, relevant to people in the South and the North'. This would address 'sustainable and equitable growth in all countries, while paying particular attention to employment, inequality, sustainable development, human rights, a global social floor, and to improved global governance'. In reviewing such a broad agenda, van der Hoeven recognises that the Stiglitz, Sen and Fitoussi report contains many relevant recommendations, endorsing what is a challenging but essential need to improve measurement of economic, social and sustainable development. However, it is still not clear what is the framework for development here, or how economic progress, quality of life, the state of the environment and its sustainability all fit together.

In May 2012, UN Secretary General invited the Presidents of Indonesia and Liberia and the Prime Minister of the United Kingdom to co-chair a high-level panel on the post-2015 development agenda. The panel was tasked with providing recommendations to eradicate poverty after the Millennium Development Goals (MDGs) expire in 2015. The panel comprised 27 members, representing government, business and civil society from all regions of the world.

The High Level Panel concluded its work in May 2013. Its report, 'A New Global Partnership: Eradicate poverty and transform economies through sustainable development', echoed the views of world leaders meeting at Rio de Janeiro in 2012 (also known as 'Rio+20', being 20 years on from the original 'Earth Summit' in Rio de Janeiro). They all envision a world in which extreme poverty (defined as people earning less than $1.25 a day) can and must be eliminated by 2030. The panel also proposed eliminating preventable infant deaths and reducing maternal mortality below current levels. The panel identified five 'transformational shifts' required to achieve this aim:

1. Leave no one behind.

2. Put sustainable development at the core: for decades, the environmental and developmental agendas have been separate. The report brings them together. This means tackling climate change and making patterns of consumption and production more sustainable.

3. Transform economies for jobs and inclusive growth: growth is the only long-term solution to end poverty, meaning a much greater focus on promoting jobs through business and entrepreneurship, infrastructure, education and skills, and trade.

4. Build peace and effective, open and accountable institutions for all: peace and good governance are not optional extras. Responsive and legitimate institutions should encourage the rule of law, property rights, freedom of speech and the media, open political choice and access to justice.

5. Forge a new global partnership: poverty eradication is not just about national governments. Businesses, community groups, donors, local governments and others all need to work together to see the eradication of extreme poverty.
   (Source: United Nations, 2013, p. 7).

The panel proposed 12 illustrative (and measurable) universal goals and 54 illustrative national targets for the international community to rally around to implement these five big ideas. The final set of post-2015 goals will be negotiated between governments in the UN between 2013 and 2015.

In a statement to the UK Parliament, the Secretary of State for International Development said: 'The High Level Panel's report provides a bold and practical illustration of how an ambitious and wide-ranging agenda can be brought together in a simple and compelling set of goals. The United Kingdom will work with others to ensure that the messages contained in the High Level Panel report are reflected in the final set of UN development goals for post-2015, and have a lasting impact for the poorest people in the world' (Greening, 2013).

Wellbeing is mentioned several times in the report but it is not a phrase used anything like as frequently as sustainable development, which emerges as the report's core theme. A number of what are listed as cross-cutting issues, such as inequality, are familiar themes in the Stiglitz, Sen and Fitoussi report and elsewhere. Will poverty around the world only or predominantly be reduced through economic growth? That view is strongly argued by the protagonists of growth, such as *The Economist* magazine ('Towards the end of poverty', 1 June 2013). However, the UN panel found that the MDGs had also made significant contributions to growth and human progress in several nations. This appears to have been partly by allowing, even encouraging, those who support national and international development to draw on a wide range of means, including education, health care and political reform as well as job opportunities. The panel's report concludes that unprecedented progress in poverty reduction to date 'has been driven by a combination of economic growth, better policies, and the global commitment to the MDGs, which set out an inspirational rallying cry for the whole world' (United Nations, 2013, p. 1).

The panel's report sets out a rationale for having goals, targets and indicators, noting that they 'believe that the combination of goals, targets, and indicators under the MDGs was a powerful instrument for mobilising resources and motivating action. For this reason, we recommend that the post-2015 agenda should also feature a limited number of high priority goals and targets, with a clear time horizon and supported by measurable indicators. With this in mind, the Panel recommends that targets in the post-2015 agenda should be set for 2030' (United Nations, 2013, p. 13). Noting that setting goals is not necessarily the best solution to every social, economic and environmental challenge, the panel nevertheless recognises that goals 'can be a powerful force for change ... They are most effective where a clear and compelling ambition can be described in clearly measurable terms. Goals cannot substitute for detailed regulations or multilateral treaties that codify delicately-balanced international bargains. And unlike treaties, goals similar to the MDGs are not binding in international law. They stand or fall as tools of communication, inspiration, policy formulation and resource mobilisation' (United Nations, 2013).

Having flagged the need for measurable indicators, the panel is also aware that there is a need to strengthen data and statistics relevant to development issues, for accountability and decision-making purposes. The panel calls for a 'new data revolution' driven by the revolution in information technology over the last decade: 'There have been innovative initiatives to use mobile technology and other advances to enable real-time monitoring of development results. But this movement remains largely disconnected from the traditional statistics community at both global and national levels. The post-2015 process needs to bring them together and start now to improve development data. Data must also enable us to reach the neediest, and find out whether they are receiving essential services. This means that data gathered will need to be disaggregated by gender, geography, income, disability, and other categories, to make sure that no group is being left behind' (United Nations, 2013, p. 23) The need for better data, better statistics and better presentations of the statistics has also featured in the OECD's world forums on measuring progress, where examples of emerging best practice have been showcased.

The panel report contains a set of global goals and national targets as an illustrative framework to support its recommended direction of travel. Much more work will be needed to reach the final set and this will involve more consultation across many different stakeholder groups. Around two in five of the illustrative targets (23 out of 54) are marked as requiring further technical work to find appropriate indicators, including all four of the targets supporting the goal of ensuring stable and peaceful societies.

One suggested target, for which the indicator is not seen as problematic, is Target 9a – 'Publish and use economic, social and environmental accounts in all governments and major companies' (United Nations, 2013, p. 48). This is in the area of managing natural resource assets sustainably, but more generally neatly captures the panel's conclusion that 'the moment is right to merge the social, economic and environmental dimensions of sustainability guiding international development' (United Nations, 2013, p. 5). The panel logs some developments on these kinds of accounts that should be piloted and rolled out by 2030, which will seem a long way off only to countries already running well-established statistical systems, and even then, there are significant measurement challenges still to face. Nevertheless, the call to prepare, publish and use economic, social and environmental accounts seems to us to summarise exactly what needs to be done.

One of the main issues, however, seems to be a proliferation of international initiatives that relate to the measurement of wellbeing and progress and that these come from different disciplines each with their own concepts, measures and infrastructure for discussion and action. In broad terms, we might follow Melamed *et al.*'s categorisation of these as either developmental or environmental (Melamed *et al.*, 2012). We welcome their call for a roadmap to move from separate strands to a single, coherent approach to development and the environment. But this also needs to engage the multiple international initiatives in each strand. As well as the UN work on successors to the MDGs, the heads of State and Government and high level representatives meeting at the UN Rio+20 Earth Summit tasked the UN Statistical Commission with launching a programme of work to develop 'broader measures of progress to complement GDP in order to better inform policy decisions' (UN, 2012b, p. 6). This recognised that there was already much work under way and the UN work should proceed in consultation with relevant organisations within the UN and beyond, to build on existing initiatives. With so much going on, some sort of overall roadmap will be essential, not only covering 'beyond GDP' initiatives but all related work. For example, the OECD continues to work on sustainable development and green growth indicators, as well as its Better Life Index.

There are some signs that international organisations are working together. In June 2013, the Conference of European Statisticians (CES), which fits in the UN system as part of the UN Economic Commission for Europe (UNECE), endorsed a set of recommendations for a framework to measure sustainable development and associated sets of indicators. The full set comprises 90 indicators across 20 themes, within which there is a subset of 60 indicators to describe wellbeing in three dimensions (current, future and 'elsewhere') and one of 24 summary or headline indicators, for communication and international comparisons. The UNECE says that this framework is 'a key step towards harmonising the various approaches and indicators already used by countries and international organisations to measure sustainable development. It is expected to contribute to the UN processes for setting Sustainable Development Goals (SDGs) and defining a post-2015 development agenda' (UNECE, 2013). It is reassuring that this report has been developed by a Task Force set up jointly by three international organisations and that it takes into account various initiatives undertaken by them as well as by individual countries. We are encouraged to see that the terminology used brings together wellbeing and sustainable development, with references to the wellbeing of future generations alongside how the wellbeing of people in other countries are affected by the activities of a country. We see all of this as pertaining to the national wellbeing of a country.

3.3 A new global movement?

'Measuring progress is possible, and it is already happening. Of course, to measure progress, one needs to know what progress looks like. And there is no single answer: progress means different things to different societies and spans different aspects of life – social, environmental and economic. But many societies are now designing sets of progress measures that are objective and/or subjective to help citizens assess whether or not life is getting better.' (OECD)

'African societies, like any other societies indeed, have to measure progress. But more importantly they have to define what is meant by progress. They have to hold a dialogue in a way that has not been done before'. (Pali Lehohla, Director General of Statistics South Africa)

(Source: Both quotes from the 'frequently asked questions' page of OECD global project on measuring progress, see Appendix)

In this section, we reflect on the 'second wave' of concern with wellbeing, which Bache (2013) saw building from around 2000, boosted by the Stiglitz, Sen and Fitoussi report in 2009, and which is still ongoing. (The first wave, in Bache's terms, was linked with the rise of social and subjective measures in the 1960s). Kroll observed around 2 years on from publication of the report that 'the current debate on measuring progress and well-being is rapidly gaining importance throughout the world' and without question was a new global movement (Kroll, 2011, p. 1). As we saw in the previous chapter, there was some increasing interest in wider measures of progress from the early 2000s onwards. We can only speculate that this might in part have been prompted by the arrival of a new millennium in those parts of the world following the Common Era calendar.

Typical of many events and reports was the international conference held in Brussels in November 2007 by the European Commission, European Parliament, The Club of Rome, WWF and OECD. It was aimed at going 'Beyond GDP' to measuring progress, true wealth and the wellbeing of nations (see Appendix for website). While this raised awareness and generated a significant amount of media coverage, the most tangible outcome was probably the European Commission communication 'GDP and beyond: Measuring progress in a changing world' (Commission of the European Communities, 2009). The subtle change from 'beyond GDP' to 'GDP and beyond' was to ensure that no one was in any doubt that GDP remained important.

The European Commission communication identified a number of actions that could be taken in the short to medium term to develop more comprehensive indicators to complement GDP, critically to measure environmental sustainability and social inclusion. A statistical work programme was put in place. We will return to this in Chapter 6, but at the time of writing this book in 2013, it is relevant to note that the statistical base compiled by European Union countries and collated through the statistical office of the European Union, Eurostat, has not altered greatly from that in place before the 2009 communication. While much detailed work is proposed and some has started, the statistical issues are complex and may be costly to resolve.

Reports to the World Economic Forum have presented wellbeing as the new concept of progress (Anderson *et al.*, 2012) and as something to be taken into account in the next set of development goals (Dolan and Harrison, 2013). Both reports call for better measures of wellbeing, including within companies as well as to influence public debate.

It might be helpful to examine the second wave of concern with wellbeing and progress from the different points of view. In a simplistic description of national statistical systems, we tend to see 'producers', such as national statistical offices, and 'users' of their output and data. The user community or communities can be large and diverse. Some users are in government, as government ministers and policy advisers. Other users are in industry or commerce, trade unions, civil society organisations, education or the media, as well as individual citizens. There is a concept of 'the public realm', the space in which democracies conduct public discussion. In practice, there are likely to be many, interconnecting public realms because no one has access to all the discussions in parliaments, in news media or in journals, to name just a few aspects of public debate, let alone social media – we gather there are currently some 500 million tweets every day, for example. Despite all this activity, we should also forget that not everyone has the same access to the public realm: some voices may be silent or even missing.

Looking at how the debate on measuring wellbeing and progress is being played out, we might perhaps see three groups of players:

- Producers of new measures, especially national statistical offices and the international organisations concerned with developing standards for the new measures. They are responding in various ways to emerging demands for new statistical measures. As part of their consultation, research and development, they may propose new measures to the following two groups;

- Governments and their advisers, who may (or may not) start to make policy and delivery decisions taking into account a wider set of measures. (We might include the senior committees and councils of international organisations here, because they also act in a governmental way, albeit made up of representatives from their member states). In theory, the demand for new measures should come at least in part from these 'end-users'. However, their requirements might not be specified as clearly as the producers would need. So, the role of the following group is vital;

- Mediators and influencers include international leaders and organisations who are championing a new way of assessing wellbeing and progress, along with political parties, research organisations and 'think tanks', academics and parts of the media.

One key area of interest missing from the three groups above is the public. Formulations such as the OECD's aim for its statistical work – 'better statistics for better policies for better lives' – might also, mistakenly, lead us to ignore the importance of individual citizens making more informed decisions about their own lives and those of their families. So, let us add a fourth group:

- Individual citizens, the 'public at large', as described in the Stiglitz report. This is not only about the public making 'a better assessment of the problems facing their societies' but also about each of us being able to make a more informed assessment of our own life.

The importance of this fourth group – and in reality, of course, this is everyone on the planet apart from the relatively tiny number of people in the other three groups – can be seen from how the assessment reports of the Intergovernmental Panel on Climate Change are presented, discussed and acted on. The chairman of the panel was reported in the media saying that 'he was confident the report would convince the public on global climate change' (McGrath, 2013), which suggests that he is aware of some scepticism about climate change and some resistance to changing behaviour, for example, in transport use. A summary for policymakers accompanies the contribution to the fifth report from the working group dealing with the physical science basis for action on climate change (Alexander *et al.*,

2013). This provides evidence about climate change and the benefits of green energy, with a scientific assessment that there is a strong likelihood that human activity is changing the climate adversely. Policymakers, especially politicians, will invariably consider what will be done based not only on the evidence but also on assessments of public – or more strictly, electorate – opinion.

National statistical offices looking at the four groups of players just described may well turn to a stakeholder analysis to help identify who needs to be involved in establishing new measures of wellbeing and progress. This analysis must be robust and not based on just one understanding of the economy and society. Those committed to a pure, free market in goods and services will, for example, only see individual producers and individual consumers as having a legitimate interest in how the market works, possibly labelling anyone else wanting to have a stake in this as representing vested interests. Conducting a comprehensive stakeholder analysis, however, means embracing all points of view without giving emphasis to any one.

The Measures of Australia's Progress (MAP) programme, started in 2002, is a good example of what national statistical agencies are doing in response to concern about wellbeing and wider measures of progress, and to contribute to the debate (see Appendix for website). MAP is a programme of work of the Australian Bureau of Statistics (ABS), including public consultation, and it results in a dashboard of summary indicators, developed by the ABS working with data users and academia. The ABS has, like other national statistical offices, published social indicators and volumes reporting on social trends since the early 1970s, also contributing to the OECD's social indicators programme. As ABS says on its MAP website, 'Setting out a suite of social, economic and environmental indicators that aim to measure a country's progress continues to be one of the most important and challenging tasks that a national statistical agency undertakes.'

Note that the statistical agency provides indicators. It sets them out on its website and draws attention to them through news releases, briefings, reports and other communications. Whether or not governments and the public respond to these indicators is less clear. It would be quite challenging to do so. The 2012 MAP report lists 17 headline areas, of which 7 were not available to assess progress over a 10-year period (either no indicator or no time series), 6 indicators showed progress, 3 showed regression and 1 showed no significant change over the last 10 years (this was also the tally in the 2011 report). The ABS is continuing to develop MAP. Meanwhile, ABS must leave the topic with a question mark on its website: is life in Australia getting better?

MAP is among many existing initiatives on measuring progress. At the national level, Kroll reports not only on Australia but also on the United Kingdom, Germany, Italy, France, the United States, Canada, Spain, Bhutan, China and India (Kroll, 2011, p. 5). We will look at the United Kingdom in Chapter 7 and draw on other countries in Chapter 6, and we give links to many developments in the Appendix. As the Istanbul Declaration (OECD, 2007) was careful to recognise, there are many commercial or not-for-profit regular publications and developments, in addition to those of the national statistical agencies. So we will also note examples such as the Gallup World Poll, Legatum's Prosperity Index, the World Values Survey and the European Social Survey in later chapters.

Insights on the producer point of view can be gained from an interview given by John Pullinger, on becoming President of the Royal Statistical Society (Pullinger, 2013). Pullinger identified measuring progress as one of his priority areas of innovation for his term of office. Recalling representing the United Kingdom at a UN meeting in New York on the system of national accounts earlier in his career, Pullinger noted the feeling that traditional methods for measuring performance were not as adequate as they need to be: 'Now it is becoming very urgent since the financial crash. Levels of employment are puzzling considering economic output. We need numbers that help us make sense of what is going on. I have no qualms about the quality of the figures being produced but there is a serious need to stand back and think what is it that we are trying to measure that will help us in decision-making?'

Pullinger recalled that, two years previously, the British Prime Minister had announced a decision to measure happiness and wellbeing as official statistics (see Chapter 7). While it was not yet clear how these new statistics would be used, Pullinger was convinced that statisticians should be involved in analysing them, as well as collecting them, so that they can in turn guide policies. This had happened during the twentieth century, with GDP helping inform many improvements, reducing serious poverty in many countries. Pullinger concluded 'Statisticians need to have a seat at these decision-making tables as once you understand the political imperatives, you can think what the statistical questions are and what are the methods to answer them. Our challenge is to bring these worlds together to guide progress over the next 100 years' (Pullinger, 2013).

One way of meeting this challenge is, for producers, to harness the power of social and environmental statistics and indicators, especially when pictured or presented imaginatively and perhaps interactively. Tufte (e.g. 1990) showed what could be done to display complex, dynamic and multidimensional data on paper effectively and there continue to be developments in eye-catching and thought-provoking visualisation.

Online presentations and video graphics, such as those by Hans Rosling on the gapminder.org website, take visualisation to another level (see also Yau, 2013). Cartograms such as those on the worldmapper.org website take a conventional map of the world and distort it so that the area of each country is proportional to the variable of interest, say its child mortality rate. The OECD's interactive visualisation of the Better Life Index compares wellbeing across countries, with the option to create your own index with your choice of weights. This won one commentator's 'top visualisation of the year' commendation in 2011 (Grant, 2013, p. 34). Dynamic and interactive visualisation is a rapidly developing field in which data owners can produce innovative websites using toolkits such as 'D3' (Bostock *et al.*, 2011).

It may be justified to recognise a new global movement from the producer perspective, in the development of new and wider measures of progress and wellbeing. However, it is still early days in the use of such measures in public policy and debate. Much hangs on how mediators and influencers carry forward any new global movement in the use of wellbeing and progress measures. With a number of countries in difficult economic conditions, the overwhelming discourse has been about delivering economic growth. Even though the 'second wave' started in less difficult economic conditions, it has been presented as the desire for a new economics and yet many governments seem tied to traditional economic thinking.

One leading 'think and do tank' that has done much to encourage adopting wider measures of wellbeing and progress is the New Economics Foundation (we abbreviate this to NEF, the brand is 'nef'). Its publication 'National Accounts of Well-being' made the case for national wellbeing measurement using a wider framework than just the national economic accounts. A chapter of this report explains 'how governments *will* use national accounts of well-being' – our italics to draw attention to what is actually a proposal and an intention by NEF 'to shift the goal posts for what nations regard as success. The aim is to bring about change in how societies shape the lives of their citizens. If they are to be successful, National Accounts of Wellbeing therefore need to influence the design of policy made by international, national and local government' (NEF, 2009, p. 44). By providing guidance on the role of national accounts of wellbeing in the policy process, NEF is here acting as a mediator and influencer, connecting the producers of statistics with users in government.

NEF and others are partners in the BRAINPOol initiative (see Appendix for website), seeking to bringing alternative indicators into policy. BRAINPOoL is a pan-European 2.5-year-long research and knowledge brokerage project, funded by the European Commission FP7 research programme. The project assesses the impact of 'GDP and beyond' indicator initiatives, and will then work with both indicator producers and potential users to help bring such GDP indicators into the policy world, through a series of road shows, action research case studies and knowledge brokerage events.

The OECD, the international organisation for *economic* co-operation and development, has taken a leading role and provided stewardship of a broader approach to economics. From around the end of the twentieth century, the OECD has been leading the development of wider measures of wellbeing and progress, including initially through a Global Project on Measuring the Progress of Societies, then regional and international conferences, reports, papers and handbooks, and latterly through its Better Life initiative and website of relevant indicators (see Appendix for website details). We will draw on OECD work particularly in Chapter 5, as we explore how to measure national wellbeing and progress.

At the end of the OECD's second world forum on statistics, knowledge and policy, with the theme 'measuring the progress of societies', the OECD and other international organisations issued a declaration. This 'Istanbul Declaration' (OECD, 2007) was addressed to all the players we identified above. It is a commitment to measuring and fostering the progress of societies in all their dimensions and to supporting initiatives at the country level. The declaration in particular reinforces the role of national statistical authorities 'as key providers of relevant, reliable, timely and comparable data and the indicators required for national and international reporting'. Governments were encouraged to 'invest resources to develop reliable data and indicators according to the Fundamental Principles of Official Statistics adopted by the United Nations in 1994'. The action areas are to

- 'encourage communities to consider for themselves what "progress" means in the twenty-first century;

- share best practices on the measurement of societal progress and increase the awareness of the need to do so using sound and reliable methodologies;

- stimulate international debate, based on solid statistical data and indicators, on both global issues of societal progress and comparisons of such progress;

- produce a broader, shared, public understanding of changing conditions, while high-lighting areas of significant change or inadequate knowledge;

- advocate appropriate investment in building statistical capacity, especially in developing countries, to improve the availability of data and indicators needed to guide development programs and report on progress toward international goals, such as the Millennium Development Goals'.

The conclusions of the fourth OECD world forum held in India in 2012, record both strong momentum and the need for further research and development. The OECD concludes that its Better Life Initiative, based on existing data and research, provides 'the first collection of internationally comparable well-being indicators tailored to the needs and concerns of developed countries. This initiative, based on a framework drawing from the Stiglitz, Sen and Fitoussi report, has served as a basis to develop a common language for the many wellbeing initiatives undertaken around the world, proposing a core set of universal well-being dimensions that could be adapted, through the inclusion of more specific items and indicators, to the priorities of different countries and regions of the world' (OECD, 2012b, p. 1). On the statistical work front, there are a number of areas relevant to the measurement of wellbeing and progress that are 'lacking a sound conceptual and statistical foundation' such as indicators of governance, civic engagement and social connections (OECD, 2012b, p. 2). However, 'Probably most important of all is the need to use better well-being metrics to inform policies' not just the policies of government but also the behaviours of citizens and businesses (OECD, 2012b, p. 3).

On the important issue of building statistical capacity, there is a consistent, strong message through international development initiatives that this should be delivered within the country concerned and under national control and direction. This should obviously especially apply in the development of measures of national wellbeing and progress. This line can be traced from the 2004 Marrakesh Action Plan for Statistics, through the 2005 Paris Declaration on Aid Effectiveness, the Accra Agenda for Action of 2008, and the Busan Action Plan for Statistics in 2011. While this may be more complicated for agencies supporting capacity building, there are clear long-term benefits in embedding processes, structures, ownership and 'statistical literacy' within each country.

Nevertheless, efficiencies can be achieved through the use of standard resource material. The World Bank provides training material, including an online training programme on the management and implementation of capacity building projects for national statistical systems. Other agencies, including, for example, the Statistical Institute for Asia and the Pacific, the Southern African Development Community, the South Pacific Commission and many other statistical training institutes with a regional mandate also have substantial training and teaching material, as do some universities. In March 2007, some of the organisations dealing with statistical capacity building came together to discuss a Virtual Statistical System (VSS) and this online resource has now been established, to allow easy access to preselected and structured information, especially for building or modernising national statistical systems. VSS is aimed at national statistical offices, other data producing agencies, data users, including policy makers, academics, students, and anyone who wants to know more about official statistics (see Appendix for website link).

There is a huge literature, both academic and more popular, about wellbeing and progress. While much of this is based on the premise that economic growth continues to be crucial, and indeed how wellbeing drives growth, other work questions the focus on GDP, with titles such as *Addicted to Profit* (Sim, 2012) and *How Much is Enough?* (Skidelsky and Skidelsky, 2012). This is essentially about 'assessing the possible trade-offs between different goals' (OECD, 2012b, p. 3), once we have reliable and relevant data on each of these goals, of course. Another popular and related issue is how income and wealth are distributed across society, with titles like *Injustice* (Dorling, 2010) and *The Spirit Level* (Wilkinson and Pickett, 2010).

These issues were taken up by Adair Turner when he gave the 2010 series of Lionel Robbins lectures at the London School of Economics. In the first of his lectures, Lord Turner asked whether the conventional emphasis on maximising GDP growth makes sense. He noted that the existence of a direct link between per capita income and welfare has become a shibboleth on both left and right of the political spectrum, and that direct evidence for such a link is anyway limited. He concludes that 'more rapid growth [in GDP per capita] should not be the overriding objective for rich developed countries' and that other things that might concern us are whether and how much inequality there should be (Turner, 2012, p. 33).

So what is the objective of economic activity? This is quite some question. There is considerable political debate about what capitalism really means, with calls for example for 'responsible' capitalism. There are undoubtedly business leaders who, when asked, say that the point of a business is to make a profit, not to make the world a better place (e.g. Aitkenhead, 2013). However, a number of commentators have called for governments to draw back from doctrine of neo-liberalism – 'the ultra-individualistic market ideology judged to be economically reckless and socially corrosive when turbocharged by deregulation', as Jesse Norman MP described it (interviewed by Rafael Behr in *New Statesman*, 5–11 October 2012). The view that more responsible capitalism is 'not an anti-business agenda, rather an agenda for a healthier and more productive capitalism' (Osmond, 2012) is widely held. However, this appears a less than full endorsement of the view attributed to UK Prime Minister David Cameron, that 'economic growth is only a means to an end' and that 'the end' is wellbeing (World Economic Forum, 2012, p. 4).

There is no shortage of advice and analysis of new economic models that retain growth as the engine (e.g. McWilliams, 2012) or on economic development models that ensure the sustainability of natural resources and ecosystems (e.g. Rifkin, 2011). Elaine Kamarck and Robert Reich's take on this for the United States is that America needs 'to return to the level of jobs and rate of growth that we had before the Great Recession', aiming to achieve 'at least a 3 per cent annualised rate of growth for at least two consecutive quarters' as the first priority. Their key concern, whether in the way in which any government budget deficit reduction is implemented, or from a more progressive tax code, is to do 'more to decrease the inequalities which we have seen' (Kamarck and Reich, 2012). Like others (e.g. Wilkinson and Pickett, 2010) they observe that societies which reach high levels of inequality are not societies which grow or prosper. Such findings are not always readily accepted. Wilkinson and Pickett address their critics in a postscript ('Research Meets Politics') in their book, standing by their conclusion that the 'important link between income inequality and social dysfunction' is inescapable.

A specific reason for this is an economic observation that the marginal propensity to spend 'is far less among the wealthy, because they have most of what they want already' than among the 'middle classes' (who in US terms are the 50% of people between the 25th and 75th percentile in the income distribution). With a declining median wage, the 'vast middle class in the US doesn't have enough purchasing power to lift the economy out of recessionary orbit' (Kamarck and Reich, 2012). Reich also features in documentary film 'Inequality for All'. One reviewer asked: can the film do for economics what 'An Inconvenient Truth' did for green issues?

Political philosopher Elizabeth Anderson explains that 'Concerns about distribution can be derived from relational inequality, but the relational egalitarian agenda is much wider than distributive concerns alone'. It may be necessary to have a target of a lower Gini coefficient but this is not sufficient. 'Relational equality is about conceiving of society as, ideally, a place where people can meet and interact with one another on terms of equality'. Thinking more narrowly about distribution, 'we want to figure out what is generating massive inequality. We have concerns about the way in which people manage to accumulate vast fortunes' (Pearce, 2012).

Others have approached the issues by looking at wellbeing and mental health. They see a need to challenge the idea that happiness depends on individual attainment. Susie Orbach has concluded that 'Consumerism – putting our faith in objects – has not provided us with ever-greater satisfaction. Growing the economy on the basis of selling more and more goods is not only unsound, it also does not account for the economic, psychological and environmental costs of the failures of such policies. We need a grown up conversation [about psychological wellbeing, mental health and mental health services]' (Orbach, 2012).

Are governments responding to these calls for policies that are addressed towards well-being and sustainable development, rather than just economic growth? As we said in Chapter 1, this is not a book about wellbeing policy. However, we do recognise that governments and policy makers help shape the requirements for new measures of wellbeing and progress. Governments will have helped draft the United Nations General Assembly 65/309 adopted in August 2011 and entitled 'Happiness: Towards a holistic approach to development' that we quoted in Chapter 1. This resolution clearly looks to those countries for which the MDGs have been important, because these goals are explicitly included in the resolution. But all countries in the General Assembly are now aware of this resolution, and the follow-up res-olution in 2012 (66/281) proclaiming 20 March as the International Day of Happiness. All Member States, international organisations, civil society and individuals are now encouraged to observe this day, including through education and activities to raise public awareness of happiness and wellbeing as policy objectives, and 'a more inclusive, equitable and balanced approach to economic growth' (United Nations, 2012a).

The Kingdom of Bhutan, a small Himalayan country, is mentioned in the 2011 UN resolution. It offered to convene a discussion on the theme of happiness and wellbeing. This will not be a surprise to anyone who has been following the wellbeing scene. Bhutan has long adopted a new economic paradigm in which it 'is now trying to measure progress not by the popular idea of Gross Domestic Product but by Gross National Happiness (GNH)', according to its website (see Appendix for details). GNH is measured through surveys of the Bhutanese people and survey results are presented to policy areas of government, such as education, as well as the headline measure of progress. The breadth of GNH can be seen by its four 'pillars': good governance and democratization; stable and equitable socioeconomic development; environmental protection; and preservation of culture. In reporting on the development of GNH in Bhutan, Bok (2010, p. 1) concludes that 'all is not perfect in Bhutan ... All in all, however, the record of Bhutan remains impressive'. Note also that GDP is not ignored. From the same official website that we took the introduction to GNH, we also see that 'Despite Bhutan's small population, there has been much economic development in recent years and the economy is growing rapidly'. Bhutan may have rejected GDP as the *only* way to measure progress, but it still appears to be measuring and using GDP alongside GNH in measuring progress.

Senge *et al.* (2008, p. 40) also discuss Bhutan and note that over recent years, the country has consistently been rated at the top of the performance index maintained by the World Bank for all countries that receive financing from its International Development Assistance arm, an index that includes measures of governance as well as social and economic conditions in the country. This points to the possibility that use of GNH as a goal within Bhutan has led to a high level of wellbeing and progress that is also recognisable by a measurement process applied *outside* the country, one that looks in at Bhutan and at other countries in a comparable way. However, it is also noticeable in Senge *et al.*'s book that national statistics do not feature widely in their prescription for creating a sustainable world. Apart from the mention of GNH and the World Bank index, and the occasional reference to GDP, usually as an indicator of the size of an economy, these authors are more focussed on what business enterprises can do.

In Chapter 6, we will see that many countries are beginning to implement the Stiglitz proposals and we have already noted some immediate steps taken in France, for example, to raise awareness among policy officials. Developments within the United Kingdom are covered in Chapter 7, including the use of wellbeing measures in the cost-benefit appraisal of UK government policy, and the attention given to wellbeing and sustainable development in the national programmes of the Scottish and Welsh governments.

The position in the United States appears to be that the case for bringing wellbeing into policy, and especially the role of measures of subjective wellbeing, is under review by a group outside of government but well connected and influential. The point of departure for the panel on measuring subjective wellbeing in a policy-relevant framework, convened by the Committee on National Statistics of the US National Academy of Science, was to examine the American Time Use Survey (ATUS), conducted by the Bureau of Labor Statistics. The ATUS included a Subjective Well-Being (SWB) module in 2010 and 2012; the module, funded by the National Institute on Aging (NIA), was being considered for inclusion in the ATUS for 2013. The panel was asked to evaluate measures of self-reported wellbeing and offer guidance about their adoption in official government surveys. At the time of writing, the panel had not concluded its assessment of the policy usefulness of including one or more kinds of self-reported well-being measures on a regular basis in government surveys, but did 'see a value to continuing the ATUS SWB module in 2013. Not only will another year of data support research, but it will also provide additional information to help refine any SWB measurements that may be added to ongoing official statistics' (National Research Council, 2012, p. 1).

It will be interesting to see what the US panel concludes and what advice it offers on how wellbeing measures might be used in policy. This is also under consideration by a UK panel that is similarly outside of government but close to it. In 2012, Legatum Institute set up a Commission on Wellbeing Policy to explore how wellbeing analysis can be usefully applied to policy. The Institute recognised that there has been a lot of progress in wellbeing measurement and analysis, but that 'a lot remains to be done on how best to apply these data to policymaking'. Chaired by former UK Cabinet Secretary Lord Gus O'Donnell, who was also the head of the civil service and is an economist, the Legatum Institute Commission will run for approximately a year. The final Commission report 'will illustrate the strengths and limitations of wellbeing analysis and provide original and authoritative guidance on the implications for public policy. The Commission is politically independent, and includes an international perspective in its work' (see Appendix for website details).

The position in Canada, at least at the end of 2010, was that the jury was still out on the question of happiness as a goal for public policy. Several areas, for example mental health policy, are being transformed by the inclusion of wellbeing data. On the other hand, there were arguments presented that 'happiness is not yet ready for the public policy arena' and that 'a more robust framework is needed' before happiness data play a role (CSLS, 2011, p. 13). Outside of government, however, the Canadian Index of Wellbeing is promoted by civil society and aims to empower Canadians 'to advocate for change, and to hold government accountable for the decisions they make', according to Roy J. Romanow, the chair of its advisory board, speaking to the OECD Fourth World Forum (OECD, 2012b, p. 28).

China is rapidly becoming a major part of the global economy. There has been much written about the development and the future of China, though mainly from outside commentators and observers. As a recent leader in The Economist opined: 'Nobody doubts that China has joined the ranks of the great powers: The idea of a G2 with America is mooted, albeit prematurely' (*The Economist*, 30 March 2013, p. 14). China's position on wellbeing and progress will be important, as will how to measure these in a vast and complex country seemingly already facing challenges in measuring its national accounts (*The Economist*, 2013a).

Some insight was gained at the OECD Fourth World Forum. Jiantang Ma noted that China's National Bureau of Statistics has not undertaken any formal measurements of societal wellbeing at the national level but could refer to an initiative undertaken in China's largest province, the formulation and release in 2011 of the Guangdong wellbeing index. This is being seen as a pilot for possible expansion at the country level. Ma pointed out that a country needs 'enough GDP' to be happy (perhaps an echo of an earlier aim of building a 'xiaokang [moderately well-off]' society) and he emphasised the need to go beyond GDP, urging statisticians and economists to help maximise the benefits of both GDP and wellbeing measurements. He concluded that 'happiness is a matter of philosophy and perception, and statisticians and economists should be aware of the significant challenges that this poses' (OECD, 2012b, p. 28).

To some commentators, China's affluence could turn into a trap. Wang Shaoguang (2012) draws on JK Galbraith's classic work on the 'affluent society' to draw lessons on inequality and consumption for China. Kuhn (2012) recalls ancient Chinese philosophy that the perfect society is 'living in harmony, treating others as family ... there is love and caring for the elderly ... nourishment and education for children ... kindness and compassion for widows, orphans, the disabled and the sick' and contrasts this with the position after vast economic development, where the big four social concerns are now education, healthcare, housing and retirement.

Michael Sandel has taken his writings and discussions on 'the moral limits of markets' to China as well as around his native United States. He promotes moral and ethical reflection and discourse in public life, noting that there is nowadays a popular misconception that markets represent the public good. Sandel recognises the need for a market economy and economic growth but, in developing these, the distinction between a market economy and 'a market society' needs to be maintained. 'A market economy is a tool: it's a valuable and effective tool for organising productive activity, and it has brought prosperity and economic growth, and rising living standards to the countries round the world. But a market society is a place where everything is up for sale. It's a way of life in which the market values dominate every corner of social life'. Sandel is concerned that increasing marketisation both increases the impact of inequality in income and wealth, and tends to crowd out non-market values that are worth caring about. According to Sandel, most of the assumptions that he has challenged are now also being questioned in China. 'What is required is a change in the public culture and attitudes and assumptions towards markets and market logic, and this means trying to appeal to non-market values in various domains' (Chen Yingqun, 2013).

Perhaps at this point, a word of caution against over-optimism might be timely. Although the producers of national statistics strive to publish trusted data, their findings are not always accepted. Politicians may 'know' that the economy is reviving even if the GDP figures do not show this, for example! It is rare for statistics to be contested, but more often there is a sense that they can be set aside in favour of other 'evidence'. Peston talks about the relationship between statistics and real life, saying 'as a society we may have become too respectful of experts and certainly too in awe of the claims to scientific certainty of economists. Which is not to say that genuine experts and social scientists should be ignored. But when their views seem to be at odds with observations of what is actually happening in the world, we should trust our observations and experience' (2012, p. 178).

Peston contrasts the 'views' of social scientists with the 'observations and experience' of say central bankers and finance ministers. We think this is dangerous territory. The distinction is not between statistics and real life, but between statistics and other perceptions of real life. We need to ask how valid, representative and accurate are each of them, and we should prefer, for example, well designed and conducted survey of business compared to informal soundings. We accept that when out orienteering, we soon learn that, when faced with a discrepancy between the map and the terrain, we should trust the terrain. Map-makers may have got it wrong, showing say a small stream when we arrive at a wide river to cross. In such circumstances we can see our immediate surroundings in more detail than any map can show. This is not the same as trying to see how the economy and society are doing by putting aside the economic and social statistics.

Without overplaying the power of statistics, one of the reasons we are writing this book is to explore how we paint a statistical picture of wellbeing and progress in any country, covering domains in addition to the market economy. Can better statistics lead to better public discourse and policies, for better lives?

3.4   Commentary

In many countries, the interest in wider measures of measuring progress and wellbeing, stimulated for example by the OECD's programme and by the Stiglitz report, came to be considered at the end of the first decade of the twenty-first century in a time of reduced economic growth, even economic recession, and severe pressures on public finances. While the headlines were about growth, or how to return to it, there are nevertheless signs that the search for a wider understanding, and better measurement of, national wellbeing and progress is continuing. As Lodge and Paxton (2012) put it, 'As yesterday's orthodoxies give way to new thinking, the chances of transformative change are the greatest for a generation – but only if progressive forces have the imagination and strategic ambition to grasp the moment'. In other words, action is needed beyond conference and assembly resolutions.

The title of the Stiglitz report when published as a book – *Mismeasuring our lives* – appeals both to the individual and to us all, collectively. The same can be said for other explorations mentioned in Section 3.3, such as asking whether we are addicted to profit. (This may be explicit addiction, enthusiasm to face challenge, or desire for sense of achievement, but the end result is the same). There are many calls for change in how we define and measure progress. Seidman (2012) recalls the business adage that 'you manage what you measure' and points out that while measures such as GDP remain necessary, they are no longer sufficient for measuring progress. He says 'In an interdependent world, we need a reliable method for measuring how we forge healthy interdependencies, how organisations operate and relate to society, the way in which they treat their people and how their staff behave and treat others'.

People do continue to search for the good life, the good city, the good society. One general trend, which we obviously welcome as statisticians, is greater acceptance of the role of data as part of the evidence base used to help inform policy development. The OECD now presents its mission as 'Better policies for better lives' and summarises its statistical work as 'Better data for better policies for better lives' (see the OECD website, details in Appendix).

One example recently reported in the British press was even headlined 'Better data means better care in the national health service'. Jeremy Hunt, UK Secretary of State for Health wrote that 'Transparency, rather than targets, will improve our healthcare – and people's trust in the National Health Service will soar'. He went on to place transparency as key to a culture of continuous improvement, not solely a tool for performance management and recrimination. By publishing more unbiased data, results in all areas of healthcare will improve, clinicians will work better, and people's trust in the NHS will soar he said, speaking on the launch of Dr Foster's 11th annual Hospital Guide, in which statistical data on individual hospitals and consultants are published (Guardian, 2012a). There are those, nevertheless, who warn of the dangers of oversimplifying these statistics. Game (2013), for example, has looked at the hospital standardised mortality ratios (HSMRs) published in the Dr Foster's guides and noted that there has been 'continuous criticisms of both HSMR methodology and interpretation – from health care professionals, the media and academia – particularly after 2007, when some of Dr Foster's (purely statistical) ratios contradicted the inspection-based assessments of the Care Quality Commission'.

But is any of this reflected in the way people live their lives these days? Evidence is hard to find. Here are three vignettes we found interesting while we were planning this book:

1. Ron Green runs a furniture shop stocking mid-twentieth century design items in Salt Lake City. When interviewed on how he saw the shop in 10 years' time, he said: 'Honestly, not much will change. People are always asking when I'm going to open another store. I'm not. The simpler I can keep the business, the better it is for me. I like my lifestyle and I don't want to make it more complicated than it is now. I'm not business oriented, I'm happiness oriented' (Green, 2012).

2. Costa Coffee is the United Kingdom's biggest coffee house chain, with more branches than Starbucks in Britain (at the time of writing). Their plan for an outlet in the main street of the Devon town of Totnes had been approved by the district council but, in October 2012, Costa abandoned it in face of a campaign by local people and businesses protesting that Costa did not fit with a town with a long history of independent retailers, especially as there were 42 existing businesses in the town selling coffee. Costa had argued that it would 'add to the vibrancy of the town and support the local community ... complementing what Totnes already offers'. Costa's statement said that it is 'proud to be a successful British company employing 10,000 people ... in all communities in which we operate we seek to be a force for good, contributing to growth, creating jobs and supporting the local economy [for example in their use of milk and food from the area]'. Totnes was the first 'transition town' in the United Kingdom, aiming to strengthen the local community, reduce the cost of living and prepare for the future with less oil and a changing climate. One campaigner was quoted in the press as saying that Costa's decision said something positive about a company engaging with a local community rather than making a corporate decision, adding that: 'The idea of communities standing up and saying "you're not right for us" has now got a lot more traction than it would have done before' (*Guardian*, 2012b).

3. Many museums in Scandinavia are open only for the busy, high summer period. At other times, Jorunn Sem Fure, director of Telemark Museums, told us: 'Low visitor

numbers combined with high employment costs and administration and security costs have reduced opening hours gradually over the years to a minimum'. It is also no longer feasible to heat historic wooden buildings in traditional ways. However, things are being kept under review. Tourism trends may bring more between-seasons visitors. Museum staff work with other destinations and tourist operators on this. The societal benefits of cultural facilities are also recognised. Telemark Museums are committed to give access to their local and regional population and so they open regularly to schools and other groups. Rather than having long opening hours, with small numbers of casual visitors, they now try to hold more events. At the Ibsen Museum, for example, this would be staging readings, plays, poetry evenings and concerts. Economic, social and environmental costs and benefits are being considered in the case for future funding of museums, to better meet the interests of visitors and residents. This will take time, but Jorunn Sem Fure concluded: 'I hope things will look different, let's say five years from now' (personal communication).

It is interesting that businesses that are driven by an ethos beyond 'the bottom line', and so seek to do more than maximise shareholder value (or may even not include that in their aims) tend to be called 'social enterprises'. It is difficult not to conclude that they are seen as fringe or auxiliary contributors to the economy: nice to have if circumstances allow. The United Kingdom's social value legislation discussed in Chapter 2, seeks to redress the balance at least in public sector procurement and so may stimulate a more mixed economy.

The financial institutions forming the Global Alliance for Banking on Values (GABV) pledge to comply with sustainable banking principles. There are a number of these, the most significant of which is that they should be committed to social banking and the triple bottom line of people, planet and prosperity (Korslund and Spengler, 2012, p. 4). This sees sustainability in a number of guises, including how far banks reach into the 'real' economy, rather than remain within financial markets, and how far the banks support people and prosperity without damaging the planet. Simple metrics are initially drawn from data available in the management information systems of the banks but there is clearly a long journey to make in terms of deriving and using more robust and more relevant measures of sustainability.

There is nevertheless a clear signal of intention here, to focus more on the value of value, not just the value of money. This suggests that investment decisions can then be made according to a 'value set', which might include aspirations to be 'world class', or to give prominence to design, for example, even though these are difficult to quantify. Seaford *et al.* (2013, 3) have proposed a 'British Business Bank' with a mandate to include supporting an industrial strategy to deliver good, sustainable jobs. The performance measurement framework for the bank would include indicators designed to measure sustainability, wellbeing and a fair distribution of income, as well as more conventional measures of financial and economic performance.

We find similar commitments among larger companies building their corporate social responsibility using the notion of a multiple bottom line, measuring success by more than just their profit margin. Barclays Bank, for example, states in its 'Citizenship Report' that one of the ways it does business is to 'proactively manage the environmental, social and governance impacts' of its business, and it also aims to deliver product and service solutions 'to help more people and society progress in a sustainable way' (Barclays Bank, 2013, p. 9). The report records, for example, how the organisation manages carbon emissions and energy use in its buildings and gives financial support to community programmes. As with any bank, though, the greatest potential impact is through the lending it does. Barclays examines the environmental and social risks in lending for large projects (applications for above US$10m). A total of 277 assessments were made by the bank's specialist team in 2012 (Barclays Bank, 2013, p. 45). Barclay's processes and its citizenship reporting are audited, although we have not learned how these risk assessments were carried out, to see if there are measurement strategies that could be applied more broadly in determining national wellbeing and progress. Sportswear brand PUMA published its first environmental profit and loss account in November 2011. Its metrics are intended for use by the company in mitigating its carbon footprint, and for shareholders to take a broader view of the company's performance and forward planning (PUMA, 2011).

Readers may well know of many more examples like this, where large or small decisions and trade-offs are made involving more than simply the economics. There is some cynicism that, while corporate social responsibility as a concept captures the importance of the responsibilities of business to the environment and to societal stakeholders, its implementation is 'frequently a tokenistic gesture' (Fleming and Jones, 2013, p. 3). And yes, GDP continues to get the headlines and to grab political attention. Although the OECD is at the forefront of the development of wider measures of national wellbeing and progress, it still generally takes the view that a return to growth is essential to leave the economic and financial crisis behind. Governments faced with large budgetary deficits see economic growth as the priority for reducing the deficits by target dates that they have set.

Many of us think what matters most are things like our health and having a secure income. Having a healthy or even a surging economy may well underpin those things, but the state of the economy is not necessarily at the forefront of our minds. Unless, that is, you are a politician. The maxim 'It's the economy, stupid' has been much quoted in political circles over the last 20 years (attributed as the view of US President Bill Clinton's campaign strategist James Carville in 1992). 'The global crisis happened' said the fictional Prime Minister in an episode of the Danish television series Borgen, justifying why social, environmental and climate change policies were being downgraded in importance. So, if GDP is growing, then we are doing well, and if it is falling then we are not. This makes progress sound as if it is a variable with potential infinity – a 'variable quantity knowing no limit to its growth ... always growing into the infinite and never reaching it' as described by Bolzano in the first half of the 19th Century (Clegg, 2003, p. 131). It is difficult to square this with a political agenda of general wellbeing, which nevertheless still seems to be around.

Reviewing the recent economic and financial crises, Peston remains largely focussed on economic sustainability. He sees as unsustainable, for example, growth in a country generated by borrowing, rather than producing goods and services the rest of the world wants. He concludes that relatively rich countries currently experiencing low economic growth may have to live with low growth for some years. This will mean deferring gratification and learning patience as investors, consumers, and users of public services – the 'end of "have-it-all-now" society ... Citizens will want political parties to offer more than proof of competence. They may be required to offer competing visions of the good society that are more differentiated than have been seen since the 1980s ... revised set of values' (Peston, 2012, p. 401).

The idea of continuing growth, indeed growth as a race between nation states, is widely held. In Prime Minister David Cameron's 2013 New Year message, he said 'On all the big issues that matter to Britain, we are heading in the right direction and I have the evidence to prove it. Britain is in a global race to succeed today. It is race with countries like China, India and Indonesia; a race for the jobs and opportunities of the future' (Cameron, 2012). We are not yet clear what evidence the Prime Minister was referring to, rather it is the analogy of progress and success as a race that interests us. Financial journalists have also been known to compare emerging markets, such as China, India, Russia and Brazil, with champion sprinters.

But to most people, a race has a start and a finish. As Sophie Elmhirst as commented, 'This "global race" idea has been around for a while ... What race? Who else is in it? *Everyone*? Where is the finishing line, and what do we get if we win? The questions pile up unanswered, but in any case, I suspect most of us aren't worried about a fictitious international league table ... new jobs and growth all wrapped up in a seductive promise of speed. The faster we go, the better everything must be, so the logic goes' (Elmhirst, 2013).

Andy Beckett has also written about the increasing use of the global race idea, and how it does not necessarily support a more complex understanding of the global economy, in which 'most big corporations are archipelagos of employees and share holdings' (Beckett, 2013).

In her book *The Failure of Success: Redefining what matters*, Jennifer Kavanagh tackles questions like these on a more individual basis in addressing her two basic reflections: how real is success? Does dependence on material success condemn most of us to failure? She explores some of the stereotypes on which these concepts are based, and reveals through case studies what some people feel really matters in their lives. Drawing on spiritual and other ideas, Kavanagh suggests ways of enriching lives and relationships, of reaching contentment by letting go of 'any striving for success ... allowing life to evolve' (Kavanagh, 2012, p. 119). This emphasis on living echoes John Ruskin's assertion that 'There is no wealth but life' in his political essays and reflections on the good society in the 1860s.

Pope Francis has been reported calling for a global system that puts people and not 'an idol called money' at its heart. He referred particularly to suffering that comes from joblessness, a problem that went far beyond the Italian island on which he was speaking: 'It is the consequence of a global choice, an economic system which leads to this tragedy' (*Guardian*, 2013). Other church leaders have suggested to businesses that they have social obligations to meet as well as a financial bottom line to make. For example, the Archbishop of Canterbury said that 'A flourishing economy is necessary but not sufficient', when interviewed after delivering a sermon in Nairobi about what makes a healthy society (Pflanz and Kirkup, 2013).

For all the recognition of limits to growth in some quarters, there remains unabashed optimism elsewhere, or at least the view that everything depends on our economic performance, with the implicit assumption that this performance needs to be as strong as possible. Promoting Malta as a vibrant economy and a solid investment, one company draws attention to the 'endless potential' that it has to offer, continuing 'Given that we keep giving potential investors the regulatory security they require; plus Malta's membership of the EU, the sky has no limits (Frank Salt Real Estate Ltd, 2013). We also note that projected economic growth of 1.6% in Canada in 2013 is described by *The Economist* magazine (30 March 2013, p. 49) as 'paltry', which seems a little overstated given that the 65-year average increase in real GDP per capita in Canada, between 1945 and 2010, was a fraction under 2% per annum (according to Statistics Canada database, see Appendix for website), which was also the long run average in the United Kingdom and the United States. As well as broader measures of wellbeing and progress, it looks as if we will also need a new language for how to report on specific values of wellbeing and progress, and how these are changing.

The leader of the Opposition in the UK Parliament seems similarly focussed on economic growth, albeit with concern over the distribution of income. Mr Miliband wants to fight an election in which voters ask themselves which party most wants to unite the country in shared economic and social endeavour. He has spoken about 'One Nation' in which social and income inequalities are reduced, and living standards increased, through nurturing 'responsible capitalism' (e.g. Miliband, 2011). There was no mention here, or in subsequent media coverage, of the environment. One article along these lines in early 2013 was even at a time when parts of the United Kingdom were suffering from relatively harsh environmental conditions. An article adjacent to the political one reported on 'The drowned world', noting that, as the planet warms, extreme weather is becoming part of our daily life (Platt, 2013).

This is the kind of 'new political economy' that commentators such as Kelly and Pearce see as needing to replace the single issue of how to secure growth: 'Our goal must be a more resilient and stable British capitalism, with more productive, regionally balanced investment, dynamic markets, and demand generated from higher productivity and rising real wages, rather than speculative bubbles, rent-seeking and debt-financed increases in living standards' (Kelly and Pearce, 2012). Their analysis includes living standards, household debt and capital asset bubbles, but again no reference to the environment, climate change or sustainability.

News reports can also be found in which people feel that 'things are massively swayed to the environment side'. This quote is from the development director of a Scottish island, reported to be striving to raise island incomes and find jobs to stem steady emigration, and trying to get the local economy and the environment in balance. It is of course actually an example of the real difficulties in managing a triple bottom line. Social issues caused by emigration from the island are likely to be in people's minds, as well as their economic prospects and the benefits and downsides of environmental designations such as having a marine conservation area in local fishing grounds (*The Economist*, 2013b).

There are others, such as Rifkin (2011), who have addressed the big picture. He drew particularly on European Union approaches to fossil fuel-driven activities and their consequences, proposing how the convergence of communication technology and renewable energies could create the infrastructure for a 'third industrial revolution'. He sets out a high-level economic narrative for a more equitable and sustainable future. The metrics needed to help develop and monitor different models of growth are not explored in detail (although interestingly GDP is discussed from a thermodynamic perspective). Reading Rifkin, one comes to the conclusion that most people in businesses and civic organisations, and individuals in society mainly respond to changes around them, especially in his study in the way in which energy is available, rather than adapt behaviour in the light of what national statistics say about trends in progress and wellbeing. If anyone reads the national statistics, it is heads of state and CEOs and their advisers, who may be using data to help shape political, entrepreneurial and governmental action. And we are also well aware that politicians and business leaders make decisions based on their own views, principles, ideologies, opinions (and those they anticipate in their constituents and stakeholders) as well as on statistics and other factual evidence. That is the system of government and of business in many countries: that government is responsible to the electorate and businesses to their shareholders, but this is usually only tested at general elections and at annual general meetings.

So, is national wellbeing too large a concept to embrace? It sounds simple to ask how a country is doing. However, we may need to draw a very big picture – including environmental sustainability and climate change – to see coherently how a country is doing. And that may turn out to be too big to envisage, to measure and to manage. We think the many different initiatives already under way clearly demonstrate that it is worth striving for the big picture, but we should be under no illusion as to the challenges ahead in painting the picture and in using it to make a difference.

We have checked that 'national wellbeing' is a search term that people use on-line. Evidence from Google Trends (http://www.google.co.uk/trends) is that this term and variants of it ('national well-being' in the United States) has been used in a small but broadly steady proportion of their English language searches from around 2007 onwards. Data are available from 2004 and the more general term 'wellbeing' has been searched from 10 countries, throughout the period, accounting for a fairly constant proportion of searches in English up to 2008 and a slightly increasing proportion from then onwards.

We should also touch on why *national* wellbeing? Policy initiatives to improve wellbeing may be focussed on a city or a neighbourhood, and again there are many such under way. The level of geography depends on the use to which the measures are to be put. We concentrate in this book on national wellbeing because we recognise that national governments provide the anchor for economic, social and environmental policy. Measures of national wellbeing should of course be replicated, and supplemented where necessary, at sub-national levels. Similarly, part of the development of national wellbeing measures will be to agree and use measures that are comparable internationally, where these are needed, alongside the measures that are most appropriate to each country's requirements.

Having looked at a history of ideas of national wellbeing, and at current developments in the measurement of wellbeing, development and progress, we conclude there is a very real need for wider measures not only to be developed but to be used as part of ongoing debate of political, social, ethical and environmental issues. Andrew Marr has described Homo sapiens as 'a clever ape, a very clever ape, albeit in a spot of bother' (Marr, 2012, p. 565). One of the clever things we have done is to consider the nature of time as potentially infinite, though that does not mean that our planet or universe is. Marr argues that, with 7 billion people on the planet, the decisions we make in the next 50 years may well decide our fate, so that we are potentially on the verge of the most interesting part of history.

That sounds like a good reason to take a wider and more measured view of the wellbeing and progress of all nations. We have already seen that there are wider measures available and that there are calls for the definition of wellbeing and growth to be extended to embrace these additional measures. There is, however, a circle that we all need to break into. At present, the focus on economic growth and GDP is self-perpetuating, operating in ways that reflect the weakness of peer review, the difficulty of establishing a change of direction to the current hegemony. Perhaps rather than asking how wider measures of national wellbeing fit with the prevailing view, we need to ask about their fitness for purpose – which may prompt us to identify how they will be used. In the following chapters, we will attempt to draw this out, though it always seems easier to look out from the viewpoint of the statistical producer and set out the stall of available measures than to suggest how to engage in wider debate.

But to conclude this chapter, we turn to the leadership shown by the Secretary-General of the United Nations, who stated in 2012 that 'I have made sustainable development my top priority'. Mr Ban went on to say that 'We must also find better ways to measure progress that goes beyond Gross Domestic Product … It is time to recognize that human capital and natural capital are every bit as important as financial capital' (Ban, 2012).

References

Aitkenhead D. (2013). Iceland's Malcolm Walker: 'We're not here to make the world a better place'. http://www.theguardian.com/business/2013/nov/15/iceland-boss-malcolm-walker-interview (accessed 26 November 2013).

Alexander L. *et al.* (2013). Working Group I Contribution to the IPCC Fifth Assessment Report. *Climate Change 2013: The Physical Science Basis.* Summary for Policymakers, http://www.ipcc .ch/report/ar5/wg1/ (accessed 25 April 2014).

Anderson P., Cooper C., Layard R., Litchfield P. and Jane-Liopis E. (2012). *Well-being and Global Success.* Report prepared by the World Economic Forum Global Agenda Council on Health and Well-being for the World Economic Forum Annual Meeting, January 2010. World Economic Forum, Switzerland. http://www.weforum.org/reports/well-being-and-global-success (accessed 20 June 2013).

Bache I. (2013). Measuring quality of life for public policy: an idea whose time has come? Agenda-setting dynamics in the European Union. *Journal of European Public Policy*, **20**(1), 21–38.

Bache I. and Reardon L. (2013). An idea whose time has come? Explaining the rise of well-being in British politics. *Political Studies.* http://onlinelibrary.wiley.com/doi/10.1111/1467-9248.12001/abstract;jsessionid=80F08AF389E4380B8EB4429346B756B5.d03t02 (accessed 25 October 2013).

Ban K. (2012). Secretary-General's remarks to high-level thematic debate on 'The State of the World Economy and Finance and its Impact on Development', United Nations, New York, 17 May 2012. http://www.un.org/sg/statements/index.asp?nid=6057 (accessed 1 December 2013).

Barclays Bank (2013). *Tough questions, honest answers: Barclays PLC Citizenship Report 2012.* http://reports.barclays.com/cr12/servicepages/welcome.html (accessed 17 October 2013).

Beckett A. (2013). On your marks, get set ... http://www.theguardian.com/politics/2013/sep/22/what-is-global-race-conservatives-ed-miliband (accessed 23 September 2013).

Bok D. (2010). *The Politics of Happiness: What Government can Learn from the New Research on Well-Being.* Princeton University Press, Princeton.

Bostock M., Ogievetsky V. and Heer J. (2011). D3: Data-Driven Documents, *IEEE Trans. Visualization & Comp. Graphics (Proc. InfoVis)* http://vis.stanford.edu/papers/d3 (accessed 25 April 2014).

Cameron D. (2012). 2013 New Year Message. https://www.gov.uk/government/news/david-camerons-2013-new-year-message (accessed 13 August 2013).

Chen Yingqun (2013). Markets put in the dock, *China Daily European Weekly*, February 1–7, 2013, p. 30.

Clegg B. (2003). *A Brief History of Infinity.* Robinson, London.

Commission of the European Communities (2009). *GDP and beyond: Measuring progress in a changing world.* COM(2009) 433 final, Brussels.

CSLS (2011). *Happiness as a Goal for Public Policy: Ready for Primetime? A Synthesis of the CSLS-ICP Conference on Happiness and Public Policy*, CSLS Research Note 2011–1, http://www.csls.ca/notes/Note2011-1.pdf (accessed 4 July 2013).

Dolan P. and Harrison O. (2013). *How do you measure happiness?* http://forumblog.org/2013/01/how-do-you-measure-happiness/ (accessed 25 April 2014).

Dorling D. (2010). *Injustice: Why Social Inequality Persists.* The Policy Press, Bristol.

Economist (2013a). Consumption in China may be much higher than official statistics suggest. *The Economist*, 30 March 2013, 63–64.

Economist (2013b). Clash of nature, *The Economist*, 30 March 2013, 33–34.

Elmhirst S. (2013). Our high-speed politicians need to learn the quiet, unassuming virtue of patience. *New Statesman*, 1–7 February 2013, 62.

Fleming P. and Jones M.T. (2013). *The End of Corporate Social Responsibility: Crisis and Critique.* Sage Publications Ltd., London.

Frank Salt Real Estate Ltd. (2013). Malta – the Mediterranean's best kept secret, advertising promotion, *New Statesman*, 15–21 February 2013.

Game C. (2013). Dr Foster's day out in the sun: The use and abuse of hospital mortality rates. http://www.psa.ac.uk/insight-plus/blog/dr-foster%E2%80%99s-day-out-sun-use-and-abuse-hospital-mortality-rates (accessed 13 August 2013).

Grant R. (2013). A life in statistics: Nathan Yau. *Significance*, **10**, 32–35.

Green R. (2012). Utah Bound, *Dwell* magazine, October 2012, 112–114.

Greening J. (2013). The UN High Level Panel Report on the Post 2015 Development Framework, Written statement to Parliament. https://www.gov.uk/government/speeches/justine-greening-the-un-high-level-panel-report-on-the-post-2015-development-framework (accessed 17 June 2013).

Guardian (2012a). Better data means better care in the NHS. http://www.theguardian.com/commentisfree/2012/dec/02/data-care-nhs-transparency-trust?INTCMP=SRCH (accessed 13 August 2013).

Guardian (2012b). Costa Coffee drops plans for Totnes outlet after protests. http://www.theguardian.com/business/2012/oct/25/costa-coffee-totnes-outlet-protests?INTCMP=SRCH (accessed 13 August 2013).

Guardian (2013). Pope condemns idolatry of cash in capitalism. http://www.theguardian.com/world/2013/sep/22/pope-francis-idol-money (accessed 23 September 2013).

Kamarck E.C. and Reich R.B. (2012). American political futures. *Institute for Public Policy Research Review (Juncture)*, **19**(3), 174–180.

Kavanagh J. (2012). *The Failure of Success: Redefining what Matters*. O-Books, Alresford.

Kelly G. and Pearce N. (2012). After the Coalition: what's left? *Institute for Public Policy Research Review (Juncture)*, **19**(2), 92–101.

Korslund D. and Spengler L (2012). *Global Alliance for Banking on Values: Strong, Straightforward and Sustainable Banking: Financial Capital and Impact Metrics of Values Based Banking*. http://www.gabv.org/wp-content/uploads/Full-Report-GABV-v9d.pdf (accessed 11 September 2013).

Kroll C. (2011). *Measuring Progress and Well-being: Achievements and Challenges of a New Global Movement*. Friedrich-Ebert-Stiftung, International Policy Analysis, Berlin. http://library.fes.de/pdf-files/id/ipa/08509.pdf (accessed 28 November 2013).

Kuhn R.L. (2012). The 'big four' concerns of Chinese, *China Daily European Weekly*, September 21–27, p. 10.

Lodge G. and Paxton W. (2012). Editorial. *Institute for Public Policy Research Review (Juncture)*, **19**(2), 82–83.

Marr A. (2012). *A History of The World*. Macmillan, London.

McGrath M. (2013). IPCC climate report: humans 'dominant cause' of warming. http://www.bbc.co.uk/news/science-environment-24292615 (accessed 28 September 2013).

McWilliams D. (2012). *A New Theory of Economic Growth*. http://www.gresham.ac.uk/lectures-and-events/a-new-theory-of-economic-growth (accessed 12 August 2013).

Melamed C., Scott A. and Mitchell T. (2012). *Separated at birth, reunited in Rio? A roadmap to bring environment and development back together*. Overseas Development Institute, http://www.odi.org.uk/publications/6513-environment-sustainable-development-post-2015 (accessed 25 April 2014).

Miliband E. (2011). Speech to Labour Party Conference, Liverpool, 27 September 2011, http://www.labour.org.uk/ed-milibands-speech-to-labour-party-conference (accessed 14 August 2013).

National Research Council (2012). *The Subjective Well-Being Module of the American Time Use Survey: Assessment for Its Continuation*. Panel on Measuring Subjective Well-Being in a Policy-Relevant Framework. Committee on National Statistics, Division of Behavioral and Social Sciences and Education. The National Academies Press, Washington D.C.

NEF (2009). *National Accounts of Well-being: Bringing Real Wealth onto the Balance Sheet*. New Economics Foundation, London.

OECD (2007). *Measuring the Progress of Societies World Forum on Statistics, Knowledge and Policy: Istanbul Declaration*. http://www.oecd.org/newsroom/38883774.pdf (accessed 12 August 2013).

OECD (2012a). *Draft OECD Guidelines on the Measurement of Subjective Well-Being*. OECD Publishing.

OECD (2012b). *4th OECD World Forum, New Delhi, India 2012: Highlights and Conclusions*. http://www.oecd.org/site/worldforumindia/OECD-World-Forum-2012-India-proceedings.pdf (accessed 12 August 2013).

OECD (2013). Statistics: Experts to continue work of Stiglitz-Sen-Fitoussi Commission on measuring progress. http://www.oecd.org/newsroom/statisticsexpertstocontinueworkofstiglitz-sen-fitoussicommissiononmeasuringprogress.htm (accessed 8 August 2013).

Orbach S. (2012). The Sad Truth. *The Royal Society of Arts Journal*, Spring 2012, 16–19.

Osmond J. (2012). 1980s individualist zeitgeist falls from grace. *The Welsh Agenda*, **47**, 1.

Pearce N. (2012). *Juncture* interview: Elizabeth Anderson. *Institute for Public Policy Research Review (Juncture)*, **19**(3), 188–193.

Peston R. (2012). *How Do We Fix This Mess? The Economic Price of Having it all, and the Route to Lasting Prosperity*. Hodder & Stoughton, London.

Pflanz M. and Kirkup J. (2013). 'Economic growth is not enough to make Britain healthy, says Archbishop of Canterbury', *The Telegraph*. http://www.telegraph.co.uk/news/religion/10392659/Economic-growth-is-not-enough-to-make-Britain-healthy-says-Archbishop-of-Canterbury.html (accessed 25 October 2013).

Platt E. (2013). The drowned world, *New Statesman magazine*, 4–10 January 2013, 21–23.

Pullinger J. (2013). *Statisticians need to have a seat at decision-making tables*. http://www.statisticsviews.com/details/feature/4364371/Statisticians-need-to-have-a-seat-at-decision-making-tables-John-Pullinger-on-hi.html (accessed 10 December 2013).

PUMA (2011). PUMA Completes First Environmental Profit and Loss Account which values Impacts at € 145 million. http://about.puma.com/puma-completes-first-environmental-profit-and-loss-account-which-values-impacts-at-e-145-million/ (accessed 10 December 2013).

Rifkin J. (2011). *The Third Industrial Revolution: How lateral power is transforming energy, the economy, and the world*. Palgrave Macmillan, New York.

Scott C. (2012). Text of deal between Colombia's government and rebel group FARC to end armed conflict. *Columbia Reports*, http://colombiareports.co/agreement-colombia-government-and-rebel-group-farc/ (accessed 16 December 2013).

Seaford C., Prieg L. and Greenham T. (2013). *The British Business Bank*. New Economics Foundation. http://www.neweconomics.org/publications/entry/the-british-business-bank (accessed 27 November 2013).

Seidman D. (2012). Not Business as Usual. *The Royal Society of Arts Journal*, Winter 2012, 42–43.

Senge P., Smith B., Kruschwitz N., Laur J. and Schley S. (2008). *The Necessary Revolution*. Nicholas Brealey Publishing, London.

Sim S. (2012). *Addicted to Profit: Reclaiming our Lives from the Free Market*. Edinburgh University Press, Edinburgh.

Skidelsky R. and Skidelsky E. (2012). *How Much is Enough? The Love of Money, and the Case for a Good Life*. Allen Lane/Penguin Books, London.

Stiglitz J.E. (2006). *Making Globalization Work*. Allen Lane/Penguin, London.

Stiglitz J.E., Sen S. and Fitoussi J-P. (2010). *Mismeasuring Our Lives: Why GDP doesn't Add Up*. The New Press, New York.

Tufte E.R. (1990). *Envisioning Information*. Graphics Press, Cheshire, Connecticut.

Turner A. (2012). *Economics After the Crisis: Objectives and Means*, The MIT Press, Cambridge, Massachusetts.

UNECE (2013). Conference of European Statisticians endorses recommendations to assist countries in measuring sustainable development, at http://www.unece.org/index.php?id=33019 (accessed 14 December 2013).

United Nations (2012a). UN General Assembly Resolution 66/281: *International Day of Happiness*.

United Nations (2012b). *The Future We Want:Outcome document adopted at Rio+20*, United Nations, New York at http://www.un.org/en/sustainablefuture/ (accessed 10 December 2013).

United Nations (2013). *A New Global Parnership: eradicate poverty and transform economies through sustainable development: The Report of the High-Level Panel of Eminent Persons on the Post-2015 Development Agenda*, United Nations, New York at http://www.post2015hlp.org/the-report/ (accessed 10 December 2013).

United Nations Development Group (2003). *Indicators for Monitoring the Millennium Development Goals: definitions, rationale, concepts and sources*, United Nations, New York at http://unstats.un.org/unsd/publication/seriesf/Seriesf_95E.pdf (accessed 10 December 2013).

van der Hoeven R. (2012). *MDGs post 2015: Beacons in turbulent times or false lights?* Background paper was prepared for the UN System Task Team on the Post-2015 UN Development Agenda at http://www.un.org/en/development/desa/policy/untaskteam_undf/rolph_van_der_hoeven_2.pdf (accessed 10 December 2013).

Wang Shaoguang (2012). Chinese socialism 3.0. In: M. Leonard (ed.) *China 3.0*. European Council on Foreign Relations, London, pp. 60–67.

Wilkinson R. and Pickett K. (2010). *The Spirit Level: Why Equality is Better for Everyone*. Penguin Books, London.

World Economic Forum (2012). *Well-being and Global Success: a report prepared by the World Economic Forum Global Agenda Council on Health and Well-being*. http://www3.weforum.org/docs/WEF_HE_GAC_WellbeingGlobalSuccess_Report_2012.pdf (accessed 10 December 2013).

Yau N. (2013). *Data Points: Visualisation That Means Something*. John Wiley & Sons, Inc., New York.

4

Measuring individual wellbeing

Atoms of pleasure are not easy to distinguish and discern; more continuous than sand, more discrete than liquid.

Edgeworth (1881, p. 8)

There have been fluctuations over time in the relative importance accorded to broad societal wellbeing on the one hand and individual wellbeing on the other. Wilkinson and Pickett comment: 'Politics was once seen as a way of improving people's social and emotional wellbeing by changing their economic circumstances. But over the last few decades the bigger picture has been lost. People are now more likely to see psychosocial wellbeing as dependent on what can be done at the individual level, using cognitive behavioural therapy – one person at a time – or on providing support in early childhood, or on the reassertion of religious or "family" values.' (Wilkinson and Pickett, 2010, p. 238). The growing worldwide interest in wellbeing as an alternative to merely relying on economic measures such as GDP is indicative of a swing back towards higher level measures. However, even if the pendulum may be swinging back towards higher level 'population' notions of wellbeing, such measures are inevitably based on low-level notions of individual wellbeing, which can then be combined to produce or at least contribute to the aggregate measure. Individual wellbeing lies at the heart of societal wellbeing, and in Chapters 5 and 6, we will explore whether the latter is more than the sum of the individual wellbeing 'scores' of the members of society.

Individual and societal or 'national' wellbeing are not the only possible levels: they are points on a continuum. Global wellbeing would be another point and, in many contexts, household wellbeing might be more pertinent. Indeed, Recommendation 2 of the Stiglitz report was that measures to improve the relevance of GDP as a measure of living standards should emphasise the household perspective. The fact is, however, that individual wellbeing constitutes the basic building block from which higher level measures (along with their emergent properties, not possessed by the elementary blocks, such as inequality) are constructed. Individual wellbeing was outlined in Chapter 1, but here we explore it in more depth.

The Wellbeing of Nations: Meaning, Motive and Measurement, First Edition. Paul Allin and David J. Hand.
© 2014 John Wiley & Sons, Ltd. Published 2014 by John Wiley & Sons, Ltd.

In Chapter 1, we remarked that different researchers will have different intended uses for measures of wellbeing. This will mean that they have different views on what is relevant or important in a measure of wellbeing, and also have different views on how the various aspects should be combined. These differences, inevitably and properly, would lead to different measures of wellbeing. The issue is not, therefore, really a question of whether one measure is 'better' or 'more accurate' than another. There is generally no ideal gold standard which a measure is seeking to estimate, and deviation from which can be used to assess the quality of a wellbeing measure. Rather, it is a question of being very clear and explicit about how one's chosen measure is defined. Then, and only then, can other people see if that particular measure could serve the purpose they seek to use a wellbeing measure for. Put more bluntly, we should expect and encourage the development of multiple different wellbeing measures.

The fact that there is no single underlying *true* notion of wellbeing upon which we can seek to construct an explicit definition explains comments such as:

> 'There is no accepted, universally used definition of wellbeing.' (Hird, 2003)

> 'There is no agreed definition of wellbeing, although there is general agreement that an intersecting range of physical, social, environmental and psychological factors influence wellbeing, and there is some uniformity across definitions.' (*Mental Health Foundation*, 2010)

> 'Wellbeing remains a contested concept, enjoying a variety of definitions.' (McAllister, 2005)

In Chapter 1, we gave some definitions of individual wellbeing. Here are three more:

> ' "A positive and sustainable state that allows individuals, groups or nations to thrive and flourish." This means at the level of an individual, wellbeing refers to psychological, physical and social states that are distinctly positive.' (Huppert *et al.*, 2004)

> [Subjective wellbeing] is 'a broad category of phenomena that includes people's emotional responses, domain satisfactions, and global judgements of life satisfaction.' (Diener *et al.*, 1999, p. 277)

> [Subjective wellbeing is] 'good mental states, including all of the various evaluations, positive and negative, that people make of their lives and the affective reactions of people to their experiences.' (OECD, 2013, from http://hdr.undp.org/en/statistics/hdi)

The Mental Health Foundation (2011) has also collated several definitions:

> 'a positive physical, social and mental state. Good wellbeing does not just mean the absence of mental illness – it brings a wide range of benefits, including reduced health risk behaviour … , reduced mortality, improved educational outcomes and increased productivity at work.' (The UK coalition government's Public Health White Paper, Department of Health, 2010).

> 'The idea of mental wellbeing includes both how people feel – their emotions and life satisfaction – and how people function – their self acceptance, positive

relations with others, personal control over their environment, purpose in life and autonomy.' (*Towards a Mentally Flourishing Scotland: Policy and Action Plan 2009–2011*, Scottish Government, 2009)

'a positive physical, social and mental state, requiring that basic needs are met; individuals have a sense of purpose; and they feel able to reach personal goals and take part in society.' (Welsh Assembly Government, 2010)

'a dynamic state, in which the individual is able to develop their potential, work productively and creatively, build strong and positive relationships with others, and contribute to their community. It is enhanced when an individual is able to fulfil their personal and social goals and achieve a sense of purpose in society.' (UK Government Office for Science, 2008)

'the extent to which people experience happiness and satisfaction, and are functioning well.' (Abdallah *et al.*, 2011)

The last of the definitions comes from the New Economics Foundation, which also defines wellbeing as a process:

'more helpful for policy-makers to view well-being itself as a *dynamic process*, in which a person's external circumstances interact with their psychological resources to satisfy – to a greater or lesser extent – their psychological needs and to give rise to positive feelings of happiness and satisfaction.' (Thompson and Marks, 2008)

Note that, although for conventional reasons, and in accordance with other authors, we have informally used the word 'definition' to describe these characterisations of wellbeing, that is not really a very good choice of word. The above are really mere *descriptions* of what wellbeing is. A definition will have to be much more precise. In particular, as described in Chapter 1, a definition of wellbeing will have to say how it is actually measured, since different ways of measuring will yield very different concepts. This is made evident simply by looking at any of the above 'definitions' and imagining constructing a measuring instrument which captures its meaning: each of the 'definitions' could be instantiated in many ways. The aim of this chapter is to look in more detail at how those informal descriptions of what different authors mean by wellbeing are translated into measurable concepts, and how numerical measures can be extracted.

We pointed out in Chapter 1 that wellbeing had multiple aspects, and this is also apparent from the above descriptions. The existence of such multiple aspects means that, broadly speaking, there are two approaches to measurement. On the one hand, as outlined in Chapter 1, we could seek to measure the separate components and then combine them, or, on the other, we could simply go directly for a global measure.

In the first case, one could go even further: having measured each of the distinct multiple aspects, one could simply report a wellbeing profile. For the Scottish Government extract quoted above, one could report measures of emotions, life satisfaction, self acceptance, positive relations with others, personal control over their environment, purpose in life and autonomy. Such a profile would be invaluable for a deep understanding of wellbeing and in studying how different aspects were related. But it could be of limited value in policy considerations, simply because of its complexity. For policy, and to serve as a general measure analogous to GDP, there are advantages to reducing these multiple aspects to a single measure.

And this is where the pragmatic 'clinimetric' notions outlined in Chapter 1 come in. Intrinsic in such a single measure are the relative importance, the trade-offs, and the balances that those using the measure regard wellbeing as having. Again we stress that different researchers, or people with different aims, may well balance the importance and trade-offs of different aspects differently. This is entirely legitimate, and should be expected. As we said in Chapter 1, wellbeing is an intrinsically more complex concept than, for example, weight.

In the second approach to finding a global measure of wellbeing, one combines the multiple aspects into a single measure by simply asking the respondents to do it: ask the individuals themselves how they feel. This is not done by explicitly asking them about the separate components and then asking them to combine them, but is rather done by a single question: along the lines of 'Overall, how satisfied are you with your life nowadays?'

The single global question approach is clearly intrinsically subjective, not because it asks for introspection, but because it goes directly for an expression of extent of subjective feeling. The approach based on externally combining multiple aspects opens up the possibility of tapping into objective measures. In particular, if we believe that external circumstances have a causal effect on wellbeing (such as the external circumstance of income might impact wellbeing, for example), or are external consequences of wellbeing (such as satisfaction with life might be, for example), or are simply correlated with wellbeing (such as autonomy might be considered to be, for example), then we can try to use measures of those to improve our measure of wellbeing.

The approach to measuring wellbeing based on measuring and combining component characteristics, causes and effects may be based on a *theory*: the notion of an underlying wellbeing 'factor' related to other more easily measurable characteristics, so that inverting this relationship allows one to determine the extent of wellbeing from the measured values of those characteristics. As noted in Chapter 1, this sort of approach is what underlies *psychometric* measurement procedures, since it is common in psychology.

In contrast, however, this approach to measurement may instead be based on a simple ('pragmatic') determination of what one believes contributes to or indicates wellbeing, followed by an operational decision on how to combine the measures of these components (e.g. in a weighted sum, though this form is not a necessary form). This is the *pragmatic* approach described in Chapter 1 (or *clinimetric*; so-called because it is common in clinical medicine).

The theory-based, psychometric approach is beneficial to the extent that the theory is sound. A good theory, which accurately represents the structure of the reality it models, and for which accurate measures of the component indicators can be obtained, will yield a sound definition and measurement of wellbeing. On the other hand, if the component indicators cannot be measured accurately, or if the theoretical construct fails to model reality well, then the resulting measure of wellbeing could be a poor one.

The pragmatic approach is susceptible to the same criticism about the accuracy or lack of accuracy in the component indicators, but not to the same criticism about weak representation of reality, simply because it does not seek to represent reality in the same way. Rather the pragmatic approach gives the *definition* of whatever one is measuring: the measurement operation tells you what the property you are measuring is. The hope, and indeed the aim, is that a pragmatic construct, formed by definition rather than explicit modelling of an underlying reality, might be correlated with other characteristics and properties and hence be useful for prediction, diagnosis, and the assessment of the effectiveness of interventions.

This chapter is about how to measure individual wellbeing, but it is not intended to be a manual. Rather, it is a review of the issues, methods, challenges, and tools used in constructing such measures. For more details and further discussion, the reader should consult the excellent and extensive OECD practical guide to the measurement of subjective wellbeing (OECD, 2013).

4.1   On quantification

Measurement is ubiquitous, and its methods and properties span disciplines and applications. To lay the foundation for what follows, this section discusses some of these universal aspects.

Students of psychology, statistics, and other areas are introduced to the notion of 'measurement scales' when beginning their studies. Typically, these will be the four scale types described by S.S. Stevens (Stevens, 1946): nominal, ordinal, interval, and ratio. These four scale types are defined by the relationships between the objects whose attribute values we are aiming to represent by numbers. So:

– for a nominal scale, one seeks to represent only the fact that different objects are *different* on some property. We may represent the possible different categories of response by numbers, but the order or relative size of the numbers used is irrelevant in the sense that such numerical relationships do not correspond to any empirical relationships between the objects. An example would be the numbers one might assign to examination candidates, in the random order in which they enter the exam hall. The nominal scale is the most basic form of measurement scale, to the extent that some would argue it is not actually a scale at all. Any one-to-one mapping of the numbers assigned by such a scale would yield an equally legitimate scale.

– for an ordinal scale, the order property of numbers (e.g. that $1 < 3 < 4$) represents some corresponding order relationship between the objects. We might be able to order experiences in terms of pain intensity, for example, although we might not be prepared to go so far as to say 'this pain is twice as bad as that': only the order relationship matters. Or, for our purposes, we might ask respondents to decide whether they feel more or less cheerful this week than last week. Objects which lie on an ordinal scale can be ranked. The class of transformations which may be applied to the numerical values of an ordinal scale and which yield an alternative legitimate set of values is more restricted than the arbitrary one-to-one transformations of nominal scales. In the ordinal case, since the order relationship must be preserved, monotonic transformations are allowed. (This is rather tautologous: a monotonic transformation is defined as one which preserves order.) Any monotonic transformation will preserve the order structure. For example, we can map the values (1,3,4) above to the values (1,2,4) or the values (1,2,100) and the order is preserved in both new sets of values. Note that, with the three values (1,3,4), the fact that $4 - 3 = 1$ while $3 - 1 = 2$ does not mean that the difference between the third and second object was less than that between the second and first. The sizes of differences are meaningless for an ordinal scale – only the sign matters (telling us that object A has a greater value than object B, or vice versa). Ordinal scales are particularly important in the social and behavioural sciences because, while it is often possible to decide if an attribute is larger or smaller for some other object than another, it is often not possible to say any more. The pain example is an illustration of this. Over a century ago, Francis Ysidro Edgeworth saw the potential for an ordinal scale for happiness: 'We cannot *count* the golden sands of life; we cannot *number* the "innumerable smile" of seas of love; but we seem to be capable of observing that there is here a *greater*, there a *less*, multitude of pleasure-units, mass of happiness; and that is enough' (Edgeworth, 1881, pp. 8–9).

- for an interval scale, the differences (or 'intervals') between any two values *do* correspond to some magnitude of the objects being studied. If the scale was interval and if the numbers (1,3,4) had been assigned to represent the magnitudes of some attribute of three objects, the fact that $4 - 3 = 1$ while $3 - 1 = 2$ would make sense. In particular, it would mean that the difference between the third and second objects was only a half of that between the second and first objects. For interval scales, the set of transformations of the assigned numbers which yield equally legitimate alternative numerical representations is further restricted. Clearly, the set of arbitrary monotonic transformations is too general: if the objects had the values (1,2,4) instead of (1,3,4), it would suggest that the difference between the third and second objects was twice that between the second and first objects, not half. If we transformed the numbers from one of these sets to the other, our description of the relationship would not be the same. In fact, the transformations which preserve the relationship are the linear transformations: multiplying the values by any constant, and then adding another arbitrary value. Thus, for example, if we multiply each of (1,3,4) by 3 and then add 5 we obtain the set (8,14, 17). And we see that $17 - 14 = 3$, which is half $14 - 8 = 6$. So the relative sizes of the intervals between values are preserved by this transformation. Time scales are examples of interval scales: the starting point is arbitrary (we could choose the beginning of this century or the start of the Gregorian calendar, for example) and so are the units of measurement: we could multiply by 7 to convert from weeks to days.

- ratio scales go one step further, one step more restrictive in terms of the sets of transformations which preserve the information in a set of numbers representing the relationships between the objects being studied. For ratio scales, only rescaling transformations are allowed: that is, multiplication by a constant, or changing the units. Ratio scales are especially familiar in the natural sciences: weight and length, for example, are measured in ratio scales. If a set of three objects have the respective lengths (1,3,4) when measured in inches, then they have the lengths (2.54, 7.62, 10.16) when measured in centimetres. These new values are found by multiplying (rescaling) (1,3,4) by 2.54. Multiplying just changes the units of measurement. One can think of ratio scale values as being multiples of a standard unit object. Thus in our trio (1,3,4) the first object has a magnitude equal to that of the unit object, the second is three times its size, and so on.

The various transformations corresponding to the different measurement scales (one-to-one in the case of nominal; monotonic in the case of ordinal; linear in the case of interval; and rescaling in the case of ratio) are called 'admissible' or 'permissible' transformations, since, given the scale type, such transformations preserve the information in the numbers describing the set of objects beings studied.

Stevens produced his set of measurement scales around the middle of the twentieth century, based on rather *ad hoc* arguments. Since then, a great deal of work has been undertaken, much of it fairly mathematical, to the extent that a full understanding of possible scale types, the relationships which they preserve, and the legitimate transformations associated with them has been developed (see e.g. Krantz *et al.*, 1971; Roberts, 1979; Suppes *et al.*, 1989; Luce *et al.*, 1990; Hand, 2004). It turns out that, broadly speaking, Stevens was right. This explains why his four-category classification has been so persistent, and almost universally adopted in elementary presentations.

The discussion of measurement scales, and in particular, the subsequent development of rigorous mathematical foundations, has led to a very solid body of theory. But one must recognise that our aim in studying wellbeing is to study an aspect of the real world, and the real world is not the same as a mathematical model. We can construct an axiom system to model the world, and explore consequences and constraints of that system and model, but we should avoid being overly zealous. To illustrate, consider the definition of an ordinal scale above. This begins from the premiss that only the ordinal aspects of the numerical measurements are relevant and that the only fact that is captured is that the objects can be ranked in terms of the attribute values. Because only the ordinal aspects matter, it is argued, *any* order-preserving transformation, that is *any* monotonic transformation, will be legitimate, since all such transformations preserve the order information. But in any real application, even though one felt that the order (1,3,4) effectively represented the information, one might well not feel that (1,3,1000000) represented it equally well. This alternative numerical assignment would be saying that the difference between the first two objects is negligible compared to their difference from the third. It seems that our initial numerical assignment, (1,3,4), may often capture more than mere order – but not sufficient to justify an interval scale.

The general point here, that the model is not the reality, becomes particularly relevant when we consider the application of statistical tools to derive higher level national measures from the individual measures. Here is a simple and doubtless familiar example.

Suppose an attribute is measured on an ordinal scale, yielding the values 1, 2, and 6 for the three individuals in one social group and the values 3, 4, and 5 for those in another. The mean of the first group is 3, and that of the second group, 4. It thus looks as if the second group has the higher average. But now recall that, for an ordinal scale, any monotonic transformation will yield an equally valid numerical representation: provided we preserve the rank order, any set of assigned numbers will capture the relationships (of 'greater than') between the objects. In particular, suppose we transform the six values (1,2,3,4,5,6) to (1,2,3,4,5,12). The order is still preserved – if an object had a greater value than another on the original scale, then it also does on the new scale. But now the averages of the two groups are, respectively, 5 and 4. Now it looks as if the *first* group has the higher average.

In general, if we believe that the individual magnitude of wellbeing can be captured only up to order relationships (that one person has a higher degree of wellbeing than another), then our conclusions about group or national *means* seem suspect: they will depend on our arbitrary choice of (order preserving) numerical values.

Something seems to be amiss here. If our conclusions vary between equally legitimate numerical representations, then they can have no real empirical force: we could get any result we wanted by choosing the scale values (still preserving their order) to yield that result.

This example is a particularly simple one, but it is symptomatic of much deeper issues – and much more sophisticated examples can easily be generated. Consideration of such apparent contradictions led to a controversy stretching over several decades, which was only adequately resolved towards the end of the last century. At first glance, it looks as if the fact that the conclusions can vary as one applies permissible scale transformations restricts the type of statistical operations which can be applied with different measurement scales. For example, while in the example calculating means for ordinal data led to problems, it is easy to see that the same problems would not arise if medians were used: the object with the median value stays the same if and when arbitrary order preserving transformations are applied to a data set (even if its numerical value changes).

The issue is clearly a fundamental one, affecting the very foundations of science. It stirred deep passions. An early, and classic paper was that of Frederic Lord (Lord, 1953), an expert in psychological test theory. He imagined two groups of American college football players, freshman (in their first year) and sophomores (in their second year), who had been assigned numbers by a machine. Since the only aim of the numbers was to identify the players (because 'the television audience had to have some way to tell which player it was who caught the forward pass') they lay on a nominal scale: any one-to-one transformation would have been equally valid. Trouble arose, however, when the freshmen complained that their numbers were lower than those of the sophomores. A statistician, from whom advice was sought, computed the means of the two groups and found that this was indeed the case: the means of the freshmen's numbers was smaller than that of the sophomores. But this caused consternation in the retired psychology professor who was responsible for distributing the numbers. Since they lay on a nominal scale, he argued, it is meaningless to add them up and calculate means – the situation is even worse than our simple ordinal example above. And he became more agitated when the statistician proceeded to square the numbers, compute their standard deviation, and perform a t-test to compare the two groups. When he remonstrated, the statistician replied (in a line which has now become immortal): 'the numbers don't remember where they came from, they always behave just the same way, regardless.'

The moral of this little tale is that we must distinguish between the numbers and what they represent. We can draw conclusions about the numbers that, for example, the mean of one group is significantly lower than that of another, in a perfectly valid way using any tools of arithmetic and statistics that we like (subject, of course, to any distributional assumptions made by the statistical tools). But any inference to underlying objects and properties represented by the numbers goes further than this. In particular, it relies on the link between the numbers and what they are intended to represent. It relies on the measuring instrument. As Burke (1953) put it: 'The statistical technique begins and ends with the numbers and with statements about them. The psychological interpretation given to the experiment does take cognizance of the origin of the numbers but this is irrelevant for the statistical test as such.' But some preferred finer interpretations: 'Since psychologists are presumably more interested in the behaviour they describe with numbers than in the numbers themselves, they will learn more if their statistical techniques correspond with the properties of the set of numbers as a measurement scale …' (Senders, 1953). Behan and Behan (1954) added: 'if the empirical procedure does not contain an operation that corresponds to one of the mathematical operators, then that operator may not be used to manipulate the numbers obtained.'

A detailed review of the debate is given by Hand (2004, Section 2.5). It turns out that it is not so simple a matter as requiring that the measurement scale proscribes the legitimacy of the statistical operations. Rather, whether a statistical operation is legitimate or not depends on the context: it is not the statistic *per se* which matters, but the use made of that statistic. In particular, a statistical operation is legitimate within the context of a particular statement if the truth or falsity of that statement is invariant to permissible transformations of the data.

The notions of measurement scales presented above have their roots very much in the representational aspect of measurement operations. In each case, we look at the empirical system of objects being studied and seek to represent the relationships between objects in terms of a certain attribute of those objects by corresponding relationships between numbers. For example, object A is 'larger' in some sense than object B; or that objects A and B, when placed on one pan of a weighing scale, just balance object C. But the pragmatic aspects of measurement are not quite like that. In the extreme pragmatic case, we define the attribute being measured by the measurement procedure. That means, in particular, that the set of numbers which are produced are the *only* legitimate set of numbers which could be assigned. If we transformed the numbers (e.g. by an arbitrary order-preserving transformation, or even by something so simple as rescaling), we would be defining our measurement scale differently, and so would be talking about a different attribute. So pragmatic measurements are not constrained by these issues of permissible transformations; for pragmatic measurement, all that matters is whether or not the resulting numbers are useful.

The pragmatic perspective on measurement is very similar to the operational perspective, which defines scientific concepts in terms of the operations used to identify them. Operationalism was originally devised by Percy Bridgman, the Nobel laureate physicist, who was responding to the developments in physics which occurred at the beginning of the twentieth century.

Since transformations of a pragmatic measurement yield a different scale, questions of alternative, equally legitimate representations resulting from transformations do not arise. If you transform the scale, you are talking about a different definition of the measurement. One consequence of this for notions of wellbeing is that any statistical operations we may choose to use, or statistical statements we may choose to make, do not have to be invariant to a set of permissible transformations, for there are none. In particular, that means that we can take averages, calculate standard deviations, and so on, *provided* we are explicit about what definition of wellbeing we are using. We can meaningfully talk about the average wellbeing of the people in a group.

4.2   Single measures of wellbeing

Easterlin (2003) regards wellbeing as being measured by the answer to a question such as that asked in the United States General Social Survey: 'Taken all together, how would you say things are these days – would you say that you are very happy, pretty happy, or not too happy.' This is the strategy mentioned previously of skipping the middleman and letting the respondent subjectively combine the various aspects of wellbeing, to produce an overall value.

We introduced the notion of face validity in Chapter 1. A measurement procedure had face validity if it looked as if it should measure what one wanted to measure. The straightforward single question approach certainly looks (at face value!) as if it should do the trick. But looking appropriate is not the same as having been proven to be appropriate, so care must be exercised.

Such simple single questions on life satisfaction measures are common in surveys. For example, Dolan *et al.* (2008) refer to '19 major national and cross-national data sets that included measures of [subjective wellbeing]', including the following surveys and questions:

America's Changing Lives survey: 'Now thinking about your life as a whole. How satisfied are you with it?'

The British Household Panel Survey: 'How satisfied are you with your life overall?'

The Canadian General Social Survey: 'Presently, would you describe yourself as very happy, somewhat happy, .…?'

The Eurobarometer: 'On the whole are you very satisfied, fairly satisfied, …, with the life you lead?'

The German Socio-Economic Panel Survey: 'How satisfied are you at present with your life as a whole?'

Russian Longitudinal Monitoring Survey: 'To what extent are you satisfied with your life in general at the present time?'

Such a strategy – asking a single question – has many attractive properties. It is simple to understand and quick to administer, and it is very widely applicable. From a pragmatic measurement perspective, it is very clear what is being asked (though questions of interpretation or comprehension may arise, so that the question might not be capturing exactly what you intend it to capture; different groups may have different inbuilt biases, responding differently to the same wording). But it has its limitations. It does not separately capture the different components or aspects of wellbeing – the hedonic and eudemonic aspects mentioned in Section 1.3, for example. Moreover, one has to live with its intrinsic variability: basic statistics would lead us to expect that single questions would have greater measurement error than an average of several questions. There are also further complications such as question wording (very different responses can be elicited by even slight changes in wording) and framing (no question is asked in isolation, and the context can have a significant impact on the result).

For this latter reason, various statistical tools have been developed which combine multiple individual statements, items or questions, even within the context of a single one of the factors of wellbeing. For example, even if one is aiming solely to measure hedonic aspects of wellbeing, there are advantages in using multiple questions. In particular, as well as reducing measurement error variation in the overall response, this better ensures that the scale captures the concepts it is intended to capture: it helps to ensure content validity.

Methods based on this idea have been in use in the social and behavioural sciences for around a century (e.g. the Likert scale was described by Rensis Likert in his PhD thesis in 1932). Such methods include.

Likert scaling. A Likert scale consists of a number of items, often bipolar five-point semantic differential scales themselves, the scores of which are added to produce an overall score. Typically, the categories of the individual items are balanced positively and negatively (e.g. strongly agree, disagree, neither agree nor disagree, agree, strongly agree). An example of a wellbeing instrument which uses this approach is the Warwick–Edinburgh Mental Well-being Scale (Stewart-Brown and Janmohamed, 2008).

Thurstone scaling. An initial set of a large number of statements describing the strength of the attribute to be measured is collected. Several judges then assign each of the statements to a position on an 11-point scale indicating their rating of the strength of agreement. Since the judges will typically not all agree on the scores which should be assigned to each statement, each statement will have a distribution of scores. If a distribution has a large spread, that statement is dropped, since the judges clearly disagree on how it should be interpreted. The other statements are then assigned a numerical value equal to the median of their distribution. From this set, a subset is then chosen to span the range of levels of agreement. A respondent's score is then the mean of the statements with which he or she agrees.

Guttman scaling. Like Likert and Thurstone scales, a Guttman scale consists of a series of items. However, whereas in the former two the scores on the separate items are combined to yield an overall score, in a Guttman scale, the items are selected so that they have a natural order, and endorsement of one of the items implies endorsement of all those which precede it. A technique sometimes called *scalogram* analysis is used to assign numbers to the items, based on the answers of a collection of respondents.

4.3   Combining aspects of wellbeing

Scale construction methods such as Likert scaling, Thurstone scaling, and Guttman scaling combine multiple items to yield an overall score, but they are really aimed at tapping into one concept. Wellbeing, however, has several rather distinct strands and, if we are seeking to produce a single measure of wellbeing, we must devise ways to combine these distinct strands. In Chapter 1, we introduced one important, even fundamental, distinction: that between subjective and objective aspects.

If one takes the view that wellbeing is intrinsically subjective, then objective measures can only really be measures of cause, effect or simply correlates of wellbeing, and not of wellbeing itself. Kahneman (2003, p. 5) illustrates this with objective happiness: 'Objective happiness is not to be confused with objective good fortune, which is an assessment of the circumstances of someone's life.' 'Objective good fortune' might well be a cause of wellbeing, but it is not wellbeing itself, and is not a fundamental aspect of it. More generally, causes would be familiar things such as income, housing standard, employment, education, poverty and so on. Such things are clearly objective, clearly not an intrinsic part of wellbeing, but potentially able to enhance or degrade it. Such objective and external indicators can be, and indeed are, regularly collected by statistical surveys. Wellbeing apart, they have clear roles to play in measuring the state of society and the effectiveness of public policy. The Stiglitz report explicitly recommended that both subjective and objective indicators of wellbeing should be included in national surveys (Stiglitz *et al.*, 2010, '*Recommendation 6: Quality of life depends on people's objective conditions and capabilities. Steps should be taken to improve measures of people's health, education, personal activities and environmental conditions. In particular, substantial effort should be devoted to developing and implementing robust, reliable measures of social connections, political voice, and insecurity that can be shown to predict life satisfaction*' and '*Recommendation 10: Measures of both objective and subjective well-being provide key information about people's quality of life. Statistical offices should incorporate questions to capture people's life evaluations, hedonic experiences and priorities in their own survey*').

Even if objective measures might not of themselves be regarded as *aspects of* wellbeing, by virtue of the fact that they are correlated with it, they can certainly be used in improving estimates of it – that is, in helping to measure it. However, it is worth noting that one should not expect too much from them: 'Several decades ago, social scientists began large-scale investigations of individuals' satisfaction with their lives and with their society. One of the robust findings of this research was that the correlations between global judgements of the quality of life and objective conditions of living are often quite low.' (Kahneman *et al.*, 2003, p. x).

4.3.1   Causes, effects, and correlates

In Chapter 1, we quoted McAllister (2005) as describing physical health, income and wealth, relationships, meaningful work and leisure, and personal stability and (lack of) depression, as 'drivers' of wellbeing. The term 'driver' suggests they are external to wellbeing – that they are influences or causes of it. Likewise, she describes objective measures as relating to material and social circumstances 'which may foster – or detract from – wellbeing' and gives examples of income, housing, educational attainment and access to and use of public services. So like the drivers, these 'circumstances' are potential influences on wellbeing. They are not by themselves aspects of wellbeing, but they could add to or detract from it. This is perhaps further supported by the fact that, as also noted by McAllister, changes in these indicators 'have not provided a coherent explanation for trends in wellbeing', citing the familiar example of rising GDP per capita not necessarily leading to improvement in life satisfaction.

From the other side, some objective measures may also be consequences of or effects of wellbeing: 'There is a wealth of evidence that positive wellbeing influences a wide range of outcomes for individuals and communities, including better physical and mental health, higher educational attainment and more social cohesion'. (Mental Health Foundation, 2010).

As a further alternative to causes or effects, some objective measures might be regarded as simple proxies for wellbeing. That is, they might be expected to be correlated with it, though it might be difficult to argue for causal links.

It will be apparent from all of these that it will not always be easy to identify a particular indicator as uniquely a cause, an effect or a mere correlate. For example, we cited the Mental Health Foundation as commenting that 'positive wellbeing influences ... mental health', but Friedli (2009, p. iii) says 'mental health influences a very wide range of outcomes ... [including] improved quality of life'. There is the potential for two-way influence.

One must also bear in mind the fact that cause/effect relationships between objective indicators and wellbeing are (if they exist) statistical. The fact that someone's income has increased does not necessarily imply that their wellbeing will increase. This is one reason why multiple indicators must be combined and why combining multiple indicators leads to improved measurement procedures and indeed improved definitions of what is meant by wellbeing.

Going further, however, even if the causal relationship were deterministic, absence of a cause does not mean absence of the effect: perhaps something else has caused the effect. If enhanced wellbeing promotes better social interactions, the mere presence of better social interactions does not necessarily mean that wellbeing has been enhanced. It could simply be that other life circumstances have changed, leading to more ready social interactions. Again, combining multiple indicators helps to focus a measure on the core which one is trying to tap.

Objective indicators typically have the striking merits of being relatively clearly defined, easily measured, and also often of being clearly quantitative (income, for example). Those attractive properties can sometimes outweigh the merits of alternative indicators which, while apparently more closely related to the thing we actually wish to measure, are themselves difficult to measure. An example in another area is the use of body weight to see if a slimming regime is working. Weight is clearly defined, easily measured (hop on a weighing machine), and is quantitative (number of pounds or kilograms). In fact, the use of weight in this context is so attractive that it disguises the fact that we are not really after weight at all, but body image or health, and these are difficult to capture in simple measures.

Objective measures are necessarily model-based. If wellbeing is an intrinsically internal attribute, measuring it using objective measures requires that one can link those objective measures to the underlying internal attribute which is actually the target of the exercise. Subjective measures attempt to do this by asking questions along the lines of 'what is the value of your internal wellbeing attribute?' In contrast, objective measures say 'we know that internal wellbeing is related to external attribute X in such-and-such a way, so, given the value of X, we can seek to deduce the value of internal wellbeing'.

One might put this in another way by saying that objective measures *make assumptions* (about the relationships between the measure and the target).

Although the objective circumstances in which we live can help us to measure wellbeing, they cannot, by themselves, completely capture it. They can tell us the circumstances, but not how different people will react to them. To take just one example, cultural differences can have an effect. The classic example is of a male consulting a doctor, and, on being asked 'How are you?', he replies 'I'm fine'. Clearly they are not 'fine' or they would not have been visiting their doctor in the first place.

We mentioned above an elegant model produced by the New Economics Foundation and included in their report *Measuring Our Progress* (Abdallah *et al.*, 2011, 13). This is a causal network (a psychometric model), two of the nodes (good functioning and good feelings) of which show aspects of wellbeing while the others (external conditions and personal resources) impact on them. In fact, the model shows both cause and effect relationships between good functioning and external conditions, and between good functioning and good feelings, and shows good feelings impacting personal resources which in turn impact good functioning. Although this is a psychometric model, wellbeing measurements based on it would need to combine good feelings and good functioning in an appropriate way, and the relative weights would reflect the pragmatic concerns of those constructing the instrument.

4.3.2   Subjective components of wellbeing

Subjective wellbeing measures are subjective because they relate to internal states – how people feel about things. It is not the fact that they are scores provided by the subjects themselves which makes them subjective. Indeed, objective measures can also be measured in a subjective way. For example, we might ask someone to give an estimate of their likely income on retirement: here, while the income is objective, the way of determining an estimate of it is subjective.

In Chapter 1, we noted the distinction between hedonic and eudemonic wellbeing. Pleasure and happiness constitute hedonic wellbeing; achievement, fulfilment, and a sense of meaning constitute eudemonic happiness. As in any area where the measurement procedure is primarily pragmatic, however, one can develop refined aspects and components of the thing being measured. So, for example, Parfit (1984) defines three perspectives as follows:

1. The hedonic perspective, regarding wellbeing as synonymous with pleasure;

2. The desire-based or life satisfaction perspective, concerned with satisfying desires or preferences;

3. The achievement-based perspective. This is concerned with improvement or realisation of aims or meeting needs.

Kahneman and his co-authors (Kahneman *et al.*, 2003, preface) describe hedonic psychology as 'The study of what makes experiences and life pleasant or unpleasant'. They go on to say 'It is concerned with feelings of pleasure and pain, of interest and boredom, of joy and sorrow, and of satisfaction and dissatisfaction. It is also concerned with the whole range of circumstances, from the biological to the societal, that occasion suffering and enjoyment.' Kahneman (2003, p. 12) also points out that hedonic scales are bipolar and that 'pain or distress differs qualitatively from pleasure', rather than being intrinsically unidimensional, like length.

There is often suspicion that subjective hedonic characteristics cannot be effectively measured. The OECD has something to say about this in its *Guidelines on Measuring Subjective Wellbeing* (OECD, 2013). It says: 'These Guidelines mark an important turning point in our knowledge of how subjective wellbeing can, and should, be measured. Not long ago, the received wisdom was that "we don't know enough" about subjective well-being to build it into measures of societal progress. However, as the evidence documented in these Guidelines shows, we in fact know a lot – perhaps more than we realised until we gathered all the relevant material for this report – and in particular that measures of subjective well-being are capable of capturing valid and meaningful information.'

These guidelines also make the revealing point (e.g. p. 62): 'Perhaps *because* of concerns about their use, quite a lot *is* known about how subjective well-being measures behave under different measurement conditions – in some cases more so than many self-report measures already included in some national surveys.'

The doubt about the feasibility of measuring subjective phenomena may be an inherited consequence of familiarity with the strongly representational measurement procedures of the natural sciences: we all agree on what we mean by length, and have a clear and very familiar representational approach based on concatenations of unit length objects. But such suspicion does not reflect advances in measurement technology. Kahneman *et al.* (1997, p. 379) put it strongly: 'The view that hedonic states cannot be measured because they are private events is widely held but incorrect. The measurement of subjective experiences and the determination of the functions that relate subjective variables to features of present and past stimuli are topics in the well-established field of psychophysical research … The loudness of a noise and the felt temperature of a limb are no less subjective than pleasure and pain.'

That psychophysical phenomena can be measured is indicated by weather forecasts which now give, in addition to the actual air temperature, a 'feels like' temperature. 'Feels like' temperature is a combination of wind chill factor and heat index, which takes into account not only the actual air temperature but also the wind speed and dew point, so that it captures the rate of evaporation of sweat from the body, and hence what the air actually feels like. The complexity underlying that condensed explanation illustrates the depth of theory which now underlies such measurement procedures.

In fact, the drive to measure subjective phenomena in psychophysics was one of the prime drivers behind early theoretical understanding of notions of measurement. It goes back a long way – see, for example, Weber's Law relating the 'just noticeable difference' of physical phenomena to the absolute level of the physical magnitude of a stimulus, described in 1846 (Weber, 1846).

Another example of how subjective attributes can be measured was mentioned in Chapter 1. There we noted that although people's degree of wellbeing could adapt as circumstances changed, it often tended to revert to a previous level (e.g. after a lottery win). Such hedonic adaptation can be tapped into by measuring the extent of aversion or attraction to particular stimuli.

Eudemonic perspectives on wellbeing are heavily based on psychological theories, and many theories could be, and indeed have been, put forward. We briefly describe some below. The theories tend to have some common ground, but differ in the details. This should probably be taken as meaning that they go some way towards capturing some underlying truth – but that it is extremely difficult (compared, perhaps, with the natural sciences) to measure the various attributes with high accuracy and, in particular, free of and uncontaminated by other influences. This means that the classifications and ontologies they use are not simply a reflection of the reality they seek to partition and structure, and the measuring instruments constructed from them necessarily involve significant pragmatic aspects.

Some examples of theories underlying approaches to measuring eudemonic wellbeing are as follows:

Maslow's hierarchy of needs: One possible starting point for defining individual wellbeing is from the perspective of human 'needs': an unmet need implies a wellbeing deficit. Maslow (1943) developed a hierarchical structure of such needs. Level 1, the most basic level, consists of biological and physiological survival essentials, such as the need to breath, for food and drink, shelter, warmth and sleep. Level 2 is concerned with safety and includes things like security, law, stability and protection from the elements. Level 3, the need for belongingness and love, including things such as work, and family and intimate relationships. Level 4 covers such things as self-esteem, achievement, and status. Finally, level 5, the top level, includes things like the need to realise one's potential for personal growth and so on. One can see that the higher levels tie into things often taken to represent aspects of wellbeing.

As one might expect, this basic theory has been expanded and modified by subsequent researchers, even to the extent of extending it to more levels. For example, two levels have sometimes been inserted between levels 4 and 5 to cover, on the one hand, the need for knowledge and meaning, and on the other 'aesthetic needs' for beauty and so on. Likewise, a level has been added at the top, reflecting a need to help others achieve 'self-actualisation'.

Self-Determination Theory: Self-Determination Theory has been described as a 'macro-theory of human motivation, personality development, and well-being' (Ryan, 2009). Like Maslow's hierarchy, it postulates a set of underlying psychological needs, in this case for autonomy (recall the notion of 'being in control' mentioned in Chapter 1), competence (the ability to do things), and relatedness (social connectedness: it is well established that having supportive social relationships is protective against depression). Wellbeing is maximised when all three needs are met:

Ryff's Psychological Wellbeing Theory: This theory proposes that eudemonic wellbeing is composed of six aspects: autonomy, personal growth, self-acceptance, life purpose, mastery, and positive relatedness. (Ryff and Singer, 1998).

4.3.3 Weighted sums

A particularly popular pragmatic way of combining different indicators or aspects of wellbeing is as a weighted sum. Scores for each aspect are derived – which themselves may be based on psychometric models or on pragmatic procedures – and then they are weighted according to their relative importance before being added to give an overall score. For convenience, we shall illustrate with three components, but the generalisation is immediate. If we now construct a weighted sum of the components, $y = w_1 x_1 + w_2 x_2 + w_3 x_3$, then, in terms of its impact on y, a unit difference in x_1 between two people is equivalent to a difference between them of w_1/w_2 in x_2: changing x_1 by d units has the same effect on y as changing x_2 by dw_1/w_2 units. In what follows, we will assume that y has been standardised so that it has zero mean and unit standard deviation: $y \rightarrow (y - \mu)/\sqrt{V(y)}$, where $V(y)$ is the variance of y. This represents no loss of generality, but makes the exposition more straightforward. It is equivalent to rescaling the weights by multiplying them all by the same constant value.

Such weighted sums sound straightforward enough and appear to be very readily interpretable. If we think that feelings of optimism are twice as important as feeling full of energy, then we multiply the score on the first by two before adding the weighted scores together. But this apparently straightforward process conceals multiple ambiguities which have to be resolved before the method can be adopted with confidence. What this means in practice is that considerable thought has to be given to a number of issues.

Perhaps the most obvious issue is that the scales of the different components of the score may have different ranges. To illustrate with an artificial and exaggerated example, suppose that one component, x_1 (extent of feelings of optimism, for example), is measured on a scale ranging from 0 to 100, while another, x_2 (extent of feeling full of energy, for example), is measured on a scale from 0 to 1. If we simply add these two scores together, weighting them equally, then differences in x_2 will barely contribute to our overall score: differences between people on their x_2 component will be irrelevant compared to differences on the x_1 component. Now it may be that this is what we intend. But we must recognise that the range of a scale is rather artificial: the pragmatic (as opposed to representational) nature of the component scales used in wellbeing measurement means that typically they can be multiplied by an arbitrary constant without losing any meaning. So, for example, we could have rescaled x_1 to lie on the unit interval without changing the comparison between individuals on x_1. But, clearly, if we used this rescaled x_1 in an (unweighted) linear combination with x_2, we would get an overall score with very different properties.

A common way to tackle this is to start by standardising all the component scales by subtracting their (population) mean and dividing by their (population) standard deviation: $x_i \rightarrow (x_i - E(x_i))/\sqrt{V(x_i)}$. Now a unit change on any of the components corresponds to a change of one standard deviation on that component. Here, we will assume that this standardisation has been adopted, but we should note that it is not the only possible standardisation.

A second and rather more subtle issue concerns the relationships between the components.

The weight w_i in the weighted sum tells us how much impact a one unit difference in x_i will have on y provided a difference in x_i does not imply that there are also differences in the other component scores. But the different components are typically correlated. A difference of one unit in x_1, for example, *is* likely to be associated with some difference in the other x_i values. What this means is that the actual impact on y of a unit difference in x_1 is unlikely to be simply w_1.

A common measure of the impact of a component variable on the overall score is the correlation between these two: for example, $\rho(y, x_1)$. Recalling that, for simplicity and without loss of generality, we have assumed that y had been rescaled to unit standard deviation, and we transformed each of the x_i to have unit standard deviation, then, if x_1 is not independent of the other components,

$$\rho(y, x_1) = \rho(w_1x_1 + w_2x_2 + w_3x_3, x_1) = w_1 + w_2\rho(x_2, x_1) + w_3\rho(x_3, x_1).$$

It follows that, unless the components are independent, the weights w_i may be poor indicators of the relative importance of the components, if this importance is to be measured by the correlation between the component score and the overall score.

The situation is precisely the same as in regression. The weights w_i correspond to partial regression coefficients from a multiple regression (often interpreted, rather loosely and inaccurately, as the effect on y of unit change in x_i, *keeping the other xs constant*), while the correlation coefficient between y and x_i corresponds to the coefficient in a simple regression of y on x_i alone (given that both y and x_i have been standardised to unit variance).

Another way of looking at this, and one which is attractive because it permits ready generalisation, is to use the familiar interpretation of $\rho(y, x_i)^2$ as the proportion of variance of y explained by x_i, $V(E(y|x_i))/V(y)$, which is equal to $V(E(y|x_i))$ since we have standardised y to unit variance.

Now, the correlation between two variables is the strength of *linear* relationship between them. It implicitly fits the model $E(y|x_i) = \alpha_i + \beta_i x_i$. If we take a more elaborate model for $E(y|x_i)$, then we can still use the proportion of variance of y explained by x_i, $V(E(y|x_i))$, as a measure of the importance of x_i in y, even though we cannot use the squared correlation coefficient for this measure. Paruolo *et al.* (2013) have explored this in detail, using a nonparametric kernel regression model for $E(y|x_i)$.

The main cautionary message from this is that the raw weights, the w_i, will not be appropriate measures of the relative importance of each component, x_i, to the overall measure y, if you regard the correlation, or more generally, the proportion of variance of y explained by x_i, as a suitable measure of the magnitude of that relative importance. Unless, that is, the separate components are only weakly mutually related.

Once one has decided on the relative importance one wishes each component to have, and given that the relative importance is to be measured by proportion of variance explained, a natural question is whether one can find a suitable set of weights in $w_1 x_1 + w_2 x_2 + w_3 x_3$ which will lead to those proportions of variance explained. Paruolo *et al.* (2013) show that one can indeed find such a (unique) set of weights. If the correlation matrix between the x_i is $\mathbf{C}$, then a vector proportion to the marginal correlations $\rho = (\rho_1, \rho_2, \rho_3)^T$ is obtained by using the weights $\mathbf{w} = \mathbf{C}^{-1}\rho/(\mathbf{1}^T \mathbf{C}^{-1}\rho)$. Note, however, that these weights may not always be positive – and constraining the weights to be positive is often natural, since then each can be expressed as a proportion of the total weight $\sum w_i$.

As an example, suppose we had three components, and regarded the second and third as equally important, but the first as less important – in the sense that we wanted it to explain only one-fifth of the variance of the overall weighted sum that the other two components each explained. That is, we wanted to choose a set of weights so that the vector of squared correlations was proportional to $(0.1, 0.5, 0.5)^T$. Suppose also that the correlation matrix between the x_i was

$$\mathbf{C} = \begin{bmatrix} 1 & 0.1 & 0.1 \\ 0.1 & 1 & 0.9 \\ 0.1 & 0.9 & 1 \end{bmatrix}.$$

Then we have

$$\rho = \left(\sqrt{0.1}, \sqrt{0.5}, \sqrt{0.5} \right)^T = (0.316, 0.707, 0.707)^T$$

and hence, from the above, $\mathbf{w} = (0.254, 0.373, 0.373)^T$.

Using this $\mathbf{w}$ we see that the marginal correlations of the weighted sum with the x_i are given by

$$\mathbf{Cw}/\sqrt{\mathbf{wCw}} = (0.328, 0.734, 0.734)^T/0.795 = (0.413, 0.924, 0.924),$$

so that the squared correlations are equal to

$$(0.413^2, 0.924^2, 0.924^2) = (0.171, 0.854, 0.854) \propto (0.1, 0.5, 0.5).$$

4.4   Components of individual wellbeing

There are many objective indicators which could be chosen, spanning many domains. The choice is largely a pragmatic one, reflecting how individual researchers want to define wellbeing: you choose those you think are relevant to capturing what you mean by wellbeing. Nonetheless, it is reassuring to note that there is considerable overlap between different researchers.

Dolan *et al.* (2008) reviewed wellbeing papers published in economics journals since 1990, along with some key psychological reviews and unpublished papers and identified seven types of potential influences on wellbeing: income, personal characteristics, socially developed characteristics, how we spend our time, attitudes and beliefs towards self/others/life, relationships, and the wider economic, social, and political environment. We shall make a few brief comments about each of these. General conclusions are typically difficult to draw as the research is usually not unanimous. This might be because the studies relate to different populations, have differences in the way they define base characteristics, use different pragmatic definitions of the individual characteristics being explored, or are complicated by interactions – or for all three of these reasons and others. Even so, simple and universal a tool as multiple regression can lead to different coefficients for a given characteristic as others are included or excluded from the model: a characteristic may appear to be positively or negatively linked to wellbeing according to whether some completely different characteristic is or is not in the model. Unfortunately, there is no absolute way of determining what should be in the model – or deciding what has been inadvertently omitted.

Furthermore, the so-called *ecological fallacy* can have an impact. This is the phenomenon that a relationship (such as a positive correlation) found *between* individuals might not hold *within* individuals. Larger values of characteristic x might be associated with larger values of characteristic y in the population as a whole, but an increase in values of characteristic x might be associated with smaller values of y in all individuals.

One implication of all this is that the assertions made below might not hold in particular cases: they are illustrative rather than definitive. The diversity of the results and relationships drives home the importance of agreeing on a common pragmatic definition which captures the important aspects when public policy is the objective.

> *Income:* Clark *et al.* (2008) gives a recent review of the relationship between income and subjective wellbeing. As is fairly well known, there appears to be a positive relationship, but (as presumably must be the case if wellbeing is defined on a finite scale while income is potentially unlimited) one which decreases in rate as income increases. Of particular interest is that the relationship also appears to be moderated by the size of income relative to others: an increase in income only results in an increase in wellbeing if others' income is not also increased. This is clearly tied in with the adverse effects of inequality on national wellbeing, as described by Wilkinson and Pickett (2010).

Personal characteristics: this covers age, gender, ethnicity, and personality. As we have commented in Section 1.1, there appears to be a U-shaped relationship between age and wellbeing, with a trough in the middle years of around 30 to 50. The relationship between gender and wellbeing is not clear, with reported relationships varying between studies. There do appear to be ethnic differences, though these are bound up with social, cultural, and environmental contexts. There is extensive work on the relationship between personality and wellbeing, and we shall say more about it at the end of this section.

Socially developed characteristics: Dolan *et al.* (2008) use this to cover education, health, type of work, and unemployment. Broadly speaking a higher level of education seems to have a positive benefit on wellbeing, though studies are not unanimous. The potential for education to interact with other factors, including health, social networks, and personality, is obvious: Dolan *et al.* (2008) comment that 'the coefficient on education is often responsive to the inclusion of other variables within the model'. Studies appear to consistently show a positive impact of good health on wellbeing and a negative impact of unemployment on wellbeing. Note, however, that as we have already commented, the impact of unemployment appears to be greater than might be expected from the financial impact alone. Note also that we have chosen to use the word 'impact' there, implicitly assuming a causal direction.

Health is a particularly compelling example of a characteristic for which it is difficult to tease open whether it should be regarded as a cause, effect or correlate of wellbeing. It seems best to regard it as potentially all three: we have already cited studies showing how low degrees of wellbeing can adversely impact health, and it is obvious that poor health will adversely impact wellbeing. Furthermore, if one regards some individual objective characteristics as intrinsic aspects of individual wellbeing, then health would be a good candidate: then one would regard it as not causing, resulting from or being correlated with wellbeing, but being part of it.

How we spend our time: this includes hours worked, commuting, caring for others, community involvement and volunteering, exercise, and religious activities. Broadly speaking, the results of different studies are heterogeneous except in the predictable domains: longer commutes decrease wellbeing, transition to care-giving is associated with decreased wellbeing, membership of organisations appears to be associated with increased wellbeing, exercise has positive results, and religious activity is associated with enhanced wellbeing. We make no comments about possibly tangled causal directions in any of this.

Relationships: there appears to be substantial evidence that being in an intimate relationship enhances wellbeing, as does regular socialising with family and friends.

Wider economic, social, and political environment: inequalities in society appear to have a detrimental effect (on many aspects of life) in aggregate (again Wilkinson and Pickett, 2010). However, as we have already commented, in individuals, an increase in income relative to others can enhance wellbeing. As one might expect, concerns about physical safety where one lives is associated with decreased wellbeing.

Environment: studies have shown that natural environments – access to green spaces, for example, have a beneficial impact on wellbeing.

Attitudes and beliefs towards self/others/life: a positive perception of one's circumstances, trust in others, and religious beliefs tend to be associated with positive wellbeing.

In contrast to the earlier factors, the last, on attitudes and beliefs, is internal, though not necessarily subjective – attitudes and beliefs are manifested in behaviour and introspection is not a necessary requirement in a measurement instrument.

As far as subjective measures are concerned, various authors (e.g. Dolan *et al.*, 2011) have distinguished three broad types of measure: evaluative, experience, and eudemonic. Hicks (2011) stresses the importance of separating evaluative and experiential questions, as the results can differ. The OECD (2013) definition of subjective wellbeing also covers these three aspects.

Evaluative measures are global assessments of some aspect of an individual's life. Examples are single overall measures, such as, 'overall, how satisfied are you with your life nowadays?' or the Cantril Ladder (a visual analogue scale styled as a 'ladder' with 10 rungs, ranging from 0 (worst possible life) to 10 (best possible life). We have already remarked on the prevalence of single global measures in surveys. Other examples are subjective assessments of particular domains, such as health or work.

Experience (affect) measures are attempts to tap into feelings such as anxious, excited, happy, and sad. Degree of wellbeing has been described as the extent of 'pleasure over pain'. It has also been suggested that experience questions should tap both positive and negative affect. A single experience question might be 'Overall, how happy did you feel yesterday?', and a single negative affect question might be 'Overall, how worried did you feel yesterday?' (Hicks, 2011). Note that each of these questions specifies a time period. This is an important issue and we shall discuss it in more detail in Section 4.5.

Eudemonic measures seek to tap into things like purpose, meaning, achievement, and engagement in life – to find out the extent to which, overall, the respondent regards their life as 'worthwhile'. Example of possible single high level eudemonic questions which have been suggested are 'Overall, how much purpose does your life have?' or 'Overall, how worthwhile are the things that you do in your life?' (see e.g. Hicks, 2011). We prefer the second of these two examples: the first seems to us to be ambiguous, confounding attempts to achieve some goal with whether or not life has a purpose or meaning.

Kahneman and Ris (2005) distinguish between two aspects of subjective wellbeing: the evaluative and the hedonic aspects. For them, evaluative aspects require people to think about particular topics, as in 'How satisfied are you with your job?' and this sort seems to be most commonly used in practice. In contrast, hedonic aspects are concerned with emotional experience, as in 'how happy are you?' The two aspects have been characterised as being about 'life as remembered' and 'life as experienced' respectively, and the two styles can give different results. The terms 'remembered' and 'experienced' bring us back to the issue of time frames.

Pavot and Diener (1993) distinguish between affective measures, likewise splitting them into positive and negative affect, and a 'cognitive component, which is referred to as life satisfaction'. Diener's Life Satisfaction Survey combines five simple items, each scored on a 7-point scale from strongly agree to strongly disagree. For example: 'The conditions of my life are excellent' and 'so far I have gotten the important things I want in life'.

Waldron (2010) has described a similar categorisation of subjective wellbeing questions found in social surveys, but takes it into slightly finer detail, into five categories: global evaluation, domain evaluation, general affect, domain-specific affect, and psychological wellbeing.

Waldron also gives an appendix listing the wellbeing questions on major UK social surveys. The categories are defined as follows, with examples of the questions from each category to show the sort of things they cover:

Global evaluation: questions aim to generate overall cross-cutting measures of people's experience of life. These are the single measures of wellbeing discussed above. Such measures are also used in addition to questions tapping into particular aspects, such as those below.

Examples:

All things considered, are you satisfied with your life?

Have you recently been feeling reasonably happy, all things considered?

How dissatisfied or satisfied are you with your life overall?

How do you feel about life as a whole?

Overall, how would you rate your own wellbeing?

Domain evaluation: questions aim to generate overall measures of people's experience with particular aspects of life (e.g. work, health, material wellbeing, relationships, social support, quality of local area, environment).

Examples:

How satisfied are you with your standard of living?

How satisfied are you with your future financial security?

How satisfied are you with your health?

How often during the past two weeks have you felt unsafe or threatened?

In the past 12 months have you experienced harassment, abuse or violence from anyone because of your age?

General affect: questions aim to generate measures of peoples' experience of emotion and affect (e.g. sadness, joy, anger, affection).

Examples:

How much do you agree or disagree with the statement 'I spend a lot of time worrying about things'?

How much of the time over the past two weeks have you been feeling cheerful?

Over the past few weeks have you been able to concentrate on whatever you're doing?

Over the past few weeks, have you lost much sleep over worry?

Domain-specific affect: questions aim to generate measures of people's experience of emotion and affect associated with particular aspects of their life (e.g. fear of crime, enjoyment at work).

Examples:

Do you agree or disagree with the statement that 'I draw comfort and strength from my religious beliefs'?

> Over the past two weeks, have you been feeling close to other people?
>
> How safe or unsafe do you feel ... at home after dark?

Psychological wellbeing: aim to measure the underlying or protective factors affecting people's mental health. These could include questions about autonomy, resilience, self-esteem, optimism and so on (e.g. Would you describe yourself as a resilient person? Do you feel connected to others?).

> All things considered, how satisfied are you with your ability to influence what happens in your life?
>
> How much do you agree or disagree with the statement 'I spend a lot of time worrying about things'?
>
> How often during the past few weeks have you felt engaged or focused in what you were doing?

A rather different, but related, aspect is a feeling that one is in command of one's life, sometimes called *autonomy*.

> *Autonomy*: in general, a lack of control, a feeling that one is a leaf blown by the winds of events, induces a sense of uncertainty, possibly even anxiety. As an example of just one study on the relationship between autonomy and aspects of wellbeing, Bosma *et al.* (1997) conducted a prospective investigation of 10,308 civil servants. In particular, they examined the relationship between degree of job control and cases of angina, severe chest pain, diagnosed ischaemic heart disease, and any coronary event. Even allowing for employment grade, negative affectivity, and classic risk factors, they found that people with low degrees of job control had a higher risk of newly reported coronary heart disease at follow up. The demands of work were not related to the risk.

Various researchers have explored the relationship between wellbeing and personality constructs, such as repressive defensiveness, trust, emotional stability, including desire for control. DeNeve and Cooper (1998) carried out a meta-analysis of studies of the relationships between subjective wellbeing and 137 such personality traits, reduced by factor analysis to ('the big') five dimensions: extraversion, agreeableness, conscientiousness, neuroticism, and openness to experience. They commented that 'one problem with utilizing the Big Five is that researchers do not agree on the precise definitions of the five factors'. They gave the following theoretical descriptions (p. 199):

> 'Extraversion was defined to include personality traits that focused on the quantity and intensity of relationships (such as sociability and dominance), energy level, positive emotionality, and excitement seeking (such as play and sensation seeking). Agreeableness included personality traits that focused on the quality of interpersonal relationships, such as empathy and warmth. Conscientiousness included goal-directed behaviour (such as efficacy and rule conscious) and control-related traits (such as internal locus of control and impulsivity). Neuroticism focused on adjustment variables (such as psychoticism and distress), as well as negative emotional and behavioural traits (such as ambivalence over emotional expressiveness and aggression). The controversial final factor, Openness to Experience was designed to include measures of intelligence, openness, and creativity. In

addition, Openness to Experience was broadened to include any personality variable that is primarily cognitive in nature, such as belief in a just world, mental
absorption, and rigidity.'

They distinguished between four 'conceptualisations' of subjective wellbeing, again similar to
those described above: happiness, positive and negative affect, and life satisfaction. Happiness
was 'the preponderance of positive affect over negative affect with a focus on the affective
evaluation of one's life situation'. In contrast, positive and negative affect focus on 'the recent
occurrence of specific positive and negative emotions' and do not involve appraisal. Life
satisfaction is 'primarily a cognitive evaluation of the quality of one's experiences, spanning
an individual's entire life'.

The disagreement about precise definitions of the five personality factors and the flexibility
in how aspects of wellbeing are defined, along with the different instruments and questions
researchers have used to tap into these various aspects illustrates the pragmatic nature of the
measurement procedures associated with these concepts.

DeNeve and Cooper (1998) concluded from their meta-analysis that while health and
socioeconomic status were important correlates of subjective wellbeing, personality also
was. We have already quoted Oliver James, in Chapter 2, as saying that 'politico-economic
and cultural factors are vital' in causing mental illness, and, by complementarity, we might
expect them to be central to wellbeing as well.

We should perhaps comment here that personality is at least partly a result of genetic constitution, as well as external influences (nature as well as nurture). One's genetic constitution
is immutable, so that will presumably constrain the impact that policy can have on improving wellbeing. In his book *Happiness*, Richard Layard says 'Since we vary in happiness, it
would be good to be able to say how much of the variation came from differences in genes
and how much from differences in experiences. Unfortunately, this cannot be done in any
neat way ... people with good genes tend to get good experiences. Their parents are good at
parenting. Their own niceness elicits good treatment from other people. And as time passes,
they themselves are good at seeking out good experiences. These effects are in truth effects
of experience, but they are also correlated with a person's genes. There is no clear way of
parcelling them out between the two influences.' (Layard, 2011, p. 58).

4.5   The frailty of memory

It will have become apparent from our discussion that time is critical in evaluating wellbeing.
Are we talking about wellbeing 'now', over the past week or some other specified period, or
over life as a whole? 'Are you happy now?' and 'How happy have you been over the past
week?' might quite correctly elicit entirely different responses.

As if that was not enough, the human memory plays various tricks. It is not a biological
equivalent of a recording device, faithfully copying the signals impinging on it. Rather it
processes them as they arrive, matching, saving, rejecting and even distorting them. As
Tiberius (2006, p. 496) puts it: 'The problem here is that people's retrospective evaluations of
their experience often do not correlate well with the experience itself because retrospective
evaluations are biased by irrelevant features of memory and attention.'

A particularly pertinent example of this for us is what Kahneman *et al.* (1997, p. 381)
call the 'peak-end' rule. They found that 'the remembered utility of pleasant or unpleasant

episodes is accurately predicted by averaging the peak (most intense value) of instant utility (or disutility) recorded during an episode and the instant utility recorded near the end of the experience'. In general, self reports are heavily biased towards the last experienced state. One consequence of this is that the duration of an experience is largely irrelevant to the *remembered* utility so that the remembered utility can be decreased by adding a less pleasurable period to the end of an episode. This means that remembered utility contravenes an additivity property. One might have hoped that adding a further pleasurable experience to an already pleasurable experience might make the whole thing even better, but it seems that this is not the case: remembered utility of a pleasurable episode can be decreased by extending its length by a less pleasurable albeit still pleasurable experience.

From the perspective of measuring national wellbeing, such issues are clearly of paramount importance. Do we want to measure what people experience at the time, or what they remember and report afterwards? Kahneman *et al.* (1997) describe two measures of 'experienced utility'. The first, 'remembered utility', is based on retrospective subjective recall of the pleasure experienced over a period of time, while the second, 'total utility', is based on the idea of integrating the level of pleasure or 'instant utility' over an interval of time.

This idea of integrating instant wellbeing over time is not a new one. Writing in 1881, Francis Ysidro Edgeworth (Edgeworth, 1881, p. 1) said: 'Utility, as Professor Jevons says, has two dimensions, intensity and time', and (Edgeworth, 1881, p. 100): '... imagine an ideally perfect instrument, a psychophysical machine, continually registering the height of pleasure experienced by an individual, exactly according to the verdict of consciousness, ... From moment to moment the hedonimeter varies; the delicate index now flickering with the flutter of the passions, now steadied by intellectual activity, low sunk whole hours in the neighbourhood of zero, or momentarily springing up towards infinity. The continually indicated height is registered by photographic or other frictionless apparatus upon a uniformly moving vertical plane. Then the quantity of happiness between two epochs is represented by the area contained between the zero-line, perpendiculars thereto at the points corresponding to the epochs, and the curve traced by the index'.

Modern approaches, such as the Princeton Affect Time Survey approach, ask people for their feelings at randomly selected times during the day (e.g. alerted by a buzzer or mobile phone call), so that these instantaneous reports can be properly integrated.

It is worth commenting that all integration requires a measure. Implicit in the above procedures is that all equal-sized intervals of time are weighted equally. But perhaps this is not appropriate. In particular, if wellbeing at the end of an episode (the end effect) is what is used when subjectively evaluating wellbeing, then perhaps one should calculate wellbeing by weighting the instantaneous measure by the probability that life will end at that time.

The idea of evaluating subjective happiness by integrating instantaneous happiness over time is obviously related to the notion of 'Quality-Adjusted Life Year'. This is a measure of overall benefit to be obtained from a medical treatment in which the time spent in each state of health is weighted by the utility of that state of health (see, e.g. Fayers and Machin, 2000).

4.6   The devil's in the details

We have so far said little about the *characteristics* of the low-level items which will be combined, either to yield an overall wellbeing measure or to yield one of the components of wellbeing discussed above. These individual items will be chosen on the basis of how well they combine to yield the intended definition, so their precise meaning is critical. But, they must also have properties beyond their simple meaning. In particular, they must have good measurement properties themselves, or at least lead to good measurement properties when combined. 'Good', here, is in terms of validity, reliability, data quality, and so on. It is also necessary to consider how practicable it is to measure a given item. An ideal item, which requires an elaborate measurement procedure or which is very expensive to measure accurately, may not be useful, and it may be better to settle for a less than ideal one which can actually be measured.

One might summarise all of this by describing it as a matter of compromise. All of which needs careful thought.

Data quality issues are especially important. One of these is the extent to which missing values are likely to arise in any of the items. We might prefer not to include one which is particularly prone to having missing values. Causing yet further complications, a question such as 'Have you had problems doing X?' could well be answered negatively by people who never had cause to do X, whereas one might prefer it to be recorded as a missing value – and if items which are likely to have many missing values are to be avoided it might be better to think of a different question altogether. Unfortunately, despite our best efforts, missing values will occur.

The problem of missing values can be tackled by various imputation methods. The oldest strategies of dropping respondents who have missing values from the analysis, or substituting the mean for the missing values, are not to be recommended. The first risks causing selection bias. For example, if respondents who would have low values on some component characteristic are more likely not to give an answer to this component, then the importance of this component to the overall measure of wellbeing may be missed. The second basic approach, substituting the mean of the observed values, leads to an underestimate of the variance of the component in question.

More elaborate tools based on the nature of the potential relationship between the probability of a value being missing and the value itself have been developed. But it is important to recognise that such methods, no matter how clever, cannot create data from thin air. The best they can do is ensure that the imputed values do not distort the conclusion and give misleading results. And they can only achieve this best at the cost of making certain assumptions (e.g. so-called 'missing at random assumptions') with the risk that, if the assumptions are not satisfied, the conclusions may be misleading.

When we discussed wellbeing measures which were constructed as a weighted sum of item scores, we assumed for simplicity that the individual raw items had been standardised so they all had unit variance. But we pointed out that this was not the only possible standardisation – and made the very important point that the standardisation method was a conscious decision, and not one to be taken without considerable thought. Different methods imply that different assumptions are being made about the way the individual components relate to each other and to the overall measure. There are various alternatives to the unit variance standardisation. They include

- transforming the raw data scale to a standard interval: $x \rightarrow (x - x_{min})/(x_{max} - x_{min})$, where x_{min} and x_{max} are, respectively, the minimum and maximum values that the raw scale can take;

- transforming to quantiles (e.g. deciles);

- transforming to (binary) indicators;

- ranking;

- normal scores.

Skewed distributions can cause particular problems, since then the bulk of the data may lie in some very narrow range, with just a few cases taking very large (or small) values. In such situations, it is probably sensible to apply a nonlinear transformation to symmetrise the distribution first (such as, e.g. a log transformation). Similarly, strongly leptokurtic distributions, with heavy tails on both sides, can also produce extreme outliers, again meaning that the bulk of the data are concentrated in a very narrow range, so that some sort of initial nonlinear transformation makes sense. Initial transformation to normal scores (Blom, 1958) can be a good idea, since then variance has a particularly useful interpretation.

Many of the raw item scales used in wellbeing measurement are categorical, but analogous transformations can easily be applied.

All of the above is all very well, but we still have to find the numerical values to start with: we have to map or assign numbers to represent the values of the attribute we wish to capture. This can be done in various ways, all hinging on how one captures a numerical answer to a question.

It is well known that the way questions are worded can have a substantial effect on the way people respond, and examples of dramatic differences resulting from apparently minor changes are easily found. Even subtle changes in wording can impact responses. Other influences, such as social desirability, the extent to which non-native speakers or those with limited education understand words, and the way the questions are introduced can have unexpected effects. This is why, in the exploration of possible subjective wellbeing questions carried out by the UK Office for National Statistics (ONS) in 2012, various question wordings were explored. For example, the questions in the following pairs were compared with each other:

- overall, to what extent do you feel that the things you do in your life are meaningful?

- overall, to what extent do you feel that the things you do in your life have purpose?

- overall, how anxious did you feel yesterday?

- overall, how worried did you feel yesterday?

And for the 'life satisfaction' question, three different endings were

- overall, how satisfied are you with your life nowadays?

- overall, how satisfied are you with your life these days?

- overall, how satisfied are you with your life?

The ONS study also reported small but statistically significant changes corresponding to things like heat waves, a royal wedding, demonstrations, strikes, the death of Osama Bin Laden, the eruption of the Icelandic volcano Eyjafjallajökull and announcements of growth in the economy. They also found significant differences between different days of the week for 'worthwhile' and 'happy yesterday' ratings.

Because of such subtleties, while care should be taken in constructing instruments which have the most desirable practical properties, it is important that, once chosen, a particular instrument is used consistently.

General advice when constructing measurement instruments is as follows:

– make questions brief;

– use simple language;

– make them relevant to all potential respondents;

– avoid double negatives;

– avoid ambiguity;

– avoid leading questions;

– make specific any potential time interval the question is intended to cover.

Questionnaires can be administered in various ways, including face-to-face interviewing, telephone interviewing, by mail or email, and, increasingly, over the web. The different methods have their pros and cons.

Face-to-face or telephone wellbeing measurements would normally be as part of a larger survey, so the mode of data capture will be determined by wider considerations. Email and the web permit shorter and more targeted investigations. The web, in particular, is susceptible to quality issues – though, as one might expect, things are improving over time as more sophisticated procedures are being developed. (Though this does not prevent very poor studies continuing to be made, even while superior designs are being developed in parallel.)

Standard survey methods to minimise non-response should be used. And the impact of this should be investigated to assure oneself, insofar as it is possible, that any potential non-response bias has in fact been minimised.

Working out what questions are to be asked, and how they are to be worded is much of the battle, but it is not the end. The numeric responses can be elicited in various ways. One popular way is by means of a *visual analogue scale*. In such a scale, respondents indicate their level of agreement with a statement by identifying a point on a horizontal line segment: the distance (often measured in millimetres) from one end of the line segment is taken as the value of the response. It is visual because the line segment is shown. It is analogue because it consists of a continuum (any point on the interval could be chosen, rather than any one of just a small number of points, as we illustrate below).

A variant of this is the semantic differential scale, in which respondents indicate their position relative to two bipolar or opposite adjectives. For example, a respondent might be asked to indicate their position on an interval with 'worthless' at one end and 'valuable' at the other.

Visual analogue scales have a number of attractive properties (McCormack et al., 1988): they are simple to construct and easy to use and score, they are quick to use and can be used repeatedly, are easy to explain to respondents, and minimal training is needed.

It is also common to use such an approach without explicitly giving a visual line segment. Thus we could ask 'On a scale where 0 is "not at all anxious" and 10 is "completely anxious", overall, how anxious did you feel yesterday?' (see e.g. Ralph et al., 2011). Often the range of possible responses is given as a preamble to several questions, such as (very x, fairly, x, a bit not-x, very not-x), (strongly agree, moderately agree, neither agree nor disagree, moderately disagree, strongly disagree), (none of the time, rarely, some of the time, often, all of the time), (better than usual, same as usual, less than usual, Much less than usual), (never, at least once, on a few days, most days, every day).

When presented visually, occasionally numbers are used to indicate points on the scale. More commonly, however, the continuum is replaced by a small set of ordinally related categories and associated statements, such as: better than usual, same as usual, worse than usual, much worse than usual; or none of the time, rarely, some of the time, often, and all of the time. Occasionally, simple numbers are replaced by other ordered symbols, such as cartoon faces ranging in expression from smiling to sad. When such discrete categories are used, it is necessary to decide how many to have. Five and seven are common.

When categories of response are used in this way, a representational perspective would regard the scale as ordinal. However, such scales are often treated as pragmatic scales, with the possible responses coded as integers – which can then be added or manipulated by other arithmetic and statistical operations as discussed above.

We would like to stress that results should be accompanied by measures of uncertainty. A single raw wellbeing value without some indication of the confidence one can put in it, and the range it really reflects, is of limited worth. All too often we have seen comparisons, either between different groups or over time, where the intrinsic uncertainty associated with the estimate meant that no reliable statement of difference could really be made. This sort of thing is, of course, particularly important if wellbeing measures are to be used to evaluate the effectiveness of government policy.

Since, as we remarked above, many wellbeing measurements are embedded in broader surveys, issues of framing need to be considered. Will the wellbeing questions be asked with those concerned with health? Their position relative to religious affiliation, employment, leisure activities and so on needs to be considered, as the mindset engendered by considering those issues can influence the responses to the wellbeing questions. In general, the impact of the order of questions needs to be thought through – and indeed tested during development.

The OECD set of guidelines on measuring subjective wellbeing (OECD, 2013) has extensive discussion of the issues described in this section.

4.7   Conclusion

It should be unnecessary to say that extensive testing and refinement, a fundamentally iterative and cyclic process, is necessary to develop effective wellbeing measures. Unfortunately, it is probably not unnecessary to say it, since one does occasionally see poorly developed wellbeing measures in surveys. In general, sensitivity analysis should be undertaken in which instruments are distorted to see how grave an impact such distortion produces on the overall measures and to identify weaknesses in the construction. Uncertainties should be characterised, and all reported values should have an accompanying indication of confidence or uncertainty. This should at least cover sampling variation, but ideally other sources of uncertainty as well. Explicit statement about what the uncertainty bounds represent is important. (Even at the most basic of levels, we have often seen 'error bounds' reported with no indication of whether they are ± 1 standard deviation, ± 2 standard deviations, 1% or 5% confidence intervals, likelihood intervals, or what.)

The various instruments referred to in this volume are typically characterised by the fact that they have undergone lengthy development processes. Testing can pick up ambiguity in questions.

Individual wellbeing lies at the core of national wellbeing – even if the latter also includes aspects and properties which do not exist at the individual level. This means that effective measures of individual wellbeing are vital for effective measures of national wellbeing.

References

Abdallah S., Mahony S., Marks N. *et al.* (2011). *Measuring Our Progress: The Power of Well-Being.* New Economics Foundation, London.

Behan F.L. and Behan R.A. (1954). Football numbers (continued). *American Psychologist,* **9**, 262–263.

Blom, G. (1958). *Statistical Estimates and Transformed Beta Variates.* John Wiley & Sons, Inc., New York.

Bosma H., Marmot M.G., Hemingway H., Nicholson A.C., Brunner E. and Stansfeld S.A. (1997). Low job control and risk of coronary heart disease in whitehall ii (prospective cohort) study. *The British Medical Journal,* **314**, 558.

Burke C.J. (1953). Additive scales and statistics. *Psychological Review,* **60**, 73–75.

Clark A., Frijters P. and Shields M.A. (2008). A survey of the income happiness gradient. *Journal of Economic Literature,* **46**, 95–144.

DeNeve K.M. and Cooper H. (1998). The happy personality: a meta-analysis of 137 personality traits and subjective well-being. *Psychological Bulletin,* **124**, 197–229.

Department of Health (2010). http://www.dh.gov.uk/prod_consum_dh/groups/dh_digitalassets/@dh/@en/@ps/documents/digitalasset/dh_122347.pdf (accessed 27 December 2013).

Diener E., Suh E.M., Lucas R.E. and Smith H.L. (1999). Subjective well-being: three decades of progress. *Psychological Bulletin,* **125**, 276–302.

Dolan P., Layard R. and Metcalfe R. (2011). Measuring subjective wellbeing for public policy: recommendations on measures. Special Paper No. 23, March 2011, Centre for Economic Performance, London School of Economics.

Dolan P., Peasgood T. and White M. (2008). Do we really know what makes us happy? A review of the economic literature on the factors associated with subjective well-being. *Journal of Economic Psychology,* **29**, 94–122.

Easterlin R.A. (2003). Building a better theory of well-being. Discussion Paper No. 742, Institute for the Study of Labour, Bonn.

Edgeworth F.Y. (1881). *Mathematical Psychics: An Essay on the Application of Mathematics to the Moral Sciences.* C. Kegan Paul and Co, London.

Fayers P.M. and Machin D. (2000). *Quality of Life: Assessment, Analysis and Interpretation.* John Wiley & Sons, Ltd, Chichester.

Friedli L. (2009). *Mental Health, Resilience, and Inequalities.* World Health Organization, WHO Regional Office for Europe, Denmark.

Government Office for Science. (2008). Foresight report, Mental Capital and Wellbeing: making the most of ourselves in the 21st century, Executive Summary. http://www.bis.gov.uk/assets/bispartners/foresight/docs/mental-capital/mentalcapitalwellbeingexecsum.pdf (accessed 27 December 2013).

Hand D.J. (2004). *Measurement Theory and Practice: The World Through Quantification.* John Wiley & Sons, Ltd, Chichester.

Hicks S. (2011). *The Measurement of Subjective Well-Being*. Paper for the Measuring National Well-Being Technical Advisory Group, 4 February 2011. Office for National Statistics, UK.

Hird S. (2003). Individual wellbeing: a report for the Scottish Executive and Scottish Neighbourhood Statistics. NHS Health Scotland.

Huppert F.A., Baylis N. and Keverne B. (2004). Introduction: why do we need a science of well-being?. *Philosophical Transactions of the Royal Society (B)*, **359**, 1331–1332.

Kahneman D. (2003). Objective happiness. In: D. Kahneman, W. Diener and N. Schwarz (eds) *Well-Being: The Foundations of Hedonic Psychology*. Russell-Sage Foundation, New York.

Kahneman D., Diener W. and Schwarz N. (eds) (2003). *Well-Being: The Foundations of Hedonic Psychology*. Russell-Sage Foundation, New York.

Kahneman D. and Ris J. (2005). Living and thinking about it: two perspectives on life. In: F.A. Huppert, N. Baylis and B. Keverne (eds) *The Science of Well-being*. Oxford University Press, Oxford, pp. 285–304.

Kahneman D., Wakker P.P. and Sarin R. (1997). Back to Bentham? Explorations of experienced utility? *Quarterly Journal of Economics*, **112**, 375–405.

Krantz D.H., Luce R.D., Suppes P. and Tversky A. (1971). *Foundations of Measurement, Volume 1, Additive and Polynomial Representations*. Academic Press, New York.

Layard, R. (2011). *Happiness: Lessons from a New Science*. Allen Lane, Penguin Group, London.

Lord F.M. (1953). On the statistical treatment of football numbers. *American Psychologist*, **8**, 750–751.

Luce R.D., Krantz D.H., Suppes P. and Teversky A. (1990). *Foundations of Measurement, Volume 3, Representation, Axiomatization, and Invariance*. Academic Press, New York.

Maslow A (1943). A theory of human motivation. *Psychological Review*, **50**, 370–396.

McAllister F. (2005). *Wellbeing Concepts and Challenges*. Sustainable Development Research Network.

McCormack H.M., Horne D.J. de L. and Sheather S. (1988). Clinical applications of visual analogue scales: a critical review. *Psychological Medicine*, **18**, 1007–1019.

Mental Health Foundation. (2011). *Need 2 Know: Measuring Wellbeing: A Introductory Briefing*.

OECD. (2013). *Guidelines on Measuring Subjective Well-Being*. OECD.

ONS. (2012). *Summary of results from testing of experimental Subjective Well-being questions*, December 2012, Measuring National Well-being programme, ONS. www.ons.gov.uk/well-being (accessed 28 April 2014).

Parfit D. (1984). *Reasons and Persons*. Oxford University Press, Oxford.

Paruolo P., Saisana M. and Saltelli A. (2013). Ratings and rankings: voodoo or science? *Journal of the Royal Statistical Society, Series A*, **176**, 609–634.

Pavot W. and Diener E. (1993). Review of the satisfaction with life scale. *Psychological Assessment*, **5**, 164–172.

Ralph K., Palmer K. and Olney J. (2011). Subjective well-being: a qualitative investigation of subjective well-being questions. Working paper for the ONS Measuring Wellbeing Project, Technical Advisory Group, 29 March 2012.

Roberts F.S. (1979). *Measurement Theory*. Addison-Wesley, Reading.

Ryan R. (2009). Self-determination theory and wellbeing. In: *Wellbeing in Developing Countries Research Review 1*. Centre for Development Studies, University of Bath, UK.

Ryff C.D. and Singer B. (1998). The contours of positive human health. *Psychological Inquiry*, **9**, 1–28.

Scottish Government. (2009). Towards a Mentally Flourishing Scotland: Policy and Action Plan 2009–2011. http://www.scotland.gov.uk/Resource/Doc/271822/0081031.pdf (accessed 27 December 2013).

Senders V.L. (1953). A comment on Burke's additive scales and statistics. *Psychological Review*, **60**, 423–424.

Stevens S.S. (1946). On the theory of scales of measurement. *Science*, **103**, 677–680.

Stewart-Brown S. and Janmohamed K. (2008). The Warwick-Edinburgh Mental Well-being Scale: User Guide, Version 1. http://www.cppconsortium.nhs.uk/admin/files/1343987601WEMWBS%20User% 20Guide%20Version%201%20June%202008.pdf (accessed 2 August 2013).

Stiglitz J.E., Sen S. and Fitoussi J-P. (2010). *Mismeasuring Our Lives: why GDP doesn't Add Up*. The New Press, New York.

Suppes P., Krantz D.H., Luce R.D. and Tversky A. (1989). *Foundations of Measurement, Volume 2, Geometrical, Threshold, and Probabilistic Representations*. Academic Press, San Diego, CA.

Thompson S. and Marks N. (2008). *Measuring Well-Being in Policy: Issues And Applications*. New Economics Foundation, London, http://s.bsd.net/nefoundation/default/page/-/files/Measuring_well-being_in_policy.pdf (accessed 16 December 2013).

Tiberius V. (2006). Well-being: psychological research for philosophers. *Philosophy Compass*, **1**, 493–505.

Waldron S. (2010). *Measuring Subjective Wellbeing in the UK: Working Paper, September, 2010*. Office for National Statistics, UK.

Weber E.H. (1846). Der Tatsinn und das Gemeingefühl. In: H.E. Ross and D.J. Murray (eds) (1978) *E.H. Weber: The Sense of Touch*. trans. D.J.Murray, Academic Press, New York.

Welsh Assembly Government (2010). *Sustainable development*. http://wales.gov.uk/topics/sustainable development/?lang=en (accessed 28 April 2014).

Wilkinson R. and Pickett K. (2010). *The Spirit Level: Why Equality is Better for Everyone*. Penguin Books, London.

5

Preparing to measure national wellbeing

For it so falls out
That what we have we prize not to the worth
Whiles we enjoy it, but being lack'd and lost,
Why, then we rack the value, then we find
The virtue that possession would not show us
Whiles it was ours.

William Shakespeare (*Much Ado About Nothing*, 1600)

Every journey begins with a single step. A journey to put in place a new statistic should start with a question like 'what is it we are trying to measure?' We learn on basic statistics courses how to derive the best estimator and how to choose the criteria for deciding this. If we are designing a survey, then similarly there are criteria – especially timeliness, cost and accuracy – to identify and to balance. For many official statistics, there are further questions to ask, such as 'who will use this new statistic?' and 'what are they going to do with it?'

Questions like this help us shape a 'user requirement'. This is usually regarded as the first step in the design and delivery of a quality product, whether that product is a new statistic or any other good or service. If quality can be summarised as 'fitness for purpose', then we need to know the purpose for which the product is being designed. Where the statistical product is, say, a consumer price index, then it seems reasonably straightforward to start addressing detailed questions as we build the user requirement.

However, we can already see that journeys towards the measurement of national wellbeing are tending to be more of a process than an event. Definitions and common understandings of national wellbeing and progress are emerging as part of the process. There are strong political aspirations for new measures, but relatively little detail on what the measures are to be used for. It also appears that many countries and organisations have started with a step that says we are heading not towards a single statistic but towards a manageable number of indicators

The Wellbeing of Nations: Meaning, Motive and Measurement, First Edition. Paul Allin and David J. Hand.
© 2014 John Wiley & Sons, Ltd. Published 2014 by John Wiley & Sons, Ltd.

to summarise clearly how a country is doing, preferably in a way that people will recognise and find useful.

In this chapter we will examine how to navigate through all of this, especially through the process of teasing out an actionable user requirement for measures of national wellbeing. This will contrast with the established statistical approach. That would be to state, define or at least describe the thing to be estimated before exploring how best to estimate it. We will seek to retain the rigour of setting out in advance our criteria for what 'best' means. We also need to recognise that building new measures of wellbeing and progress may require several iterations, as an initial set of indicators may need further development and refining. It seems helpful for users to see some 'real', but still provisional, indicators so that they can 'get their hands on' some data and try it out. The danger of course is that could lead to statistics driving use, rather than the other way round, if there is not time for consultation and further development.

We will mention in this and later chapters several frameworks that have been proposed to measure the progress of societies. While it might be tempting for us to choose 'the' definitive framework, we refrain from that. The point we would rather make is simply that there are potentially useful frameworks that seek to capture the definition and scope of national wellbeing. They provide potential starting points. However, the framework that is most suitable for a given locality, country or group of countries should be determined through a process of deciding and meeting user requirements, which we explore in this chapter.

5.1   Towards a user requirement for measures of national wellbeing and progress

There is no generally agreed definition of national wellbeing or of progress, although, as we summarised in Chapter 2, people have been thinking about what these things mean for at least 2000 years. Runciman (2010, p. 20) maintains that 'there are no agreed criteria by which to measure the health of a human society as there are to measure that of a human body'. While Deaton, a member of the Stiglitz Commission, has written a book with the measurement of wellbeing at its heart, rather than define wellbeing he appears to focus on the conditions for wellbeing, leaving each individual to define what a good life is for them: 'In this book, when I speak of freedom, it is the freedom to live a good life and to do the things that make life worth living' (Deaton, 2013, p. 5). Nevertheless, over recent decades, the view seems to be gaining ground that measuring national wellbeing and progress needs to take account of more than economic performance, 'an emerging consensus on the need to undertake the measurement of societal progress in every country, going beyond conventional economic measures such as GDP per capita' in the words of the 2007 Istanbul Declaration (see Appendix).

A number of high-level visions have been presented over the years. For example, the vision of the New Economics Foundation (NEF) is 'a more just and sustainable world' and in their work on wellbeing over more than a decade they have come to define a successful society as one where 'people have high levels of well-being which is sustained over time' (Abdallah *et al.*, 2011, p. 2). According to NEF, progress can be considered in terms of three key 'spheres'. The first, which they call 'Goals', is summarised as universally high levels of individual wellbeing. The second sphere is 'Resources', requiring sustainable use of environmental resources. The third sphere is 'Human systems', which embraces activities that achieve intermediate objectives such as a stable and productive economy, a cohesive society, good housing and so on. This approach is broadly similar to the 'triple bottom line' of sustainable development, discussed in Chapter 2, where the impact on society, the environment and the economy are all considered in measuring progress.

The existence of these visions presents a challenge for producers of statistics. It means that there are needs for statistics for political and advocacy purposes, as well as for use in policy. We notice that official statisticians tend to anticipate their statistics being used primarily in policy. While working with policy-makers does have challenges, it is perhaps a somewhat more familiar environment for some official statisticians than meeting the wider needs of politics, the media and the public.

To support such visions for national wellbeing we will need a fuller structure, to make things clearer and to ensure we share a common understanding. While the NEF vision of progress provides a comprehensive coverage, defined in terms of three spheres, it is still at a high conceptual level. Visions have to be supported by a fuller structure in particular so that a measurement framework can be specified and implemented. Only then can the route towards the vision be plotted and progress along the route tracked. We need to operationalise the vision, by defining and using agreed measures. The agreement should be about what we intend to measure, as well as what our measurement procedures should be (and, it needs to be said, we need to agree that we are measuring what we intended to measure!).

A common feature of approaches to the measurement of wellbeing and progress is that they have a number of dimensions or spheres. This is not a new idea. The United Nation's Universal Declaration of Human Rights urges member nations to promote a number of human, civil, economic and social rights. Eight Millennium Development Goals (for 2015) were set out in the United Nations Declaration in 2000 (see Appendix), to tackle the needs of the world's poorest people. All of the examples of societal wellbeing measures that we have seen cover a number of attributes, often grouped into broader domains.

One way of visualising these domains and attributes is to see them as different dimensions. Atkin (1981, p. 148) argues that we live in a multi-dimensional world, not just in the three dimensions that define physical space. He demonstrates how aspects of our lives such as employment status, the industrial classification of our employment and the characteristics of the area in which we live can be associated with us, so that we each live in a broader 'space' than that defined by our physical location. While this interpretation may be debateable, the use of domains and dimensions seems widespread and helpful. Having set out a number of domains, some approaches to measuring wellbeing and progress then attempt to produce a single summary measure. This seems largely for ease of communication of headline results, rather than as a precise measurement of wellbeing or progress.

It would be simpler, in an already complex area, to use the same framework to measure both wellbeing and progress in a particular nation or region. That seems achievable, given that progress is generally taken as a measure of how wellbeing changes over time. To NEF, progress means achieving improvements to national wellbeing (Abdallah et al., 2011, p. 4). Researchers at the Organisation for Economic Co-operation and Development (OECD) have similarly defined societal progress as occurring when 'there is an improvement in the sustainable and equitable well-being of a society' (Hall et al., 2010, p. 15). One might pause over the slight nuance that they define the variable of interest, progress, as something with a positive connotation ('improvement'), rather than defining a variable – say, 'change' – that has no directional implications. (We talk about measuring temperature, not about measuring 'hot-ness' or 'cold-ness'). Leaving that aside as confirmation of the underlying ethos of member nations of OECD, the main thing we take from this is that the main requirement is to measure wellbeing: measures of progress then follow from seeing how wellbeing changes over time. We will see later that there are a couple of important caveats to this, to recognise sustainability and equity.

Defining progress by the change in wellbeing might not fully reflect the nature of progress and how it is perceived. There have been several examples from history where an initial assessment of a period, say the 'Dark Ages' or the 'fifties' (in which it was claimed we in the United Kingdom had 'never had it so good'), is later contested, as additional evidence comes to hand, either about the period in question or for a fuller comparison with other times. This could be down to the arrival of better information, such as when time series of economic variables are revised when initial estimates are replaced by more robust ones. This is perhaps inevitable in the writing of any history: what actually happened does not change, but what is known about what happens, or what is captured as an assessment of events, may well change over time. But it could also be that looking back from a 'better' time leads us to downgrade the assessment of the quality of life that people would have made at the time. If, therefore, we have a problematic relationship with history, do we also have a problematic relationship with progress?

Sticking with the formulation that progress is equated with an increase in the wellbeing of a society, we still need to consider the time period over which we measure change. How far apart are the points between which we assess change? Put another way, if we measure wellbeing every year, because many constituent variables will be available annually, then how far back should we go for an earlier year with which to compare the latest year?

We understand that a trend in meteorological terms is defined as a consistent shift over 30 years. Economic statistics are routinely analysed over much shorter periods than this, even quarter on quarter, though economic growth is usually measured year on year. Is that the right frequency for measuring wellbeing and hence progress more widely? One response is that it depends on the frequency that users want. But we also need to bear in mind the statistical properties of the variable being measured. Does the wellbeing of society as a whole change from quarter to quarter, or even from year to year? How accurate are the measures likely to be for a quarter or for a full year? Are we in danger of interpreting 'noise', in the form of random or other error, as meaningful progress? We will of course want to see estimates of variability of the estimates of national wellbeing. However, even when such descriptions of the accuracy of published statistics are produced, they can be ignored in the rush for political or media headlines.

Historians may be able to identify points at which there was a step change in the quality of life, but are more likely to compare much longer periods of time. Heath provides one example of the long-term view: 'It was during the Neolithic Age that agriculture was introduced into Britain and people began to settle in permanent farming villages, whilst in the Copper and Bronze Ages the secrets of metalworking were discovered. The combination of these two activities provided a potent force for change and it is beyond doubt that, ultimately, the establishment of agriculture and metalworking had a profound impact on the development of modern civilisation' (Heath, 2010, p. 10). Does this suggest different degrees of progress, with changes between epochs being identified only long after the event, and progress on a much smaller scale captured by statistical measures of the recent past?

Looking at the reams of statistics now published each year, it is apparent that the conventional approach is to produce and analyse time series that track economic, social and environmental aspects in near real time. In practice, statistics are invariably published in arrears, because it takes time to collect, check and analyse the data and publish results. Statistical outputs appear some months or even years after the end of the time period to which they refer. Nevertheless, they are then taken as the current assessment of the state of the nation, and comparisons are made with immediately preceding periods. It is difficult to envisage how statistics on national wellbeing and progress would be handled any differently. We might therefore implicitly be building a process where the initial assessment of wellbeing and progress might be supplemented with later assessments, revisiting and reviewing the results decades or even centuries later.

Who should measure wellbeing? The potential scale of the task suggests that this will require considerable resources. Perhaps more importantly, measuring wellbeing sounds like something that should result in a public good, that is something that is freely available not only for governments but for all in society to use. The Istanbul Declaration put it like this:

> A culture of evidence-based decision making has to be promoted at all levels, to increase the welfare of societies. And in the 'information age', welfare depends in part on transparent and accountable public policy making. The availability of statistical indicators of economic, social, and environmental outcomes and their dissemination to citizens can contribute to promoting good governance and the improvement of democratic processes. It can strengthen citizens' capacity to influence the goals of the societies they live in through debate and consensus building, and increase the accountability of public policies. (See Appendix for link.)

While there are commercial operations, notably Gallup's World Poll available on the world wide web (see Appendix for link), and many community initiatives, the measurement of societal wellbeing is being seen as something for which national statistics offices should be responsible. Across Europe, for example, national statistical offices are working together with Eurostat, the statistical office of the European Community, and OECD to deliver an ambitious and wide-ranging set of developments around measuring national wellbeing and progress.

The Istanbul Declaration put statistical offices first in the list of organisations able to take this forward. It also gives a strong steer to make the new measures official statistics:

> We affirm our commitment to measuring and fostering the progress of societies in all their dimensions and to supporting initiatives at the country level. We urge statistical offices, public and private organisations, and academic experts to work alongside representatives of their communities to produce high-quality, facts-based information that can be used by all of society to form a shared view of societal well-being and its evolution over time.
>
> Official statistics are a key 'public good' that foster the progress of societies. The development of indicators of societal progress offers an opportunity to reinforce the role of national statistical authorities as key providers of relevant, reliable, timely and comparable data and the indicators required for national and international reporting. We encourage governments to invest resources to develop reliable data and indicators according to the 'Fundamental Principles of Official Statistics' adopted by the United Nations in 1994. (See Appendix for link.)

While the UN fundamental principles are open to any organisation producing statistics to follow, the principles are the guiding light for every national statistics office. They set out high-level quality criteria for official statistics. Drawing on UN material, we can summarise the scope of the 10 principles as in Table 5.1.

Table 5.1 The fundamental principles of official statistics.

Principle 1 seeks to ensure relevance (practical utility), impartiality and equal access

Principle 2 calls for professionalism, using scientific principles and professional ethics in the collection, processing, storage and presentation of statistical data

Principle 3 addresses accountability, so that statistics producers present information according to scientific standards on the sources, methods and procedures of the statistics

Principle 4 envisages what statistical agencies should do to prevent misuse of their statistics – not only by following the principles above but also by considering the comments by statistical agencies on erroneous interpretation and misuse of statistics

Principle 5 recognises cost-effectiveness – which means choosing the source (statistical surveys or administrative records) with regard to quality, timeliness, costs and the burden on respondents

Principle 6 requires that confidentiality must be ensured if statistical operations are to be trusted – individual data collected for statistical compilation are to be strictly confidential and used exclusively for statistical purposes

Principle 7 recognises the role of relevant legislation – laws, regulations and measures under which statistical systems operated are to be made public, as part of the openness needed to maintain trust and credibility in statistical agencies and in the statistics they produce

Principle 8 is about national co-ordination – co-ordination among statistical agencies within countries is essential to achieve consistency and efficiency in the statistical system

Principle 9 describes international co-ordination – the use of international concepts, classifications and methods by statistical agencies in each country promotes the consistency and efficiency of statistical systems at all official levels

Principle 10 captures international statistical co-operation – bilateral and multilateral co-operation contributes to the improvement of systems of official statistics in all countries.

Source: UN Statistics Directorate. See Appendix for link

© United Nations 2007, reproduced with the permission of the United Nations.

These 10 principles should underpin the design, production and delivery of all official statistics and they help to shape the process of creating new statistics on national wellbeing and progress. There are many examples of how statistical agencies are seeking to ensure that the statistics will be useful, neatly summarised in an OECD strapline of better statistics for better policies for better lives. Kroll (2011, pp. 5–14) has collated examples from a number of countries, suggesting how people and organisations with an interest are able to participate in the process of developing national measures of wellbeing and progress. These include public consultations as well as steering groups and parliamentary commissions.

The UN principle of international co-ordination needs to be followed thoughtfully if a requirement for international comparability of national wellbeing is not to overwrite national requirements. The Istanbul Declaration quoted above treads this line carefully, but there still needs to be due caution in the development of international standards and guidance on this topic, so that national approaches can evolve to meet national needs, as well as support international comparisons and aggregation.

There is a connection here with how shared or common natural resources can be managed and used effectively. We should be able to learn how to develop better measures from how practical challenges have been faced in seeking better lives and sustainable use of common resources such as fresh water, ocean fish or petroleum reserves. Much of Elinor Ostrom's work, for example, was about the governance of common resources, suggesting there is no one right way to do these things, and that the best solution was for communities to develop their own approach to managing shared resources. This is a sophisticated perspective, which does not advocate only local community solutions but recognises that effective government, private and community mechanisms can be found in different settings. National policy does have a significant role, including to affect 'factors such as human migration rates, the flow of capital, technology policy, and hence the range of conditions local institutions must address to work effectively [and to …] cope with the ramifications of civil or international war'. (Ostrom *et al.*, 1999).

Does our introduction of the UN fundamental principles mean that this book should only be read by official statisticians? Certainly not! At the heart of the Istanbul Declaration, and echoed in the Stiglitz Report and elsewhere, is the aim to 'encourage communities to consider for themselves what "progress" means in the 21st century … stimulate international debate, based on solid statistical data and indicators, on both global issues of societal progress and comparisons of such progress … produce a broader, shared, public understanding of changing conditions, while highlighting areas of significant change or inadequate knowledge' (see Appendix for link to the Declaration). This is at the heart of why we have written this book: to take stock of the current debate and to highlight issues for further discussion and agreement.

If we see national statistical offices as the primary producers of national wellbeing measures, this is not to close down on measures also being produced and published by other organisations. Measures produced by other organisations, whether they draw on official statistical sources or other data, including their own research, can add to our understanding of national wellbeing and progress, including by reminding us of different perspectives. However, in order to ensure quality, the UN principles should still apply, so that, for example, sample sizes and sampling methodology are transparent.

To take just one example, British Future's State of the Nation Reports (e.g. British Future, 2013) focuses on immigration, integration and identity issues. They are published by a non-partisan think tank that is seeking 'workable solutions to make Britain the country we want to live in'. The title of their annual report promises much. It is based on some 25 questions conducted by a major opinion survey company. There are certainly many eye-catching elements, such as the survey question about whether or not Britain is heading in the right direction, which seems a relevant question to ask about the progress that a country is making. (The actual question was 'Generally speaking, would you say things in Britain are heading in the right direction or off on the wrong track?', so respondents are limited to a simple binary choice.) We are not denying that this report is a description of the state of the nation, but readers of that report might want to consider how the authors selected the questions to be included, and how the report differs from what we might consider a wider measurement of national wellbeing. We should also note that it is based on around 2500 online interviews conducted during one week in late November, and we could not find any sampling error information quoted in the report.

5.2   Towards a framework to measure the progress of societies

Some years into the current wave of interest in wider measures of progress, it was noted (e.g. by Boarini *et al.*, 2006, p. 6) that, beyond the system of national accounts and associated satellite accounts, the measurement of the wellbeing and progress of societies was lacking a coherent conceptual and statistical framework. Various indicator sets provide information that is relevant for the assessment of wellbeing. However, at that stage these were essentially descriptive exercises, bringing together and summarising (or perhaps just indicating) different aspects of wellbeing.

Reviewing the scene in 2010, Jon Hall, Enrico Giovannini, Adolfo Morrone and Giulia Ranuzzi wrote an OECD working paper (Hall *et al.*, 2010, p. 7), concluding that over the last three decades there had been a number of frameworks developed, on which to build. These frameworks were variously to promote and measure wellbeing, quality of life, human development and sustainable development. The authors presented one high-level framework for measuring the progress of societies. Their framework 'does not aim to be definitive, but rather to suggest a common starting point ... broad-based and flexible enough to be applied in many situations around the world'. They do not want to suggest that there should just be a single view of what progress is, but nevertheless to 'provide a head start to future initiatives wanting to measure the progress of a society'. The OECD itself has not adopted this framework to define and measure wellbeing in its *Better Life* Initiative (see Appendix for website link) and its *How's Life?* reports published every 2 years (e.g. OECD, 2013, 21). These reflect a conceptual framework for the 'well-being' of a given population that distinguishes between current – that is, individual wellbeing – and future wellbeing, or the sustainability of wellbeing over time.

The approach adopted by Hall *et al.*, rather than their end product, is the important thing. They draw on examples from around the world and distil them into a broad description of the many dimensions or components of societal progress. This is often the way in which international statistical standards emerge. It seems intuitive to build on existing work and available data, and expedient to minimise any adjustments needed for existing systems to conform to the new standard. Indeed, that is what the OECD has done in devising the framework for measuring wellbeing in their *Better Life* initiative. This 'attempts to operationalise the capabilities approach and to make it measurable through indicators that can be collected and used by policy-makers and National Statistical Offices to monitor well-being conditions in the population and their evolution over time' (OECD, 2013, 22). However, there are implications, such as the potential danger of 'first-mover advantage' if this shapes an emerging field to fit a particular view or available data, especially in a field as wide-ranging as the measurement of progress.

Three basic elements in the measurement of progress identified by Hall *et al.* do seem, as they say, 'incontestable' (Hall *et al.*, 2010, 9). The first is that progress is a multi-dimensional concept. It is made up of material aspects, necessary to meet basic needs, and a moral component, which aims to turn material wellbeing into happiness and a good life. We have already touched on this point several times. It is certainly the case that wellbeing and progress are generally treated as multi-dimensional concepts, apart from by those who conclude that happiness, measured as subjective wellbeing, is *the* ultimate goal and therefore the overall measure of wellbeing (e.g. Layard, 2006, p. 113).

The second element is that progress is about change. Hall *et al.* (2010, p. 10) expand on this to suggest that 'to properly assess progress one needs to look not only at the past and the present, but also to the future: any serious assessment of the current well-being of society should pay attention to what might happen to societal well-being in future given current trends, as some development paths may not be sustainable'. Although this may be 'incontestable', it does certainly lead statisticians into unfamiliar territory. Measuring the recent past is usually as far as statistical exercises go. We can only *forecast* or *predict* the future, not *measure* ahead of time how things will turn out. (All of these involve uncertainty in differing forms and extents, of course.) Some subjective wellbeing surveys do ask respondents to assess what their wellbeing will be in say 5 years' time. Question testing suggests that people captured in surveys do respond well to subjective wellbeing questions (e.g. Tinkler and Hicks, 2011, p. 13), though we have not found evidence on the reliability of questions about future wellbeing. There is some evidence that respondents make an assessment of their wellbeing more broadly than at a point in time, particularly if the questions evoke trait-like emotions (e.g. Krueger and Schkade, 2007, p. 12). Some business surveys ask companies to anticipate what sales or profits might be in future, but otherwise statisticians are firmly looking over their shoulder, at conditions in the recent past.

The third element to the measurement of progress proposed by Hall *et al.* is that progress of societies refers to the experiences of people and what they value as important for their lives and societies. The evidence that this is incontestable is covered in Section 6.5, where we mention outreach and consultation exercises being widely conducted around the measurement of progress, stimulated by the Stiglitz, Sen and Fitoussi report. We also recognise the leadership shown by the OECD in organising its series of world and regional forums and meetings. One nuance might be to think about communities as well as individual people or the whole society. Hall *et al.* conclude that communities should be evaluated 'by virtue of what they bring to the people living in them'. This is where the concept of social capital that we included in Chapter 2 may particularly have something to contribute, not least because of the understanding that we may live simultaneously in several different communities (family, locality, faith, workplace, networks of interest etc).

Hall *et al.* discuss the desirable attributes or key characteristics of frameworks to measure societal progress. Drawing on the work of Alkire and Sen, they conclude that a framework should have five characteristics (Hall *et al.*, 2010, p. 12), two of which we might describe as 'scientific' and three as more 'pragmatic'.

The first 'scientific' characteristic is that a framework should be built on solid conceptual ground. This sets the bar high because, as we have already suggested several times, concepts of national wellbeing and progress are still evolving and may vary according to different moral and political values. The essence of this characteristic is perhaps more that the conceptual basis for a framework should be explicitly described and that the framework should reflect prevailing social, economic and environmental systems.

The second 'scientific' characteristic seems to contain a large dose of pragmatism, because it starts with the assumption that the framework should include broad domains and more detailed dimensions. This is taken as given – how else can a framework or structure be built? – and is justified by the authors because frameworks for measuring societal progress are usually made up like this. There is circularity in the argument here, though it may be justified by the need to start somewhere. What is more clearly a scientific angle to the characteristic is the requirement that domains and dimensions must be 'incommensurable, irreducible, non-hierarchical and valuable'. These are sound measurement principles but there may still be room for debate over the necessity of such features in the context of a framework for measuring wellbeing and progress, especially during a transition from gross domestic product (GDP) to 'GDP and beyond'.

Turning to what we described as the more fully 'pragmatic' characteristics, we welcome the requirement that frameworks should 'not require too much precision, nor be too pre-scriptive'. This sounds like a good understanding of the need to make progress in measuring progress. But what is 'too much'? Surely we need to give more attention to what is perhaps an implicit or implied characteristic, that the framework should be built to meet understood needs, and that how the framework is to be used is clear from the outset. The need to identify and meet user requirements is recognised in OECD's subsequent work, which we will examine later in this chapter.

The second 'pragmatic' requirement is to 'focus on outcomes (or ends) rather than outputs (or means)' for the domains and dimensions. There are two reasons put forward to this: to keep the framework at the level of values or 'reasons for action', and to help with cross-national comparability through the use of broad and common values. This seems intuitively right for measuring something as high level as national wellbeing and progress. We just wonder if this sets too great a challenge for a number of potential domains where measures, if not the concept of the domain, are likely to be tethered more to outputs than to outcomes.

The treatment of public or government services in the national accounts points to the difficulty of defining and measuring outcomes directly attributable to activities such as the provision of education, health and security services. While there have been some developments in moving away from measures based on outputs, resolving these issues 'is not entirely straightforward and they are ongoing agendas' (Grice, 2011, p. 626). As Grice says, 'What is it from public services that society actually wants? In the case of schools, is it increased educational attainment that is the objective? Or is it to produce well balanced, cultured citizens that can contribute to and benefit from society as a whole? Or is it, at least in part, to provide reasonable quality childcare?' – these are questions that apply equally to the understanding of the wellbeing of a country as well as to the sound measurement of the national economic accounts.

The third pragmatic requirement for a framework for measuring societal progress suggested in the OECD working paper, and the last of the requirements suggested there, is that 'the process that leads to the development of this framework should involve consulting relevant stakeholders for greater legitimacy'. We have already touched on this, which is very much in the spirit of the Istanbul Declaration and the approach proposed in the Stiglitz, Sen and Fitoussi Report. How this requirement is met must be down to each country to decide. We can see a leadership role for national statisticians and heads of national statistical offices here, working with many people and organisations within and outside government.

Having set out the key desirable characteristics of a framework to measure the progress of societies, Hall *et al.* then present a framework. Their working paper describes how the framework came about and makes some important points about it, notably that it is not 'a model of how the world works' but is a selection of dimensions of societal progress that can be influenced by human beings and by their (our!) activities (Hall *et al.*, 2010, p. 13). The framework they present has human wellbeing as the key domain. Human wellbeing is shown as the combination of individual wellbeing, such as one's state of health, and social wellbeing, where factors such as the cohesion and resilience of society are identified: that is, human wellbeing is associated with both individual and social outcomes. In this framework, human wellbeing is supported by just three domains: the economy, culture and governance of the individuals and of society.

Hall *et al.*'s framework adopts a systems approach. Hall *et al.* consider that societies are supported by a 'human system' alongside an 'ecosystem' that services the human system, with the human system responsible for managing resources in the ecosystem. Although they describe an increase in human wellbeing as 'the final goal of progress', they conclude that societal wellbeing is 'the sum of human well-being and the ecosystem condition' (Hall *et al.*,

2010, p. 15). In coming to this representation, Hall *et al.* recognise that there is a view that subjective wellbeing should be the only thing that is important. However, we rather like their formulation that it is asking too much for subjective wellbeing assessments to reflect a full understanding of the objective state of society and the ecosystem. We know that many if not all of us are far from the rational decision makers, with access to full information, that economists assume for the workings of the market economy. It seems entirely reasonable, therefore, to at least start developing measures of societal wellbeing and progress with the assumption that subjective wellbeing measures need to be supplemented with objective measures. This may in theory introduce some overlap between the subjective and objective measures, counter to the requirement of incommensurability, but we feel that this is justified by the current state of how we humans see others and the rest of the world.

We are struck by the way in which this framework appears to avoid assuming that economic growth is the essential driver of human activity and wellbeing – what might be seen as the hegemony of GDP. The search is for ways of moving beyond GDP, and GDP itself does not feature explicitly in the framework: the economy is one component supporting human wellbeing. If the argument goes that growth is needed for investment, for example, this framework should enable that to be tested, and the full social and environmental impacts to be considered, not just the economic benefits. Setting out a framework like this also seeks to cut through what would otherwise be an ongoing debate about 'what is growth?' and enter a process to come to a consensus.

At this stage, the reader might wonder what all the fuss is about! After all, what else is there that is not captured in a framework involving human systems and the ecosystem? The point is to gain more general acceptance that this is indeed how to view wellbeing and progress. There have always been visionaries who see the 'big picture'. Beatrice Webb, for example, argued over 100 years ago that poverty is a problem of social structure and economic management, rather than a weakness of individual character (Knight, 2011, p. 11). Among contemporary examples, one would be the architect Richard Rogers, who 'believes passionately in the power of architecture to shape and change society, a conviction that guides his philosophy and practice ... fairness is the single most important guiding ethic for a healthy society' (Royal Academy of Arts, 2013).

There is, however, much to be done to develop a framework like this, if it is to be implemented in the production and use of measures of wellbeing and progress. What are the geographical boundaries around each of the human system and ecosystem spaces in the framework, for example? Should they be co-terminous, or does the human system of a country draw on, and impact, an ecosystem beyond its borders, such as the oceans?

Similarly, by including the economy, is that the domestic economy (all economic activity within the borders) or the economy that gives rise to the national income of the country (which takes into account income from assets held outside the country, and flows of income to owners abroad of domestic businesses and other assets). There is a balance to be stuck between getting an agreed, workable framework with producing and using new measures of wellbeing and progress. Many new measures are now being produced. It is unrealistic to put them on hold until the framework is more fully developed. Indeed, the emerging measures are already highlighting the relevant issues and offering insights on how to resolve them. We are reminded of the length of time that has been needed to produce and update the manuals of the system of national accounts. Working collaboratively, we anticipate much effort will be made over coming years to produce a manual of economic, social and environmental accounts, to underpin the publication and use of measures of wellbeing and progress.

If we have one criticism of Hall *et al.*'s framework it is that it is derived primarily from the views of experts, rather than grounded in what matters to people. This is not to deride expert views (nor to suggest that they are not aware of what matters) but simply to encourage full interaction with politicians, the media, civil society, individuals and special interest groups, all of whom have a stake in how progress is defined and measured. This is something we will pick up in the discussion of process, in Section 5.3.

Hall *et al.* add two other aspects to their framework: their intention is to recognise in the measurement framework how each of these domains is distributed across and within societies and geographical regions (equity) and between generations (sustainability). This leads to their final definition of societal progress as 'an improvement in the sustainable and equitable well-being of society' (Hall *et al.*, 2010, p. 15). Drilling down into each component of the proposed framework, Hall *et al.* list 26 'dimensions of progress' (Hall *et al.*, 2010, Box 3, p. 17). Some of these are grouped into 'final goals', such as the condition of the atmosphere and human freedom and self-determination and 'intermediate goals' (e.g. national income, national wealth, human rights and cultural heritage). Other dimensions relate to the links between the human system and the ecosystem and to the cross-cutting dimensions of equity and sustainability. There is little explanation of these dimensions or how they were derived, other than that they resulted from an analysis of work 'from around the world'. As high-level concepts to cover wellbeing and progress, there is little if anything that appears to be missing.

The final section of the OECD working paper gives a flavour of the sources they have used for the proposed framework and its dimensions, and how these compare to other frameworks. The sources are as follows (we discussed the first six of these in Chapters 2 to 4 and we will look further at specific national developments in Chapters 6 and 7):

- Maslow's Hierarchy of Needs

- Capability approach

- Sustainable development

- Gross National Happiness (Bhutan)

- National Accounts of Wellbeing (NEF)

- Stiglitz, Sen and Fitoussi Commission

- National initiatives in Australia, Canada, Ireland and Hungary.

The authors acknowledge that the fit is not perfect, indeed how could it be with already so many different sources on which to draw. We are reassured, nevertheless, that they conclude that there is 'a considerable degree of overlap in how the different initiatives view progress and well-being' and we compliment the authors especially on presenting a set of guiding principles for work nationally, locally and internationally from now on, as well as for proposing one framework by which to measure the progress of societies.

For the wellbeing conceptual framework that the OECD actually adopted, individual wellbeing is defined through eight quality-of-life domains (including health status, environmental quality and subjective wellbeing) and three domains for material conditions (income and wealth, jobs and earnings, housing conditions). These are to be measured using specific indicators, presented as population averages and differences across population subgroups.

The 11 domains or dimensions of current wellbeing are considered by the OECD to be 'universal, i.e. as relevant to people living in all societies'. The OECD recognises that the relative importance of dimensions may 'vary between individual and countries' and that countries 'may adjust this framework to better reflect the well-being of their population', including by adding dimensions. 'More importantly', as the OECD says, 'the selection of indicators used to reflect achievements in these dimensions may also differ to reflect specific country conditions, history and challenges'. So the intention is that the framework should not constrain national initiatives but provide 'a benchmark for meaningful international comparisons' (OECD, 2013, pp. 23–24). The assessment of future wellbeing in the OECD framework requires the measurement of four types of capital (natural, economic, human and social). A separate, complementary dashboard of indicators is being developed in conjunction with an international task force for measuring sustainable development (OECD, 2013, pp. 175–6).

But as we noted in the previous chapter, the devil is in the detail! Whatever framework is adopted by a country or international organisation, there is much to do to produce specific measures or indicators of wellbeing that will turn the conceptual framework into statistical information to meet user needs and gain the trust of stakeholders.

We will look further in the following section and in the next chapter at how any framework can be operationalised, considering the process and the selection of measures respectively. We will also look at how the United Kingdom is approaching this in Chapter 7. However, we can already see a number of challenges faced by many approaches to the measurement of progress. For example, the authors of the OECD working paper refer to 'an improvement' in something defined in a number of domains. What is the logic to be applied in reaching an overall assessment based on all the available information? Is there no improvement unless every domain improves (or at least human wellbeing and the ecosystem condition both improve)? How do we square changes in distributions with changes in the overall or average position? And as flagged previously, how can we assess the sustainability of the activities of the current generation ahead of seeing how things turn out for the next generation?

One way to answer the latter question could be to focus attention on the state of various stocks or assets, rather than base our thinking on flows of resources or transactions. The dimensions of progress proposed in the OECD working paper are a mix of flows and stocks; the OECD *Better Life* framework turns to stocks as the sole basis for assessing future wellbeing, which they separate from current wellbeing. That echoes Stiglitz *et al.* (2010, 19), who emphasise that the assessment of sustainability 'must be examined separately' from the question of current wellbeing. But why the distinction? It strikes us that one way of assessing national wellbeing would be to examine the state of all stocks and assets, including how they are held, or accessed, by different groups in the population. This would provide one way of producing a picture of how a country is doing.

It is not, however, a way that commends itself to Stiglitz *et al.* or to the OECD, and we respect their view that capital stocks are not aspects of wellbeing, but the means to sustain wellbeing in the future. This leads them to specify separate scoreboards for sustainability and for assessing wellbeing at a given point in time. Perhaps this is only semantics. It is commonly accepted that sustainability and inequalities can bring in different perspectives from those identified by focussing on personal wellbeing, especially if personal wellbeing is driven by self-interest. But to take a broader view, the things that matter can only be gleaned by what people say matters to them, whether they are thinking about their individual wellbeing or are acting in some community, entrepreneurial or governmental role in which they might give more weight to distributions and sustainability. Conceptually, therefore, it is important that the same dimensions of wellbeing and progress are used to assess both person and national wellbeing.

The distinction between stocks and flows is crucial in the national economic accounts, reflecting, of course, a distinction equally important in everyday life. Headline measures such as GDP are measures of flows and transactions, summarising economic activity within a given period like a year or a quarter. These activities result in additions to, or reductions in, the stock of various assets associated with the national accounts. Household wealth, for example, is usually considered to comprise property, goods and financial assets including pensions. Wealth is not the same as income and, although there is likely to be a correlation between the two, there can be occasions when there are marked differences, such as when sources of income are reduced despite having wealth, which may be difficult to release.

When Adam Smith wrote his economic treatise he referred to the wealth of nations, suggesting that wealth was the goal of his work and of economic activity generally. More recently, the EU's Beyond GDP initiative, seeking wider measures of progress, is described as 'measuring progress, **true wealth**, and the well-being of nations' (our emphasis, see Appendix for website link).

As we saw in Chapter 3, Stiglitz *et al.* (2010, p. 19) recommend a 'well-identified dashboard of indicators' for sustainability assessment. The indicators to be chosen for this purpose, they recommend, should be 'interpretable as variations of some underlying stocks'. So, while they start from stocks, the indicators that are likely to be most useful are those that look at changes in stocks and can act as warning lights.

This suggests that 'leading' indicators would be particularly helpful, that is indicators chosen because they have a good track record of anticipating when current patterns of growth are becoming unsustainable, so that corrective action can be taken. This is probably going to be more difficult than it sounds. To take just one issue, we suspect that depletion of natural resources is invariably measured from the point when concerns are raised, not from a baseline of abundance. While the analogy of a car dashboard, used in the Stiglitz report, is useful in a number of ways, we humans know rather more about the workings of a car engine than we do about planet Earth, so the prospect of constructing a dashboard for assessing sustainability is challenging.

In the development of the economics of sustainable development, considerable attention has been given to how the total capital stock (human-made or physical capital, natural capital and human capital) supports human welfare. An early lesson was that this is not just through the traditional economic process, the production of goods and services, but in other ways as well. Pearce and Barbier (2000, p. 20) identify these as the built heritage, aesthetics and life support, and human knowledge. While Ostrom's framework for analysing social-ecological systems identifies the transactions that occur, its core subsystems and settings are described in terms of resources and their characteristics, which is another way of thinking of stocks and capitals (Ostrom, 2009, p. 420).

Stocks may be difficult to conceptualise and to quantify. However, the idea of preserving and even enhancing stocks and capitals does appear to resonate with the public and with policy-makers. We will look further at stocks and capitals in the following chapter, so just a couple of examples here. First, we see that the British countryside is often described as 'our greatest natural asset', although we are not sure what 'greatest' means here. Second, there is considerable support for various 'public things', be they forests, libraries or cultural heritage sites, whether or not people regularly (or ever) visit them. These and other examples suggest to us that the assessment of wellbeing and progress overall, not just in terms of sustainability, may well be informed by focussing on the total capital stock.

Turning from sustainability to the other cross-cutting perspective, concerned with equity and inequality, the authors of the OECD working paper explain that this depends 'on the way which the various items that shape people's lives are distributed in society' (Hall *et al.*, 2010, p. 15). Statisticians are used to thinking in terms of the underlying distributions of attributes and variables, not just summary measures such as averages. Distributions are often summarised by comparing the 10 deciles in any population (think of organising the population in order of the variable of interest and counting off into 10, equally sized sub-groups).

As well as assessing equity and inequality by comparing wellbeing and progress between different groups in the population, we may also be interested in how specific groups are managing in their own right. In all of this, it seems simplest to start from the assumption that frameworks for population subgroups should simply mirror whatever we develop for society as a whole. This should help maintain comparability as well as deliver efficiency.

One sub-group that may need additional attention in the content of measures and in the process of compiling them is children and young people. We expect different levels of care to apply and we might envisage that children are not engaged in paid employment, for example. Appropriate ways are also needed to give children a voice. UNICEF, the United Nations Children's Fund, and many national agencies are exploring the state of wellbeing of children and young people. A series of report cards produced by the UNICEF Office of Research provides a comprehensive assessment of child wellbeing in 29 nations of the industrialized world (member countries of the OECD). The 2013 report was accompanied by an online interactive version, providing a visual representation of the latest data and key findings (see Appendix for link).

One signal of the importance of involving children themselves in the process is given by Rys Farthing (2012, p. 1), who suggests that involving young people in policy production might lead to quite different approaches from those included in official strategies. In research on child poverty, many issues repeatedly identified by young people were not mentioned at all in their government's child poverty strategy. Conversely, issues heavily cited by the government did not even rate a mention among young people. There were remarkably few places where both young people and the government agreed on policy directions. This research shows that young people have very distinct opinions about child poverty policy, rooted in their lived experiences, and that they can – and want to – take part in designing policy responses.

Measuring children's wellbeing is an important and growing field, supporting debate, research and action into what makes a good childhood. Minujin and Nandy (2012), for example, review concepts, measurement, policy and action, including on the link between wellbeing and child poverty. Rees *et al.* (2010) report on developing an index of children's subjective wellbeing in England.

5.3   Constructing measures of progress and national wellbeing: Identifying and meeting user requirements

As well as their framework working paper, the OECD Statistics Directorate has also published a working paper that is a practical guide to developing societal progress indicators (Trewin and Hall, 2010), on which we are pleased to base this section. The paper had previously been proposed as a handbook to measuring societal wellbeing and progress, which would have been an adventurous and ambitious undertaking. The idea of a practical guide fits much better with the present state of play in the development of societal progress indicators. It fits well with the idea that measuring national wellbeing is a process, and it suggests six steps to take to make such a process as effective as possible.

There are many initiatives already underway around the world and it may well be that they are following a process like the one we will review. In which case, we would value hearing of your experiences. We also hope that this section will point others to what we believe is helpful and actionable guidance.

Capturing user requirements for a new set of official or public statistics is always challenging (and it is no easier to determine who uses an existing set of statistics, and how they use them). There are some specific requirements, such as needing statistics about the population, to help plan and deliver education and healthcare services. These may be relatively straightforward to identify and the temptation is to see such requirements as the bedrock and main component of the user requirement. Another example of this is where legislation requires certain statistics to be produced. However, beyond such uses there are many and diverse uses and potential applications of a set of statistics. When national statistical offices seek to reach to the user community, they need to be aware that there are in reality many different communities of interest. As we discussed in Chapter 3, the media plays a major role as an intermediary to the public or, in effect, acting as the public user of statistics.

Politics are an added dimension when it comes to specifying the user requirement for measures of national wellbeing and progress. These statistics will be used in the political arena, so it is important that the measures are designed to be used by all political parties and movements, otherwise the measures will be dismissed as partisan or biased. For example, when a Prime Minister says, 'we'll start measuring our progress as a country, not just by how our economy is growing, but by how our lives are improving; not just by our standard of living, but by our quality of life' (see Chapter 7), then the national statistical office concerned must provide statistics that both meet this requirement and address the other issues that matter to people and have a bearing on their wellbeing and progress, such as the state of the environment.

To get a feel for the breadth of the things that matter to people, just turn to news media reports to see the social and environmental issues frequently bought into discussion of economic growth and the state of an economy. Unemployment, poverty, inequality (not just in income but in life chances), educational attainment, social exclusion, depression, despair and other mental health problems all feature in our daily newspapers and online reports. Any framework for measuring wellbeing and progress should allow issues like this to be identified. The development of national systems should start from a user requirement reflecting the issues of concern in the country.

In discussing how individuals and organisations are working together to create a sustainable world, Senge *et al.* (2008, p. 255) also look at how people use data, along with their own experiences, to reach conclusions and, subsequently, to change those conclusions. The authors describe how we might start by selecting from the available (or observable) data and experiences before adding meanings, making assumptions and drawing conclusions, on which we may or not act. They describe something that is far from an objective or scientific process for most people and reflects the very recognisable, subjective way in which many of us see the world. Our beliefs can affect what data we select, for example, but we are also capable of adapting those beliefs in light of new data. We can suspend our assumptions and seek more data to check something out, or we can seize on data that confirm our view. The message to take from this in designing measures of national wellbeing and progress is to recognise the way people see things, rather than seek to identify the way things are. If, say, a national statistical office sets off to assess the way things are, the result will be a set of statistics describing the way the national statistical office sees things.

Step 1: Defining the issues: what matters most to a society

Our guides, Trewin and Hall (2010, p. 9), see the production of 'a clear framework mapping out the territory one is seeking to measure' as the first step towards being able to answer questions such as 'how is the nation doing?' and 'are we making progress as a society?' They rightly suggest we need to know what matters most to a society in order to build the framework. They observe that such frameworks can use a conceptual approach, and are 'derived from a particular view of what progress means' or can use a consultative approach, 'in which the components are selected through discussion and agreement'. Their paper gives further guidance on the consultative approach under the next step.

Discussions about 'what matters' are taking place in many different contexts, only some of which are in exercises with the declared purpose of defining new measures of national wellbeing and progress. For example, we have heard people from Africa talking of their efforts to reconnect with what their country meant to them before they were under colonial rule. In such cases the dialogue may be about 'how to be ourselves', to be self-confident and to trust in the ability of citizens to build the country and the continent.

It might also be argued that 'what matters' is inevitably hammered out during a parliamentary or local election (or, indeed, in a revolution). We have certainly seen some evidence of this in the form of policy statements from political parties and their leaders (e.g. see some UK examples in Chapter 7). Such political ideals may well shape the overall vision for what wellbeing and progress means in a country, but we suspect that more detailed work will inevitably be needed to move from this to a fuller and actionable specification based on 'what matters' to the population at large.

We strongly encourage as much consultation as possible. We have been involved with the UK measuring national wellbeing programme (see Chapter 7) and we see that as an exemplar in consultation that could be followed and adapted elsewhere. (We have mentioned this several times already, including how it chimes with Stiglitz, Sen and Fitoussi's encouragement of global debate and national roundtables to discuss and prioritise societal values.) Clearly the OECD is also doing much to encourage debate. What is slightly more problematic is when we move on from Step 1 and start producing and using new measures of wellbeing and progress. It is not clear how this happens, perhaps through some 'big bang', or by reaching a tipping point, or as a more gradual evolution from GDP to 'GDP and beyond'. There could be more than one iteration through the six steps discussed here, in order to refine the framework, the measures and how they are used. The downside to that, of course, is that the process is extended, becomes more costly and results in a longer period of uncertainty over how we are measuring wellbeing and progress if not through GDP.

One of the complicating factors is the issue of international comparability. Much of what is written about measuring progress is in terms of the needs of a country, its citizens, communities, businesses and government. However, these needs may include a requirement to compare the country with others. International organisations have obvious needs for cross-national comparability, including seeing the overall position. Trewin and Hall point out that 'it is unlikely that any international initiative will include all aspects that are important to any one country' (2010, p. 10). This means we could end up with many views of the wellbeing of a particular nation – the nationally derived measure, the assessments made by other nations according to their own criteria of what matters and what international organisations come up with, using criteria that are common across nations.

Although an initial framework is drawn up under this step, it is only the first step in the process.

Step 2: Identifying possible partners, consultation and collaboration

Trewin and Hall emphasise the importance of consultation, the second step in the process. It is 'a vital prerequisite for a successful initiative on measuring progress'. We could not agree more, as will be apparent from our comments about consultation above, in putting Step 1 into practice. In this section of the paper, Trewin and Hall say more about this and, most importantly, they point to lessons that have been learned in OECD and in member states about the pace of collaboration and consultation, and interaction between stakeholders. There is a balance to be struck – and it will vary in different times and in different places – between taking time (and money) to consult and coming to decisions. Although the literature often talks of reaching agreement, this might be more about acceptance then full agreement. Transparency is a powerful tool in keeping stakeholders on board.

Step 3: Producing an initial set of indicators

A framework tells us nothing about the wellbeing and progress of a society, only about the aspects we need to get some data for. Each framework needs to be put into operation, invariably by the selection of a set of indicators. Trewin and Hall (2010, p. 15) suggest several stages to be followed within this step of producing a set of indicators and they illustrate problems that commonly arise in selecting indicators. They point to two criteria that should help decide which indicators to include: seek indicators that focus on outcomes, and choose only indicators that can unambiguously be associated with progress. Trewin and Hall also discuss the pros and cons of selecting indicators to enable comparisons between regions and nations.

We think it is also worth considering the provenance of indicators to be in scope for measuring wellbeing and progress. While there is much to commend the fundamental principles of official statistics, we suggest it would be counter-productive to draw from this that national statistical offices should be the only producers of the indicators to be used for measures of wellbeing and progress. We would certainly want national statistical offices to be the places where these measures are accessible by anyone, and that the measures should draw on the official data wherever possible, both to allow the credibility of the data to be examined and to recognise that national statistical offices generally have a large store of data, collected at public expense, that should be used as fully as possible. We have in mind, then, the idea that what is needed to measure national wellbeing and progress is a set of public statistics, which should draw on national statistical offices' own data and the data of other organisations where this fills a gap without compromising the quality standards set by the fundamental principles.

This step is about producing an initial set of indicators first time round the course. The aim, of course, is to gain feedback on that set and refine it where necessary in any subsequent iteration of the six steps.

Trewin and Hall (2010, p. 18) discuss the problem of summarising different aspects of one dimension of progress using just one indicator (and indeed they offer the suggestion of summarising each dimension using one or two indicators). They are silent on whether or not to produce a single overall measure of well-being, and hence a single overall measure of progress. Similarly, the framework proposed by OECD is designed not to produce a single measure. This may well be right, conceptually, but it leaves open two issues: the need for a single overall measure for effective communication, and if more than one measure is needed, how to keep the headline indicators to a manageable number.

As Fender *et al.* (2011, p. 8) note, when wellbeing is being measured in non-monetary terms, the most common way of producing an aggregate measure is to construct a synthetic index: 'Synthetic indices are typically constructed as weighted averages of summary measures of economic or social performance in various domains. Weighting allows many domains to be expressed within a single indicator.' (One of the challenging details, of course, is to make meaningful aggregations of domains with separate and distinct units of measurement, the well-known 'apples and pears' problem.) We saw in Chapter 2 that many such indices have been produced and we will look at some more in Chapter 6.

Synthetic indices appear mainly to be used because they are perceived to have presentational advantages: they allow easy comparison over time and between areas. Fender *et al.* reckon that one of the reasons for the wide use of GDP both with the public and policymakers is that 'it allows the whole economy to be described by a single number' (2011, p. 9). This sets a standard for any measure going beyond GDP. With its Better Life Index, the OECD invites users to select the weight to be applied to each dimension, to give an overall score. This also demonstrates that a synthetic index, and any ranking of such an index for different countries, is highly dependent on the weightings applied to the different selected domains. Without such transparency and flexibility, Fender *et al.* warn that 'weightings are subjective and depend on the choices of those who create the index meaning the index is open to abuse and manipulation. This lack of robustness of weightings applied in synthetic indices is a major problem' (2011, p. 9).

If more than one measure is adopted, then we are in the territory described by Stiglitz *et al.* (2010, p. 19) and others, as 'a well-identified dashboard of indicators'. The primary concerns in populating the dashboard with indicators will be about the validity and relevance of the chosen indicators, following criteria such as those outlined above. However, from a presentational point of view, the number of headline indicators is also a factor. Common sense suggests seeking parsimony, so keep the number of indicators small enough for people to absorb in a single reading; otherwise the dashboard becomes a repository of information that people have to browse or find their way through.

More specifically, we are drawn to George A. Miller's work of the mid-1950s, partially reprinted in the 1990s, concluding that humans 'possess a finite and rather small capacity' for making uni-dimensional judgements, with 'small', here meaning seven, plus or minus two, pieces of information (Miller, 1994, p. 345). That research was about distinguishing sound tones, loudness or various visual attributes, each one the single dimension that Miller refers to. However, it seems appropriate to consider any potential dashboard as a single 'dimension' or set of measures (although we know each measure is a separate dimension) because that is what the user would face. Further support for keeping the number of headline measures to a small number might come from our understanding that, despite the complexity of an aircraft cockpit, there is a 'big five' set of flight instruments that pilots need constantly to monitor.

Step 4: Communication – getting the information 'out there'

We sincerely hope that national statistics offices and other statistical producers are now well aware of the importance of communicating their data and findings, rather than devoting all their efforts to publishing their outputs. This is certainly addressed in the UN's fundamental principles shown in Section 5.1, and there is much evidence (e.g. see the websites in the Appendix) that initiatives to build better measures of wellbeing and progress are being communicated through innovative and effective channels. The OECD's world forums have also provided an opportunity to showcase communication tools. Trewin and Hall (2010, p. 26) set out some basic principles, including to design an effective strategy for communicating and disseminating new measures of wellbeing and progress.

We note that one of their examples is of communicating with business leaders. We see this as important not just to spread the word about new measures of wellbeing and progress but also to actively encourage major companies and organisations to extend their own reporting to embrace the kind of economic, social and environmental accounts envisaged by the UN High Level Panel (see Chapter 3).

Trewin and Hall (2010, p. 30) give the example of a fictional radio news broadcast in which the Canadian Index of Wellbeing (CIW) is reported as if it was *the* measure of wellbeing and progress of that country. Key economic, environmental, societal and health indicators are presented and discussed, giving a rounded picture of the state of the nation. We do know that the CIW is reported by the media, although this is in reality just one of many media reports of published statistics each year, including those from Statistics Canada, responsible for the Canadian national economic accounts and GDP. Our point is that much needs to be done in terms not only of how the CIW is reported but also how all other relevant headline statistics, notably GDP, are presented. Getting the information on wellbeing and progress 'out there' is something that has to be managed in a coherent way across the statistical outputs of each country and not just left to the compilers of national wellbeing measures.

Step 5: Building knowledge with the indicators

As with the previous step, we would like to take it as given that nowadays statistical outputs are accompanied with helpful analysis and interpretation. We know there are tensions here, as Trewin and Hall (2010, 31) acknowledge, especially to avoid damaging the impartiality that is so important for national statistics offices to maintain. The OECD authors suggest five questions that could be asked of each indicator of wellbeing and progress, as a checklist for better statistical 'story telling'. As several national and international statistical offices are also finding, interactive online graphics and tools can be particularly effective both in communicating the 'big picture' and in providing a structured way of drilling down for more detail.

Step 6: Ensuring continuity and relevance

Trewin and Hall include this step to recognise that there may well need to be 'a continuous revisiting and adaptation of the previous five steps' (2010, p. 39). They recognise a number of interlinked issues: enabling long-term trends to be measured while keeping the selection of indicators relevant to current requirements; adequate resources for building, maintaining and developing systems and processes to deliver measures of wellbeing and progress; continued stakeholder engagement; and adapting to developments in communication and presentation.

5.4 Commentary

We are in no doubt that the practical guidance offered in the OECD working paper is sound, useful and grounded in experience of measuring national wellbeing and progress. In their final comments, Trewin and Hall (2010, p. 40) conclude that 'There is no single right way to run an indicator project' to measure the progress of a given society. Many countries are already a considerable way down the path of publishing wider measures of wellbeing and progress, as well as their national accounts and headline GDP statistics. We reported in Section 5.2 that the OECD's *Better Life* initiative delivers regular *How's Life?* reports, which are accompanied by a much-used, interactive index on their website, although OECD also points out that their indicators 'should be understood as being experimental and evolutionary' (OECD, 2013, p. 24). This then begs the question, how should all this work be taken forward, embracing national and local initiatives, as well as the international programmes of work?

There is clearly a role for international organisations and there is much evidence that they are taking this forward, encouraging and leading their member states, as well as supporting them through guidelines and fostering the exchange of good practice. Only by considerable international collaboration, as envisaged in the fundamental principles of official statistics, will new measures of wellbeing and progress be suitable for comparisons between countries and aggregation over regions of the world. Collaboration freely and openly conducted also allows for difficult conceptual and practical issues to be solved more effectively, drawing on a wider range of experience and expertise.

Compared with the system of national economic accounts, any system of internationally based, national wellbeing accounts is still in its infancy. The framework proposed by Hall *et al.* and discussed in Section 5.2 wants for more structure, clarity and definition. For example, we anticipate the need for a common boundary within which societal, economic and ecosystems are measured, in the way that a production boundary is defined for the economic accounts. Topics such as this will certainly benefit from international discussion and agreement, so that the boundary for each country's accounts fits with those of other countries.

Several cross-national processes appear to be running. This may result in a richer set of developments, but we are also concerned that it could lead to duplication of effort and potential conflicts in approaches, both internationally and within countries. The current processes we particularly have in mind are the OECD's long-standing work on measuring progress and the processes now in play to agree what should replace the current set of Millennium Development Goals, when the deadline for those goals is reached in 2015.

We recognise that the OECD's work on measuring progress is evolutionary because, for example, it is punctuated with regular world forums, where topics of great and mutual interest are explored and national developments reported on. The OECD's work, including the recommendations of the Stiglitz, Sen and Fitoussi Commission which we link to the OECD process through ongoing High Level Expert Group (see Chapter 3), is being carried forward by world regional statistical bodies, such as Eurostat, as well as by national statistical offices. However, there is a distinction between current and future wellbeing in the OECD work that we understand, but still find somewhat concerning. This is, to reiterate, because we are not convinced of the separation between current wellbeing and future wellbeing.

It is not only in the OECD that there is parallel working. At the time of writing, in 2013, we understand that there are two separate UN processes working on post-2015. One process was initiated at the 2010 Millennium Development Goals summit and is concerned with the global development agenda beyond 2015. The first tangible output from that process is the High Level Panel Report we discussed in Chapter 3. The other UN process was initiated in the 2012 Rio+20 Conference on Sustainable Development and is concerned with sustainable development goals (see Appendix for website). We gather there is broad agreement that the two processes for sustainable development goals and the post-2015 development agenda should be closely linked and should ultimately converge in one global development agenda beyond 2015 with sustainable development at its core.

From what we have seen, UN processes are extremely thorough in their involvement of all UN agencies and in supporting the process with much technical coordination. Member states oversee the process and have the opportunity to participate in a number of work streams. However, we need always to remember that the capacity for many countries to meet the data requirements for the existing Millennium Development Goals is limited. Alongside, and ideally in advance of, work on new measures of wellbeing, progress and sustainable development, there needs to be statistical capacity building, for example, as proposed in the Busan action plan (see Appendix for website link). Measures that assume a household survey large enough to collect data on all relevant dimensions, for example, will raise many and different challenges from those that are based on existing indicators or administrative data.

Does it matter that there is more than one international process in play? We can see pros and cons in the current situation. An obvious advantage is that there is much to do; so the more people involved, the better the solutions are likely to be. There are many different players, each with their own interests, angles and expertise, with varying degrees of overlap. On the other hand, we are concerned that a proliferation of activities might allow the 'Friends of GDP' to say that GDP should continue to be the way to measure wellbeing and progress, at least until there is a consensus on how to move beyond just GDP. However, our main concern is with the pressures on national statistical offices when they have to engage with multiple initiatives, especially in countries where there is much need for improvement in statistical capacity and capability.

We are reminded of traditional organisational charts, where delivery units form the bottom row. Above them, in a sharply reducing pyramid of a tree, are the supervisory, management and leadership positions. What is sometimes described as the international statistical system, comprising the United Nations Statistics Division, a number of world regional and other international organisations and national statistical offices, is far from a single organisation. However, it is sometimes seen as following the traditional hierarchical structure. Whenit comes to working together on measures of progress, we would prefer to see national statistical offices treated as the top tier in the organisation, supported by regional and global statistical agencies and standards, to help get the right balance between national and cross-national needs.

Despite all the activity on the producer side, we are left with concerns that the use of societal progress indicators and measures has yet to gain momentum. There is a lack of progress in recognising progress and development as anything other than something spearheaded by strong and sustained GDP growth. Part of the reason for this may well be an inevitable lag between intention and reality: new indicators take time to develop and to enter political and policy debate, let alone everyday conversations.

It is also worth considering the pace at which new measures should be developed and introduced. Professor Daniel Kahneman is a behavioural economist who has long worked on measures of subjective wellbeing. He is one of the advisors to the UK National Statistician on the measuring national wellbeing programme. After hearing him give a lecture at the London School of Economics on his book *Thinking, fast and slow* (Kahneman, 2011), we asked him whether a programme to develop measures of national wellbeing should be done fast or slow. The tension is between managing experimental work in what is still an emerging science against the understandable interest of users in getting to grips with the data and starting to build time series, longitudinal and other models in which continuity will be essential. Kahneman was inclined to advise 'slow and reversible'. He noted that 'the costs of premature decisions in surveys are enormous. The unquestionable merits of consistency and the need to observe trends encourage conservatism and cause mistakes to be perpetuated'. Set against this, 'the appetite of sponsors for results, including trends, makes it difficult to follow this precept and the constraints of budgets and sample sizes constrain the ability to experiment' (personal communication, 2011). We endorse his advice that experimentation should be retained for as long as possible and we note that the UK work is still described on the Office for National Statistics (ONS) website as a 'long term statistical development programme'.

This all presents a real challenge to national statistical offices and others, to reach out and engage with everyone with an interest in the wellbeing and progress of society, in order to make the development of new measures as effective as possible. The process to develop societal progress indictors proposed by the OECD and reviewed in this chapter encourages those producing new measures to consult and collaborate widely with potential users. We cannot emphasis strongly enough the importance of this. Such consultation must seek to engage everyone with a stake in the new measures. Without wanting to sound too grandiose, it seems to us, and to many others, that we all have a stake in how our nations develop and progress, so the new measures need to be developed in ways that enter public and political life.

As we write these words in the autumn of 2013, UK political parties are holding their annual conferences. They are being held against a backdrop of a government already committed to economic growth and a fairer, more decent society. One of the coalition parties in government tells its party members, and the public more generally, that it is the party to deliver a stronger economy and a fairer society. We are not sure exactly which comparisons are being made by 'stronger' and 'fairer', presumably than the conditions that currently prevail. However, we note that at least one of the domains (the economy) and one of the cross-cutting themes (equity) in the OECD framework are featured in this particular political vision, so perhaps our pessimism should be tempered.

References

Abdallah S., Mahony S., Marks N. *et al.* (2011) *Measuring Our Progress: The Power of Well-Being.* New Economics Foundation, London.

Atkin R. (1981) *Multidimensional Man: Can Man Live in 3-Dimensional Space?* Penguin Books, Harmondsworth.

Boarini R., Johansson A. and d'Ercole M.M. (2006) *Alternative Measures of Well-Being*, DELSA/ELSA/WD/SEM(2006)2 http://dx.doi.org/10.1787/713222332167 (accessed 26 November 2013).

British Future (2013) *State of the Nation: Where Is Bittersweet Britain heading?* http://www. britishfuture.org/wp-content/uploads/2013/01/State-of-the-Nation-2013.pdf (accessed 13 September 2013).

Deaton A. (2013) *The Great Escape: Health, Wealth, and the Origins of Inequality.* Princeton University Press, Princeton.

Farthing R. (2012) *Young People's Thoughts on Child Poverty Policy.* Child Poverty Action Group and Webb Memorial Trust, http://www.cpag.org.uk/content/young-peoples-thoughts-child-poverty-policy (accessed 16 September 2013).

Fender V., Haynes J. and Jones R. (2011) *Measuring Economic Well-being.* Office for National Statistics at http://www.ons.gov.uk/ons/guide-method/user-guidance/well-being/publications/previous-publications/index.html (accessed 29 July 2013).

Grice J. (2011) National accounts, wellbeing, and the performance of government. *Oxford Review of Economic Policy*, **27**(4), 620–633.

Hall J., Giovannini E., Morrone A. and Ranuzzi G. (2010) *A Framework to Measure the Progress of Societies, OECD Statistics Directorate Working Paper No. 34, STD/DOC(2010)5*, http://search. oecd.org/officialdocuments/displaydocumentpdf/?cote=std/doc(2010)5&docLanguage=En (accessed 26 November 2013).

Heath J. (2010) *Sacred Circles: Prehistoric Stone Circles of Wales.* Llygad Gwulch, Pwllheli.

Kahneman D. (2011) *Thinking, Fast and Slow.* Allen Lane, London.

Knight B. (2011) Introduction. In: B. Knight (ed.) *A Minority View: What Beatrice Webb Would Say Now*, Webb Memorial Trust series on poverty, vol. **1**. Alliance Publishing Trust, London, pp. 9–20.

Kroll C. (2011) *Measuring Progress and Well-being: Achievements and Challenges of a New Global Movement.* Friedrich-Ebert-Stiftung, International Policy Analysis, Berlin. http://library.fes.de/pdf-files/id/ipa/08509.pdf (accessed 28 November 2013).

Krueger A.B. and Schkade D.A. (2007) *The Reliability of Subjective Well-Being Measures.* http://dataspace.princeton.edu/jspui/bitstream/88435/dsp01d217qp50q/1/516.pdf (accessed 13 September 2013).

Layard R. (2006) *Happiness: Lessons from a New Science.* Penguin Books, London.

Miller G.A. (1994) The magical number seven, plus or minus two. Some limits on our capacity for processing information. *Psychological Review*, **101**(2), 343–352.

Minujin A. and Nandy S. (2012) *Global Child Poverty and Well-being: Measurement, Concepts, Policy and Action.* The Policy Press, Bristol.

OECD (2013) *How's Life? 2013: Measuring Well-being.* OECD Publishing. http://dx.doi.org/10.1787/9789264201392-en (accessed 2 December 2013).

Ostrom E. (2009) A General Framework for Analyzing Sustainability of Social-Ecological Systems. *Science*, **325**, 24 July 2009, 419–422. doi:10.1126/science.1172133

Ostrom E., Burger J., Field C.B., Norgaard R.B. and Policansky D. (1999) Revisiting the commons: local lessons, global challenges. *Science*, 9 April 1999, **284** (5412), 278–282. doi:10.1126/science.284.5412.278

Pearce D. and Barbier E.B. (2000) *Blueprint for a Sustainable Economy.* Earthscan, London.

Rees G., Goswami H. and Bradshaw J. (2010) *Developing an Index of Children's Subjective Well-being in England.* The Children's Society, London.

Royal Academy of Arts (2013) *Richard Rogers RA, Inside Out, Gallery Guide*, Royal Academy of Arts, London.

Runciman W.G. (2010) *Great books, Bad Arguments: Republic, Leviathan, and The Communist Manifesto.* Princeton University Press, Princeton.

Senge P., Smith B., Kruschwitz N., Laur J. and Schley S. (2008) *The Necessary Revolution*. Nicholas Brealey Publishing, London.

Stiglitz J.E., Sen S. and Fitoussi J-P. (2010) *Mismeasuring Our Lives: Why GDP Doesn't Add Up*. The New Press, New York.

Tinkler L. and Hicks S. (2011) *Measuring Subjective Well-being*. Supplementary paper to the National Statistician's Reflections on the National Debate on Measuring National Well-being, at http://www.ons.gov.uk/ons/guide-method/user-guidance/well-being/publications/previous-publications/index.html (accessed 13 September 2013).

Trewin D. and Hall J. (2010) *Developing Societal Progress Indicators: A Practical Guide*, *OECD Statistics Working Papers*, No. 2010/06, OECD Publishing. doi:10.1787/5kghzxp6k7g0-en

6

How to measure national wellbeing?

> a man who knows the price of everything and the value of nothing.
>
> Oscar Wilde (*Lady Windermere's Fan*, 1891)

In this chapter, we will explore various measurement approaches that have been proposed and are being pursued around the world. We will also take stock of a number of important issues in the measurement of national wellbeing that have arisen during these developments.

Analysing the available data for some 30 countries of the Organisation for Economic Co-operation and Development, the OECD, Boarini *et al.* (2006, p. 6) concluded that measures of economic growth are necessary but not sufficient for 'any assessment of well-being'. Their findings suggest a typology for prospective measures of national wellbeing:

- GDP and other measures of economic resources, both for the economy as a whole and for households (but data availability and reliability restrict the scope for cross-country and intertemporal comparisons);

- Calculations to extend national accounts, for example, to include leisure time, the sharing of income within households and distributions across households;

- Indicators to measure specific social conditions (which we take to include environmental conditions as well) that are related to wellbeing;

- Survey-based data on happiness and life satisfaction.

Fleurbaey (2009, p. 1030) does not refer to Boarini *et al.*'s paper but discusses four approaches to measuring 'social welfare' beyond Gross Domestic Product (GDP) that are very similar to these groups drawn, like the earlier paper, from an extensive body of economic literature. He does not explore the existing alternatives to GDP within the existing accounts,

The Wellbeing of Nations: Meaning, Motive and Measurement, First Edition. Paul Allin and David J. Hand.
© 2014 John Wiley & Sons, Ltd. Published 2014 by John Wiley & Sons, Ltd.

the first group of Boarini *et al.*'s measures. He calls their second group 'corrected GDP' and the fourth group 'Gross National Happiness'. Fleurbaey also makes the distinction between Sen's Capability Approach and other 'synthetic indicators', rather than the single group of indicators in Boarini *et al.*'s list.

Fleurbaey concludes that the different approaches are unlikely to converge in the near future: 'It probably makes more sense to abandon the illusion that a unique consensual measure of well-being will emerge and to assign economists the task of thinking rigorously about the alternatives to GDP that each school of thought may inspire and of developing concrete proposals for each of them.' While we welcome this and his final words, that 'serious alternatives to GDP are around the corner' (Fleurbaey, 2009, p. 1070), we would encourage many people, not just the profession of economists which he targets, to 'think rigorously' about alternatives to GDP. It is for us all to engage with economists in developing and using new measures.

Boarini *et al.* (2006, p. 6) also talked of measures (i.e. plural) to complement measures of economic growth, to present a fuller picture of wellbeing. They decided that how to integrate measures to produce a coherent picture was an open question, and it remains so at the time of writing this book, though it is apparent that a 'pragmatic' solution will be required so it would be unreasonable to expect to find a single 'right' method. We will therefore look separately at the ways in which each of the four approaches that they identified can be, and are being, taken forward. The Stiglitz, Sen and Fitoussi recommendations (see Chapter 3) provide a checklist of what needs to be done to build an extensive set of measures.

6.1   Drawing on the national economic accounts

The danger with starting with the national accounts is that it may appear that we are reluctant to go beyond them and the headline measure of GDP. We are reminded of the old joke, about asking for directions and being told: 'Well, I wouldn't start from here!' However, as we are approaching the measurement of national wellbeing in the spirit of complementing existing measures of economic growth, this is where we will start. We will see that the first two of the Stiglitz, Sen and Fitoussi recommendations, as well as some of their other observations, are being addressed through developments within the national economic accounts.

The national accounts produced and published regularly by many national statistical offices reflect a particular model of the economy. It is a model that identifies supply of, and demand for, certain goods and services within a market economy. Whether these concepts actually replicate real life can be disputed (e.g. do we as consumers actively demand products or services, or do we demonstrate that we did want them by purchasing them?) With the oft-quoted warning in mind that all models are wrong, but some are useful, this is how the United Nations Statistics Division describes the national accounts:

> 'The System of National Accounts (SNA) is the internationally agreed standard set of recommendations on how to compile measures of economic activity. The SNA describes a coherent, consistent and integrated set of macroeconomic accounts in the context of a set of internationally agreed concepts, definitions, classifications and accounting rules.
>
> In addition, the SNA provides an overview of economic processes, recording how production is distributed among consumers, businesses, government and foreign nations. It shows how income originating in production, modified by

taxes and transfers, flows to these groups and how they allocate these flows to consumption, saving and investment. Consequently, the national accounts are one of the building blocks of macroeconomic statistics forming a basis for economic analysis and policy formulation.

The SNA is intended for use by all countries, having been designed to accommodate the needs of countries at different stages of economic development. It also provides an overarching framework for standards in other domains of economic statistics, facilitating the integration of these statistical systems to achieve consistency with the national accounts.' (Source: UNSD website, see Appendix for link)

The headline measure most often identified with the SNA is Gross Domestic Product, which is the market value of goods and service produced by an economy. It is often calculated by national statistical offices in stages. The first estimate of GDP is called the preliminary estimate and, in the United Kingdom, for example, it is produced about three and a half weeks after the end of the quarter. An estimate of GDP this close to 'real time' is based solely on estimates of the economy's output. The second GDP estimate is produced in the United Kingdom eight weeks after the end of the quarter, and is based on output, income and expenditure data from the economy. The third estimate is the full national accounts, and is produced 12 weeks after the end of the quarter (Source: ONS website, see Appendix for link).

The reason for the focus on GDP is that 'expansion is the normal state of the economy' (Harvey, 2012), at least as far as economists and central bankers are concerned, so that the quarterly and annual series of GDP numbers are scrutinised by everyone with an interest in whether the economy is behaving 'normally' or not. If the economy is not behaving normally, then this is usually because it is contracting (or, very rarely, if the economy is overheating by expanding too quickly). When an economy is temporarily contracting, then this is called a 'recession' and various definitions are used to avoid labelling say just one quarter in which GDP is smaller than in the previous quarter as a recession. We have also seen at least one example in which a politician referred to 'growth this year of minus 0.1%' (Osborne, 2012), technically correct but potentially confusing to the audience, and also without reference to the confidence limits to be applied to this estimate or to its likely pattern of revision.

GDP can be seen as a measure of the size of an economy. In measuring the overall size, we can also learn much about the shape of an economy, in terms of its structure and the productivity of component sectors, for example. Compiling the national economic accounts is a significant operation for national statistical offices, requiring data from firms, the public sector and individuals as well as considerable processing, checking and analysis in the statistical office. The statistical product is an extensive set of accounts, especially in the annual publications, as well as quarterly updates, which in some cases are updated monthly. From all this data, analysis and output, the 'bottom line' for many people is simply about how the latest GDP total differs from the figure in previous and earlier periods: in short, whether or not there has been economic growth, as defined by $GDP_{t+1} > GDP_t$.

We note in passing that, as with many time series, the figure for the most recent time period is invariably the least reliable of the full GDP series. Revisions may continue over many years. The comparison of GDP_{t+1} and GDP_t is not therefore strictly on a comparable basis. National statistical offices do analyse their history of revisions (e.g. Guerrero et al., 2013, examine Mexican data) but we are not aware that GDP estimates are routinely presented by comparing GDP(first estimate)$_{t+1}$ with GDP(first estimate)$_t$.

Research effort continues to be put into improving the timeliness and reliability of GDP estimates. Guerrero *et al.* (2013) report on how a first estimate of Mexican GDP (or PIB, Producto Interno Bruto, as it is referred to in Spanish) could be produced no more than 30 days after the end of a quarter, compared with the current delay of 50–52 days. They note that their procedure 'comes as a response to users' demand of timely data for decision making, a need evidenced by the 2008 world financial crisis. In fact, most users prefer timely estimates, even at the expense of precision' (Guerrero *et al.*, 2013, p. 397).

As the authors also note, such 'rapid estimates' are also called 'flash estimates' and the authors record some of the 'many international meetings [that] have taken place in order to discuss different issues and technicalities related to this topic, the trade-off between timeliness and precision being of utmost relevance' (Guerrero *et al.*, 2013, p. 398). We believe that the authors are referring to current users of GDP statistics, not necessarily to users of economic, social and environmental statistics more generally. There are many other trade-offs to be made in the allocation of limited resources to improvements of official statistics and it would be interesting to see a cost–benefit analysis that addressed that.

There are a couple of obvious, standardising operations that can be applied to GDP before comparisons are made. First, changes in population size can be taken into account by dividing total GDP by the total population of the country, to give a figure called GDP per head (or per capita). In certain circumstances, this would also represent the average, or mean, GDP per person in the country, although that is not a concept (or an amount) that any of us would recognise as relating to our own personal circumstances. It does, though, reflect that GDP is likely to be associated with population size, through either the size of the working population available for the supply side or the size of the consuming population (or both).

Data on GDP per capita, expressed in current US dollars for comparison, are available for nearly all countries in the World Bank's online databank (see Appendix for link). The figures for 2011/2012 range between US$ 107,500 in Luxembourg and US$ 250 in Burundi, a ratio of nearly 430:1.

Looking at GDP per capita, rather than just GDP, may also help us think more about what GDP measures. By this we mean that GDP is a measure of economic activity during a given period, usually a year. That activity meets the needs of the population, not just by providing goods and services but also generating income to be spent, invested or saved. For economic wellbeing to remain level, GDP in the following year must be sufficient to meet all those needs again, though this time the population will be slightly different from that in the first year. The size of the population will be different, due to births, deaths and migration. There will also be more subtle changes within the population, as people enter or leave the labour force, for example, or enter partnerships and set up new households. This suggests that, even if GDP per capita remains static, there are nevertheless still some underlying dynamics in how that economy is serving the needs of the population of the country. It is possible that GDP per capita does not have to grow in order for the population to pursue their needs – this might provide a possible counterfactual to the view that GDP growth is inevitable. However, accounting for population dynamics is only part of the story.

It is also possible that many producers of goods and services in market economies have got used to population growth as a driver for economic growth. Drawing on the work of Angus Maddison and www.worldmapper.org, Danny Dorling has shown how average GDP per capita annual growth rates started to increase in the 1800s (Dorling, 2013, 359). Taking 11 time periods from year 1 to 2000 (these start very long and get shorter over time) and splitting the world into 12 regions (e.g. Central Africa, North America, Western Europe, Asia

Pacific) gives 132 observations of average annual GDP per capita growth rate in a region in a time period. These average rates are numerically below 1% in 101 cases, that is more than three quarters of all 'times and places'. (We use the one per cent cut off, rather than a growth rate of zero for GDP per capita, to allow for uncertainties in the data). Moreover, there is a pattern of how and when higher average growth rates, above 1%, emerged at the world regional level: starting in North America in 1821–1850, spreading to a further five regions by 1940, peaking with 11 of the 12 regions above 1% on average during 1941–1970, in some regions markedly so, and retrenching somewhat, apart from Asian regions, in 1971–2000.

So what has been happening? Dorling links economic per capita growth mainly to population growth: population growth provides opportunities for trade in goods and services beyond that needed to keep pace with changing demographic characteristics of the population. Added to this is the zest for speculating by bringing new goods and services to market. As Adam Smith noted, if a project – 'the establishment of any new manufacture, of any new branch of commerce, or any new practice in agriculture' – succeeds, then profits are 'commonly at first very high. When the trade or practice becomes thoroughly established and well known, the competition reduces them to the level of other trades' (Smith, 1776/2000, p. 132). It looks as if the capitalist business model has evolved over the centuries into one that relies on population growth and expects economic growth.

Looking ahead, Dorling anticipates population slowdown, that is, the total population number continuing to rise but less rapidly than hitherto. He concludes that: 'In the future, our collective fortunes may depend far more on how well we share out what we do have, rather than on trying to grow our profits ever higher' (Dorling, 2013, p. 360). This suggests a need to look at distributions, which are not routinely published in national economic accounts. We will return to this in Section 6.2.2.

A second set of adjustments that can be made to aggregate GDP figures is to remove the effects of price differences. If we are looking at a country over time, then we might want to remove the effect of price changes (inflation). If we are comparing countries, then we might want to remove the effect of overall differences in the levels of prices in each country, using 'purchasing power parities' (PPP). These kinds of adjustments result in GDP amounts that are presented in so-called 'real terms' (real here meaning underlying or basic, rather than actually as seen in the economy). We will look at some PPP figures for another headline measure shortly.

If we can make adjustments like this, have we got better measures than GDP alone? The answer to this is a resounding no! Two of the Stiglitz, Sen, and Fitoussi recommendations take us much further into looking at the national economic accounts from viewpoints other than the headline of GDP:

- When evaluating material wellbeing, look at income and consumption rather than production – because material living standards are more closely associated with measures of real income and consumption than with production;

- Emphasise the household perspective to track trends in the material living standards of citizens, as well as tracking the performance of the economy as a whole.

We will see that GDP is only one of a number of headline measures defined in the SNA. Using the others, in the ways steered by the two recommendations, will help us to see how well an economy and its citizens are doing. Some measures are directly in the national accounts, and we turn to them next. We also recognise that measures can be derived from national accounts and other data, notably measures of productivity such as GDP per hour worked. Productivity measures can be compared over time and between countries, to get some indication of how effective countries are in producing goods and providing services.

To go beyond GDP, or rather to move to 'GDP and beyond', we bring other summary measures centre-stage. First is the set of measures obtained by varying the concepts of Gross and Domestic in GDP, because each concept has an alternative – it can be Gross or Net, and Domestic or National. The four measures that result from all combinations of these two concepts are fully described by Chiripanhura (2010), who also demonstrates how international league tables of economic performance vary according to which measure is used.

The 'gross' in GDP means that no deduction has been made for the 'wear and tear' of machinery, buildings and other capital products used in the production process during the period under consideration. That such depreciation of capital assets happens is recognised in the SNA, where it is referred to as the consumption of fixed capital. In general, the more resources that are needed to replenishing a nation's capital stock, the fewer resources are available for consumption in the short run. Subtracting the consumption of fixed capital from GDP gives NDP (N for Net, or net of the consumption of fixed capital). This may be a better measure of material economic wellbeing than GDP as it is designed to precisely cover the new wealth created during the period. However, measuring the consumption of fixed capital is not a precise art (typically conventions are applied in company accounts, to write off a proportion of their fixed capital each year) so that in saying that NDP is superior to GDP we need to be sure that it is a more reliable measure.

The second concept we can vary is about accounting for international income flows. The 'Domestic' in GDP indicates that activity is measured within the economic territory of the country concerned. This refers in the main to the physical geography of the country, with some minor adjustments for places such as foreign embassies and military bases hosted in country but strictly seen as territory of the overseas nation.

Gross National Income (GNI), formerly known as Gross National Product, reflects cross-border ownership of economic assets of nationals of the particular country. GNI is calculated by adding to GDP the income received from abroad by that country's resident units and deducting from GDP the income created by production in the country but transferred to units residing abroad. We know we live in an increasingly global economy where many enterprises operate across a number of countries. For any one country, the net amount of income received from abroad and income transferred to units residing abroad is called in the SNA that country's 'net factor income from abroad'.

GNI is theoretically a better measure of the welfare of the people of a country than GDP because it indicates how much production in the economy and abroad is available to nationals of that country. It excludes resources within the economy that do not ultimately benefit residents. However, it is difficult to measure remittance flows between countries, with the further complication that some take place outside of the formal financial system.

To complete a quartet of headline measures of economic wellbeing, we can account both for international income flows and for consumption of fixed capital. The combined adjustment to GDP gives Net National Income, NNI. It shows the net value of income obtained from resources owned by nationals of a country and thus, in theory, is a better indicator of material wellbeing than GDP, NDP or GNI. It also, though, carries all the measurement difficulties identified in considering each of the two kinds of adjustment.

It may be that totalling GDP across countries reduces the difference between GDP and GNI for the aggregate. For example, *The Economist* magazine regularly publishes estimates of 'World GDP', drawing on IMF data. 'World GDP' is here defined as the sum of the GDP of 52 economies, amounting to 90% of actual world GDP, using their GDP at purchasing power parity. Many, but clearly not all, of the international income flows of these 52 countries will be with other countries included in the total, so as a first approximation, this is 'World GNI' as well as 'World GDP'. The approximation will begin to break down again as individual countries (e.g. United States, China) and country groupings are identified within the total position.

The World Bank's world development databank covers 214 countries. We downloaded the data for GNI per capita for 2012, expressed in international dollars using purchasing power parities (PPPs), for the 172 countries for which this item was available. (In doing so, we had to use the 2011 figure for 11 of these countries because 2012 was not included.) The Democratic Republic of the Congo, the largest country by area in sub-Saharan Africa, had the lowest GNI per capita, of $370. The small state of Qatar, some 5000 km distance from the Congo, had the highest GNI per capita, of $81 300 or some 220 times that of the figure for the Congo. This is a large difference and it is even greater than that suggested by looking at GDP per capita. This is because moving from GDP to GNI reduces the resources available to the Congo as a nation by over 10%, while there is less than a 2% difference between GDP and GNI in Qatar, where flows of resources into and out of the country are more in balance.

Figure 6.1 shows the average GNI per capita for each decile group among 172 countries. The median GNI per capita across the countries was $8780 and, as is often also the case for the distribution of income within countries, the distribution of GNI per capita between countries shows a marked skewing towards the upper-end of the distribution.

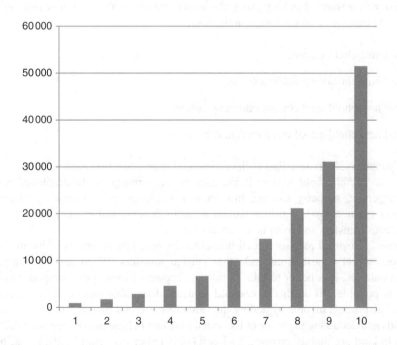

Figure 6.1   Average GNI per capita by decile, 2012, international dollars using PPPs. Data source: World Bank.

While we have moved on from just looking at GDP, we have remained with measures of national income, aggregated across all of the actors in the economy, including companies, institutions, the public purse and individuals. The Stiglitz Commission argued that 'while it is informative to track the performance of economies as a whole, trends in citizens' material living standards are better followed through measures of household income and consumption' (Stiglitz *et al.*, 2010, p. 12). The point here is that national wellbeing comes down, in the final judgement of the Stiglitz Commission and many others, to the wellbeing of people in the country.

The SNA allows for this by segmenting the economy into a number of sectors, such as financial corporations, nonfinancial corporations and general government. Another sector is the 'household sector'. The first broad cut of the economy into sectors in the SNA includes 'nonprofit institutions serving households (NPISH)', for example charities, in the 'household sector'. We need to be able to look at national accounts data for households as commonly understood, remembering that 'households' are also found when people live in communal establishments, such as nurses' homes or nursing homes. In defining the household sector of interest, we therefore need to exclude the nonprofit institutions allocated to the national accounts 'household sector'. In measuring the household sector of interest, we find that many surveys are limited to households living in houses or apartments, with communal establishments less well covered.

We are still within the SNA, so economic rules and rationales apply. The thinking is that households have the choice of improving their current welfare by allocating more resources to consumption, or improving future welfare by increasing savings and wealth accumulation. Such economic welfare decisions are submerged within overall analyses of GDP and the other headline measures. Looking just at the household sector, there are four main measures of household income or consumption in the SNA:

- total household income;

- total household disposable income;

- total household final consumption expenditure;

- total household actual consumption expenditure.

Chiripanhura (2010) describes each of these and shows how they each vary across OECD countries. *Total household income* is the sum of the earnings of the employed and self-employed people, property income, interest and dividends, gross operating surplus (e.g. of business partnerships), pensions, social security benefits (other than pensions), some miscellaneous transfers and insurance claims received.

Household disposal income is total household income less payments of income tax and other taxes, social contributions and other current transfers. When making comparisons between countries, it is better to take as full an account of their social support and benefit systems as possible. To do this, household-adjusted disposable income is calculated from household disposable income by adding the value of the social transfers in kind received by households and deducting the value of the social transfers in kind paid by households. (Social transfers in kind are mainly received by households rather than paid by them, but because we are in the national accounting framework we must always allow for any such transfers, for example, arising from adjustments in payments when households buy services and have them reimbursed.) Household disposable income provides a measure of both the present and future consumption amounts available overall to households.

Turning to consumption, the SNA makes a distinction between consumption intended to be used up in the relatively short term and expenditure of items, notably property, analogous to fixed capital formation by businesses, which helps households function in the longer term. *Household final consumption expenditure* consists of the expenditure, including imputed expenditure, incurred by resident households on individual consumption of goods and services, including those provided at nonmarket prices. This covers all purchases made by consumers: food, clothing, housing services (rent), energy, durable goods (notably cars) and spending on health, on leisure and on miscellaneous services, but excludes households' purchases of dwellings.

Household actual consumption expenditure gives the value of the consumption goods and services acquired by households, whether by purchase in general or by transfer from government units or NPISHs, and used by them for the satisfaction of their needs and wants. It is derived from household final consumption expenditure by adding the value of social transfers in kind that households receive. Eurostat, the European Commission's statistical body, calls this measure *actual individual consumption* (AIC) and it publishes estimates of AIC per capita for countries inside and outside the European Union (EU), presenting this as an alternative to GDP per capita as a way of measuring living standards.

At the time of writing, the World Bank's databank of world development indicators showed values in 2011 or 2012 for both household final consumption expenditure (HFCE) per capita (expressed in dollars, using purchasing power parities, PPPs) and GNI per capita (also in dollars using PPPs) for 115 of the 214 countries covered in the databank. (It is smaller countries that tend to be missing.) Figure 6.2 is a scatter plot for the available data. By restricting this chart to those countries with relatively up-to-date data for both variables, we are presenting a chart that is not strictly comparable with the GNI data in Figure 6.1 as HFCE is less widely available than GNI. Nevertheless, Figure 6.2 shows, at first glance, that there is broadly a linear relationship between HFCE and GNI, and that HFCE per capita is typically under half of GNI per capita. However, for many countries, knowing the current size of an economy, its GNI per capita, would not be a good predictor of the total financial resources available to households there, measured by HFCE per capita. There is clearly not a straight-line relationship between the two variables, and a number of countries sit well

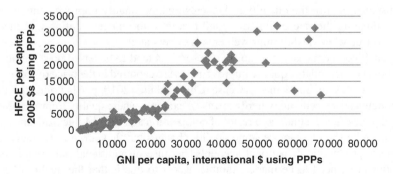

Figure 6.2   Per capita GNI and HFCE for 115 countries, 2011/2012.
Data source: World Bank.

away from the line. (The two countries that appear as outliers in the bottom-right corner of Figure 6.2 are Singapore and Macao SAR, China: they have high GNI per capita but values of HFCE per capita are more typically found in countries with half their GNI per capita.)

We have now identified eight potential headline measures of economic wellbeing, each of which could further be expressed in variants such as per capita measures. This begs the obvious question of how to use many rather than just one measure. This is a question that has arisen for producers and users of official statistics beyond the national accounts. For example, the United States has one official definition and measure of unemployment but 'some have argued that this is too restrictive and does not capture the full range of labour market problems', so the Bureau of Labor Statistics also publishes a set of alternative measures of labour underutilisation (Bureau of Labor Statistics, no date given).

The Stiglitz Commission is clear that a 'dashboard' of measures of wellbeing and progress is preferable to a single metric. The commission concludes that there is 'no single indicator that can capture something as complex as our society' and that the goal then is 'to construct a simple set of metrics that captures much that is of central concern' (Stiglitz et al., 2010, p. xxv). This suggests to us that there is much still to discuss during the process of building new sets of measures. The debates and the determination of user requirements envisaged in our previous chapter must lead to the identification of the central concerns, and how many of them are to be measured, with how many measures. (We will return to this, but first we have more to do to collate material that is becoming identified as contributing to our wider understanding of national wellbeing. We realise that this only complicates the question further.)

The Stiglitz Commission says much about what can be done with the existing set of national accounts that many countries routinely publish, including giving greater prominence to the additional statistical measures we have discussed in this section. As Chiripanhura observes (2010, p. 56), there are limitations with national income as a measure of welfare that affect all of these headline measures. Nevertheless, they can be used to build greater understanding of current economic performance and how the country as a whole benefits from this.

The commission's report also contains some 'main messages' that focus on the current system of national accounts and how it would anyway have to develop to cope with structural changes 'which have characterised the evolution of modern economics' (Stiglitz et al., 2010, p. 9). First is the issue of capturing quality change in the goods and services that we consume, which the commission accepts is a 'tremendous challenge' in making national income measures better reflect quality of life. The commission notes, 'In some countries and some sectors, increasing "output" is more a matter of an increase in the quality of goods produced and consumed than in the quantity ... Underestimating quality improvements is equivalent to overestimating the rate of inflation, and therefore to underestimating real income. The opposite is true when quality improvements are overstated.'

National income measures of goods and services tend to be based on price and volume. While it may be argued that quality improvements are captured in the price of some goods and services, this does not apply in every case. Chiripanhura (2010, p. 61) points to information and communication technology hardware as an example where quality improves greatly over time, and price often declines, as a result of competition and technological advances. Hedonic methods can be used to capture some quality changes but they are not routinely applied in the primary production of national accounts, because of additional data requirements and assumptions that need to be made. Another aspect to this is that the quality of goods and services can vary between countries, making cross-national comparisons and aggregates based on national data less reliable.

The second main message in the Stiglitz Commission report is that government services, whether of a collective nature like national security, or individual services such as medical services and education, remain 'badly measured'. These services are often only measured using inputs (such as the number of doctors) rather than on actual outputs (such as the number of particular medical treatments), let alone the outcomes in terms of improvements in the health, knowledge and skills of the nation. Changes in the quality of public services, and in the efficiency with which they are delivered, tend to be ignored, with an impact on the estimation of economic growth and real income. This matters because government output and total government expenditure are a significant component in the total GDP of many OECD countries, so measuring the performance of government is important in measuring and understanding the wellbeing of the nation. While some work has been done on this (e.g. Grice, 2011, p. 624), and there is some broad support for tackling the issues, there is not yet agreement on how to take these forward in the regular production of national accounts.

The international mechanism for tackling these two measurement issues, and other improvements and enhancements to the national accounts that inevitably arise, recognises that the SNA needs to be updated from time to time. This is delivered through a research programme and the release of new versions of the SNA, overseen by the UN Statistics Division. National statistical offices and others contribute to the research and, after consultation with their users, shift their national accounts outputs to the latest version. For example, US GDP was revised in 2013 (back to 1929!) by including intangibles like research and development spending (McCulla *et al.*, 2013). Much attention is now being given to capturing in the national accounts the intangible investment by companies, including design and branding. This is covered in the latest version of the SNA: SNA 2008 replaces the previous, 1993, version. European and other country blocks, as well as the United States, are engaged on managed moves to using the latest version in published statistics. There are, however, still many aspects of modern life, for example, the value of consumer online activity, for which better measures are needed.

6.2   Extending the national accounts

In the previous section, we looked at some ways of delving within routinely published national accounts, for example, by focussing on the household sector, to help assess national wellbeing. In this section, we turn to what might be seen as a wider system of national accounts, including supplementing the core accounts. We seek to overcome limitations of GDP and the regularly published national accounts as measures of wellbeing.

When we buy something, the transaction in theory contributes to GDP. If we buy more in one year than in the previous year, then that will contribute to the growth in GDP and hence to progress. In practice, this is measured at different stages in the supply chain, so the economic benefits to others of our transaction, in terms of income and employment, are captured. However, this assumes a number of things. For example, it assumes that we value what we have paid for, so that economic welfare can be accepted as overall wellbeing. It also assumes that there are no disbenefits in the supply chain, such as the depletion of scarce resources or deterioration in work–life balance, because these are not measured in GDP. The move towards wider measures of national wellbeing seeks to provide systematic ways to quantify such areas.

Another issue with the system of national accounts is that it incorporates illegal as well as legal actions. There is no distinction, in theory, between any transactions in which there is mutual agreement between the parties. Sales of, for example, illegal drugs or stolen goods are in scope of the national accounts. (Theft should not be included, because it is not a mutually agreed transaction.) Including such transactions should lead to internal consistency in the accounts (e.g. between financial holdings and transactions) and, over time, between countries, as well as covering the whole economy.

The economy as measured by the core system of national accounts excludes many unpaid service activities. Any shifts in society to undertake these activities in the market bring them in scope of the core national accounts and GDP in particular. Supporting of satellite analyses can extend the coverage of national accounts. However, it has been claimed that the exclusion of unpaid activities reflects current cultural norms, that it is a value judgement about such work and about the wide section of society, mainly women, who undertake it (e.g. Fioramonti, 2013, p. 56), effectively giving zero value to services beyond those paid for in the market or provided by government.

It is initially re-assuring that national statistical offices do not take into account any ethical or moral considerations when compiling national accounts. However, these data then form part of the calculation of GDP – still the headline measure of wellbeing and progress. Is it right, from an ethical or moral viewpoint, that wellbeing is measured, judged and acted on, partly on the basis of illegal activities and without greater recognition of the value of unpaid activities?

Many books, articles and blogs have been written on all of this. Fioramonti, for example, concludes that GDP continues to dominate the economy but that it fails to define progress and has little relevance to moral principles such as equity, social justice and redistribution. He notes (2013, p. 110) that while revisions to the system of national accounts have recognised satellite accounts, these are outside of the central framework used for policy making, and that the definition of GDP itself goes unchanged because of 'reluctance to add any further imputations to the national accounts'. A more optimistic view is that of the Stiglitz Commission, which decided that there is a case to identify resources such as leisure time, and how they are being used, even if they cannot be valued in the market (Stiglitz *et al.*, 2010, p. 14).

We noted in the previous section that work is needed to improve some aspects of the core national accounts. Fender *et al.* (2011, p. 2) and Chiripanhura (2010, p. 62) summarise the further limitations of the core national accounts as measures of wellbeing. Regularly published national accounts

- exclude determinants of wellbeing outside the 'production boundary' defined for the measurement of core national accounts: there are activities, attributes, social institutions and relationships that will feature in the framework for measuring the progress of societies that we will not find in the national accounts, such as household work, leisure, the quality of social relations, health and longevity and how well we are governed;

- include economic activities that either reduce wellbeing or that arise as costs of economic growth: crime, war, pollution and car accidents all cause people to spend money – and hence add to GDP – but we have yet to find anyone who would say that these also increase national wellbeing;

- do not help us assess whether wellbeing can last over time;

- give most attention to measures of income rather than of wealth: the national income measures discussed in the previous section are all essentially about transactions measured over a given period of time. Stock concepts are also important for well-being, including net wealth (consisting of physical, financial, property and private pension wealth), as well as environmental resources, human capital and social capital that are not measured in the main national accounts;

- and tend not to help understand inequality and how income and wealth are distributed. In looking at the wellbeing and progress framework, we saw how the idea of social justice was to be included. For the things captured in the national accounts, this means looking at the distribution of income, expenditure and wealth across society but such distributional analyses are seldom provided as part of the presentation of a nation's set of accounts. There is also the danger that presenting national income measures on a per capita basis (which is technically an average measure) can be misleading as the income of a representative or typical individual, because distributions of income and wealth are very unequal in most countries. In some developed countries, there is evidence that they are becoming more unequal in terms of income and wealth.

Three Stiglitz, Sen Fitoussi recommendations relate to these issues:

- Consider income and consumption jointly with wealth;

- Give more prominence to the distribution of income, consumption and wealth;

- Broaden income measures to nonmarket activities.

6.2.1   Consider income and consumption jointly with wealth

GDP and the alternative measures discussed in Section 6.1 are all measures reflecting income and expenditure, or consumption more generally. Economic wellbeing is also determined by wealth. To understand wealth, you have to look at all your assets and liabilities at a point in time. Wealth is not the same as income, though they are sometimes confused. For example, a financial newspaper recently reported latest GDP per capita figures for EU member states as 'Italy slips in EU wealth measure' (City A. M., 2013). Wealth is an indication of the resources at one's disposal, and therefore is also used popularly to gauge status. Senge *et al.* (2008, p. 174) give a nice example of how knowing only about income tells us very little about wealth: they show how annual fish catches (i.e. income) may only start to decline long after the stock of fish in the ocean has been drastically reduced.

The distinction between income and wealth is well understood in company financial reporting. A vital indicator of the financial status of a company is its balance sheet, showing its wealth. To construct the equivalent balance sheet for a country, we need comprehensive accounts of its economic and financial assets and its liabilities (what it owes to other countries). Many countries already publish sector balance sheets as part of their national accounts, including for the household sector. Reading the Stiglitz, Sen and Fitoussi report as a whole, it is clear that the balance sheet for a country should also include human, natural and social capital: they are steering us towards the 'triple bottom line' (with economic, social and environmental dimensions) that has emerged in understanding sustainable development (see Chapter 2).

Many studies have shown that wealth, like income, tends to be unequally distributed within and between countries, and such inequality tends to be passed down through generations.

Of particular interest are longitudinal studies allowing for analysis of levels of wealth and material wellbeing varying over time. However, collecting reliable data on the value of household wealth is challenging. Current methods are based on attempting to draw either on administrative data relating to household wealth and assets or on household surveys of wealth and assets. Without some form of linking together data for the same household, administrative sources can only be used to produce aggregate measures of wealth. The advantage of a survey is that the household can be asked to identify all of their assets, debts, borrowing, saving and plans for retirement. This allows for richer statistical analysis of the wealth of households. However, surveys to ask about these things can be time-consuming and costly to run. The wealth and assets survey run in two waves in Britain during 2006–2010 took an average 90 minutes per household, for those households from which full information was collected (Chamberlain and Black, 2012, Chapter 1, technical details).

There are many examples of wealth statistics around the world, drawing on these kinds of sources. The OECD has published an internationally agreed set of guidelines for producing statistics on household wealth (OECD 2013b). (These guidelines refer to 'micro statistics', which means collecting data from individual representative households, analysing it and publishing reports on how wealth is distributed across households. Ideally, anonymised data at the household level should also be available in safe settings for further analysis.) The guidelines were prepared by a group of experts, mainly from national statistical offices or central banks, and they address the many conceptual, definitional and practical problems in producing statistics on household wealth.

The thrust of the Stiglitz recommendation is not just to collect wealth data but also to consider how income, consumption and wealth are inter-related aspects of economic wellbeing. The OECD has published an internationally agreed framework to support the joint analysis of micro-level statistics on household income, consumption and wealth (OECD 2013c). Guidelines such as both of the OECD publications are aimed at improving the comparability of country data, as well as meeting national needs.

Different kinds of stocks and capital vary in how difficult they are to measure as items in themselves. Any farmer will know how much livestock is on the land, and the area of growing crops. To measure the total amount of natural capital in an area is more challenging. In most cases, putting a value on stocks and capital is the most difficult part. We tend to resort to market prices, but these only exist when assets are sold in the market. Indeed, a tenet of the OECD guidelines is that household assets, liabilities and transactions should be valued at their current market value at the date to which the statistics refer (or an average value over a period of say three months is usual for transactions data).

The guidelines explore in some detail how to achieve this, or more realistically how to come up with approximate market values. Within the confines of the system of national accounts this is what to do for measures of household wealth, as well as for measures of income and consumption. However, this does not necessarily give the full picture, for a number of reasons. We will briefly explore one of these here – the difficulty of attributing a market value to items not currently in the market. In later sections, we will cover the broader point, about activities and assets beyond the reach of the market that nevertheless may contribute to wellbeing.

Capitalism is synonymous with market economies. Economic considerations of production, consumption and wealth need a theory and definition of value that is effectively tied to the idea of market transactions, and in markets we can see the prices at which goods and services are bought. However, price is not necessarily the same as value. Price is realised as an exchange value, the value that the buyer and seller put on something at the time it changes hands. This may not be the real value if we think there is a measure of worth that is based purely on the utility derived from the consumption of a product or service, such as satisfaction with it. We might only come to know this after a long time. There is much in the popular saying about people who know the price of everything and the value of nothing. On the other hand, we as consumers may make an assessment of the value of something at the point of purchasing it, especially if we agree with the producer's assessment of value, even where these cover, for example, intangible attributes such as authenticity, craftsmanship, elegance or tradition.

There is also a practical consideration in using market prices in valuing household assets in a statistical exercise. Consider putting a value on the property that a household owns (the same applies to stocks and shares). Only a small proportion of properties will actually be offered for sale at the reference point for the valuation. The price of those properties will reflect the market conditions at the time. Prices will tend to rise if there are more active buyers than sellers, and fall if more sellers than buyers. Whatever the market price, this is not a good indication of the price that every household would get if they sold their property at the same time. Even if the market could cope with this huge increase in volume of activity, the first thing that is likely to happen is that prices would fall due to the influx of sellers. However, the ultimate point is where every household selling their property would also be in the market to buy another, adding another dynamic to the market process.

At best we can say that attributing current market prices is indicative of value. It may be illusory. The alternative, and no less easy, is to invite households to value their assets in their own terms of utility and value to them. Eatwell (2012) points out that we should be indebted to Adam Smith for capturing the problem of how to value things, by having both natural prices and market prices, but also that Smith's definition of natural price is not a theory of value. It is the specification of what the theory of value is to determine. Economists have been going over this ever since (for a progress report in the second half of the twentieth century, see Debreu, 1959).

Weale (2009, p. 3) noted that governments have tended not to have policies relating to overall saving in the economy. He proposed a number of ways in which savings can be defined and measured, including going beyond the national accounts definition of income and savings and constructing comprehensive balance sheets for each 'generation' (i.e. cohorts of households according to age). Weale also included the environment as a capital asset available for current adults and future generations, building balance sheets for each sector covered in the national accounts. These enable many issues to be examined, including household, government and national solvency (or indebtedness). Current and future generations can be compared, along with an assessment of the sustainability of current consumption and hence issues of fairness between generations.

6.2.2 Give more prominence to the distribution of income, consumption and wealth

Figures of average income, consumption and wealth per capita or per household do not tell the whole, or even an accurate, story about living standards and how these are changing for households with different levels of resources. The interest here is actually broader than this recommendation relates to, and ties up with a later recommendation on the need to assess inequalities in all dimensions of quality of life (see Section 6.3.2). The issue is whether or not societies are becoming fairer as well as richer, and, increasingly, this question is being asked by including health and the quality of life, as well as income, consumption and wealth. Deaton, for example, explores the 'interplay of progress and inequality', noting that 'Inequality is often a *consequence* of progress' and that 'Inequalities in turn affect progress', sometimes in positive and sometimes in negative ways (Deaton, 2013, p. 1). Deaton also notes that 'economic growth has been the engine of international income inequality', of widening gaps between country averages as well as within countries (Deaton, 2013, p. 5). He is clear that 'Wellbeing cannot be judged by its average without looking at inequality, and wellbeing cannot be judged by one or more of its parts without looking at the whole' (Deaton, 2013, p. 9).

Household survey data are usually needed for distributional analyses and, to follow Deaton's advice, these data need to cover all aspects of wellbeing, not just material living standards and health. Hills *et al.* (2013), for example, have examined the distribution of household wealth in Great Britain using national survey data, gaining insights to policy options. They conclude that considerable wealth inequality exists overall, across the lifecycle and within age groups. Wealth gives people greater life choices and can bring greater political freedom. The authors show how wealth affects not only current standards of living but also prospects throughout life, from education and early career choices through to retirement, and the legacy passed to later generations. This illustrates well the point that seeing distributions, rather than just averages, inevitably prompts us to ask why there are differences in income, consumption and wealth. We recognise that this opens up a potentially huge area of analysis, both at the individual or household level, as well as how political and social systems and structures function. (Some data and analysis requirements may also be at the individual business level, given interest in some places in linking the salaries of the highest- and the lowest-paid employee of a company.)

Jacob Hacker (2011) approached the distribution of resources in society by introducing what he calls 'pre-distribution' – the idea that the state should try to prevent inequalities occurring in the first place rather than seeking to reduce inequalities through the tax and benefits system once they have occurred (the so-called redistribution of income and wealth). The data needs for pre-distributional analyses are not yet clear.

Chiripanhura (2010, p. 62) reminds us that median income analysis should be used to complement the more readily available analyses of average (mean) income per household. The median gives a better indication of the level of economic wellbeing of the 'typical' household, in the middle of the distribution by definition. Since income distributions are invariably positively skewed, mean analysis is influenced by extreme observations at the top-end of the distribution, resulting in the mean exceeding the median. In fact this more pertinently argues for the distributions of income, consumption and wealth to be measured, presented and considered, which Chiripanhura goes on to do by analysing real household income data in quintiles for OECD countries. However, that analysis had to be based on household surveys and the figures are not exactly comparable with the aggregates in national accounts. An OECD/Eurostat taskforce is tackling this and developing measures of income distributions in a national accounts framework. This involves decomposing household national income accounts by type of household, using information from surveys about both the mix of household types and the distribution of income for each household type. The methodology should then also be applicable to consumption and wealth.

When constructing distributions of income, consumption and wealth for the analysis of wellbeing, we need to give some thought to the unit of analysis. This usually results in analysis at consumption unit level, typically a household, because at least some income (e.g. some benefits), consumption (e.g. of heating) and wealth (e.g. household electrical goods) are shared. Taking households as the unit, though, is in effect making the assumption that all income, consumption and wealth are shared within the household. Understanding the detailed dynamics of distribution within households seems something more suited to small-scale research than to large-scale household surveys, because of the detail that might need to be collected from each household member independently. However, we recognise that there are various ways of approaching this, and that one of the occasional questionnaire modules used for EU Statistics on Income and Living Conditions (EU-SILC, see Appendix) does collect data on this topic.

Some household-level analyses are adjusted for size and composition. Although household income can be adjusted for the size of the household (called 'equivalising'), there appears to be no consensus on what this actually represents. Also, even though 'equivalised' income reflects the sharing of consumption goods, it 'does not allow broader assessment of the consequences of living with others' (Boarini *et al.*, 2006, p. 21).

We must also remember that this section is about extending the national accounts, so we must not see income, consumption and wealth, and how they are distributed, purely in financial terms and market activities, within the existing production boundary of the national accounts. Pearce (2013b, p. 102) reminds us that focussing on 'abstract patterns of distribution tells us little about what constitutes a good life, or indeed how to achieve our goals'. He points to relational egalitarianism, which 'seeks equality in social relations'. This is complex, covering, for example, how people relate to each other, participation in civic society, social integration, where power is held and the nature of democracy within the country. We will pick up these kinds of issues later, but first we can look at taking one step beyond conventional national accounts.

6.2.3   Broaden income measures to nonmarket activities

One way into this issue is to think about building a comprehensive picture of living standards, including goods and services not provided by the market, or by the public sector. This particularly matters when services previously provided within the household, say preparing meals from basic ingredients, start to be purchased on the market, in this case in the form of meals out or the purchase of ready-prepared meals. Looking only at the national accounts would suggest that things have gotten better, because various economic measures would have increased. However, from the point of view of the services consumed by the household, things may hardly have changed: still the same number of meals, for example, with around the same calorific value.

National income over a year is the total market value of production as defined in a country's economy during that time. It is now generally accepted that there are productive activities that contribute to societal wellbeing that do not have an explicit market value. Services provided by government and the public sector are within the production boundary of the national accounts, but we saw in Section 6.1 that there are measurement problems in valuing outputs and outcomes. Some productive activities are treated as outside the production boundary and so not counted in the national accounts. The main categories are 'household production', such as housework, caring, preparing meals, leisure activities (though this is debateable) and what economists call 'externalities' (though these could well be considered part of market activity but are effectively treated as nonmarket when they are not accounted for).

While non-market production in the household and nonmarket leisure activities are not included at all in the national accounts, there is a 'third-party' criterion, first developed by Reid (1934), that can be used to identify activities that might be included in a wider measure of production and which still reflects national accounting conventions. Reid suggested that, if someone *could* be paid to provide this service for the household, then it should be measured. So, not all activities would be included – only *you* can go for that walk in the countryside, for example! – but many more activities would be in scope. If we can estimate it, then 'full' income, consisting of household income, household production and at least some leisure activities, more accurately approaches a measure of societal wellbeing than does a measure solely of income from the core national accounts.

Pullinger (1998, p. 2) proposed taking account of 'the contributions made by women and men to society' in a system of social contributions that would include, for example, volunteering, to complement the economic contributions from paid work. It is not clear how this differs from Reid's third-party criterion. For example, the defining feature of voluntary work is that it is done voluntarily and, on the face of it, no one would be paid to do it in the absence of volunteers. However, it is not as simple as that. There are, for example, situations where volunteers take over when paid services are discontinued, perhaps under public sector funding constraints. The International Labour Office has published a definition of volunteer work, with examples of activities within and outside scope of it (ILO, 2011, p. 13). Pullinger's focus 'remains on the economy' (Pullinger, 1998, p. 2), seeking to explore the things that make the economy, rather than society as a whole, function. He highlights the importance of quantifying, or at least identifying, social contributions in various areas of policy, also calling for the need, like SNA, for this to have a conceptual basis.

Pullinger estimated social contributions in Britain using data from a time use survey. This process has been explored for estimates of the value of nonmarket production more generally, using the 'household satellite account' methodology developed as part of the SNA (see Appendix for SNA website). This methodology calls for assumptions to be made, such as the use of market rates, say for child care, to be applied to nonpaid work. In 2002, ONS produced an experimental household satellite account for the United Kingdom that suggested that the value of household production was around the same size as conventional GDP (ONS, 2002). This has not been fully updated and there are no immediate plans to conduct another time use survey necessary to derive these estimates, largely because time use surveys, like wealth surveys, are expensive. The methodology can, of course, be applied in specific policy areas as required (see Chapter 7 for an example of this).

Time use surveys are carried out in a number of countries, including the United States where the American Time Use Survey (ATUS) is carried out by the Bureau of Labor Statistics. In an article published by the Bureau around 15 years ago, Joyce and Stewart (1999, p. 5) noted that the potential uses of time use data included better measures of real income and wellbeing, by permitting 'a more complete assessment of changes in quality of life'. They give the example that working fewer hours with a drop in wage income may not amount to being worse off, if extra time for household and leisure activities leads to a compensating increase in quality of life. Here there appears to be no restriction on how time is spent in considering quality of life, in contrast, say, to Pullinger (1998, p. 6), who took the line that leisure is needed and valued, but should be outside any wider production boundary drawn to extend the SNA to a system of economic and social accounts: 'the role of leisure ... more in terms of a counterpoint to work than a replacement for it'. Joyce and Stewart also looked to time use data to improve understanding of inequalities, extending analyses usually based on earnings and other financial income: 'With time-use data, it is possible to measure a family's command over a broader set of resources', they observe (Joyce and Stewart, 1999, p. 5).

More recently, and drawing on the ATUS, Krueger *et al.* (2009, p. 11) have developed 'national time accounts' to complement, not to replace, the regular national accounts. Their time accounts reflect the satisfaction people report with each activity and time period. The authors argue that 'evaluated time use provides a valuable indicator of society's well-being, and the fact that our measure is connected to time allocation has analytical and policy advantages that are not available from other measures of subjective well-being, such as overall life satisfaction'. Their approach seems particularly amenable to evaluating public policy, such as laws limiting overtime, and public infrastructure projects – investing in roads or in high-speed rail will affect leisure and commuting travel times as well as business travel, for example.

Gershuny (2011) also describes the potential uses of time use data. The concept of 'full' income can be translated into accounting for the full use of time, the 24 hours in each day. After considering the options for measuring time use, the paper focuses on the diary studies method. Time diaries provide information on who does what, when they do it and how much of each activity they do, allowing measures of household production and leisure time. Along the lines envisaged by the American researchers, time diaries can also be extended so that activities are linked with subjective evaluations, so respondents score their enjoyment of each diary event. The paper concludes by highlighting that time diaries provide a means for integrating various distinct, potentially opposing, views of economic output and aggregate wellbeing.

Most European countries have participated voluntarily at some point in the Harmonised European Time Use Survey (see Appendix for website), which is coordinated by Eurostat, and there is a plan for European countries to deliver time use statistics by 2020 as part of 'Beyond GDP'. However, this is far from the formal requirement that applies to the production of many established economic time series, for example. Before we leave these studies, we note that in calling them 'time use' studies, survey managers appear to subscribe to a view that time is a commodity or resource, all of which needs to be accounted for. While this is a widely held view (e.g. 'time is money'), it is not universal.

Richard Stone made a number of significant contributions in the 1960s and 1970s to the formulation of 'an integrated system of demographic, manpower and social statistics' (e.g. Stone, 1973, p. 143). It was envisaged that such a system should include three aspects. The first two aspects were 'a detailed treatment of human stocks and flows in different areas of social interest, such as education, employment, health, delinquency and so on [and ...] a means of accounting for the services provided, often by the state, in these areas, the costs incurred and the resources engaged in them' (Stone, 1973, p. 143). This seems to cover all human activities, not just those engaged in market or nonmarket production because, for example, services are provided in the form of conserving the natural environment. The third aspect of the integration system would be, as others have demanded, 'a means of recording the distribution of these services over various classes of beneficiary' (Stone, 1973, p. 143).

The idea of 'human stocks and flows' is interesting and, although Stone's experimental matrices appear not to have been taken up by national statistical offices, the matrices were perhaps the seeds for later work on various forms of capital, which we will consider later. Stone started from the position that, at any point in time, each person could be described by where they were in each of many different personal and family characteristics (e.g. their age, where they were living, etc.) and these characteristics could be broadly grouped into a number of 'states', such as being in full-time education, at work or within the criminal justice system.

The choice of characteristics and states would reflect policy needs (his detailed example was about education).

Having measured the stock of the population according to the selected characteristics and states, the 'flows' were the changes in stock between points in time, such as from year to year or, again more broadly, according to position in the life sequence or life cycle. Stone recognised what we have seen in the national accounts as the need for a boundary: 'defining the compartment of life to which a sequence relates it is convenient to make use of the concept of a boundary as exemplified by the economic concept of the production boundary' (Stone, 1973, p. 144). However, at least in his example, Stone settles on where the boundary should be drawn on the pragmatic grounds of what data are available. This is a problem we often encounter in seeking to go beyond GDP, that data are not available because they are not required for GDP.

The final category of what are seen as nonmarket activities is 'externalities'. These are acknowledged by-products of economic or human activity, such as pollution, litter or vandalism, and so they may well in theory be included within the production boundary. However, they are rarely costed or accounted for, so they are treated as external to the production boundary unless there is some direct compensation paid by the person or organisation involved. Externalities are increasingly being recognised and counted as 'social costs' in cost–benefit analyses, at least where they can be given some monetary value. Externalities can also be positive. For example, benefits can spill over to other firms when there is diffusion of knowledge and openness in innovation, as reviewed by Roper *et al.*, who also note 'Estimating externality effects raises a number of conceptual and econometric difficulties' (Roper *et al.*, in press).

6.3   Indicator sets describing social and environmental conditions relating to wellbeing

Indicators, indicator sets and composite indices are being invented all the time. *The Economist* magazine (13 April 2013) published a 'misery index' defined as the annual average percentage unemployment rate plus the inflation rate (retail prices index percentage change on year earlier) in each year in the United Kingdom from 1970 to 2012. In doing so, it was replicating the United States Misery Index (see Appendix for link), created in the 1960s by economist Arthur Okun, an adviser to President Lyndon Johnson. It is an indicator, assuming not unreasonably that increasing unemployment and higher inflation lead to deterioration in economic and social conditions beyond their immediate reporting of the situation in the labour market and in retail prices.

However, while the 'misery index' (not least its title) may grab the attention of the reader by combining two well-known, socio-economic indicators, each soundly constructed in their own right, the resulting index is not as statistically robust as we envisaged for measures of wellbeing in Chapter 1. This illustrates to us the power of the Stiglitz, Sen and Fitoussi recommendations relating to environmental and social indicators. We will therefore structure this section around their six recommendations relating to such indicators:

- Quality of life depends on people's objective conditions and capabilities. Steps should be taken to improve measures of people's health, education, personal activities and environmental conditions.

- Quality-of-life indicators in all the dimensions covered should assess inequalities in a comprehensive way.

- Surveys should be designed to assess the links between various quality-of-life domains for each person, and this information should be used when designing policies in various fields.

- Statistical offices should provide the information needed to aggregate across quality-of-life dimensions, allowing the construction of different indices.

- Sustainability assessment requires a well-identified dashboard of indicators.

- The environmental aspects of sustainability deserve a separate follow-up based on a well-chosen set of physical indicators.

6.3.1   Improve measures of people's health, education, personal activities and environmental conditions

This is quite a tall order! As Stiglitz, Sen and Fitoussi observe in their recommendation, quality of life depends on people's objective conditions and capabilities. The statistical task is not just to ensure that areas such as health and education, already well covered in many countries, have improved measures: the full recommendation calls for substantial effort to be devoted to developing and implementing robust, reliable measures of social connections, political voice and security, because these have also been shown to predict life satisfaction.

As we saw in Chapter 2, there is no shortage of indicators to cover many areas, although the three topics just mentioned remain relatively poorly defined and measured, at least in regular outputs from national statistical offices. There are a number of initiatives to assess quantitatively the governance of countries. These provide insights for the problematic areas of quality of life by using expert advice and drawing on available data. Examples include the Ibrahim Index of African Governance, the Fraser Institute Index of Economic Freedom and the World Bank 'Doing Business Indicators' (see Appendix for links). Maplecroft (2013) is an example of a consultancy assessing and quantifying human rights risks and responsibilities, in this case in 197 countries.

There is an extensive academic and practitioner literature on indicators, including at least one journal dedicated to social indicators research (see Appendix). Later in this chapter, we look at where to find local, national and international sets of indicators about quality of life. Anand and Roope (2013) selected seven national or international 'comprehensive wellbeing surveys' or composite indicator sets. The authors offered eight examples of how such data could be used to inform key policy decisions, for example, around the quality of work. They also made their own recommendations for further work, including that 'All countries around the world develop dashboards of life quality indicators', along the lines reflected in their selected examples. They recognise that 'The development of these indicator sets requires time and thought'. We would add the need for transparency, inclusive consultation and engagement, so that concepts, frameworks and definitions are aired and discussed before indices and dashboards are finalised.

Shortly before the Stiglitz, Sen and Fitoussi report, Bandura (2008) had listed 178 composite indices measuring country performance, ranking or assessing countries according to some economic, political, social or environmental measure. A number of these were one-off reports, but many are repeated measures over time and covering large numbers of countries. Within this inventory, we can see indices that tackle almost every aspect of people's lives and the environment in which they live. Only a small proportion comes from national statistical offices. So, we wonder if a useful way forward under this Stiglitz Report recommendation would be for national statistical offices to draw on the information and research already available from such indices for their countries, before perhaps honing the data and adding to it, to meet current requirements.

This is not to understate the huge amount of statistical work that is undertaken in every country. We can see this, for example, from the 2013 Human Development Report (UNDP, 2013), which includes 14 statistical tables aimed at providing an overview of key aspects of human development in 187 countries (and eight other countries or territories, but where the statistical data is too sparse to include them in the main analysis). The tables include composite indicators estimated by the Human Development Report Office (HDRO), which we will refer to later, and nine tables presenting sets of indicators relating to aspects of human development. The HDRO gets the data from 26 named organisations, most of which are international data agencies with 'the mandate, resources and expertise' (UNDP, 2013, p. 140) to collect national data on specific indicators. We can see one source, the Gallup World Poll, where the organisation itself collects data in the countries. Otherwise, the international data agencies invariably rely on national statistical offices and other national official bodies.

To get a feel for the effort needed to improve coverage for the indicators selected by the HDRO and hence produce a complete statistical picture for those indicators, we looked at the pattern of missing values in one table (Table 9 in UNDP, 2013, pp. 174–177), relating to social integration. We saw this as an example of a topic highlighted for improvement by the Stiglitz, Sen, and Fitoussi recommendation. We are also aware that this does not address the full extent of work to be done to improve measures in this topic area because HDRO's selection of indicators will itself have been constrained by available data. With that caveat, we found that 72% of the cells in the table were completed. There was only one of the 14 indicators, the homicide rate, with a figure for all 187 countries. Three indicators were only available for around half of countries, with all other indicators in this table available for roughly 70–80% of countries. Scrolling down the table, as countries are ranked in decreasing order according to their overall Human Development Index score, we found something of a U-shaped distribution for the number of indicators available by country. Countries with the highest HDI rankings had the fullest coverage. But it was countries just below the middle of the ranked order that had the least coverage, while countries in the lowest decile of the rank had, on average, better coverage than other countries below the median. This may be some tentative, and incomplete, evidence of statistical improvements resulting from development assistance, although we have not examined this further by looking at the nature of aid to these countries.

One feature of a composite indicator designed to compare many countries is that it can appear as if the organisation compiling the index is detached from the countries. Organisations like the UN and the OECD are, of course, member organisations and work through extensive dialogue and discussion with countries. We wonder if in other cases there are organisations out in the country that select indicators with little dialogue. We noticed that *The Economist* magazine, in conjunction with Freedom House, has listed five items by which to assess the extent of democracy in Arab countries. The items presented in a report on the Arab Spring (*The Economist*, 13 July 2013) are as follows:

- Monarchy or republic;

- Elected head of state or not;

- Elected legislature or not;

- New constitution issued since 2010, or not;

- Serious political violence since 2010, or not.

This is presumably meant to be a one-off assessment. Each indicator is designed as a binary variable, so there will be no change in the 'index' until one or more of the items change. But actually it turns out that the items cannot all be scored yes or no: approaching one in three (7 out of 19) countries have a qualification against one of these items. And we cannot help noting that Western European countries include monarchies and republics. Although French revolutionaries guillotined their king, many other Europeans still love their reigning monarchs, so we are not sure what this tells us about democracy.

The Stiglitz, Sen and Fitoussi recommendation we have been discussing in this section calls for improvements across the board in quality-of-life measures and we do not, of course, dissent from that. But national statistical offices and other producers have limited financial and other resources and capabilities. How, when and which measures are tackled needs national priorities and international coordination and collaboration, such as that set out in the Busan Action Plan that is driving statistical developments in countries receiving international aid.

6.3.2   Quality-of-life indicators in all the dimensions covered should assess inequalities in a comprehensive way

Stiglitz, Sen and Fitoussi note that it is often necessary to produce measures of inequality to accompany indicators that measure quality of life overall or 'on average'. Two indicators may each record that, say, 25% of the population fail to meet a given marker of the quality of life. However, without further information on the underlying distribution of each aspect, we fail to appreciate the true extent of the inequality or the fairness captured within each headline indicator. Exploratory data analysis techniques seem a good place to start, as well as making use of summary measures of inequality, such as the Gini coefficient.

There is a related aspect to this, as Stiglitz, Sen and Fitoussi also acknowledge, which is that indicators must be measured over the whole population; otherwise inequalities can remain hidden. Before telephones were widely found in American or European homes, for example, survey researchers learned to assume that telephone surveys were not necessarily representative of the population as a whole. Telecommunications have moved on, but the issue still remains. Surveys, censuses and administrative data sources can all exclude groups of the population. Surveys conducted as 'household' surveys may well miss people living in communal accommodation. Working out which groups of the population are not covered by a statistical indicator sounds like an impossible task, that of finding the unknown unknowns. However, by trawling over different types of source, working with local authorities and agencies and using multiple channels of communication and outreach, statistical offices can seek to maximise their population coverage.

6.3.3   Surveys should be designed to assess the links between various quality-of-life domains for each person, and this information should be used when designing policies in various fields

Surveys, whether described as household, social or micro-surveys, are widely used in many statistical offices in the upper half of the countries, as ranked by the UN Development

Programme. Around the world, there are many centres offering training in survey skills and there are often publicly funded programmes to support innovations in survey methodology.

But surveys are not a panacea and they are under pressure as governments re-assess their priorities for statistics and the balance between timeliness, accuracy and cost in meeting their requirements. See Babbie (2013), for example, for a review of current practices of social research, looking at design, methods, operations and ethics. He also discusses how 'the political context in which we live and conduct social research affects that research', including the example of debate leading up to the 2010 US Census (Babbie, 2013, p. 80). It seems that for effective surveys to be conducted, we need policy makers to be confident in commissioning surveys, as well as having capacity to be able to deliver reliable surveys, either by statistical offices or by specialist centres or companies working for them.

Many surveys are either one-off or are repeated as free-standing surveys on a more or less regular basis. These so-called 'cross sectional' surveys have many advantages: for example, they can be prepared reasonably quickly, perhaps using pre-tested questions from a question-bank; they can be tested for representativeness against a sampling frame; and they are relatively easy to analyse using standard statistical software and analysis packages. However, for some purposes cohort studies or longitudinal surveys are more appropriate, particularly if the measurement of change over time is the focus of the research, especially when there may have been a policy or other external intervention between successive sweeps of the study.

The downside is that longitudinal studies tend to be more costly to run, they need effort to maintain the cohort, or to refresh it appropriately, and the analysis is more complex. Schuller *et al.* explore these issues in a review of 18 longitudinal sources in the United Kingdom relevant to an understanding of wellbeing, concluding that these studies 'are a ready and cost-effective resource for investigation into the antecedents and outcomes of subjective well-being as well as the distribution of well-being across the population, throughout the life course and over a long historical period'. They also provide the opportunity to test the validity of subjective wellbeing measures being used in the national statistical office's own surveys (Schuller *et al.*, 2012, p. 19).

It also seems unavoidable, and some would say desirable, that alternatives to surveys and censuses have to be considered. Following a framework for measuring wellbeing and progress, and the Stiglitz, Sen and Fitoussi recommendations, leads to the search for a mix of objective and subjective measures. National statistical offices are beginning to investigate alternative ways of compiling economic and social statistics and we anticipate there will be developments that will help with the measurement of wellbeing and progress in future. Improvements in technology and in government data sources offer opportunities to either modernise existing statistical processes, such as to run surveys and censuses mainly or fully online, or develop alternative processes that re-use existing data already held within government, perhaps supplemented with surveys. Following extensive research, two main options for providing population statistics in England and Wales along these lines were proposed in a public consultation from the UK Office for National Statistics in 2013.

6.3.4   Statistical offices should provide the information needed to aggregate across quality-of-life dimensions, allowing the construction of different indexes

The thrust of the OECD's framework for measuring wellbeing (OECD, 2011a, p. 18), and of the Stiglitz, Sen and Fitoussi recommendations taken together, is for a limited number of carefully chosen indicators, presented as a set or 'dashboard' rather than as a single index.

Nevertheless, as we have already seen, the demand remains for aggregate measures, so this recommendation aims to provide ways for users to construct their own overall index, using pragmatic measurement ideas as described in Chapters 1 and 4, rather than necessarily leading to a definitive single index of national wellbeing in a country. For an online example of how such pragmatic measurement can be presented, see the OECD's *Better Life* index website (see Appendix). Here the OECD does not set weights but users are given the opportunity to vary the importance of 11 aspects of national wellbeing, to see how their and other countries would then be ranked overall. (Aspects are initially rated equally, although this should not be interpreted as the 'official' view of wellbeing, simply a reasonable default opening position.)

There is a history of presenting alternative single measures to replace, or supplement, GDP (rather than using a dashboard, as the *Better Life* index does). We look at one in particular, to follow the thinking in generating new headline measures of wellbeing and progress. The Index of Sustainable Economic Welfare (ISEW) starts from an established economic indicator that is then subject to a series of adjustments, with the aim of coming to a new economic variable that should show more clearly whether or not economic welfare (or wellbeing) is increasing in a sustainable way. While these adjustments allow the compilers of an ISEW to explore trade-offs, the presentation of an ISEW is invariably the result of the set of weights finally used. To follow the spirit of the Stiglitz *et al.* recommendation, we wonder if the ISEW could also be presented more as a framework allowing users to explore trade-offs, similar to varying the weights in the *Better Life* index?

Nordhaus and Tobin (1972) produced the seminal Measure of Economic Welfare (MEW). Daly and Cobb (1989) extended their work by adding several other 'costs' into the definition of ISEW. There are now many different versions of the index (including Genuine Progress Indicator, see Appendix), produced largely by academics and other research centres and for a range of countries, states and regions within countries, including in the United States, Canada, Thailand, Chile, Austria, Belgium, Germany, Italy, Sweden and the United Kingdom. This diversity of measures illustrates the intrinsically pragmatic nature of the exercise.

The adjustments included in the ISEW seek to address criticisms of GDP. First, GDP itself is not the starting point, but personal (i.e. household) consumer expenditure, anticipating the Stiglitz, Sen and Fitoussi recommendations to focus on consumption and on the household perspective in measuring wellbeing. Adjustments are then made to exclude the 'defensive' or 'regrettable' expenditures that have been included in the national accounts, and to include things that are not taken account of, such as household production and the use of natural resources. Again in line with current thinking, there is a further adjustment to take account of inequality in the distribution of incomes. A summary of how ISEW could be calculated is as follows:

> ISEW = Personal consumer expenditure
>
> + an adjustment for income inequality
>
> + public expenditures (deemed nondefensive)
>
> + value of domestic labour & volunteering
>
> + various economic adjustments
>
> − defensive private expenditures
>
> − costs of environmental degradation
>
> − depreciation of natural capital.

(Source: Fender *et al.*, 2011, p. 8)

There are critiques that can be made of this approach, such as over how the choice of components is made. The concept of defensive expenditures is not clear-cut: some consumer expenditure on housing, food and drink could be seen as defensive, providing shelter and avoiding hunger and thirst, while some is discretionary, but how to decide this? Costs and benefits concerned with social and environmental issues not usually measured in monetary terms need to be monetised, and ways of doing this may well depend on assumptions. Is there a conceptual basis: by making adjustments to GDP, are such indices getting closer to some underlying concept of the wellbeing of a country over a given period of time – that is, is the result getting closer to a representational measurement, or is it at the hard pragmatic end of the spectrum?

There are a number of supporters of the ISEW who value what it does in questioning whether or not GDP is really measuring welfare, wellbeing and progress. In his overview of the MEW, Fioramonti also looks at other alternative indicators to GDP (2013, pp. 85–93), including noting that some of these have been funded by charitable and nongovernmental organisations in the absence of 'official' versions from national statistical offices.

Readers may be aware of many measures that aggregate across dimensions of quality of life and can see how widely they are used to summarise wellbeing and progress. The most prominent of these composite indices are probably the four human development indices now included in the Human Development Reports of the United Nations (see Appendix). The Human Development Index (HDI) combines four measures, covering the three dimensions of health, education (with two measures) and living standards. An inequality-adjusted HDI (IHDI) was introduced in 2010, taking into account the extent of inequalities in each of the three dimensions. Country-specific HDIs are available, and there are two further, currently experimental HDIs: the Gender Inequality Index and the Multidimensional Poverty Index.

Figure 6.3 is a scatter plot of the overall HDI value for each of the 187 countries covered, measured along the horizontal, against the country's GNI per capita, measured on the vertical scale. Both data series are included in the 2013 Human Development Report (and GNI per capita here is for 2012, but measured in 2005 dollars, using PPPs, rather than at current prices, also using PPPs, that we used earlier: this does not affect the overall picture). This chart shows that HDI is telling us something different about the relative state of development across countries than is shown by the economic measure of GNI. Qatar and Liechtenstein have by far the largest GNI per capita, but they are not at the very top of countries ranked by HDI value. In the lower left-hand portion of the chart, Equatorial Guinea is another country with GNI per capita considerably higher than countries which have similar HDI scores to it. Generally there looks to be some broad relationship between GNI and HDI, but HDI adds to our understanding of wellbeing and progress, both as an overall measure and through its component parts.

We should also note that the curvature in the relationship is something of an artefact. Since HDI is an almost entirely pragmatic measurement, one could define an alternative measure based on a monotonic transformation of it: such a transformed measure would be just as valid. In particular, one could define HDItrans, transformed so that the relationship was essentially linear. Of course, such a transformation would also lead to different relationships with other variables. The original (untransformed) version of HDI has the merits that it is widely used and recognised as a simple and effective summary. It does not require data on many items and it is easy to communicate. It is not appropriate here to go into detail, but we should note that there are some limitations to HDI (and indicators like it). In their full report, Stiglitz et al. (2009, 208) caution, for example, that the change in the value of a country's HDI over time can be dominated by its GDP change.

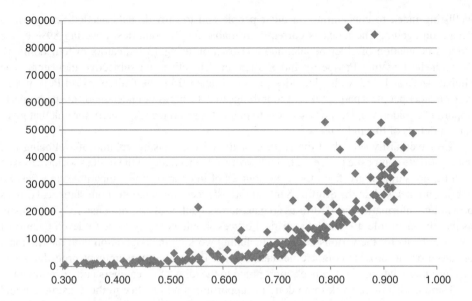

Figure 6.3 Scatterplot of GNI per capita (2012, in 2005 dollars using PPPs vertical axis) versus HDI value (2012).
Data source: United Nations Development Programme 2013 Human Development Report, Statistical Table 1.

To mention just a handful of other composite indices, the Legatum Prosperity Index (see Appendix for link) is constructed annually using information on economic growth, wealth and wellbeing. The 2012 index was available for 110 countries, with eight domains or sub-indices. The 89 variables included were selected drawing on theory and empirical research on economic growth and wellbeing. Variables are combined in a complex way, using weights derived from regression analyses. In essence, this seems to capture the extent to which a variable correlates with higher national income, measured as GDP per capita, or higher wellbeing (measured by life satisfaction data from the Gallup World Poll).

The Social Progress Index (link in Appendix) is based on social progress defined as 'the capacity of a society to meet the basic human needs of its citizens, establish the building blocks that allow citizens and communities to enhance and sustain the quality of their lives, and create the conditions for all individuals to reach their full potential' (Porter *et al.*, 2013, p. 7) and is operationalised using some 50 indicators in 12 domains, for 50 countries. The idea driving this index is that measuring the wellbeing of a country in a way that can be compared between countries means looking at particular social and environmental outcomes. The index is published by the Social Progress Imperative, whose advisory board, board of directors, funders and supporters are listed in their 2013 report. They represent a strong commitment to competitiveness, liberty and democracy. The index is intended for use by governments in national development initiatives and by businesses as a framework to articulate their impact on social progress, something echoed in the High Level Group report we looked at in Chapter 3.

HelpAge International is a network of nongovernmental organisations to support older people around the world. It has launched the Global AgeWatch Index, said to be the first wellbeing index to concentrate on older people and to provide data needed for informed debate on ageing. The index is currently available for 91 countries, covering 89% of the world's population of older people, and construction using 13 indicators in four domains. As with the Legatum Prosperity Index, there are objective and subjective indicators. The Global AgeWatch Index also includes measures taken from the Gallup World Poll, in this case on older people's perceptions of four things that the network understands are particularly important to older people, such as access to public transport (see Appendix for link that gives further details of this index).

We have hardly scratched the surface of the ever-increasing volume of wellbeing and quality-of-life composite indices, although we do note that many of the indices we have looked at draw, not surprisingly, from the same sources of internationally comparable statistics. So to bring all this back to the Stiglitz, Sen and Fitoussi recommendation about statistical offices providing 'information needed to aggregate across quality-of-life dimensions', it seems to us that the main role of national statistical offices should continue to be to develop national sources of data for the various domains, including working in cooperation with international organisations to provide comparable data as well. Pragmatic measurement procedures can then use these data to yield indices appropriate to the aims of researchers and governments.

There is also more work to be done in supporting good practice in the construction and use of composite indices, such as through the OECD's handbook on constructing composite indicators (OECD, 2008), which looks at methodology and provides a user guide. A number of fairly obvious pitfalls include the potential for bias in the selection of variables, either overtly to reflect a particular view of the world or more pragmatically by limitations in available indicators (which may in turn have been influenced by earlier decisions about the data to collect). Even where data appear to be available, there are sometimes anomalies, for example, that certain sections of the population may be under-represented by the data. There are also countries that do not feature in any of the composite indices that only draw on complete data or who show up with larger numbers of missing values in the HDI.

As we saw in Chapter 4, Paruolo et al. (2013) have looked in detail at how indicators and domains (which they call 'pillars') can best be aggregated if they need to be. They recognise the pros and cons of composite indicators, and that one of us (Hand, 2009) has already supported the pragmatic nature of composite indicators, not least that they are 'pervasive in the public discourse' (Paruolo et al., 2013, p. 630). The authors make four broad recommendations for the developers of composite indicators. If followed, these will inevitably lead to more complex, technical presentations of composite indicators and their constituent parts. But perhaps that is the direction to be followed, given the importance of building measures to go beyond GDP. However, with complexity comes the need for clear and powerful tools to help users explore the measures. We also think that publication of latest results from a composite indicator should include commentary, so that readers gain insights on the results from the people who have compiled them.

The recommendations of a Royal Statistical Society working party on measuring the processes and outcomes of public services (Bird et al., 2005, p. 2) are also relevant to the measures of quality of life. The working party called for, among other things, clear definitions to be applied in constructing indicators, and for indicators to be accompanied by measures of uncertainty. (We have found those to be missing from all the indices we have looked at.) The working party concluded that well-informed public debate does not result unless there are efforts to educate the public, as well as policy makers, in the use of indicators, and indeed about statistics more generally.

6.3.5   Sustainability assessment requires a well-identified dashboard of indicators

This Stiglitz, Sen and Fitoussi recommendation continues, 'The distinctive features of the components of this dashboard should be that they are interpretable as variations of some underlying "stocks". A monetary index of sustainability has its place in such a dashboard but, under the current state of the art, it should remain essentially focussed on economic aspects of sustainability.' We discussed dashboards in Chapter 5 and we here want to focus on the measurement of stocks because we think this is an interesting way of 'taking stock of wellbeing' as well as assessing sustainability.

We come to this by realising that one way of currently assessing how a nation is perform-ing, or the wellbeing of its citizens, is to measure the value that its citizens and organisations put on all of the goods and services that they consume. For goods and services with a market price, then the value of goods and services purchased, as included in the national accounts, may suffice. Standard economic theory suggests that, acting as rational consumers, price reflects value. (A more sophisticated approach would be to factor in customer satisfaction as well as 'the bottom line'. That is how some businesses seek to increase value. However, it would be impractical to measure this alongside the measurement of consumer expenditure. It is also rather a large leap to assume that respondents to surveys of life satisfaction take account of their satisfaction as consumers in all but the most general sense.)

So perhaps we should turn not to current consumption but to the current wealth of the nation, in the broadest possible terms and look at what the New Economics Foundation (Michaelson *et al.*, 2009) and others call the 'real wealth' of the nation. Wellbeing might then be said to comprise the kinds of capital that we reviewed in Chapter 2 (natural, produced, human and social capital; cultural capital may or not be a separate entity). We have seen a number of high-level models linking wellbeing or human welfare with these capitals (e.g. Pearce and Barbier, 2000, p. 20 and Harper and Price, 2011) but it is still far from clear what we mean by wellbeing, or how wellbeing is affected by the stocks of these capitals, or by changes in their levels. Both wellbeing and sustainable development measures effectively draw on the same broad schema using the capitals, so it does seem worthwhile to use a single measurement framework, to support the assessment of the wellbeing of the nation, and hence progress over time, as well as the sustainability of our current way of living.

Since the 1990s, there have been moves to produce a bigger picture of wellbeing and progress than that given by the conventional national accounts. The first step is 'to view the way in which natural resources and environments provide economic benefits as being similar to the way in which any valuable asset provides "services" to an economy' (Pearce and Barbier, 2000, p. 19). The second step is to recognise that human and social capital, as well as natural capital and produced capital, support the economic process. The third and final step is to accept that national wellbeing (or human welfare, in economic terminology) depends not just on the economic process but also on how all four capitals also support the things that make life worthwhile.

This is not about replacing markets but seeks to recognise their full impact over all the resources that they require to function, especially the resources and ecosystem services provided by nature. Hawken *et al.* called this 'natural capitalism' and concluded that 'future economic progress can best take place in democratic, market based systems of production and distribution in which all forms of capital are fully valued, including human, manufactured, financial and natural capital' (Hawken *et al.*, 1999, p. 4). As we can see, though, the challenge to fully value all capitals is huge. First the capitals have to be identified and quantified in some way, and then their value has to be determined.

Some argue (e.g. Helm 2012) that classical economics started with three factors of production – capital, labour and land – and that as land ran out then the population would stop growing, consumption would level off and we would be in a steady or stationary state. That clearly did not happen, but some way along the line land got dropped from the equations of modern economics. This made economics more manageable, but hid many realities, especially environmental issues and what was happening to natural capital.

It is not clear whether it is the level of capital and other stocks or changes in the level that drives wellbeing. The wellbeing of some individuals might include an element of the assessment of the sustainability of the current position, as one example of how wellbeing and sustainable development are interwoven. For relative simplicity, it might be sufficient to ensure that stocks of capital are maintained at existing levels, so that the potential for generating wellbeing is not reduced over time. The use of such 'floor levels' appears to be supported by the Stiglitz, Sen and Fitoussi report.

One important point to note is that this is not to ignore inequality. This is experienced at the individual level and, although there are implications for society as a whole, we must not lose sight of the Stiglitz, Sen and Fitoussi recommendation discussed earlier about the need to track inequality in all dimensions of quality of life. There is then the further possibility of assessing inequality in terms of capitals, to see how all resources are distributed. 'Floor levels' may not be appropriate here: who is to say how much inequality is too much?

If we are to define national wellbeing as the level of the various capitals at or around a point in time, then we need not spend too much time working through the possible links between these capitals and the individual wellbeing of all the citizens of that nation. Indeed, the current level of subjective wellbeing, and how it is distributed, could be included as a further measure of human or social capital. We are fully aware that building dashboards of measures of capital will be challenging, even for countries with extensive statistical systems and resources. Measures of income are easier to produce and could serve as interim indicators, but we are nevertheless drawn to the idea of *taking stock,* at a point in time, of the state of a nation's various capitals, assets and resources, and seeing that as the current wellbeing of the nation. Looking at how such assessments change over time will provide measures of progress. Looking at progress alongside markers of vulnerability for each stock, such as how stock levels sit against appropriate floor levels, should help build understanding of the sustainability of current development.

There are significant issues to consider in defining, measuring and valuing each capital. Developments in this area proceed at a slow pace: it is over 10 years ago that Cote and Healy (2001) recognised the role of human and social capital in the wellbeing of nations. Identifying all of a particular stock in existence may present considerable conceptual and measurement challenges. Each stock probably has its own natural unit, such as its financial value in the case of assets held in banks, or the weight or volume of natural resources. There is no clear understanding of what a unit of social capital is, however. If we want to compare or to aggregate different kinds of capitals, then we will need a common valuation. Stiglitz, Sen and Fitoussi appear to go for the pragmatic line, which is 'focussing the monetary aggregation on items for which reasonable valuation techniques exist, such as physical capital, human capital, and certain natural resources' (Stiglitz *et al.*, 2010, 20). Khan notes that there are two broad approaches to valuing total wealth: there are various 'top down' approaches, often using models, say, based on wealth being defined as the present value of future consumption, as well as the 'bottom up' approach of adding up individual capitals (Khan, 2013, p. 4).

The link between value and price for stocks or capitals is problematic, as it is generally, and valuations of stocks and capitals are likely to be contested. Many stocks simply do not have a price because they are not traded (and here we are distinguishing between the absence of a price and a price set at nil). Such stocks may still have value, seen, for example, when the countryside is described, at least by those campaigning to preserve it, as our greatest natural asset. As an example of quantifying the 'state of nature' in the United Kingdom and its overseas territories, see Burns *et al.* (2013).

The problem of defining value is an old one. In their introduction to a detailed history of value and financial markets, Goetzmann and Rouwenhorst (2005, p. 4) do not so much define value as identify the 'transfer of value through time' as a key foundation of finance and financial innovation. There are tools to calculate the 'true' value of money but just looking at the simplest kind of financial arrangement may help illuminate the idea of value. In taking a loan, the borrower gains wealth, but typically at the cost of incurring a charge, in the form of interest payments. So for the borrower, the value of the loan is realised by what they can do with the money they obtain, tempered by any interim payments they are committed to make while they hold the loan, and that they need to make arrangements to repay the loan at some time in the future. For the lender, the value comes though giving up some of their current wealth with the expectation that they will regain it later, and receive compensatory payments in the meanwhile.

Peter Drucker recognises the nature of value when he suggests that customers do not just buy a product or a service, it is always 'a utility, that is what a product or service does for' the customer that is important (Drucker, 2007, p. 15). In other words, people buy and value the benefits that products, services and their suppliers offer to them. By analogy, we might say that people do not value the environment by putting a price on it; they value the benefits that it offers to them. Building on this, and keeping in mind the core idea of price emerging from the value given to a good or service when it is exchanged, economists have developed valuations that are based on what people say they are collectively willing or prepared to pay (e.g. Pearce and Özdemiroglu, 2002). However, such techniques do not deal in market prices because money has not changed hands, and they assume rational behaviour by participants in the study, an assumption in economics that has been increasingly questioned.

An alternative approach to valuation, in place of stated or revealed preferences, is to use subjective wellbeing. Fujiwara and Campbell (2011) review the established approaches before setting out a technique that starts by estimating the change in subjective wellbeing associated with the good, service or asset in question. This would then be monetised, for example, by estimating the change in the amount of income from employment that would be needed to give the same change in subjective wellbeing. The technique has been developed for use in cost–benefit analyses of proposed changes to public services or infrastructure, where presumably potential impact can be reasonably well identified by respondents to a survey of how their subjective wellbeing would be affected. It is not clear if the technique would work as a way of valuing assets more generally, unless the choice was between all or none of the asset. Sticking with subjective wellbeing and not monetising it would chime with Oswald's proposal that we should be measuring a 'nation's emotional prosperity rather than its economic prosperity (i.e. we ought to focus on the level of mental well-being, not on the number of pounds in people's bank accounts)' (Oswald, 2010, p. 651).

Dresner notes how interest in sustainable development has waxed and waned, including criticisms of the vagueness of the concept, with consequent difficulty in putting sustainable development into operation. He concludes that, rather than agreeing upon a precise definition of sustainable development, we should be 'agreeing upon the *values* that would underlie any such definition' (Dresner, 2008, p. 70). This introduces the question of ethics, as well as intrinsic (e.g. monetary) values, into cost–benefit analyses.

When we talk of the values in this way, we are referring to something more deeply held than attitudes and opinions. Values are part of our psychology, reflecting upbringing, background and influences. Values can be measured, as in the World Values Survey and the British Values Survey – the latter started in 1973 (see Appendix for links). Using data like these, Ronald Inglehart (1977) described as 'post-materialists' a generation that was more focussed on society than economy, compared to earlier generations. In more recent work, Pecorelli identifies three main value groups. One is those who focus on a 'good society', and appear to be closest to Inglehart's postmaterialists. A second group comprises people from various backgrounds who just want results in the form of free market solutions; they are relaxed about differences in wealth. A third group values a 'secure society' that is economically secure in a world of finite resources. The relative prevalence of the different value groups may vary from generation to generation (Pecorelli, 2013).

Similar issues have emerged in the search for 'public value', a concept aimed at enabling the fullest consideration of the costs and benefits of public services and infrastructure. (We flagged the concept of public value at the end of Chapter 1.) These are the 'public things', such as parks, schools, forests, public broadcasters and the military, that political theorist Bonnie Honig has identified (e.g. Pearce, 2013a, p. 229).

Measuring 'public value', that is, the value that citizens give to public services, such as education, health services, museums and galleries, let alone less tangible 'public things', is far from easy. Not all citizens are clients of every public service or user of every public thing. Nevertheless, they may want to value these services and things in case they do need to call on them, or because they are deemed to be an integral part of the way of life.

Work on public value has proceeded in two ways over the last two decades or so. First, the managers of individual public services have been encouraged to consider public value in delivering services to the public, for example, by asking representatives of the public what they do indeed value about the service in question. This had led to guidance and good practice in creating public value (e.g. Moore, 1997). The second, and slimmer, body of work seeks to include public value in the accounts of public sector organisations or in the national accounts. Moore (2013) has developed a 'Public Value Account' that 'outlines the values that citizens want to see produced by, and reflected in, agency operations. These include the achievement of collectively defined missions, the fairness with which agencies operate, and the satisfaction of clients and other stake-holders' and he offers a 'Public Value Scorecard' to help public sector managers 'sustain or increase the value they create into the future'. Grice (2011, p. 624) has reported on work in the United Kingdom and in the OECD to include in the national accounts the assessment of 'government's own direct contribution to the generation of value, in the form of public services'.

People in the arts and cultural sectors sometimes speak of cultural value, but what is that? The focus is often on the value of individual works of art or buildings, for example, if an antique object is about to leave the country. Carey (2005, p. 167) questions the point of that, suggesting that the aim of research in the arts should switch to finding out 'how art has affected and changed other people's lives … investigate the audience not the texts'. This brings us back to the big picture, of wellbeing seemingly determined by the state of many economic, social, cultural, governmental and environmental factors.

National statistical offices and others are producing measures of some capital stocks. Measures of physical capital are already integral parts of the system of national accounts. Environmental accounts are being produced using methodologies and conventions recommended by the UN's evolving System of Environmental and Economic Accounts (SEEA; see Appendix for link) to accompany the System of National Accounts (SNA). This includes the valuation of stocks of natural resources such as sub-soil assets (e.g. oil and gas reserves), water, forest, aquatic resources and land. We understand that natural resource accounting will move up the agenda as a result of increasing international awareness, from Rio+20 as well as through the World Bank and other initiatives.

The value of the stock of human capital is also being estimated, albeit restricted initially to measuring the knowledge, skills and talents of people currently in employment, rather than for the population as a whole (see OECD statistics working papers on human capital, available on the link given in the Appendix). There would seem to be a tie-up to be made between existing measures of human capital and surveys of the literacy, numeracy, problem-solving and science proficiency among school children and adults.

There is a huge research literature about social capital, including reporting on survey work. However, this seems problematic to address at the national level. Social capital is invariably talked about as belonging to an area, such as a neighbourhood, a community of people defined through some common interest or background, or in terms of a formal or informal organisation. However, social capital is only manifest through individual attributes and can only be measured in surveys of individuals. While these can be measured over everyone in a given area, community or organisation, it is an open question as to whether the accumulation of social capital leads to societal wellbeing or not. The rules for amalgamating social capital are not clear. An organisation or an area with lots of bonding capital aids the wellbeing of those in it, but without bridging capital may detract from the wellbeing of people excluded from the organisation or area. It is for reasons like this that social capital is problematic as one of the pillars of wellbeing.

6.3.6 The environmental aspects of sustainability deserve a separate follow-up based on a well-chosen set of physical indicators

Under this recommendation, Stiglitz, Sen and Fitoussi particularly identify a need for a clear indicator of our proximity to dangerous levels of environmental damage, such as associated with climate change or the depletion of fishing stocks. As they note, 'Fortunately, a good deal of work has already been undertaken in this field'. This work ranges over sustainable development indicators, some of which we discussed in Chapter 2, green growth indicators, which seem to be a variant of sustainable development indicators, and natural resource accounting, covered in the previous section. There is also much to glean from the detailed scientific reviews of climate change reported.

One further development to note is Yale University's Environmental Performance Index (see Appendix for link). This is built with 22 indicators covering environmental policy goals (e.g. marine protected areas), outcomes (e.g. child mortality), stocks (e.g. forest growing stock) and changes (e.g. in water quality). The 2012 analysis covers 132 countries. The index and indicators are intended to be used within countries to support good practice in environmental protection, as well as raising awareness of critical natural resource and environmental constraints to be considered alongside significant economic and social challenges.

6.4   Survey-based data on subjective wellbeing

Stiglitz, Sen and Fitoussi concluded that measures of both objective and subjective wellbeing provide key information about people's quality of life. They recommended that 'statistical offices should incorporate questions to capture people's life evaluations, hedonic experiences and priorities in their own surveys'. Rifkin (2011, p. 223) sees quality of life being used increasingly to judge the overall performance of the economy: 'If quality of life requires a shared notion of our collective responsibility for the larger community in which we dwell, the question becomes, where does that community end?' It could 'encompass the biosphere itself'.

For others, the focus of measuring national wellbeing should be on individual or human wellbeing because, as Dolan and Harrison (2013, p. 1) see it, 'ultimately a good life has to be good for the individual. At some point, this requires inquiry into how people feel'. They call for measures to assess 'both how we feel on a day to day basis and how we think about life in an overall sense', using a variety of measures 'as carefully selected approaches are complementary for research and building effective interventions'.

This is also the approach adopted by the New Economics Foundation, which calls for more emphasis to be given to collecting accounts of individual functioning or flourishing. These would focus on 'a range of experiences or characteristics of life believed to be part of "living well"' (Abdallah *et al.*, 2011, p. 12).

We saw in Chapter 4 that there have been many advances in the measurement of human wellbeing through surveys in which people assess their own wellbeing. We can be confident that properly designed, conducted and analysed measures of subjective wellbeing should be reliable and should give meaningful results, including how the measures vary as circumstances change. A number of national statistical offices are now gathering subjective wellbeing data, as well as established academic studies and networks (see Appendix). A number of different approaches are being pursued. Anand *et al.* (2009, p. 147), for example, conclude that it is feasible, but nontrivial, to implement a survey instrument 'that provides indicators of capability across a wide range of life domains and issues'. We describe official UK developments in Chapter 7 (see also Hicks *et al.*, 2013, for a summary, including potential use of subjective wellbeing data in policy).

Lau *et al.* noted some 10 years ago that, 'While a plethora of QOL [quality of life] measures are available, almost all have been developed in Western countries. This poses major concerns regarding their cross-cultural validity and limits their usefulness as comparative tools' (2005, p. 404). They also saw a disjunction between QOL measures and measures of subjective wellbeing, wanting to include assessments of how people feel about their lives as well as more objective measures of the quality of life, especially when the latter are particularly drawn from a medical point of view. Lau *et al.* concluded from using it that the Personal Wellbeing Index, originally developed by Robert Cummins in 1997 (see Cummins *et al.*, 2003), 'demonstrated evidence of utility as a cross-cultural tool for measuring SWB within Asian Chinese and Western societies' (Cummins *et al.*, 2003, p. 426). Some of the many subjective wellbeing measurement tools now available are listed in the Appendix.

Measures of more objective attributes, such as health, employment status and wealth, do need to be collected as well if we are to understand the drivers or determinants of human wellbeing. We must also be careful not to describe factors as drivers when the factors may simply be associated with levels of self-reported wellbeing – see also the discussion of causes, effects and correlates in Chapter 4. Longitudinal studies will be needed in order to confirm casual relationships between, say, employment status and wellbeing. A range of data can be collected at the same time as individual wellbeing is measured. This makes for coherence and clarity in analysis, but may be costly and burdensome on respondents. We should also bear in mind that we strictly then gather subjective reports even of objective factors (survey interviewers will seldom want to check, for example, the number of vehicles that the respondent reports are available to the household). Data from other sources may be needed, with consequent challenges in data matching and analysis.

Measuring subjective wellbeing can best be seen as an emerging science. There are many open issues around content, methods and presentation. In many cases, these issues will need resolving in terms that meet national user requirements, while other aspects will be more important in working towards international standards. A subjective wellbeing measure tends to be mainly about assessing an individual's own wellbeing, but there is also scope to gather individual assessments of the wellbeing of the community and society more widely. There are choices to be made against time, resources and accuracy. It is not yet clear how frequently subjective wellbeing should be measured. We will look at some of the presentational issues in the following chapter.

As Peracchi and Rossetti (2013) note, survey respondents are often asked to evaluate various aspects of their life, such as life satisfaction or self-rated health, on an ordered scale. Although such questions are widely used, there is concern that respondents describing the same underlying position may interpret the values on the scale differently, and so answer them differently. Anchoring vignettes (King *et al.*, 2004) have been used, including when measuring life satisfaction, as a way of identifying potential variation in using an ordinal scale. However, this in turn depends on further assumptions. Peracchi and Rossetti propose a simple test of these assumptions and their results confirm the importance of testing the validity of vignettes chosen to anchor a particular life satisfaction scale. Further research, for example, on vignette design, may also help to improve the robustness of life satisfaction measures, including where cross-national comparisons are needed and which might be particularly prone to cultural differences.

To conclude, as Bok does (2010, p. 62): 'Although there are limits to the value of happiness research in making policy decisions, investigators can now publish findings about the well-being of populations that are far more useful to policy-makers than anything Bentham and his contemporaries could produce'. He explores several fields of policy in which subjective well-being measures can add to the search for policy interventions or at least raise 'especially challenging questions', including in education, healthcare and the labour market. Bok's 'most provocative issue' raised by research on happiness is whether 'Americans are wise to place such a high priority on increasing and sustaining economic growth' (2010, 63), which looks to us like an issue not just for policy makers in the United States but for governments, policy makers, businesses and the public around the world.

6.5   Developments in measuring national wellbeing and progress around the world

Initiatives to measure wellbeing in individual countries were presented and discussed at a roundtable as part of the OECD World Forum in India in 2012. The Australian statistician Brian Pink listed some 75 'indicator projects' concerned with wellbeing and progress around the world and the Australian Bureau of Statistics has compiled a list of a further 50 projects within their country. Building on these, a list of all the initiatives and related developments that we have found is given in the Appendix, with apologies for any that are missing. We encourage all readers to explore all that seem relevant to their own situation.

Looked at overall, the projects cover all of the ways in which progress has been conceptualised and each of the typologies of national wellbeing measures discussed at the start of this chapter. They draw on many different approaches, including sustainable development, human development and community development (follow the link in the Appendix to the City of Onkaparinga for an example of how to monitor comprehensively the wellbeing of communities).

There is also much rich information about how communities, civil society, businesses and policy makers are being engaged in the process of developing and using new measures. On this, the European Economic and Social Committee, part of the machinery of government of the European Union, published an 'Opinion' in 2012, which including the conclusion that 'civil society, together with the other social and institutional players, should determine the arenas in which the progress of societies is to be gauged, identifying specific areas and salient facts (in the economic, social and environmental spheres). This can be done by means of dedicated information, consultation and participation instruments' (EESC, 2012, p. 3). This is sound advice. However, it requires national statistical offices, along with others involved in building new measures of wellbeing and progress, to reach out to civil society. There are good examples of this in developments listed in the Appendix.

There is perhaps an inevitable emphasis on indicators, which are relatively easy to collate into new indexes. The Appendix includes many links to national sets of sustainable development indicators. However, United Nations Resolution 65/309, which we quoted in Section 1.1, refers to 'new indicators, and other initiatives' in producing additional measures of wellbeing and development. We (and more importantly, UN Secretary General Mr Ban) are particularly keen to see economic, social and environmental accounts, which should present a more coherent and integrated picture of wellbeing and progress. Covering human and natural capital as well as financial capital, these will inevitably take longer to develop. We are reassured, for example, that the programme of statistical developments across Europe, to support 'GDP and Beyond', includes substantive, collaborative work involving national statistical offices and international organisations on this and on the other Stiglitz *et al.* recommendations. (This is a long-term programme, with new outputs starting to appear from 2013 to 2020). Ongoing development of the System of National Accounts, particularly though the creation of 'satellite accounts', will also support wider accounting approaches. We have referred in Chapter 5 to new work on the analysis of the household sector, time use and national time accounts, and to state of nature reports.

Within the official statistical community, work is proceeding both in national statistical offices and through world and world-regional bodies, such as Eurostat. We will look at developments in the United Kingdom in the following chapter, but it is important to register here that, as in many countries, there are initiatives beyond the national statistics office. How, or even if, these are always being brought together in order to share good practice, and perhaps to produce a 'meta-analysis' of national wellbeing in a country, is not clear to us. Israel is one example of collaborative working, where the Israeli Society for Sustainable Economics, a nonprofit organisation, is leading the construction of Israel's Progress Index ('Erech'). The goal of the project is to establish an index for progress and quality of life, and promote it as a central tool for decision making in Israel. Also involved are the Israeli Central Bureau of Statistics, academic centres, the relevant government ministry, other nonprofit organisations and the Israeli public, through 'Community Assessment' reviews (see Appendix for link).

Staying with national statistical offices, we want especially to mention the French National Institute of Statistics and Economic Studies (the French acronym is INSEE) as the torchbearer for taking forward the Stiglitz, Sen and Fitoussi recommendations that were formally commissioned by France. In an update issued in February 2013 (see Appendix for website link), INSEE presented a dossier of some 50 relevant statistical outputs, working papers and reports, along with a summary schedule of work up to 2017. These are organised under the three main strands of the Stiglitz *et al.* report: developments relating to GDP (accounting for half of the material), quality of life, sustainable development and the environment.

We also want to draw attention to the work of the Italian National Statistics Office, Istat, on 'Equitable and Sustainable Wellbeing' (Benessere Equo e Sostenibile or BES in Italian, see link in Appendix). This seems to us to demonstrate many features that make a successful initiative, including leadership from the top of the organisation (Enrico Giovannini, the President of Istat, was previously chief statistician at the OECD, leading their global project on measuring progress and a member of the Stiglitz, Sen and Fitoussi Commission). Istat is working closely with stakeholders, particularly through the National Council for Economics and Labour (CNEL). The Italian public have been involved, notably through two consultations on 'what matters?' The first of these was carried out in 2011, as part of the official social survey of 24 000 households (see Appendix for link), in order to provide a basis for discussion of the domains of BES by the CNEL/Istat steering committee. The second consultation was an online questionnaire completed by 2500 people, used to help refine domains and indicators.

Istat and CNEL published their first report on equitable and sustainable wellbeing in Italy in March 2013. It was launched at the Italian Parliament in the presence of the President of the Republic, with much media coverage. Tommaso Rondinella from Istat told us that the reaction was 'very positive', both in terms of the extent and the depth of the coverage, though there were also, as in the United Kingdom, some reports simply talking about 'happiness' and the demise of GDP (personal communication, 2013). BES has also caught the public's attention, with over 1600 people registered for the BES newsletter and many other attending meetings presenting the interactive online tool and results that have been organized by dozens of local organisations and institutions across Italy.

The Italian programme of work reflects the Stiglitz *et al.* recommendations, including measuring subjective wellbeing. A single question on life satisfaction has been asked since 2011 and other questions are being considered, but the social survey is already 'too long' and there has not yet been the opportunity to ask additional subjective wellbeing questions. Tommaso Rondinella also briefed us on Istat's engagement with policymakers. (Istat is leading the EU e-Frame Project, which includes enhancing the relevance of wellbeing measures and analysis for addressing key policy issues, as well as generally fostering and supporting wellbeing measurement, see link in Appendix.) At the national policy level in Italy, things are moving slowly, although there is some movement within the Parliament towards a structured system of policy formation and evaluation based on 12 domains in BES. This contrasts with local level, where there is much more attention, in particular at city level. A network of the 15 major Italian cities has launched a project, strongly supported by Istat and by its territorial offices, to provide wellbeing indicators at local level. Some of them, like Bologna, Genoa and Venice, launched local consultations in order to better understand what wellbeing means locally and why.

Travelling around the globe, Clode (2012) reports from a conference on Asia-Pacific developments in measuring progress, including on a commission on measuring wellbeing established by the Japanese government. He also notes the recent launch of China's National

'Quality Index', which measures the economy by sustainability, social equality and ecological impact, as well as by size. 'Whilst not directly affecting government priorities, the index has provoked intense debate, especially amongst provincial leaders', he observes (Clode, 2012, p. 4). Key issues for the region include wellbeing and ageing, the wellbeing of women, governance as a dimension of wellbeing and the need for governments to measure extreme risks.

Countries still developing their national statistical systems have the opportunity to incorporate measures of wellbeing, progress and sustainable development from early on. On its twentieth anniversary in 2013, the Palestinian Central Bureau of Statistics published a strategy for the following five years that includes promoting the use of statistics in policy making by government and the private sectors. We see from a recent call to tender that a statistical centre for the Cooperation Council for the Arab Countries of the Gulf (United Arab Emirates, Bahrain, Saudi Arabia, Oman, Qatar and Kuwait), created in 2013 has 'progress and development indicators' as one of its 10 priority areas, alongside more established statistical topics such as national accounts, price indices and a population census.

There are many initiatives listed in the Appendix. This is just a small selection and we have not repeated the countries we looked at in Chapter 3 (Measuring Australia's Progress, for which updated results were published in November 2013, and developments in Bhutan, Canada, China and the United States). There has been a Parliamentary Commission of Inquiry in Germany (Kroll, 2011, p. 7) and a national round-table in Spain (Herrero and Morán, 2011), and we are sure that readers will be aware of other developments. We welcome updates on proposals, especially on those we have not been able to follow up on, such as reports of a new portal 'Turkey by Numbers'.

In 2010, two researchers at the OECD, Katherine Scrivens and Barbara Iasiello, reported on their broad overview of societal progress indicators and their uses, including case studies involving interviews with key players in five initiatives. While acknowledging that it is difficult to generalise, they did present lessons that they had learned to help deliver indicators that will be used in decision-making processes and with real impact on policy and societal outcomes. They suggest that 'three conditions need to be met. First, the indicators should be seen as *legitimate* by the intended users. Second, the indicators should be set within a wider *system* that provides "fit-for-purpose" information. Third, appropriate *incentives* must exist for stakeholders to act on that information' (Scrivens and Iasiello, 2010, p. 52).

We recognise and support their conclusions. Our take on this is that strong and sustained support for the measurement and application of national wellbeing and progress is needed from three angles: political leaders, policy making and statistical producers. Taking each in turn, we observe that political strength is gained the closer it is to the centre of government. We reckon that strength in the policy sphere requires two things: support from senior administrators and policy applications that are designed to improve the things that matter to people. Strength in the area of statistical production, we suggest, arises when it is a national statistical office that is involved in providing credible and trusted data. This is not to devalue the significant contribution of academic, commercial and nonprofit providers, but simply to ensure that, as Scrivens and Iasiello concluded, measures of wellbeing and progress can best be maintained within a wider system, which we think should be a national statistical system.

In looking at developments around the world, readers may want to reflect on how they are working, as well as what they are delivering. What, for example, are the capability or capacity requirements, such as skills in data collection and analysis? What about data quality and the frequency and timeliness of publication? How is research and development into the measurement of wellbeing and progress being funded and otherwise stimulated? What infrastructure is needed to communicate the results, and what levels of 'statistical literacy' are required of end-users and by the news media? There are also some interesting issues around the emergence of 'early adopters', the agencies who start producing new measures which may then be taken up by others.

6.6 Important issues in the measurement of national wellbeing

Despite the proliferation of wellbeing, progress and development indicators, we can see that a number of important issues have yet to be resolved. Hall *et al.* (2010, p. 10) have, for example, identified differences between various approaches that they drew on for the framework to measure the progress of societies that they proposed. This is not to suggest that there are irreconcilable differences, but it would seem to be helpful to work on these issues collectively, during the development of measures of wellbeing and progress, so that measures are fit for the purposes they are being designed for.

It is unarguably the case that there are different concepts behind each of the starting points for new measures of national wellbeing and progress. As we saw in Chapters 2 and 3, work in earlier decades can now be categorised as being about, for example, individual life satisfaction, individual wellbeing, quality of life, economic welfare, human development, the state of nature or sustainable development. We suggested earlier that there is a possible 'big picture' embracing all of these and potentially side-stepping the need to fit them together precisely. (This may, in particular, avoid the need to specify whether or not human wellbeing is the overall goal.) However, this still leaves open the need for clarity in what each of them is referring to, so that we have a common and reliable language with which to discuss different aspects of the overall picture, and how they fit together. We also recognise that there has been considerable investment in the development of communities of interest and expertise around each concept, which needs to be maintained as we go forward in measuring wellbeing and progress.

No 'big picture' will be understandable, or useful, unless it includes a manageable number of dimensions that will act as the pointers to more specific decisions that we need to make or policies that need to be put in place. As with the broad concepts, there are already many different sets of dimensions that could be adopted, each with their own advocates (and also with their own challenges). Some of the developments of national wellbeing measures have started from the position that the dimensions should reflect the things that matter to people. But such things can vary over time, unless we seek to anchor the dimensions in more deeply held values, and they may well vary between people in different places.

This feels like it needs quite a complex process to reach an accepted set of dimensions, and a process that balances user needs from within the place being considered, alongside needs for comparative or aggregate measures across a number of places. We intentionally said 'balance' international comparability with national and local needs to avoid the suggestion that this is about one or the other. Such balances have been drawn in many other areas of official statistics. Bringing national and local statisticians together to help compile international standards and guidance is a good way of understanding the various requirements and of drawing on best practice.

Some of the things that matter to some people turn out to be things that are good to have around us – thinking of the arts, culture more generally, landscape, for example – but which we tend not to use very often. Does this mean we give such things less value or is there a way in which these things can be included to reflect our underlying value of them? The definition and measurement of public value is at an early stage but we think this will have much to contribute to the measurement of national wellbeing.

A related point is how we deal with things held in common between different places, such as the oceans, but beyond the boundaries of any country. There will be lessons to learn from Elinor Ostrom's work on how communities manage common resources in practice, particularly her general framework (Ostrom, 2009) and the importance of monitoring (e.g. Ostrom *et al.*, 2012, p. 27). Although Ostrom values the way in which communities can operate to manage shared resources, this does tend to emphasise the 'bonding' aspects of social capital, things that benefit the existing members of a community, rather than the way in which social capital can 'bridge' between different communities. We suggested in Section 2.13 that all forms of social capital should be identified and measured.

Moving on to more operational concerns, the ways in which dimensions of national wellbeing and progress have been measured in practice are many and varied, as the briefest of glances at the indicator projects in the Appendix will demonstrate. There is a mix of new research and the understandable re-use of existing indicators, driven in some cases by whether or not resources and timescales allow for collecting fresh data. We want simply to recognise that there is much detail to be worked through in designing valid and useful indicators and that, as we remarked in Section 4.6, the devil is in the detail!

In talking about indicators, we are referring only to the top level of a pyramid of statistical systems and sources covered by the typology of methods listed at the start of this chapter. While there is much attention given to the design of headline indicators, these may well require substantive supporting systems, for example, to measure human capital. Those systems, as with the current system of national accounts, will draw on many different survey, census and administrative data sources, the bedrock of all statistical developments.

National statistical offices, international organisations and other institutions are devoting great attention to presenting and summarising wellbeing results. Online sites offer the most flexibility and interaction for users. Early examples of English language dashboards, balanced score-cards and other online graphical presentations include the OECD's *Better Life* index, Measuring Scotland's Progress, Measures of Australia's Progress (MAP) and the United Kingdom's Measuring National Well-being Programme.

Some of these websites encourage users to choose the weight to attribute to each of the dimensions included. However, it is still an open question as to whether or not weights can and should be applied in seeking to arrive at an overall assessment of progress. The pros and cons of a single number have been much debated, as we saw in Chapter 4 and earlier in this chapter, but this issue should still be explored in the development of each set of wellbeing and progress measures.

The assertion that a single number is easier than having a set of numbers to communicate will be difficult to overcome. Early work on looking for alternatives to GDP seemed to take as read that alternatives should have their own 'common currency' to combine different aspects into a coherent system, because GDP is constructed as a monetary measure (e.g. Pullinger 1998, p. 18, explores time use in a system of social contributions). There now seems to be more interest in providing an overview of progress than in providing a single headline measure. We are confident that ways of handling a small number of measures, in several different units, will emerge. This might, for example, result from considerations of the changing nature of value: how to capture how society values different things, and how things are valued differently over time.

We have mentioned Bhutan several times already. It is characterised as having moved to a single, 'gross national happiness' index. However, as we noted earlier, the position in Bhutan appears to be a little more nuanced than at first sight. Its national wellbeing measure sits alongside the existing national economic accounts and there may not yet be full reconciliation into a single measure or assessment (e.g. Economist, 2013).

Another issue of which we are aware is how to measure the wellbeing of sub-groups within a population. The wellbeing of children and of older people has been examined in some places, and women's development is highlighted in work to add an index of gender inequality alongside the Human Development Index.

So, it should not be surprising that there are calls for further research and more data collection in support of the development of measures of wellbeing and progress. Speaking at an OECD conference in 2011, two years on from the publication of the Stiglitz, Sen and Fitoussi report, Professor Stiglitz ran through four areas 'ripe for new work over next few years' (see Appendix for link to this conference website and presentations). These areas are as follows:

- Inequality, especially to show how individuals and households fare against all dimensions of quality of life, by making statistical distributions available, not just average measures;

- Research on the drivers and impacts on wellbeing so that public policy and commercial and personal decision making can all draw on a fuller understanding of the likely effects of specific action (and these drivers and impacts include some hard-to-measure topics, such as governance, wealth creation and climate change);

- Risk vulnerability as one way of thinking about sustainability. Assessing the sustainability of current activities seems inevitably to include some kind of appraisal of what might happen in future. Attempting to identify and to quantify key risks may help with this;

- How to ensure transfer of all of this into the policy process, the business world and everyday life. Professor Stiglitz argued the need to present trade-offs using a 'parsimonious dashboard', that is a carefully selected and limited number of indicators, rather than comprehensive indicator set.

This is a huge agenda, especially considered as a 'global project'. All of these points deserve greater discussion and research. To take just one, how are indicators to be selected 'parsimoniously' and does this mean excluding all redundancy by eliminating overlapping indicators that would otherwise provide some re-assurance and triangulation through difficult terrain?

There are a number of international leaders, including the OECD and the High Level Expert Group that we met in Chapter 3, which are now following up on these areas of further research. What is less clear to us is, as we also discussed in Chapter 3, how this will fit with the UN process to put in place development measures to succeed the Millennium Development Goals, when they expire in 2015.

Finally, we still have a concern that there is a disjunction between increasing activity by the producers of national and other statistics, and how this is perceived and will be used. In Section 6.2, we referred to a number of critiques of GDP as 'the' measure of wellbeing and progress. In seeking to supplement GDP, there is as yet no clear understanding of what national wellbeing means, and thus how things would be done differently with a new set of societal progress indicators.

There have been many concepts that have had to be defined and measured over the years. These measures have not always met every user's needs and they have sometimes been contested – measures of unemployment and of poverty come to mind here. National wellbeing and progress have all the hallmarks of also being problematic concepts. There is much good intention to measure wellbeing and progress not only by GDP but also in other ways. But how far should GDP act as an anchor for any wider set of measures; indeed, will GDP continue to be seen as real core of any new system of wellbeing accounts? We have in mind especially those users of statistics for whom 'expansion is the normal state of the economy' (as we saw in Section 6.1).

At this stage, we simply do not know if adopting the measurement framework used by the OECD in their *Better Life?* outputs (OECD, 2011a, p. 18) will provide a common understanding of national wellbeing and progress. However, we are optimistic that initiatives at local, national and international level will increasingly draw attention to a different way of looking at wellbeing, progress and sustainability and that, at some stage, governments, businesses and households will start to act differently as well. It may sound rather grand to talk about the importance of agreeing the facts about the economy, society and the environment, without which no democracy can plan its future and check its progress. But that is what awaits these new measures of wellbeing and progress. It is no less than informing the public and holding businesses, governments and all of us accountable for our actions. To be able to do that, the new measures must be robust and accessible enough to survive in political and public debate.

References

Abdallah S., Mahony S., Marks N. *et al.* (2011) *Measuring Our Progress: The Power of Well-Being*. New Economics Foundation, London.

Anand P. and Roope L. (2013) *Measuring Progress and Human Development: A Briefing Paper for Government Statisticians and Policy-Makers*. Available from the authors: p.anand@open.ac.uk or laurence.roope@dph.ox.ac.uk.

Anand P., Hunter G., Carter I., Dowding K., Guala F. and Van Hees M. (2009) The development of capability indicators. *Journal of Human Development and Capabilities*, **10**(1), 125–152, http://dx.doi.org/10.1080/14649880802675366 (accessed 26 November 2013).

Babbie E. (2013) *The Practice of Social Research* (13th edition). Wadsworth, Belmont.

Bandura R. (2008) *A survey of composite indices measuring country performance: 2008 update*. Technical Report, United Nations Development Programme, Office of Development Studies, New York, http://web.undp.org/developmentstudies/docs/indices_2008_bandura.pdf (accessed 30 September 2013).

Bird S.M., Cox D., Farewell V.T., Goldstein H., Holt T. and Smith P.C. (2005) Performance indicators: good, bad, and ugly. *Journal of the Royal Statistical Society: Series A*, **168**, 1–27.

Boarini R., Johansson A. and d'Ercole M.M. (2006) *Alternative Measures of Well-Being*, DELSA/ELSA/WD/SEM(2006)2 http://dx.doi.org/10.1787/713222332167 (accessed 26 November 2013).

Bok D. (2010) *The Politics of Happiness: What Government Can Learn from the New Research on Well-Being*. Princeton University Press, Princeton.

Bureau of Labor Statistics (no date given) How the Government Measures Unemployment, http://www.bls.gov/cps/cps_htgm.htm}def (accessed 26 November 2013).

Burns F., Eaton M.A., Gregory R.D. *et al.* (2013) *State of Nature report.* The State of Nature partnership. http://www.rspb.org.uk/ourwork/science/stateofnature/index.aspx (accessed 7 October 2013).

Carey J. (2005) *What Good Are the Arts?* Faber and Faber, London.

Chamberlain E. and Black O. (2012) Wealth in Great Britain Wave 2, 2008–2010 (Part 2). Office for National Statistics, http://www.ons.gov.uk/ons/rel/was/wealth-in-great-britain-wave-2/2008-2010–part-2-/index.html (accessed 26 November 2013).

Chiripanhura B. (2010) Measures of economic activity and their implications for societal well-being. *Economic & Labour Market Review,* **4**(7), 56–65, available at http://www.ons.gov.uk (accessed 26 November 2013).

City A.M. (2013) Italy slips in EU wealth measure. http://www.cityam.com/article/italy-slips-eu-wealth-measure (accessed 27 June 2013).

Clode T. (2012) Measuring well-being and fostering progress; an Asia-Pacific perspective. *The Statistics Newsletter, March 2012,* Issue 55, pp. 3–5, OECD, Paris.

Cote S. and Healy T. (2001) *The Well-being of Nations: The Role of Human and Social Capital.* Organisation for Economic Co-operation and Development, Paris.

Cummins R.A., Eckersley R., Pallant J., Van Vugt J. and Misajon R. (2003) Developing a national index of subjective wellbeing: the australian unity wellbeing index. *Social Indicators Research,* **64**(2), 159–190.

Daly H. and Cobb J. (1989) *For the Common Good.* Beacon Press, Boston.

Deaton A. (2013) *The Great Escape: Health, Wealth, and the Origins of Inequality.* Princeton University Press, Princeton.

Debreu G. (1959) *Theory of Value: An Axiomatic Analysis of Economic Equilibrium.* Yale University Press, New Haven.

Dolan P. and Harrison O. (2013) *How Do You Measure Happiness?* http://forumblog.org/2013/01/how-do-you-measure-happiness/ (accessed 26 November 2013).

Dorling D. (2013) *Population 10 Billion.* Constable, London.

Dresner S. (2008) *The Principles of Sustainability.* Earthscan, London.

Drucker P.F. (2007) *The Essential Drucker.* Butterworth-Heinemann, Oxford.

Eatwell J. (2012) The theory of value and the foundations of economic policy: in memoriam Pierangelo Garegnani. *Contributions to Political Economy,* **31**, 1–18.

Economist (2013) Bhutan at the polls: Happy and you know it? http://www.economist.com/news/asia/21580514-debt-and-discontent-are-growing-happy-and-you-know-it (accessed 9 July 2013).

EESC (2012) Opinion of the European Economic and Social Committee on GDP and beyond – the involvement of civil society in choosing complementary indicators, at http://www.wikiprogress.org/index.php/File:Ces814-2012_ac_en.doc (accessed 13 December 2013).

Fender V., Haynes J. and Jones R. (2011) *Measuring Economic Well-being.* Office for National Statistics at http://www.ons.gov.uk/ons/guide-method/user-guidance/well-being/publications/previous-publications/index.html (accessed 29 July 2013).

Fioramonti L. (2013) *Gross Domestic Problem: The Politics Behind the World's Most Powerful Number.* Zed Books, London.

Fleurbaey M. (2009) Beyond GDP: the quest for a measure of social welfare. *Journal of Economic Literature,* **47**(4), 1029–1075.

Fujiwara D. and Campbell R. (2011). *Valuation Techniques for Social Cost Benefit Analysis: Stated Preference, Revealed Preference and Subjective Well-Being Approaches.* Available at http://www.academia.edu/1456360/Valuation_Techniques_for_Social_Cost_Benefit_Analysis_Stated_Preference_Revealed_Preference_and_Subjective_Well-Being_Approaches (accessed 3 October 2013).

Gershuny J. (2011) Time-Use Surveys and the Measurement of National Well-Being. Available at http://www.ons.gov.uk/ons/rel/environmental/time-use-surveys-and-the-measurement-of-national-well-being/article-by-jonathan-gershuny/index.html (accessed 26 November 2013).

Goetzmann W.N. and Rouwenhorst K.G. (2005) Financial innovations in history. In: W.N. Goetzmann and K.G. Rouwenhorst (eds) *The Origins of Value: The Financial Innovations that Created Modern Capital Markets*. Oxford University Press, Oxford, pp. 3–16.

Grice J. (2011) National accounts, wellbeing, and the performance of government. *Oxford Review of Economic Policy*, **27**(4), 620–633.

Guerrero V.M., García A.C. and Sainz E. (2013) Rapid estimates of Mexico's quarterly GDP. *Journal of Official Statistics*, **29**(3), 397–423.

Hacker J.S. (2011) The institutional foundations of middle-class democracy. http://www.policy-network.net/pno_detail.aspx?ID=3998&title=The+institutional+foundations+of+middle-class+democracy (accessed 3 July 2013).

Hall J., Giovannini E., Morrone A. and Ranuzzi G. (2010) *A Framework to Measure the Progress of Societies, OECD Statistics Directorate Working Paper No. 34, STD/DOC(2010)5*, http://search.oecd.org/officialdocuments/displaydocumentpdf/?cote=std/doc(2010)5&docLanguage=En (accessed 26 November 2013).

Hand D.J. (2009) *Measurement Theory and Practice: The World through Quantification*. Wiley, Chichester.

Harper G. and Price R. (2011) *A Framework for Understanding the Social Impacts of Policy and Their Effects on Wellbeing*. Defra, London. http://www.defra.gov.uk/publications/files/pb13467-social-impacts-wellbeing-110403.pdf (accessed 26 November 2013).

Harvey C.R. (2012) *Recession*. http://financial-dictionary.thefreedictionary.com/recession (accessed 25 September 2013).

Hawken P., Lovins A.B. and Lovins L.H. (1999) *Natural Capitalism: Creating the Next Industrial Revolution*. Little, Brown & Co., Boston.

Helm D. (2012) *The Carbon Crunch: How We're Getting Climate Change Wrong – and How to Fix It*. Yale University Press, New Haven.

Herrero L.M.J. and Morán J.M. (2011) The Spanish Initiative and the OECD-Hosted Global Project on Measuring the Progress of Societies. *OECD Global Project Newsletter, July 2011*, OECD, Paris.

Hicks S., Tinkler L. and Allin P. (2013) Measuring subjective well-being and its potential role in policy: perspectives from the UK office for national statistics. *Social Indicators Research*, **114**, 73–86, http://dx.doi.org/10.1007/s11205-013-0384-x (accessed 4 January 2014).

Hills J., Bastagli F., Cowell F., Glennerster H., Karagiannaki E. and McKnight A. (2013) *Wealth in the UK: Distribution, Accumulation and Policy*. Oxford University Press, Oxford.

ILO (2011) *Manual on the Measurement of Volunteer Work*. International Labour Office, Geneva at http://www.ilo.org/stat/Publications/WCMS_162119/lang--en/index.htm (accessed 14 December 2013).

Inglehart R. (1977) *The Silent Revolution: Changing Values and Political Styles among Western Publics*, Princeton University Press, Princeton.

Joyce M. and Stewart J. (1999) What can we learn from time-use data? *Monthly Labor Review*, August 1999, 3–6, at http://www.bls.gov/opub/mlr/1999/08/art1full.pdf (accessed 30 September 2013).

Khan J. (2013) *Towards Wealth Accounting – Natural Capital within Comprehensive Wealth*. Office for National Statistics, at http://www.ons.gov.uk/ons/guide-method/user-guidance/well-being/guidance-and-methodology/index.html (accessed 17 October 2013).

King G., Murray C.J.L., Salomon J.A. and Tandon A. (2004) Enhancing the validity and cross-cultural comparability of measurement in survey research. *American Political Science Review*, **98**, 191–207.

Kroll C. (2011) *Measuring Progress and Well-being: Achievements and Challenges of a New Global Movement*. Friedrich-Ebert-Stiftung, International Policy Analysis, Berlin. http://library.fes.de/pdf-files/id/ipa/08509.pdf (accessed 28 November 2013).

Krueger A.B., Kahneman D., Schkade D., Schwarz N. and Stone A.A. (2009) National time accounting: the currency of life. In: A.B. Krueger (ed.) *Measuring the Subjective Well-Being of Nations: National Accounts of Time Use and Well-Being*. University of Chicago Press, Chicago, pp. 9–86, at http://www.nber.org/chapters/c5053 (accessed 28 September 2012).

Lau A., Cummins R. and McPherson W. (2005) An investigation into the cross-cultural equivalence of the personal wellbeing index. *Social Indicators Research*, **72**(3), 403–430.

Maplecroft (2013) *Human Rights Risk Atlas 2013* at https://maplecroft.com/themes/hr/ (accessed 26 November 2013).

McCulla S.H., Holdren A.E. and Smith S. (2013) Improved Estimates of the National Income and Product Accounts: Results of the 2013 Comprehensive Revision. *Survey of Current Business, September 2013*, US Bureau of Economic Analysis, 14–45, at http://www.bea.gov/scb/pdf/2013/09%20September/0913_comprehensive_nipa_revision.pdf (accessed 26 November 2013).

Michaelson J., Abdallah S., Steuer N., Thompson S. and Marks N. (2009) *National Accounts of Well-Being: Bringing Real Wealth onto the Balance Sheet*. New Economics Foundation, London.

Moore M.H. (1997) *Creating Public Value: Strategic Management in Government*. Harvard University Press, Harvard.

Moore M.H. (2013) *Recognizing Public Value*, Harvard University Press, Harvard.

Nordhaus W. and Tobin J. (1972) *Is Growth Obsolete?* Columbia University Press, New York.

OECD (2008) *Handbook on Constructing Composite Indicators: Methodology and User Guide*. Organisation for Economic Co-operation and Development, Paris.

OECD (2011a) *How's Life?: Measuring Well-Being*. OECD Publishing. http://dx.doi.org/10.1787/9789264121164-en (accessed 3 August 2013).

OECD (2013b) *OECD Guidelines for Micro Statistics on Household Wealth*. Organisation for Economic Co-operation and Development, Paris. http://dx.doi.org/10.1787/9789264194878-en (accessed 4 July 2013).

OECD (2013c) *OECD Framework for Statistics on the Distribution of Household Income, Consumption and Wealth*. Organisation for Economic Co-operation and Development, Paris. http://dx.doi.org/10.1787/9789264194830-en (accessed 4 July 2013).

ONS (2002) Household Satellite Account (Experimental). Available at http://www.ons.gov.uk/ons/guide-method/method-quality/specific/social-and-welfare-methodology/household-satellite-account/household-satellite-account-publications.html (accessed 25 September 2013).

Osborne G. (2012) *Chancellor's Autumn Statement 2012*, https://www.gov.uk/government/speeches/autumn-statement-2012-chancellors-statement (accessed 25 September 2013).

Ostrom E. (2009) A general framework for analyzing sustainability of social-ecological systems. *Science*, **325**, 24 July 2009, 419–422. doi:10.1126/science.1172133

Ostrom E., Chang C., Pennington M. and Tarko V. (2012) *The Future of the Commons: Beyond Market Failure and Government Regulation*. The Institute of Economic Affairs, London.

Oswald A.J. (2010) Emotional prosperity and the Stiglitz Commission. *British Journal of Industrial Relations*, **48**(4), 651–669.

Paruolo P., Saisana M. and Saltelli A. (2013) Ratings and rankings: voodoo or science? *Journal of the Royal Statistical Society, Series A*, **176**, 609–634.

Pearce N. (2013a) *Juncture* interview: Bonnie Honig. *Institute for Public Policy Research Review (Juncture)*, **19**(4), 226–234.

Pearce N. (2013b) What should social democrats believe? *Institute for Public Policy Research Review (Juncture)*, **20**(2), 101–110.

Pearce D. and Barbier E.B. (2000) *Blueprint for a Sustainable Economy*. Earthscan, London.

Pearce D. and Őzdemiroglu E. (2002) *Economic Valuation with Stated Preference Techniques: Summary Guide*. Department for Transport, Local Government and the Regions, London, https://www.gov.uk/government/publications/green-book-supplementary-guidance-stated-preference-techniques (accessed 3 October 2013).

Pecorelli N. (2013) *How One Nation Labour Can Bridge the Values Divide*, http://www.ippr.org/juncture/171/11151/how-one-nation-labour-can-bridge-the-values-divide (accessed 3 October 2013).

Peracchi F. and Rossetti C. (2013) The heterogeneous thresholds ordered response model: identification and inference. *Journal of the Royal Statistical Society*, **176** (3), 703–722.

Porter M.E., Stern S. and Loría R.A. (2013) Social Progress Indicator 2013, Social Progress Imperative, Washington D.C. at http://www.socialprogressimperative.org/publications (accessed 16 December 2013).

Pullinger J. (1998) *The Income and Wealth of Society: A System of Social Contributions*, paper prepared for the 25th General Conference of the International Association for Research in Income and Wealth.

Reid M.G. (1934) *Economics of Household Production*. John Wiley & Sons, New York.

Rifkin J. (2011) *The Third Industrial Revolution: How Lateral Power Is Transforming Energy, the Economy, and the World*. Palgrave Macmillan, New York.

Roper S., Vahter P. and Love J.H. (in press) Externalities of openness in innovation. *Research Policy*, available online http://dx.doi.org/10.1016/j.respol.2013.05.006 (accessed 30 September 2013).

Schuller T., Wadsworth M., Bynner J. and Goldstein H. (2012) *The Measurement of Well-being: The Contribution of Longitudinal Studies, Report by Longview*. Office for National Statistics, available at http://www.ons.gov.uk/ons/guide-method/user-guidance/well-being/guidance-and-methodology/index.html (accessed 1 October 2013).

Scrivens K. and Iasiello B. (2010) *Indicators of 'Societal Progress': Lessons from International Experiences*. Statistics Working Paper 2010/4, OECD Publishing, Paris. doi:10.1787/5km4k7mq49jg-en

Senge P., Smith B., Kruschwitz N., Laur J. and Schley S. (2008) *The Necessary Revolution*. Nicholas Brealey Publishing, London.

Smith A. (1776/2000) *The Wealth of Nations*. The Modern Library, New York.

Stiglitz J.E., Sen S. and Fitoussi J-P. (2009) Report by the Commission on the Measurement of Economic Performance and Social Progress, http://www.stiglitz-sen-fitoussi.fr/en/index.htm (accessed 16 December 2013).

Stiglitz J.E., Sen S. and Fitoussi J-P. (2010) *Mismeasuring Our Lives: Why GDP Doesn't Add Up*. The New Press, New York.

Stone R. (1973) A system of social matrices. *Review of Income and Wealth*, Series **19**(2), 143–166.

United Nations Development Programme (2013) *Human Development Report 2013. The Rise of the South: Human Progress in a Diverse World*. United Nations Development Programme, New York, available at http://hdr.undp.org/en/reports/global/hdr2013/ (accessed 30 September 2013).

Weale M. (2009) Saving and the National Economy. National Institute of Economic and Social Research, NIESR Discussion Paper 340, http://niesr.ac.uk/sites/default/files/publications/011009_160719.pdf (accessed 28 September 2013).

7

Wellbeing policy and measurement in the UK

We must measure what matters – the key elements of national well-being.
Jil Matheson, UK National Statistician (2010)

There are developments in wellbeing policy and measurement in many countries, with the close involvement of international organisations such as Organisation for Economic Co-operation and Development (the OECD) and the United Nations (see Appendix). We take the United Kingdom as a case study in this chapter, looking in particular at the Measuring National Well-being programme of the United Kingdom Office for National Statistics (ONS). This is because, from our close involvement with the programme, we think that there are a number of features that are worth highlighting and which should be applicable more widely.

The Measuring National Well-being programme (which we will call MNW) builds on 40 years of social reporting by the ONS, especially through an annual volume *Social Trends*, aiming to present a wider picture of life in the United Kingdom than that gleaned from looking only at economic statistics. In setting up MNW, the ONS was able to draw on trail-blazing work, including through building a close working relationship with the Centre for Wellbeing at the New Economics Foundation. The centre had been established some 10 years ahead of the ONS programme and had consistently sought to understand, measure and influence wellbeing, both directly and by alerting policy makers to the issue.

ONS became increasingly aware during the first decade of the new millennium of calls for measures of wellbeing and progress to go 'beyond GDP'. It was also apparent that meeting that interest should be without any reduction in ONS's commitment to publishing full and timely national accounts and to continue to develop those accounts in line with international developments and evolving user requirements, for example, on the treatment of the output of public services. ONS staff examined the Stiglitz, Sen and Fitoussi recommendations and quickly realised that these recommendations provided a good framework for how to proceed. The recommendations struck many chords with existing (albeit incomplete) statistical outputs

The Wellbeing of Nations: Meaning, Motive and Measurement, First Edition. Paul Allin and David J. Hand.
© 2014 John Wiley & Sons, Ltd. Published 2014 by John Wiley & Sons, Ltd.

that contribute to a fuller picture of national wellbeing and progress. For example, work on human capital, social capital, natural capital, the measurement of household wealth and analyses of the distribution of income and wealth could be brought into, and taken forward under, the MNW programme.

The United Kingdom already had a well-developed and regularly published set of sustainable development indicators (SDIs). These were not at the time the responsibility of ONS, though ONS indicators were included. This did raise the issue of the fit between measures of national wellbeing and SDIs.

There were three innovative aspects to MNW. First, it kicked off with a period of considerable public engagement and debate around the question 'what matters?' The second major development was that, for the first time, ONS included subjective wellbeing measures in its regular household surveys. The questions resulted from an intensive period of investigation, made possible by building on long-established academic research and survey work on subjective wellbeing. The questions were not just for ONS surveys, but the intention was to include them in other government surveys, to create a widespread picture of wellbeing in different policy areas. This reflects the third eye-catching aspect of MNW, that of working closely with policy makers prompted by government wanting to give greater attention to wellbeing in policy.

We will return to the MNW programme shortly. First, here is a timeline to illustrate a number of events, developments and reports across the United Kingdom that, with hindsight, we can see as the evolution of measures of national wellbeing and progress. It is a far from complete history. We have selected developments that we see as illustrative of the breadth of interest and which appear to have acted as milestones and have taken forward debate on measuring progress and wellbeing. The timeline should also be seen against a backdrop of much work on wellbeing measurement in academic centres and by researchers in nongovernmental organisations, producing many academic papers relevant to wellbeing and progress and increasing media coverage.

1941: *Analysis of the Sources of War Finance and Estimate of the National Income and Expenditure* can be read as prototype set of official national accounts, and provides foundation for UK National Accounts published from late 1940s onwards by the Central Statistical Office;

1960s: Central Statistical Office starts publishing income distributions, including annual analysis of the effect of taxes and benefits on household income;

1970: Central Statistical Office launches Social Trends as annual collection of economic, social and environmental statistics describing life in Britain;

1991: *Alternative Economic Indicators* by Victor Anderson;

1996: Questions about life satisfaction added to the British Household Panel Survey;

2000: The New Economics Foundation establishes Centre for Wellbeing, working collaboratively and producing many reports (e.g. National Accounts of Wellbeing, January 2009);

2000: Local Government Act gives local authorities the power (but not a statutory duty) to promote social, economic and environmental wellbeing in their area;

2001: Welsh Assembly Government's first national economic strategy notes that 'increasing GDP does not automatically lead to a better quality of life';

2002: ONS publishes first partial set of UK Environmental Accounts and experimental Household Satellite Account;

2002: Prime Minister's Strategy Unit publishes *Life Satisfaction: The State of Knowledge and Implications for Government*;

2005: *Happiness: Lessons from a New Science* by Richard Layard published;

2005: UK Sustainable Development Strategy *Securing the Future* commitment to exploring policy implications of wellbeing research. Sustainable Development Indicators published;

2005: ONS article about the measurement of social capital in the United Kingdom published;

2005: Audit Commission publishes list of local quality-of-life indicators;

2005: Review of the Measurement of Government Output and Productivity in the National Accounts. The Atkinson Review argued for a principled approach to the task of measuring the value of public services. ONS sets up a UK Centre for the Measurement of Government Activity;

2006: The *Economist*'s Christmas edition leads with 'Happiness (and how to measure it)';

2007: Institute for Economic Affairs research monograph argues that happiness research cannot be used to justify government intervention;

2007: ONS Economic & Labour Market Review article on Measuring Societal Wellbeing published;

2007: Scottish government includes quality of life in its principles and priorities;

2007: Conservative Party Quality of Life Policy Group includes recommendation 'for the UK to agree on a more reliable indicator of progress than GDP, and to use it as the basis for policy-making';

2008: Young Foundation publishes 'Local wellbeing: can we measure it?' as part of Local Wellbeing Project with number of partners;

2008: Climate Change Act sets target to reduce UK's greenhouse gas emissions by at least 80% (from 1990 baseline) by 2050;

2009: Report of the Commission on Measuring Economic Performance and Social Progress (led by Stiglitz, Sen and Fitoussi, with three UK members);

2009: Royal Statistical Society Statistics Users' Forum conference on measures of progress;

2010: David Cameron, then leader of opposition (Prime Minister from May 2010), sets out his views on the importance of general wellbeing, in TED talk on the next age of government;

2010: Marmot Review on reducing health inequalities in England includes key message that 'economic growth is not the most important measure of our country's success';

2010: UK government Budget Report includes commitment to developing broader indicators of wellbeing and sustainability;

2010: ONS Measuring National Wellbeing programme launched, along with conference on wellbeing policy;

2010: Economic and Social Research Council/National Institute of Ageing Workshop on the Role of Wellbeing Measures in Public Policy, Washington DC;

2010: Young Foundation report *The State of Happiness: Can Public Policy Shape People's Wellbeing and Resilience?*;

2010: The ESRC's first overview making the case for the social sciences is on wellbeing;

2011: UK participation in Eurostat Sponsorship Group and Task Forces on GDP and beyond;

2011: Liberal Democrats Policy Paper *A New Purpose for Politics: Quality of Life*;

2011: PWC and Demos report on economic wellbeing 'Good growth';

2011: House of Lords short debate on national wellbeing;

2012: Legislation enables public authorities to have regard to economic, social and environmental wellbeing in their procurements;

2012: UK participates in UN High Level meeting on wellbeing and happiness;

2012: Legatum Institute Commission on Wellbeing Policy launched, chaired by Lord Gus O'Donnell, former UK Cabinet Secretary;

2012: House of Commons Environmental Audit Committee reports on Sustainable Development Indicators;

2012: ONS publishes roadmap *Accounting for the Value of Nature in the UK* to incorporate natural capital into the UK Environmental Accounts, linked to Natural Environment White Paper commitment to developing natural capital resource accounting;

2013: Environmental Audit Committee launches enquiry on the ONS Measuring Wellbeing programme and how government policy is using wellbeing research and analysis;

2013: London School of Economics 'Growth Commission' aims to provide the authoritative contribution to the formulation and implementation of UK long-term growth strategy;

2013: UK National Statistician Jil Matheson, member of OECD High Level Expert Group, to continue work of Stiglitz, Sen and Fitoussi Commission;

2013: Prime Minister David Cameron co-chair of UN High Level Panel, reporting recommendations on eradicating poverty after the Millennium Development Goals expire in 2015.

On 25 October 2010, the British Prime Minister made a speech to the Confederation of British Industry, in which he set out a strategy for growth for the country and how 'we can create a new economic dynamism in our country' (Cameron, 2010b). Like many political leaders in the aftermath of the financial crisis and economic recession, David Cameron was concerned to answer the questions 'where is the growth going to come from – where are the jobs going to come from?' In a speech almost entirely devoted to growth, the Prime Minister also spoke about the wider role of government, touching on the issue of wellbeing that he had spoken several times about when he was the leader of the opposition, including the concept of general wellbeing (Cameron, 2010a). Mr Cameron said in his October 2010 speech, 'In the weeks ahead, we will be setting out how we will bring a new emphasis on well-being in our national life, and how we will work with business to spread social and environmental responsibility across our society'.

Less than a month later, on 20 November 2010, the Prime Minister gave a speech on wellbeing during which he said, 'today the government is asking the Office of National Statistics to devise a new way of measuring wellbeing in Britain. And so from April next year, we'll start measuring our progress as a country, not just by how our economy is growing, but by how our lives are improving; not just by our standard of living, but by our quality of life' (Cameron, 2010c).

On that occasion, the Prime Minister was speaking at the launch of the UK Office for National Statistics (ONS) 'Measuring National Well-being Programme'. ONS had established this (MNW) programme not only to meet the needs of government policy makers but generally to provide wider measures of the nation's progress beyond just focusing on Gross Domestic Product (GDP), to capture more fully economic performance, quality of life as well as environmental sustainability issues. The programme was greatly influenced by the report by the Commission on the Measurement of Economic Performance and Social Progress (the Stiglitz, Sen and Fitoussi report), published in 2009, which had concluded that 'the time is ripe for our measurement system to shift emphasis from measuring economic production to measuring people's well-being' (Stiglitz *et al.*, 2010, p. 10).

The Stiglitz, Sen and Fitoussi report contained specific recommendations to national statistics offices. Other initiatives, such as the European Commission's *GDP and Beyond* project and the OECD's *Global Project on Measuring the Progress of Societies,* were adding to the impetus to look for new approaches to the measurement of quality of life (see Appendix for links). It is a fine point, but worth making, that the ONS programme was devised to respond to these international developments, reflecting interest in the United Kingdom in wider measures than GDP, as well as to the government's request. The ONS programme has been misreported in the media as being to produce Mr Cameron's Happiness Index, which is wrong on all three counts. It is not just for the Prime Minister and was not commissioned by him: ONS initiated the programme, including bidding for funding from the government's Spending Review in June 2010; it is not just about happiness, even broadly defined to sum up psychological wellbeing, but about national wellbeing more generally; and it is designed to produce a number of measures, not a single index.

It had been 40 years since the last time that a British Prime Minister had been involved in the launch of a statistical programme. That was a much lower-key event, when Edward Heath held a reception to mark the publication of *Social Trends*. However, the context was the same, because *Social Trends* was established in 1970 to provide an annual picture of social conditions and changes, to complement the more extensive and well-known economic statistics. This was part of an effort to develop social statistics, which 'had long tended to drag behind economic statistics in priority and quality' (Moser, 2000).

The approach with *Social Trends* was novel: it was to be 'exciting, non-technical and accessible to the general public well beyond Westminster and Whitehall. It had to be authoritative with the statistical material beyond criticism. But above all it was to be written and produced by us statisticians without political interference. What we included in any issue was up to us to decide, even if the material touched sensitive political nerves, and even if our comments were not popular with our political masters' (Moser, 2000), according to Claus Moser, who was the head of the UK Government Statistical Service at the time.

The first edition of *Social Trends* recognized 'economic progress must be measured, in part at least, in terms of social benefits' and the fact that 'it is just as important to have good statistics on various aspects of social policy' (CSO, 1970) than it is to have good economic statistics. This was in part a response by the UK National Statistical Office to the social indicators movement, which was stressing the need for a wider set of 'objective' measures to allow a better assessment of the quality of life of people in the nation. It illustrated the dissatisfaction with the idea that the quality of life and progress could be measured using economic data alone, as Robert Kennedy had so eloquently expressed a few years previously (see Chapter 2).

Annual *Social Trends* reports were published for 40 years (and a quarterly publication trialled in 1998 but not continued), moving latterly to Web-based publication and rolling update of dozen or so chapters covering different aspects of life. Since 2011, ONS has evolved this publication into online outputs of the MNW programme, including an annual report on life in the United Kingdom.

The aim of the MNW programme is 'to produce accepted and trusted measures of the wellbeing of the nation' (taken from website, see Appendix). This does not in itself define the wellbeing of the nation. The programme is designed to help answer the question, 'how is the UK as a whole doing?' The concept of national wellbeing is meant to embrace everything needed to be able to answer the question in a meaningful, accepted and trusted manner, so that action and decisions at all level, from the individual to the government, can be taken. In these terms, national wellbeing, or how the nation is doing, should then address the present state of the nation, whether progress is being made and if current progress is sustainable in the longer term: all of these dimensions (and more) are wrapped up in the idea of national wellbeing.

Given the timing of the MNW programme, and its acknowledgement of the influence of the Stiglitz, Sen and Fitoussi report, it will be no surprise that MNW is also about looking at 'GDP and beyond'. It is a statistical development programme that draws on a wide spectrum of statistical sources, so an early decision in the programme was that it should include headline indicators. The indicators are being formulated in the programme and are driven by covering the areas that matter to people. We will see that they relate to areas such as health, relationships, job satisfaction, economic security, education, environmental conditions and measures of personal wellbeing (individuals' assessment of their own wellbeing, or subjective wellbeing as we called it in earlier chapters). How these indicators were to be presented, the measurement framework, was still to be decided but it does look as if taking this approach to *national* wellbeing meant that the United Kingdom and the OECD would embark on somewhat different approaches, given that the OECD's *How's Life?* reports reflect a conceptual framework that distinguishes between current and future individual wellbeing. Drawing on the capabilities approach, the OECD measures current wellbeing 'in terms of outcomes achieved in the two broad domains' of material living conditions and quality of life. The OECD assesses future wellbeing by looking at the state of 'some of the key resources that drive well-being over time and that are persistently affected by today's actions' (OECD, 2013a, p. 21).

The intention of the MNW programme is to provide a framework for evaluating progress overall or identifying priorities. But it is not just aimed at policy makers, politicians and governments. The public, the media, nongovernmental organisations in civil society and businesses are all part of the intended audience for this and for all of the output of the ONS. Moreover, the MNW programme includes giving this wider public a voice. In doing so, the programme recognises that a national debate and ongoing consultations might help people in thinking about their own lives and choices. This is as well as more broadly seeking to raise awareness and influence ideas and debate about economic performance, social progress, the state of the environment and how all these interact.

One of the first phases of the MNW programme was, therefore, for ONS to host a wide-ranging national debate on measuring national wellbeing, with the strap line 'What matters to you?' The Stiglitz, Sen and Fitoussi Commission had encouraged – though this was not a formal recommendation – that roundtables be held in each country. Between November 2010 and April 2011, ONS's interpretation of a roundtable was to hold 175 events, attended by over 7000 people, around the United Kingdom, and to surround these events with extensive online activity. The debate generated more than 34 000 responses in total, mostly through online media including social media as well as website questionnaires.

In launching the programme with the Prime Minister, the UK National Statistician Jil Matheson spoke of statistics as the bedrock of democracy, in a country where we care about what is happening: 'We must measure what matters – the key elements of national well-being. We want to develop measures based on what people tell us matters most' (this quote is on the MNW programme website; see link in Appendix). The National Statistician published her reflections on the national debate, in July 2011 (these and supporting papers are published on the MNW website; see Appendix), including concluding that individual wellbeing is central to understanding national wellbeing, but not sufficient. There is a need for objective measures about the things that matter to people, such as health, education and access to public services, as well as subjective measures of personal wellbeing. National wellbeing must also take into account equity, sustainability and locality.

Working through the responses to the national debate enabled ONS to identify the key areas that matter most to people (ONS, 2011a) and to make initial proposals of domains and headline measures of national wellbeing. The initial proposals were then subject to further, but more targeted, public consultation, from October 2011 to January 2012. The aim of that consultation was to gather feedback on whether the domains and measures proposed reflected the broad scope of wellbeing, were easy to understand and whether users felt there should be any additions or changes. The ONS published a report summarising the 1800 responses, which showed that there was broad support for the proposed domains and measures (ONS 2012a).

To develop a framework for measuring national wellbeing, the ONS drew on an OECD working paper (Hall et al., 2010), as well as on other frameworks that had emerged in UK work and in the wellbeing literature. Note that the OECD now uses, in How's Life? (e.g. OECD, 2013a, p. 21), a different framework from that suggested by Hall et al. It is not that the United Kingdom has struck out in a different direction, but simply that there was need for a framework at that point in the UK programme. The challenge was to start structuring the measurement of national wellbeing with an eye to international developments while providing some common ground on which to engage nationally, including with 'academics across the social sciences, life sciences and humanities' (Spence et al., 2011, p. 2).

The framework for measuring national wellbeing published by the MNW programme in October 2011 is shown in Figure 7.1. It placed individual wellbeing at the heart of national wellbeing, identified six broad factors (such as health) directly affecting individual wellbeing and identified three more contextual domains (governance, the economy and the natural environment). Crucial in forming a full picture of national wellbeing are the distributions of each of the domains (suggested in the diagram by a 'dimension' of equity/fairness) and the sustainability over time of each domain (the bottom axis in the picture).

Although the assessment of individual wellbeing through the measurement of subjective wellbeing sits at the core of the ONS framework, subjective wellbeing is only one component in the approach to measuring quality of life proposed by the Stiglitz, Sen and Fitoussi Commission (as we discussed in Chapter 4). However, ONS had not previously undertaken regular or extensive subjective wellbeing surveys and there was clearly an appetite for new measures of personal wellbeing, which is why this element of the MNW programme gained so much attention. (John Hall recalls that ONS published subjective wellbeing research

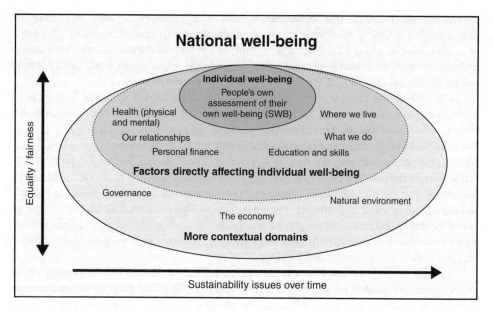

Figure 7.1 The Framework for Measuring National Well-being in the United Kingdom. © Crown copyright 2011 – used under the terms of the Open Government Licence, http://www.nationalarchives.gov.uk/doc/open-government-licence/version/2/

and results from other sources in *Social Trends* in the 1970s, see his website listed in the Appendix.)

In April 2011 – the date referred to by the Prime Minister for the start of a new way of measuring progress – four experimental subjective wellbeing questions were introduced in ONS's Annual Population Survey (APS) of UK households. This allowed the subjective wellbeing questions to be analysed using at least some of the key determinants of wellbeing, as well as by demographic and geographic attributes. ONS took the decision to use only a few questions within a large sample (165 000 adults are questioned over the course of a year in the APS). This is in contrast to many in-depth studies of subjective wellbeing, which tend to have many questions exploring wellbeing conducted with a relatively small sample: two different approaches to using a fixed amount of funding. Using only a short set of questions makes it easier for the managers of other government social surveys to include them, to build a richer data set and to extend subjective wellbeing measurement into specific areas of government. These subjective wellbeing data are not just meant for analysing personal wellbeing, they contribute to the fuller picture of national wellbeing and progress in the United Kingdom.

The four questions asked by ONS in the APS are as follows:

- 'Overall, how satisfied are you with your life nowadays?' (*This comes from the evaluative approach to measuring subjective wellbeing.*)

- 'Overall, to what extent do you feel the things you do in your life are worthwhile?' (*This is from the eudemonic approach.*)

- 'Overall, how happy did you feel yesterday?' (*This is about experience, specifically positive affect.*)

- 'Overall, how anxious did you feel yesterday?' (*This is about experience, negative affect.*)
    (*All asked using a 0 to 10 scale where 0 is 'not at all' and 10 is 'completely'*)

Source: Hicks (2011).

These are very similar to the core measures described in the OECD's Guidelines on Measuring Subjective Well-Being (OECD, 2013b).

Although there are only four subjective wellbeing questions in the APS, ONS decided to use them as a way of capturing different aspects of subjective wellbeing identified in the literature (Tinkler and Hicks, 2011), accepting the recommendations of Dolan *et al.* (2011) to do this as the best way of providing a broad overview of subjective wellbeing. As noted in parentheses against the first question above, one approach is about life evaluation or a cognitive assessment of how life is going. Positive affect is about the experience of positive emotions and negative affect about the experience of negative emotions. These three aspects of subjective wellbeing are also discussed and endorsed in the Stiglitz, Sen and Fitoussi report. The fourth approach included by ONS is taken from the eudemonic perspective, concerned with positive functioning, flourishing and having a sense of meaning and purpose in life (e.g. NEF, 2011, and Huppert and So, 2013).

Alongside the APS data collection, the ONS has continued to use its monthly Opinions Survey (OPN) to carry out testing and development of subjective wellbeing questions, and to cover aspects of subjective wellbeing in more detail. OPN collects data from 1000 respondents in each monthly sample, so it is markedly smaller than the APS. Initial estimates from several months of the OPN and the APS were published in December 2011 (ONS, 2011b) and in February 2012 (ONS, 2012b). They show that the two surveys generate broadly similar results of overall subjective wellbeing of adults in the United Kingdom.

Hicks *et al.* (2013, p. 79) summarise the testing and development of the ONS subjective wellbeing questions. The testing of the questions, and how to ask them, included through split trials on question order, question wording (see Chapter 4), the use of show-cards, preambles for the 'yesterday' questions and response variation over days of the week. Data from the APS survey were used to demonstrate how responses varied month by month when the same subjective wellbeing questions were asked throughout the year. ONS has also looked at how face-to-face interviews compare with self-completion interviews. Dolan and Kavetsos (2012) found that respondents interviewed by telephone in the APS gave consistently higher scores for their subjective wellbeing than those meeting face-to-face with an interviewer.

The APS data have already been analysed by ONS and others (e.g. Abdallah and Shah, 2012), including looking at subgroups of the population and making comparisons below the national level. As the sample grows, further detail will be available and will provide users with a large dataset to undertake further analysis. ONS publishes estimates at a more local level and for small subgroups of the population with more precision (e.g. ONS 2013). The latest data currently available are for 405 local areas across the United Kingdom. In Figure 7.2, we show the average life-satisfaction score, with confidence limits, in each of the 10 highest scoring and 10 lowest scoring areas for the 12 months April 2012 to March 2013. Some of the confidence limits are relatively wide, reflecting smaller numbers in the sample in those areas, and combining data from adjoining time periods will allow for greater precision. However,

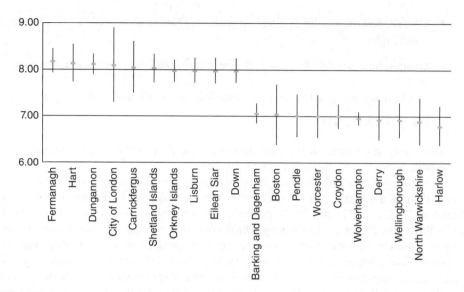

Figure 7.2   Average life satisfaction 2012/13 (on 0–10 scale) in 10 highest- and 10 lowest-scoring local areas across the United Kingdom.
Date source: ONS, 2013.

even data for 1 year allow for some clear discrimination between areas according to their average score on life satisfaction (though we would stress caution, and in particular that multiplicity be allowed for in any analysis).

One development triggered by the introduction of the ONS subjective wellbeing data has been for the Treasury, the UK Ministry of Finance, to update its 'Green Book' to include reference to using subjective wellbeing data in cost–benefit analyses (HM Treasury, 2011, p. 58). The Green Book is required reading for UK government officials assessing proposals for policies, programmes and projects, with the aim that 'public funds are spent on activities that provide the greatest benefits to society, and that they are spent in the most efficient way' (HM Treasury, 2011, page v). MNW staff are also working with government researchers to develop tools to evaluate the impact on subjective wellbeing that specific policies and publicly funded projects have made. However, the general ethos of the ONS is that it can only go so far in terms of linking their measurements to specific policies and programmes. The ONS data provide more of an overall picture and a backdrop against which policy officials are encouraged to build their evidence base. Policy officials are encouraged to add the same subjective wellbeing questions and more detailed ones to their own research surveys, and to draw on more policy-relevant indicators such as measures of poverty.

There is a slight tension here, at least during the early years of the MNW programme. The MNW programme seeks to establish standardised questions for assessing personal wellbeing and to encourage their use in many different surveys, beyond those conducted by the ONS. However, the ONS questions were described at least initially as experimental and potentially open to amendment in subsequent years. In practice this has not led to significant changes, so the use of the questions in other surveys is enabling a richer picture of wellbeing to be built up. One of the surveys adopting the ONS questions is the Cabinet Office's Community

Life Survey across England. This is also designed to be comparable with an earlier set of citizenship surveys conducted by government, so that time series of some key variables in the social and community domain can carry on. The key themes of the new survey are social action (giving, civic participation), social capital (trust, influence) and wellbeing.

Although the subjective wellbeing questions were the new element of MNW from April 2011, it will be seen from Figure 7.1 that the MNW programme is about much more than subjective wellbeing in assessing national wellbeing and progress. Similarly, the ONS programme is not about the end of using GDP. Rather, this is a pluralistic approach to measurement, to provide measures for people with different interests and to encourage the use of a set of wider measures of national wellbeing and progress overall. Those interested in economic growth and those focussing on subjective wellbeing will find each of these measures within the ONS set, but the intention is to shift attention to the full set of wider measures of national wellbeing.

The Stiglitz, Sen and Fitoussi commission was undoubtedly a significant influence on the ONS programme. Much of the content of the commission's report was not new. However, the timing and the authority with which it was delivered helped ONS draw together and build on many existing developments across the commission's recommendations, recognising the boost that the commission had given to finding and using measures to supplement GDP. In Table 7.1, we give a flavour of how the MNW programme reaches all parts of the agenda set by the Stiglitz, Sen and Fitoussi recommendations. This is not to say that everything is close to being sorted: even within a well-developed and funded national statistical system, it will still take time for some of these developments to come to fruition.

We suggested in Chapter 6 that looking at stocks and capital, though challenging, might be a way of understanding national wellbeing overall. Here is a small selection of results from the MNW programme and associated outputs that we find interesting and indicative of what can be learned by focussing on stocks and capital:

- The United Kingdom's human capital stock (an estimated £17.1 trillion in 2010) is worth more than two and a half times the value of UK tangible assets – buildings, vehicles, plant and machinery and so on – as estimated in the national accounts for the beginning of that year;

- The richest 10% of households own 44% of the combined net wealth of all private households within Great Britain (total estimated at £10.3 trillion for 2008–2010);

- Approaching 13% of the area of the United Kingdom is taken up with its stock of forest and other wooded area (woodland stock was almost 3.1 million hectares in 2012);

- The proportion of adults reporting high levels of life satisfaction varied from 34% down to 15% across some 160 districts for which reliable data were available for 2012/13 (for the United Kingdom as a whole, almost 26% of adults reported life satisfaction levels of 9 or 10, on a scale of 0–10).

The ONS MNW programme is aimed at delivering information at different levels of detail, to meet user requirements for broader, headline measures as well as being able to drill down to more detail and to reach specific statistical source material, where users can undertake further analysis of the data. This is shown in Figure 7.3, which is not quite an 'information pyramid' because the ONS is not providing a single number to sit at the top of the pyramid.

Table 7.1   Examples of how the UK Measuring National Well-Being (MNW) programme addresses the Stiglitz, Sen and Fitoussi recommendations.

Stiglitz, Sen and Fitoussi recommendations cover the following:	UK Measuring National Well-Being (MNW) programme includes the following:
Classical GDP issues Household perspective; income and consumption (rather than production) and wealth; distribution of income, consumption and wealth; income measures of nonmarket activities	• Various measures of household income are calculated and analysed e.g. for effects of the financial crisis on households' real disposable incomes • Regular measures of income inequality and analyses of how taxes and benefits redistribute income between various groups of households in the United Kingdom (articles and more recently podcasts) • Analyses from survey of wealth and assets • Developing and updating household satellite accounts e.g. valuing informal care • Exploring case for using time use data to measure national wellbeing • Improved measures of public service output, following the 2005 Atkinson Review • Wider measures of public sector debt and a generational accounting approach to long-term public finance in the United Kingdom
Quality of life Improved measures of people's objective conditions and capabilities; comprehensive assessment of inequalities; survey data on quality-of-life domains; information to aggregate across quality-of-life dimensions, allowing different indexes; subjective wellbeing data	• Developing and consulting on domains and measures • Topic reports e.g. governance, also measures of children's wellbeing • Analytical articles examining different dimensions of inequality • Regular outputs on personal wellbeing • Interactive charts and maps • Review 2005 work on development of measures of social capital measures and availability of current measures
Sustainable development and environment Dashboard of indicators of stocks; indicators of physical aspects of environment, especially proximity to dangerous levels of environmental damage	• Working with department currently responsible for UK Sustainable Development Indicators to ensure SDIs complement national wellbeing measures • Environmental Accounts (published since 2002) following methodologies and conventions recommended by UN System of Environmental and Economic Accounts (SEEA) • Roadmap for development of natural capital accounting • Estimates of UK stock of human capital and working with OECD consortium to develop methodology

Sources: Stiglitz *et al.* (2010) and ONS MNW programme outputs at: http://www.ons.gov.uk/ons/guide-method/user-guidance/well-being/publications/index.html.

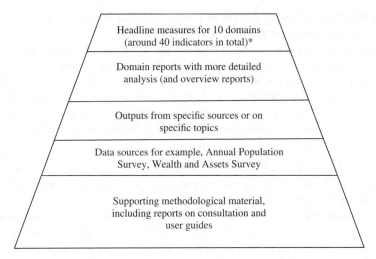

Figure 7.3 levels:
- Headline measures for 10 domains (around 40 indicators in total)*
- Domain reports with more detailed analysis (and overview reports)
- Outputs from specific sources or on specific topics
- Data sources for example, Annual Population Survey, Wealth and Assets Survey
- Supporting methodological material, including reports on consultation and user guides

Figure 7.3   The levels of information provided by the ONS MNW programme (this is not to scale!).
*With new ways of accessing statistics, for example, interactive wheel of measures, interactive graphs and maps.

The United Kingdom embarked on its MNW programme when, as is the case in several countries, there was already a set of sustainable development indicators (SDIs). The UK SDIs had been regularly published by official statisticians in the government department responsible for sustainable development policy (see Appendix for UK SDI website link and Section 15 in Chapter 2 for more on SDIs). Moreover, the SDIs had been developed nationally and internationally over the previous decade and had increasingly become presented as measures of national wellbeing and progress.

There had, for example, been a discussion meeting at the Royal Statistical Society in London in January 1998 billed as 'Alternatives to economic statistics as indicators of national well-being', where both of the papers (Levett, 1998, and Custance and Hillier, 1998) and all the discussion (Barnett *et al.*, 1998) were about SDIs and the criteria for selecting indicators. The direction of travel was to move from economic statistics only to looking at economic, social and environmental indicators, but at least initially there appeared no conceptualisation of this as national wellbeing. Rather, the SDIs were presented as tools for developing sustainable development policy and for monitoring progress towards sustainable development: as Levett had noted at the 1998 meeting, 'the development of sustainability indicators and policy are intimately intertwined' (1998, p. 301).

This intertwining is inevitable as part of a policy process. When it works well, the statistics should be informed by an understanding of the policy they are meant to measure, and how they will be used. The role of official statisticians, whether in departments or a national statistics office, is to produce statistics for policy and for public use. However, it appears to us to be more complicated if statistics are needed primarily for policy, because there is a risk that policy needs might, even inadvertently, crowd out the use of the same statistics for public debate. The emphasis in the development of measures of national wellbeing and progress should be that they are meant for use as public statistics, including helping the electorate assess the performance of government, as well as in policy.

The need to protect and, better, to enhance the wellbeing of individuals has long been recognised as important in policy. Around 2007, the UK government department responsible for sustainable development worked with other government departments, the devolved administrations and other stakeholders to develop a common understanding of what wellbeing means in a policy context. It was intended to support those wishing to take a greater policy focus on wellbeing and to promote consistency. The common understanding is that:

> 'Wellbeing is a positive physical, social and mental state; it is not just the absence of pain, discomfort and incapacity. It requires that basic needs are met, that individuals have a sense of purpose, that they feel able to achieve important personal goals and participate in society.
>
> It is enhanced by conditions that include supportive personal relationships, strong and inclusive communities, good health, financial and personal security, rewarding employment, and a healthy and attractive environment.
>
> Government's role is to enable people to have a fair access now and in the future to the social, economic and environmental resources needed to achieve wellbeing. An understanding of the effect of policies on the way people experience their lives is important for designing and prioritising them'. (Department for Environment Food & Rural Affairs, 2007)

Alongside this, some measures of subjective wellbeing were included in the UK SDIs. The department responsible for sustainable development set about developing a new set of sustainable development indicators and consulted during 2012 on its proposals. The indicators were meant to complement the ONS measures of national wellbeing, an issue that had been spotted by, among others, a Parliamentary committee scrutinising work on environmental audit. Submitting evidence to that committee's inquiry into wellbeing, the Royal Statistical Society suggested that, while there may be some advantages in letting a number of flowers bloom, it might be more productive to bring the SDI and MNW developments together, 'to work on a single measurement framework to meet a range of policy needs in a coherent and efficient way' (Royal Statistical Society, 2013).

The Royal Statistical Society also noted that Scott (2012) had reviewed the potential conflict between improving wellbeing and sustainability as two central public policy goals of government. She pointed out that there is much common ground, especially through the focus each policy area has on broadly the same set of indicators. However, she is wary of 'a simplistic win-win scenario of subjective wellbeing and sustainability' (Scott, 2012, p. 168), arguing for a clearer, democratically derived, conceptual framework for policy makers regarding different wellbeing constructs. Nevertheless, it looks as if the two sets of United Kingdom measures, SDIs and MNW, will be brought together so that one overall measurement approach can be used for a variety of public policy needs.

The ONS held a conference in 2012 to mark the first 2 years of its MNW programme. Glenn Everett, the programme director, summarised how far the programme had progressed, with many outputs and the first new annual report on life in the United Kingdom. There was also much more to do. The domains and measures of national wellbeing were still under development and open for revision and further refinement. The subjective wellbeing questions were subject to further testing and possible development. There was also the issue of how to assess the progress of the United Kingdom from these measures: was it always clear whether, say, an increase in the value of a measure meant that the United Kingdom was making positive progress in that area? ONS promised to continue cooperation with international partners, including through the UN, OECD and EU, as well as further consultation and engagement within the United Kingdom.

Turning to the use of national wellbeing measures, the ONS remains keen to encourage more of this. It does look to us that more attention is being given to understanding the drivers of personal wellbeing than to those of national wellbeing. While not wanting to detract from analysis of personal wellbeing data, we are keen to see more use made of measures to determine national wellbeing and how, and why, that is changing. Policy linked to personal wellbeing is not new. We explored health and wellbeing, for example, in Chapter 2. There are opportunities for further policy areas to develop a national wellbeing focus, such as those being identified by the Legatum Institute Commission on Wellbeing Policy (see Appendix for website link). These could, for example, concern how major infrastructure projects, such as airports or high-speed rail networks, are considered against economic, social and environmental costs and benefits.

There continues to be a strong political narrative in the United Kingdom about the need for economic growth and deficit reduction. There is also some contesting of earlier 'green' agendas. It is in this political environment that ONS must remain strongly committed to producing wider measures of national wellbeing and progress, so that these are available to use alongside the regular data on economic growth and the public finances.

For a time, wellbeing had appeared in the stated purpose of UK government departments. For example, the 2008–2009 annual report and accounts of HM Treasury, the United Kingdom's Economics and Finance Ministry, recorded that one of its strategic objectives was 'to ensure high and sustainable levels of economic growth, well-being and prosperity for all' (HM Treasury, 2009, p. 11).

The new coalition government formed in the United Kingdom after the 2010 general election published a programme for government (HM Government, 2010) with three references to 'well-being and quality of life'. Two of the references were about the importance of 'a vibrant cultural, media and sporting sector' (HM Government, 2010, p. 14) and of 'a modern transport infrastructure' (HM Government, 2010, p. 31). The third reference was to the 'need to protect the environment for future generations, make our economy more environmentally sustainable, and improve our quality of life and well-being' (HM Government, 2010, p. 17). This document did, therefore, recognise the broad agenda set by the Stiglitz, Sen and Fitoussi report and already taken up across the OECD and the EU. (At the time of writing, the United Kingdom is a member of both.)

However, the government also needed to set a number of priorities, largely shaped in the wake of the global financial crisis that began in 2007 and leaving the United Kingdom, and several more of the world's major economies, with structural deficits in their public finances. These priorities refer to economic growth rather than to wellbeing. By the time of a government report covering 2012–2013, the Treasury's objectives had been replaced by strategic priorities that include reference to 'a growing economy that is more resilient' and to reducing the structural deficit 'in a fair and responsible way' (HM Treasury, 2013, p. 9) but not explicitly to wellbeing. The only reference to wellbeing in the document is to the wellbeing of the staff of the Treasury (HM Treasury, 2013, p. 43).

Indeed, although we have not searched the strategy documents and business plans of every UK government department, it appears that the purposes and objectives of UK government departments most closely associated with wellbeing do not explicitly refer to it. A recent guide to the role and purpose 'post-April 2013' of the Department of Health does include many references to 'wellbeing', understandable in light of much national and international interest in improving health and wellbeing, though the overall role and purpose of the department is now described as 'helping people live better for longer' (Department of Health, 2013, p. 7). The language of the UK government is now predominantly about sustainable growth and sustainable development, along with a fair and equal Britain, rather than wellbeing.

Within the United Kingdom, there are currently two countries in which many governmental functions are devolved by the UK government. In both countries, the main policy focus is on sustainable economic growth. There is a flavour of wellbeing in the aim of the devolved government for Wales, which is 'working to help improve the lives of people in Wales and make our nation a better place in which to live and work' (see Appendix for website link). The devolved government for Scotland is similarly responsible for most of the issues of day-to-day concern to the people of Scotland, including health, education, justice, rural affairs and transport. The declared purpose of the Scottish government is this: 'To focus government and public services on creating a more successful country, with opportunities for all of Scotland to flourish, through increasing sustainable economic growth' (see Appendix for link). The word 'flourish' resonates with the eudemonic perspective on personal psychological wellbeing that we discussed earlier. In both Wales and Scotland, there are developments to measure national wellbeing and progress (see Appendix for links). In Wales, this covers wellbeing and sustainable development. 'Scotland Performs' measures and reports on progress of government in Scotland.

In drawing on high-level government documents, we are aware that we are not necessarily presenting a comprehensive picture of wellbeing policy in the United Kingdom. This is for two main reasons. First, underneath the strategy statements much work goes on across government to deliver specific policies, programmes, projects and services. Here there may well be examples of wellbeing being taken into account. We also discussed in Chapter 2 that there is a legal basis for some public authorities to have regard to economic, social and environmental wellbeing when letting contracts for goods and services. There does not yet appear to be any monitoring of the extent and the effectiveness of this legislation, so this would be an interesting area of future research. It would be unusual if some form of interdepartmental committee was not starting to share good practice and help build a wellbeing policy community of interest. Allin (2014, p. 438) drew on informal discussions to form a view of the kinds of areas in which officials were looking at policy through a 'wellbeing lens'. These were childhood obesity, community grants, offending reduction and personal budgets for public service users. The field of wellbeing at work appeared to be another policy area to focus on (Allin, 2014, p. 450).

We are confident that there will be considerable interest in the research community to review how wellbeing data are being applied to policymaking. This should be stimulated by the work of the Legatum Institute Commission on Wellbeing Policy mentioned earlier in this chapter, which is exploring how wellbeing analysis can be usefully applied to policy and will presumably be publicising exemplars of wellbeing policy. The commission is chaired by former Cabinet Secretary Lord O'Donnell and it promises that its reports will illustrate the strengths and limitations of wellbeing analysis and provide original and authoritative guidance on the implications for public policy.

The second reason we may have painted a less than complete picture of wellbeing policy is that we have not examined the extent to which policymakers are drawing on, or are at least aware of, the considerable volume of evidence and measurement tools provided by academic and other nongovernmental centres. There is a significant issue of knowledge transfer here, to facilitate the flow of information from policy makers on the policy areas needing development and the flow of knowledge from researchers with evidence and techniques that could usefully be brought into the policy world. The world has moved on since data about the state of Britain's economy, society and environment were summarised in the annual volume of *Social Trends*, which policymakers might (or might not) have consulted. One major way of encouraging knowledge transfer is to build a requirement for this into funding arrangement for academic research. The Economic and Social Research Council (ESRC) has, for example, identified wellbeing as a priority area in making the case for the social sciences, and the ESRC website (see Appendix) contains many 'evidence briefings' and other reports relating to wellbeing. The publication by Brown *et al.* (2009) is one example of such knowledge transfer in action in the field of wellbeing and working life.

Allin (2014, p. 422) notes that 'the United Kingdom enjoys a strong network of civil society organizations, universities, and think tanks with a real expertise in wellbeing and this has helped to enrich the political and policy debate considerably'. We have experienced this in action, especially through the meetings of the Technical Advisory Group for the ONS's MNW programme. Many UK centres play a strong role internationally, and have done so for many years. This brings challenges where, for example, methodologies have been developed but which are not fully consistent with later initiatives. However, the benefits of having a strong network to work with have proved to be considerable. We have included links to UK centres in the Appendix.

The machinery of government can move at what might seem at times a frustratingly slow pace. The announcement by the British Prime Minister in November 2010 signalled one immediate policy shift, to start measuring wellbeing. Some government policies were, of course, already engaged with wellbeing, particularly to link health with wellbeing, but in other areas progress is not so easy to spot. Although wellbeing is less in the headlines, there are a number of building blocks being put in place to support wellbeing in policy. We have mentioned the 'Green Book', public value in procurement and the Legatum Institute Commission, for example.

Bache and Reardon (2013, p. 14) have reviewed the emergence of wellbeing as a political concept in the UK government. They conclude that a paradigm shift in measurement may be taking place, especially through the ONS MNW programme, and that the wellbeing 'remains on the government agenda'. However, they also conclude that more action is required by those who support and sponsor policy inside government if 'more decisive [well-being] policy action is to follow. In short, a more effective coupling of the problem stream to policy and politics streams is needed for us to claim with confidence that well-being is "an idea whose time has come"'. As Bache also observes elsewhere that it is wellbeing measurement that is developing more than policy at the EU level (Bache, 2013, p. 35), we feel it is time for us to leave the United Kingdom as our case study and draw our thoughts to a conclusion in the following chapter.

References

Abdallah S. and Shah S. (2012) *Well-being Patterns Uncovered: An Analysis of UK Data*. New Economics Foundation, London.

Allin P. (2014) Measuring wellbeing in modern societies. In: P.Y. Chen and C.L. Cooper (eds) *Work and Wellbeing: Wellbeing: A Complete Reference Guide*, vol. III. John Wiley & Sons, New York, pp. 409–465.

Bache I. (2013) Measuring quality of life for public policy: an idea whose time has come? Agenda-setting dynamics in the European Union. *Journal of European Public Policy*, **20**(1), 21–38.

Bache I. and Reardon L. (2013) An idea whose time has come? Explaining the rise of well-being in British politics, *Political Studies*. http://onlinelibrary.wiley.com/doi/10.1111/1467-9248.12001/abstract;jsessionid=80F08AF389E4380B8EB4429346B756B5.d03t02.

Barnett V. *et al.* (1998) Discussion at the meeting on 'Alternatives to economic statistics as indicators of national well-being'. *Journal of the Royal Statistical Society Series A*, **161**(3), 303–311.

Beaumont J. (2011) *Measuring National Well-being, Discussion Paper on Domains and Measures,* UK Office for National Statistics, http://www.ons.gov.uk/ons/rel/wellbeing/measuring-national-well-being/discussion-paper-on-domains-and-measures/measuring-national-well-being—discussion-paper-on-domains-and-measures.html.

Brown A., Casey B., Charlwood A. *et al.* (2009) *Well-being and Working Life: Towards an Evidence-Based Policy Agenda*. ESRC Seminar Series, Mapping the public policy landscape, Economic and Social Research Council, Swindon.

Cameron D. (2010a) The next age of government. http://www.ted.com/talks/david_cameron.html (accessed 17 October 2013).

Cameron D. (2010b) PM's speech on creating a 'new economic dynamism' at https://www.gov.uk/government/speeches/pms-speech-on-creating-a-new-economic-dynamism (accessed 17 October 2013).

Cameron D. (2010c) PM's speech on wellbeing at https://www.gov.uk/government/speeches/pm-speech-on-wellbeing (accessed 17 October 2013).

CSO (1970) *Social Trends 1*, Central Statistical Office, Her Majesty's Stationery Office, London.

Custance J. and Hillier H. (1998) Statistical issues in developing indicators of sustainable development. *Journal of the Royal Statistical Society Series A*, **161**(3), 281–290.

Department for Environment Food & Rural Affairs (2007) *A Common Understanding of Wellbeing for Policy Makers* at http://archive.defra.gov.uk/sustainable/government/what/priority/wellbeing/common-understanding.htm (accessed 24 October 2013).

Department of Health (2013) Helping people live better for longer: A guide to the Department of Health's role and purpose post-April 2013. https://www.gov.uk/government/uploads/system/uploads/attachment_data/file/226838/DH_Brochure_WEB.pdf (accessed 24 October 2013).

Dolan P. and Kavetsos G. (2012) *Happy talk: mode of administration effects on subjective well-being*. CEP discussion paper, no. 1159. London School of Economics and Political Science at http://eprints.lse.ac.uk/45273/.

Dolan P., Layard R. and Metcalfe R. (2011) Measuring subjective wellbeing for public policy: recommendations on measures. Special Paper No. 23, March 2011, Centre for Economic Performance, London School of Economics.

Hall J., Giovannini E., Morrone A. and Ranuzzi G. (2010) *A Framework to Measure the Progress of Societies, OECD Statistics Directorate Working Paper No. 34, STD/DOC(2010)5,* http://search.oecd.org/officialdocuments/displaydocumentpdf/?cote=std/doc(2010)5&docLanguage=En.

Hicks S. (2011) *Spotlight On: Subjective Well-being,* Office for National Statistics. Available at http://www.ons.gov.uk/ons/rel/social-trends-rd/social-trends/spotlight-on-subjective-well-being/index.html.

Hicks S., Tinkler L. and Allin P. (2013) Measuring subjective well-being and its potential role in policy: perspectives from the UK office for national statistics. *Social Indicators Research*, **114**, 73–86, http://dx.doi.org/10.1007/s11205-013-0384-x.

HM Government (2010) *The Coalition: Our Programme for Government*. Cabinet Office, London, available at https://www.gov.uk/government/uploads/system/uploads/attachment_data/file/78977/coalition_programme_for_government.pdf (accessed 24 October 2013).

HM Treasury (2009) *Annual Report and Accounts 2008–09*. The Stationery Office, London. Available at http://www.official-documents.gov.uk/document/hc0809/hc06/0611/0611.pdf (accessed 24 October 2013).

HM Treasury (2011) *The Green Book: Appraisal and Evaluation in Central Government*. Available at https://www.gov.uk/government/publications/the-green-book-appraisal-and-evaluation-in-central-governent (accessed 23 October 2013).

HM Treasury (2013) *Annual Report and Accounts 2012–13*. The Stationery Office, London. Available at https://www.gov.uk/government/uploads/system/uploads/attachment_data/file/212752/hmtreasury_annual_report_and_accounts_201213.pdf (accessed 24 October 2013).

Huppert F.A. and So T.T.C. (2013) Flourishing across Europe: application of a new conceptual framework for defining well-being. *Social Indicators Research*, **110**, 837–861.

Levett R. (1998) Sustainability indicators in integrating quality of life and environmental protection. *Journal of the Royal Statistical Society Series A*, **161**(3), 291–302.

Moser Sir C. (2000) *Foreword* in Social Trends 30, Office for National Statistics, London.

NEF (2011) *Measuring Our Progress: The Power of Well-Being*. http://dnwssx4l7gl7s.cloudfront.net/nefoundation/default/page/-/files/Measuring_our_Progress.pdf (accessed 2nd August 2013).

OECD (2013a) *How's Life? 2013: Measuring Well-being*. OECD Publishing. http://dx.doi.org/10.1787/9789264201392-en (accessed 2 December 2013).

OECD (2013b) *OECD Guidelines on Measuring Subjective Well-Being*. OECD Publishing.

ONS (2011a) *Measuring What Matters: National Statistician's Reflections on the National Debate on Measuring National Well-being*. UK Office for National Statistics. Available at http://www.ons.gov.uk/ons/guide-method/user-guidance/well-being/publications/index.html (accessed 24 July 2013).

ONS (2011b) *Initial Investigation into Subjective Well-being Data from the ONS Opinions Survey*. UK Office for National Statistics. Available at: http://www.ons.gov.uk/ons/guide-method/user-guidance/well-being/publications/index.html.

ONS (2012a) *Initial Findings from the Consultation on Proposed Domains and Measures of National Well-being*, Office for National Statistics. Available at: http://www.ons.gov.uk/ons/guide-method/user-guidance/well-being/publications/index.html.

ONS (2012b) *Analysis of Experimental Subjective Well-being Data from the Annual Population Survey, April–September 2011*. UK Office for National Statistics. Available at: http://www.ons.gov.uk/ons/guide-method/user-guidance/well-being/publications/index.html.

ONS (2013) *Personal Well-being across the UK, 2012/13*. Office for National Statistics. Available at: http://www.ons.gov.uk/ons/rel/wellbeing/measuring-national-well-being/personal-well-being-across-the-uk--2012-13/sb---personal-well-being-across-the-uk--2012-13.html.

Royal Statistical Society (2013) *Memorandum to the Environmental Audit Committee Inquiry on Well-being* at http://data.parliament.uk/writtenevidence/WrittenEvidence.svc/EvidencePdf/1005 (accessed 24 October 2013).

Scott K. (2012) *Measuring Wellbeing: Towards Sustainability?* Routledge, Abingdon.

Spence A., Powell M. and Self A. (2011) Developing a Framework for Understanding and Measuring National Well-being, Office for National Statistics at http://www.ons.gov.uk/ons/guide-method/user-guidance/well-being/publications/previous-publications/index.html (accessed 17 October 2013).

Stiglitz J.E., Sen S. and Fitoussi J-P. (2010) *Mismeasuring Our Lives: Why GDP Doesn't Add Up*. The New Press, New York.

Tinkler L. and Hicks S. (2011) *Measuring Subjective Well-being*. Supplementary paper to the National Statistician's Reflections on the National Debate on Measuring National Well-being, at http://www.ons.gov.uk/ons/guide-method/user-guidance/well-being/publications/previous-publications/index.html (accessed 13 September 2013).

8

Conclusions

> We the peoples of the United Nations determined … to promote social progress and better standards of life in larger freedom
>> From Preamble to the United Nations Charter, 1945

8.1 Progress

We humans appear to have somewhat ambivalent attitudes to progress. In a number of aspects of life, winning is all. In others, drawing on a line of Grantland Rice's poetry, it matters not whether you win or lose, but how you play the game. This echoes the ancient Greek idea of good strife and bad strife: good strife, what we might nowadays call good competition, should spur us to reach greater achievements. Bad strife is all the rest. Is there a natural human competitiveness in everything we do, not just when we are playing a game?

Some people talk of 'moving on' and 'putting the past behind us', in relationships and in life more generally, while others are 'comfortable in the place they are'. Some political parties and movements are described as 'progressive', meaning that they want to change the world, while others are more conservative, reluctant to change or even striving to re-create the values, conditions and mores of an earlier time. Advertisements for financial services invite comparisons between relentless economic growth and growth in the natural world, without appearing to reflect on the cycle of natural growth. Yes, sunflowers can grow tall, for example, but they are also harvested and then die back. In his seminal work on the collapse of complex societies, Joseph Tainter (1988) shows that collapse of civilisations is recurrent. He describes how progress is associated with increasing specialisation, intrinsically nonproductive interfaces between the specialists, increased regulation and costs which increase at a faster rate than the output. In short, a greater proportion of an organisation's effort is spent on simply running it, instead of on its primary aim – with consequences which manifest in the law of diminishing returns, ultimately overwhelming societies. There is an analogy with

The Wellbeing of Nations: Meaning, Motive and Measurement, First Edition. Paul Allin and David J. Hand.
© 2014 John Wiley & Sons, Ltd. Published 2014 by John Wiley & Sons, Ltd.

the Laffer curve, where increasing rates of tax ultimately result in decreasing revenue for the state. 'Progress' is not a straightforward notion.

We should also not confuse growth with evolution. Evolution is a process of adaptation and change. We, as humans, have certainly evolved to the extent where we can invent and manufacture products, and make scientific discoveries, some of which make the world a safer place. But there are inevitable concomitant downsides, such as the way in which we can destroy other humans in warfare and use up natural resources more quickly than they can be replaced. Something which may represent progress and be good for one group may be bad for another. Rising house prices are good for property owners, but bad for those hoping to buy their first home. Fast new railways may be good for travellers, but will have damaging wellbeing implications for those living near to the track. Studies of the impact of noise from airport flight paths on psychological wellbeing and on cardiac health are a similar illustration, as are studies of the impact of particulate pollution on those living near roads with heavy traffic.

Progress comes in various flavours, and much of it is driven by technological advances. Sporting records seem regularly to fall, as athletes jump higher, run faster, and throw further, much of which is attributable to advances in training methods, in footwear and in diet. Progress in standard of living is also heavily driven by technological advance. Think of the impact on society of the successive waves of communications technologies: the telegraph, landline telephones and mobile phones. Think of the all-pervasive impact of computers, and imagine managing without the internet for a week. Carr (2010) has gone further, documenting 'how the internet is changing the way we think, read and remember'.

Cukier and Mayer-Schöenberger (2013) make a similar claim for a new technological front which appears to be opening – that of 'big data'. A McKinsey report on this subject claimed, 'we are on the cusp of a tremendous wave of innovation, productivity, and growth, as well as new modes of competition and value capture – all driven by big data as consumers, companies, and economic sectors exploit its potential' (Manyika *et al.*, 2011). Stephan Shakespeare's review of the use of public sector information in the United Kingdom, in the context of 'open data', commented that, 'from data we will get the cure for cancer as well as better hospitals; schools that adapt to children's needs making them happier and smarter; better policing and safer homes; and of course jobs. Data allows us to adapt and improve public services and businesses and enhance our whole way of life, bringing economic growth, wide-ranging social benefits and improvements in how government works … the new world of data is good for government, good for business, and above all good for citizens' (Shakespeare, 2013).

On the other hand, a French epigram from the middle of the nineteenth century has become something of a proverb that may describe a familiar feeling. *Plus ça change, plus c'est la même chose* can be understood as 'the more things change, the more they stay the same'. This points, perhaps in a slightly world-weary or even cynical way, to change in some sense being an illusion, for we are always living in a world which is as good as it can be at the time.

The early hopes that television would become a wonderful driver of mass education seem to have fallen beneath populist cultures of game shows, reality shows and celebrity culture. Technological advance does not *necessarily* imply progress. And progress, however defined, does not necessarily increase wellbeing: we are increasingly searching for new models of progress, including what else, in addition to economic growth, 'can increase the well-being of our societies' (Anderson *et al.*, 2012, p. 3).

There is also a feeling that technological change appears to be happening at an increasing rate. And when we think of modern computer-related technologies, it is difficult to argue that this is not the case. There may also be synergistic effects, accelerating this increasing rate: search engines permitting instant access to knowledge resources which would previously have required days of search, increased connectivity via social networks, enhanced online access to goods, resources, expertise and so on. These aspects of the gradual shift from material wealth to information wealth cast yet further doubt on the adequacy of GDP as a measure of progress.

Making a considerable simplification, we can see that social change has often been, and continues to be, studied in two broad contexts. First are the sociological studies of what is happening within a country, for example, as a result of increasing industrialisation or as a consequence of economic downturn with rising unemployment and poverty (e.g. Silbereisen and Chen, 2010). The second approach studies the process of international development. One reading of international development is of countries in the North encouraging countries in the South to become self-governing states and full participants in the global market, with the System of National Accounts and especially GNP as 'a universal quantifiable measure of development' (McMichael, 2012, p. 4).

Both ways of examining social change involve the development of economies as envisaged by Adam Smith onwards. But we also appear to have reached a place – really more a period of reflection than a precise point – where the key issue is 'increasingly about how we survive the future rather than how we improve on the past' (McMichael, 2012, p. 1). Back in 1999, Robert Gordon was examining changing patterns of US productivity and asking 'why did the fundamental determinants of American economic growth create such a surge between 1913 and 1972, but neither before nor after?' He predicts this 'will not be replicated in the lifetimes of our generation or that which follows us' (Gordon, 1999, p. 127) and continues to hold that view, raising basic questions about the process of economic growth (Gordon, 2012).

As we saw in Chapter 2, there is a long tradition of collecting, publishing and analysing statistics to describe different aspects of a country's economy and society. Data such as that collected in censuses of the population of England and Wales, held every 10 years from 1841 apart from in 1941, continue to be exploited. Barrett (2013), for example, describes how the industries people work in have changed over 170 years, including a marked shift from working on the land in agriculture to working in services in towns and cities. Social theorists and sociologists have also kept a close eye on how societies have been changing, adding their descriptions of what was going on, for example, during depressing times in many countries in the 1920s and 1930s. However, it now seems that the system of national accounts, especially the measurement of gross national product and gross domestic product, was the only real contender as a measure of progress. Anderson (1991, p. 17) notes how political arithmetic evolved into economics, with national income accounting 'seen by its advocates as primarily a matter of being simply more efficient and systematic about collecting statistical information'.

Anderson concluded that economic progress had emerged as a way of assessing social progress during the eighteenth and nineteenth centuries and that in the first half of the twentieth century 'for economics as a developing quantitative science, gross national product statistics appeared to offer a much more precise way of talking about economic progress' (Anderson 1991, p. 45). Stiglitz et al. (2010, p. 61) explain why it has taken so long for other measures to appear: 'While a long tradition of philosophical thought has addressed the issues of what gives life its quality, recent advances in research have led to measures that are both new and credible ... These measures, while not *replacing* conventional economic indicators, provide an opportunity to *enrich* policy discussions and to inform people's view of the conditions of the communities where they live'. Stiglitz, Sen and Fitoussi see these measures as applicable to industrialised countries as well as to developing countries and 'more importantly, the new measures now have the potential to move from research to standard statistical practice'. In particular, we have started to see these measures being taken up by national statistical offices, with support and encouragement from international agencies.

Many economists see the natural state of economies as inevitably growing: Will Hutton (2013) has described economies as having an 'inbuilt upward momentum driven by productivity and population growth'. While productivity is perhaps a simpler concept than wellbeing, it is not an entirely objective concept, because it assumes that demand is absolute. Population growth can add to demand, for example, for food and housing, but can also be taken account of in a relatively simple way, by producing statistics such as GDP per head, rather than total GDP. Dorling (2013, Figure 2.2) has analysed how the rise in the world's population began to slow down in the early 1970s and has continued to slow down, more or less, since then. (That is, the total population number continues to rise but the rate of annual growth shows a downward trend.) There is a fine line between seeing economic growth as inevitable and seeing it as necessary in order to maintain markets and capitalism. Perhaps it is time to differentiate, if we can, between different types of growth. This seems to be the notion behind the index of sustainable economic welfare and the identification of 'green growth'. Otherwise, we might be trapped into thinking that economies, as conventionally defined, will always recover from a downturn.

Companies seem to define progress as producing new products and services in response to consumer demand. Quite how this demand is identified before new brands, functionality or features are launched may be less clear, and for the most part the 'demand' is realised by the purchase of goods and services as they are advertised, recommended by friends or spotted in stores or online. There is a fine line here between what people want and what they need.

A further complication is the homeostatic effect discussed earlier. We quickly get used to 'better' products and services. This happens at the level of the individual: many of those reading this book will have grown up before the age of the internet, but would now find life difficult without it. And think of life before mobile phones! But it also happens at the community level, as the proportion of a population adopting a new technology gradually increases. The eminent physicist Max Planck had an elegant way of putting this community effect in the context of science, saying, 'a new scientific truth does not triumph by convincing its opponents and making them see the light, but rather because its opponents eventually die, and a new generation grows up that is familiar with it'. Individuals may not progress here, but the group does. Of course, science as a whole progresses by developing new theories which explain more empirical observations or which explain existing data better, but the meaning of that sort of 'progress' is relatively straightforward.

A corollary question is whether, once we have got used to new things, we then feel an urge to move on to further new things. Fashion would seem to be a primary example of this – though we have to be aware of the additional commercial driver here: persuading people that they need a new coat every year, even if the old one is barely used, owes little to 'progress'.

Economists can track changes in the characteristics and qualities of goods and services, using hedonic methods, but it is more difficult to do this for our 'quality time'. If we were to travel back in time – as some TV documentaries attempt to do, with participants living as our ancestors did – then it looks as if we would consider that wellbeing has improved. We can also make a personal judgement – the English actor Sir Cedric Hardwicke was born in 1893, close to the end of the reign of Queen Victoria. He was reported (Lyons, 1964) to have said that he would liked to have lived in the Victorian Age, but with penicillin. But such retrospective imaginings are fraught with difficulties: few if any technological advances exist in isolation, and most require an infrastructure. Manufacture of penicillin on a commercial scale would necessarily imply other differences. An iPad is built on a very extensive foundation of technical progress. There is also an inevitable whiggish tendency to look backwards and see changes as steps inevitably leading towards the present, rather than as a sequence of events which could have had other outcomes.

Similar caveats apply when we look forward, contemplating future progress – imagining, for example, a time when we have a cure for all cancers or more leisure time (that last being a particular sign of progress which seems to advance at the same rate as we move forward). Again we caution that such changes occur in the context of other changes, and it is not necessarily obvious that things which appear to be progressive will constitute progress when taken along with the concomitant changes of their context. In particular, it is not inevitable that they will increase human happiness and wellbeing.

Governments provide the necessary framework within which society functions – and this includes regulatory restrictions without which, for example, a free-market economy would run amok. But this also implies that they impede or moderate progress. Analogies are speed limits on roads and traffic-calming measures in built-up areas, which slow the progress of vehicles but lead to smoother running at a higher level. A more subtle example has arisen in agriculture. Agricultural intensification, monocultures, housing and tree-planting have had the effect of drastically reducing the amount of species-rich meadows and pastures in parts of Britain. Conservation groups have formed to help landowners re-introduce meadows, including through grants from public funds towards more traditional land management methods.

Progress, then, is multifaceted. But we should not underestimate the extent to which the story continues to be told purely in terms of economic wellbeing, and GDP in particular. Peston notes that the GDP model is played out with different attitudes and values between countries. Germany's 'shocking and traumatic [20th century] history persuaded the Germans that a stable economy and steadily rising prosperity are the sine qua nons of a healthy democracy' (Peston, 2012, p. 135). Peston also observes that for most people in Japan (and one might add, presumably for most people everywhere), 'it's the income they actually enjoy and the quality of the life they lead, rather than the aggregate GDP of the economy, which matters'. Drawing on the Japanese experience, he suggests that 'at the very least [this] leads us to re-examine our basic presumption that low aggregate GDP growth is necessarily a bad thing. What matters at least as much as the rate of increase in GDP is how that GDP is shared' (Peston, 2012, p. 139). Observing that China's overriding target is GDP growth, Peston concludes that China has learned that 'not all contributions to GDP growth are of the same quality', citing particularly examples of economic activity that may be doing long-term harm to the health of people and to the environment, although he concedes that Chinese people also tell him they can 'barely believe the astonishing economic progress of their lifetimes' (Peston, 2012, p. 272).

Despite two waves in which potential alternatives to GDP were proposed, as we saw in Chapters 2 and 3, the progress of a nation (perhaps bar the cases of Bhutan and Colombia) still typically comes down to economic performance, measured through system of national accounts (SNA) and headline measures in particular. But even within the narrow confines of the SNA, opinions differ on what is meant by progress. As we observed in Section 3.4, *The Economist* magazine recently commented on the 'paltry' GDP growth of Canada, referring to an annual increase of 1.6%, since this is below the long-run, post-war average for GDP growth. However, according to figures published by Statistics Canada (Baldwin and Macdonald, 2011), Canada's real GDP per head increased between 1945 and 2010 by a factor of 3.37, equivalent to an annual compound rate of increase of 1.9%. Within this 65-year period, the highest annual increase in real GDP per capita was 6.6% and the lowest annual change was a decrease of 4%. The recent figure quoted by the magazine may be lower than the long-run average, but does it really count as 'not worth considering' – which is the dictionary definition of paltry?

Looking at the bigger picture, we should perhaps also ask whether *sustainable* development is an oxymoron, a contradiction in terms, as Sir David Attenborough once suggested.

To us it seems that national wellbeing, progress and sustainable development go hand-in-hand. While progress might be judged from how wellbeing is changing, for some people the assessment of progress and sustainability is part of understanding current wellbeing.

If wellbeing is to be used as a national indicator, at the level of GDP, it will also be reported in the national news media. People seem to accept GDP (though we suspect that few readers could say how it is constructed), but the acceptance of the concept of wellbeing is often confused with the concept of happiness: formal technical definitions distinguishing between the two are all very well, but lay usage is a different matter (and in any case, some researchers regard wellbeing and happiness as interchangeable – e.g. Easterlin, 2003).

It will doubtless be some time before we reach the tipping point, when national statistical offices worldwide routinely collect, analyse and publish wellbeing data, treating it as one of the portfolio of measures of progress within societies.

8.2   Measuring wellbeing

If we are going to use wellbeing as one indicator of the state of a nation, then we need to have some way of measuring it. The lay response to the very notion that wellbeing might be measurable and indeed be measured is often one of scepticism. It is interesting to note that nowadays there is not a similar scepticism to the notion that pain, depression or anxiety can be measured, although these are in some sense complementary to wellbeing.

This scepticism seems to have two primary aspects. One is the notion of whether it makes sense to speak of a numerical scale for wellbeing. This reservation is a familiar one in the history of measurement. Even physical concepts which we would nowadays regard as clear examples of things which permit numerical measurement scales, such as temperature, often had their early battles, as people gradually refined the concept (see, for example, Chang, 2004). It took a long time, and much deep thought by generations of philosophers and scientists, before heat and temperature were separated, and even longer before energy, thermodynamics and the surrounding theories were developed. Less physical concepts have taken even longer.

The second aspect of scepticism concerns how one can actually construct a measurement scale for the concept of wellbeing. This is intimately tied in with how one defines it. The way wellbeing is measured and its very definition are two sides of the same coin. Furthermore, as we have seen, the concept of wellbeing defies a simple and straightforward unique definition, with different perspectives being suited to different uses – wellbeing is near the pragmatic end of the representational/pragmatic measurement spectrum. And as if all that was not enough, things are complicated yet further by the fact that wellbeing is intrinsically multidimensional. At least temperature has the advantage of being unidimensional!

There is also a third complication: the fact that wellbeing necessarily has subjective aspects. Until relatively recently, it was not appreciated that subjective attributes could be effectively and reliably measured, and this suspicion lingers on among those not versed in modern measurement technology. But even when one accepts that such things can be measured, there remains the question of how to combine the very different aspects of wellbeing to yield a single index. This is why many have favoured an intrinsically multidimensional approach – a dashboard or profile showing the different components of wellbeing.

The subjective aspects of wellbeing describe individuals. Some researchers regard the wellbeing of a nation as necessarily the collective aggregate of the wellbeing of individuals. This perspective certainly has some appeal: it is straightforward and relatively clear. One example was the British social reformer Sir William Beveridge (later Lord Beveridge), who was for nearly 20 years the director of the London School of Economics prior to the Second World War. The school's department of social policy still quotes him on its website homepage as saying, 'the object of government in peace and in war is not the glory of rulers or of races, but the happiness of the common man'.

National wellbeing, defined by aggregation of individual scores, has the singular merit of permitting its measurement for local areas and/or for population subgroups.

As we have seen, however, even what is meant by the wellbeing of an individual is far from agreed: regardless of the complications of how to go about the aggregation, there are different approaches to defining and measuring individual wellbeing. Different approaches have different merits, and further evaluation and development is needed, along with ways of analysing and presenting them, to be sure that they do the job(s) required of them. The OECD guidelines are helpful in making progress, both in detail and through a more general encouragement that this can be done, but they leave many questions.

Even if we take the restrictive view that national wellbeing is solely an aggregate of individual wellbeing, we have to think carefully about how that aggregation is to be achieved. A sum or average has its place, but one might argue that additional summary statistics are needed to capture other aspects – that, for example, national wellbeing also depends on how individual wellbeing is distributed, with less equal societies appearing to be less happy ones. Alternatively, some argue that individual wellbeing has to be the sole determinant of the wellbeing of the nation, and that if inequality influences individual wellbeing, then inequality is one possible *explanation* of the level of national wellbeing that we observe, not an additional *aspect* of it.

More generally still, many argue that we need a fuller picture of national wellbeing, beyond the simple aggregation of individual scores – for example, because some issues (such as natural resource sustainability) may have no impact on individuals currently measured, but do have a larger-scale national wellbeing implication. One of the 'key messages' in the Marmot review (on health inequalities in England) in 2010 (p. 15) was that 'Economic growth is not the most important measure of our country's success. The fair distribution of health, well-being and sustainability are important social goals. Tackling social inequalities in health and tackling climate change must go together'. (Again we come back to the importance of inequality, as described by Wilkinson and Pickett, 2010.) The separation of 'current' wellbeing from 'future' wellbeing also worries us, even if these are presented as components of an overall framework for national wellbeing. We do not see how we can call it 'progress' if our current wellbeing is doing more harm than good for future generations. We were not being glib when we mentioned turkeys and Christmas at the start of this book!

All of this suggests a very large 'big picture' embracing individual subjective wellbeing, sustainability, inequalities and economic progress. Although, naturally enough, some have suggested that this might be hoping for too much, nevertheless, it does seem to us that such issues need to be explored if an effective measure of the wellbeing of nations is to be developed. A broadening of the system of national accounts to include social and environmental accounts might be an answer. It would summarise the state of all the capital stocks – 'wealth' in its widest sense – available to a nation/society.

An example of recommendations in this direction is the 2012 Royal Society report, *People and the Planet*, which looked at global population changes and consumption patterns, and identified three pressing challenges: to raise the world's 1.3 billion poorest people out of extreme poverty, to urgently reduce unsustainable consumption in the most developed and the emerging economies and to slow and stabilise global population growth (not by coercive means). The report reviewed measures of progress alternative to GDP, covering objective, subjective and economic measures, and noted that, while there is a growing body of work looking at alternative measures, there is 'as yet, no consensus on a replacement for GDP, or if there should be one. What is clear is that very few measures of progress actually measure sustainability – a key element of development' (Royal Society, 2012, p. 90).

When measuring sustainability, the Royal Society saw it as important 'to measure a society's *wealth*, which means the value of its *entire* set of capital assets … *Sustainable development* means growth in (comprehensive) wealth *per capita*. Market prices are a misleading guide for valuing goods and services, and they *under-value* natural capital to such an extent that market signals encourage profligacy in its use' (Royal Society, 2012, p. 89). The Royal Society recommended that national governments should accelerate the development of comprehensive wealth measures. This should include reforms to the system of national accounts and improvement in natural asset accounting (Royal Society, 2012, p. 105).

The call to adjust GDP to reflect the use of natural capital is not new. Martin called the focus on GDP 'false accounting … a false view of our current balance sheet'. If natural capital was given some realistic non-zero value, then different business decisions are likely to ensue and be more geared to 'planetary well-being' (Martin, 2007, pp. 56–58).

The idea of identifying, restoring and maintaining natural assets is being taken up by increasing numbers of local authorities and amenity groups. Botanical and wildlife surveys help to quantify the state of the natural assets. What is proving more difficult is to value the assets, although we note this does not deter projects with aspirations to add value to local wildlife sites, for example.

Again we stress that we are not ignoring the measurement of individual wellbeing in all of this – but merely that, if a dashboard of measures of the state of a nation is to be used, then (aggregate) individual wellbeing is but one indicator on that dashboard of measures. It is just that we are not convinced that (aggregate) individual wellbeing should be *the* single or overall measure of national wellbeing.

Overall, the system of national accounts has a rigour which it is important to preserve, and which should be applied across the big picture, not just within the production boundary as defined in the SNA.

It is perhaps also worth asking to what extent is it necessary to resolve the significant conceptual uncertainties surrounding wellbeing, before actually using some such measure. Again we recall the example of temperature – where people found temperature measurement of great value long before the conceptual basis of temperature was properly understood – and the same is true in other areas. (Ancient Egyptians built the pyramids and ancient Britons built Stonehenge long before a formal representational theory of length measurement was developed.) More recently, measures of concepts such as intelligence and depression continue to undergo development and refinement – but this state of flux does not mean existing measures are not of great value. Recall Voltaire's adage that 'the best is the enemy of the good'.

8.3   New technologies, new data?

We live in a changing world. The very fact that we are contemplating extending and supplementing the standard economic measures of progress illustrates that. But it is not merely the high-level things that change. In particular, low-level data and also strategies for capturing those data are also evolving. In large part, this is driven by progress in electronic and computer technology. Increasingly, data is automatically added to a database, without requiring human effort. For example, medical prescription records, ticket purchases and travel details go into databases, which can subsequently be analysed (or 'mined') for valuable information about human behaviour and its condition. There is no practical limit to the size of such databases which can now be stored, since computer memory is so cheap. And neither does their size pose any practical restrictions on analysis (though there are often interesting inferential questions which arise when one has an overabundance of data). We are entering the world of 'big data', mentioned in Section 8.1.

The New York Times described big data as 'the tool du jour for tech-savvy' companies and city governments who have 'realized that lurking in the vast pools of unprocessed information in their networks are solutions to some of today's most pressing and convoluted problems'. Going hand-in-hand with big data is open data – access to data by all. In the United Kingdom, one example is the HM Revenue and Customs Datalab, which was launched in 2011 to allow approved academics (so not quite 'anyone') to access anonymised tax data in a secure environment for research purposes.

Such things open up interesting new possibilities for measuring wellbeing. The traditional approach of survey sampling is now not the only source of relevant data – it might be supplemented by, or even replaced by, information coming from administrative databases. In 2013, the United Kingdom's Economic and Social Research Council announced the launch of a £64 million initiative in big data, the first phase of which is a £34 million network of four research centres tasked with facilitating research projects using administrative data from government departments. The UK's *Beyond 2011* project is exploring ways in which the decennial UK census, next due to take place in 2021, might be replaced by alternative approaches, including using administrative data originally collected for other purposes.

It is clear that such alternative sources could be immensely valuable when measuring any 'national' indicator. We have repeatedly mentioned the relevance of health, education and income to the measurement of wellbeing, and the ability to extract data relating to those from existing databases covering the whole of the population can only lead to better measures.

These alternative sources of relevant data hold great promise for enhancing measures of wellbeing – though they do not help resolve the deep conceptual issues about wellbeing and its measurement discussed in this book. However, very little in life is an unqualified benefit, and big data and open data have other potential problems which we should be aware of (see, for example, Hand, 2013). Perhaps the most important of these are uncertainty and data quality issues.

Uncertainty in estimates arising from sampling fluctuation is well understood. Such sources of uncertainty have been studied for over half a century, and highly sophisticated methods for estimating and reducing that uncertainty have been developed in the context of survey samples drawn by formal probabilistic methods. Uncertainty in estimates based on administrative databases is more of an unknown. It will have various aspects, including uncertainty about coverage – because, although in principle such databases might be intended to be complete, they rarely are. Since the sample is not drawn in a random way, any deficiencies in coverage cannot be tackled by traditional statistical means. Essentially such deficiencies are likely to introduce systematic bias rather than variance into the estimates – and bias is more difficult to handle. The question is whether that bias is large enough to matter.

Coverage is one aspect of a broader issue – that of data quality. Errors creep into data in all sorts of ways, many known about (e.g. digit transposition, unfortunate rounding, misplaced decimal points, incorrect units and so on), but sometimes unexpected (such as the time when one of our printers failed to print the most significant digit of a column of numbers we had prepared for a student exercise). William Kruskal wrote that 'almost all – perhaps all – sizable collections of statistical material have prima facie strange contents' (Kruskal, 1981). Since wellbeing measures are condensation of large collections of data, we should be aware of the risks.

Administrative data will have been collected for a particular purpose, rather different from our aim of measuring wellbeing. For example, medical prescriptions are written with a view to give the patient the right medicine, not with a view to subsequently use the data as a possible input to a wellbeing measure. This can mean that the definitions are not ideal for our purposes. Is the definition of unemployment, as used for economic measurement, the same as the definition we would ideally like to use if using it as an input to a wellbeing measure?

Furthermore, administrative data definitions can change over time, for reasons completely unlinked to wellbeing. Unless such changes are allowed for, they could induce an apparent step change in wellbeing.

8.4   Beyond the economy

Economic policies are seen collectively as about re-shaping the political economy of the country, and not merely about re-distributing its proceeds. But economics *per se* is, nevertheless, very one-sided, at least for our purposes. For wellbeing, we need also to consider the environment, and, more generally, other social aspects of the human condition – the sorts of issues discussed throughout this book. One might say that it is time for society to come out of the economic shadow. In any case, new economic theories and case studies are challenging the established idea that economic growth, social progress and the environment are inevitable enemies.

It is true that, to a large extent, the fate of governments depends on the performance of the economy under their stewardship. But, even so, current indicators – GDP, for example – even fail to pick up on aspects of the economy which are relevant to national wellbeing, let alone noneconomic aspects. Economic equality is an obvious example. The need to see wealth widely shared, as well as created, is as likely to be a social priority of a neoclassical economic government as it is of a government of a more progressive or communitarian hue.

The choice of direction to take is a political one, and even in the same political movement there will be many different motives, opinions and approaches to the concept of progress and the wealth of the nation. Even with hindsight, it can be difficult to agree on whether or not wellbeing has been attained and progress made. Neoclassical economic policies in the 1980s may have reversed long-term economic decline and led to a 16-year boom in the United Kingdom between 1992 and 2008, but it is not so clear that wellbeing was advanced. Even economists disagree about whether or not Britain was able to pave its way in the world. And, again more generally, to others the sense of community has evaporated. One might ask if wealth was shared or if materialistic individualism was the driver of national 'success' – with anything being justified as long as it made money.

In the context of sustainability, Scott (2012, p. 62) argues that 'process is as important as product' in developing local indicators of wellbeing and sustainability. Recognising, as we have done in this book, that 'wellbeing is a complex human phenomenon and a political construct', she urges policymakers to generate 'a democratically derived account of wellbeing through working closely with the public and different interest and community groups', based on a wide range of evidence (Scott 2012, p. 169). But even process and product are not all that is needed. To be successful, measures must also be widely used.

In Junjie Zhang's analysis of China's economic, social and environmental positions (Zhang, 2012, p. 10), he discusses problems with its claim to be one of the first developing countries to implement a national strategy for sustainable development. Some inadequacies are due to 'universal shortcomings of the sustainable development concept'. Zhang notes that the final document of the 2012 Rio+20 Conference allows that 'any action that a country performs to improve social welfare can be counted toward sustainable development. However, the trade-offs among the economic, environmental, and social pillars are often ignored. For example, if poverty eradication through economic growth is accompanied by environmental degradation, is this development pattern sustainable? At the core of the issue is that there is no agreed-upon way to measure the overall state of sustainable development'. We might also ask how the sustainability of huge investment programmes, say to establish more urban centres with associated construction, transport and supporting infrastructure, can be assessed. Economic growth might be generated by such activities, but at what cost to the environment and to society?

The universal numeraire that is used (by economists) as a common currency is money. Lord O'Donnell has commented on this: 'At the moment we tend to regard the impact of GDP as a success measure. This is rarely a very sensible measure but it is particularly inappropriate for many public sector projects. Take the case of a policy designed to reduce prisoner re-offending. We want to do this because it will raise the wellbeing of individuals who will avoid being victims of crimes, it will raise the prisoner's wellbeing by leading him or her away from a life spent largely in prison and there are all sorts of gains in wellbeing for the families concerned. The reduced strain on the resources of the criminal justice system will raise wellbeing for many groups, not least the taxpayers who will not need to pay for so many prison places. So how should we add up all the gains? At the moment we attempt to translate them all into money and to come up with an overall figure of x% GDP as a saving and then compare this to the cost of the policy. But if we could measure each step in wellbeing units we could end up with the question "is x units of wellbeing worth y units of money?" In the end we have to find a way of answering this question if we are ever to make progress in using wellbeing as a "numeraire"' (O'Donnell, 2013).

A higher-level generalisation from simply monetary value was described by John Maynard Keynes, over 80 years ago. He saw 'the modern age' as reaching a time when 'We shall once more value ends above means and prefer the good to the useful' (Keynes, 1930/1963, p. 7).

He envisaged that time as a hundred years on from when he was writing (i.e. less than 20 years from when we are writing). By then, he said, we would have 'down-sized' (to use current jargon) with increased leisure time enhancing the quality of life for all. We have already commented that increased leisure time seems to be as far off as it ever was. Email, instead of leading to more efficient, and hence less extensive, correspondence, seems to have had the opposite effect – who, now, does not have a full email inbox? On the other hand, it is certainly true that the internet and World Wide Web has enhanced individual opportunities. Long gone are the days of shared cultural experience when we all watched the same television shows on the same nights. Likewise, in terms of products, Chris Anderson has argued in his book *The Long Tail* that modern technology means that mass sales of identical items is being replaced by sales of large numbers of individually customised goods (Anderson, 2006).

However, the bottom line is that wellbeing measures will not have an effect until governments and policy makers embrace them and incorporate them into the administrative and legislative machinery. The levers available to governments and policy makers include statutory regulation (which needs enforcement) and systems of incentives, which have also traditionally been provided through statutory provision. Latterly some governments have also been increasingly interested in 'nudging' their citizens and companies to act differently, for example, by requiring opt out from the preferred direction, rather than opting in: make it more costly to take action A than B, and people will prefer the latter.

Change will not happen overnight, nor as the result of a single, or even a succession of well-argued, reports. As architect Richard Rogers believes, and has led by example, 'To bring about change you need to campaign constantly. Demonstrations, Parliamentary speeches or the way you run your life and business could all be means at our disposal. It is equally important to campaign for the planting of a tree as for a just National Planning Policy' (Royal Academy of Arts, 2013, p. 2).

How far should governments reflect the preferences of their citizens? Even in a democracy, we tend to rely on the outcome of occasional elections, rather than through referenda or voting on specific issues. On the other hand, statistical opinion polls have long captured what the public reports are its preferences and a handful of national statistical offices have asked the public 'what matters' to them in the design of measures of national wellbeing and progress. Modern Web technology has increased the possibilities for a closer link between representatives and those they represent.

Recall the comment made by Joseph Stiglitz, in *Vanity Fair* in 2011, when he said that most US political representatives 'are members of the top 1 per cent [of society by personal wealth] when they arrive, are kept in office by money from the top 1 per cent, and know that if they serve the top 1 per cent well they will be rewarded by the top 1 per cent when they leave office' (Stiglitz, 2011). There is evidence of growing awareness of the opportunities here, with increasing engagement with academia, business and civil society. For example, Professor John Harries, Chief Scientific Adviser for Wales, says 'Social Sciences are important to many research areas and to policy-making. For example, we are placing increasing focus on behavioural research, in fields such as energy. A related area where we are very active is the better availability and application of data, to address links and causality across economic performance and social, health and environmental well-being. Research on people's attitudes to, and adoption of new energy sources and technologies is one example of social science work that can inform natural science research activity and policy-making' (Harries, 2012, p. 7). (On the other hand – two steps forward and one back – at the time of writing the UK government is currently without a chief social scientist.)

International organisations, whether working directly with national governments or more independently, are identifying the scale and the breadth of the challenge. According to its website, the OECD's mission, 'Better Policies for Better Lives', promotes 'policies that will improve the economic and social well-being of people around the world'. And to avoid thinking that the environment does not count, the OECD provides a unique forum in which governments work together to share experiences on what drives economic, social and environmental change, seeking solutions to common problems. The World Economic Forum has a similar mission, committed to 'improving the state of the world'.

Only the fullest understanding of popular sentiment – that is, of society as it is, rather than as we would wish it to be – can provide the firm basis for government. It is for these sorts of reasons that it is so important that official statistics should be produced independently of government: the measuring instrument must not be susceptible to distortion according to the desirability of the results. Even further, official statistics must also be *seen* to be independent. In a nutshell, they have to be both trustworthy and trusted. This is enshrined in the UN's Fundamental Principles for Official Statistics, and the United Kingdom has achieved it through its *Statistics Authority*, which reports directly to parliament, and not via the government.

Of course, this does not answer the question of whether such an independent but official body is sufficient for assessing national wellbeing. Many wellbeing measures are being produced outside official statistics – all with slightly different objectives and all defined in slightly different ways, as described earlier in this book. That is, we have a 'mixed economy' of public sector, academic, civic society and commercial providers all owning products relevant to measuring national wellbeing.

One consequence is that there is certainly the opportunity for confusion. After all, think how much confusion has been generated in the UK media over the various official price indices, such as RPI, CPI, RPIJ and so on, despite guidance from the Office for National Statistics. The question of how to present, or to bring, the different measures together for the benefit of citizens is a real one.

Sainsbury (2013) has argued for a better 'knowledge infrastructure' as one way of reforming capitalism, 'to achieve economic growth, liberty and social justice'. This infrastructure would facilitate growth by making the market potential of basic scientific and technological research clearer to companies, especially venture capitalists, as well as seeking to improve human capital through education and training more geared to market needs. We suggest that the knowledge infrastructure of future societies also needs to cover the production, analysis and use of better statistics on economic performance, social progress and environmental sustainability. The transparency agenda is a critical part of this. Note that integral to Sainsbury's proposals for progressive capitalism is competent and active government, standing for economic growth and the quality of people's lives (including the environment). The role of such governments should be to define and uphold the public interest, and to do this by supporting and enabling, not directing or controlling, markets and other human endeavours.

These are not easy issues and we should avoid thinking that there is a single 'right' answer to many public policy, commercial and personal decisions. The call for more evidence means bringing in more scientific evidence, including on the natural environment, and more social science evidence, covering quality of life as well as economics. Evidence can only inform decision-making. People take decisions not only on the evidence but also within the context of their political, ethical and religious values.

If we set national wellbeing at the heart of things, it will obviously need to be surrounded by the policy areas that governments, businesses, civic society and individuals can affect. Each of these areas will need suitable measures, to complement the overall measure of national wellbeing.

8.5   The future

We have almost reached the end of our book, but the story mostly starts from here. Our first overall conclusion is that it is far too early to draw definitive conclusions. There have been approaches to measuring the topic we call national wellbeing for over 40 years, counting Bache's 'first wave' – the social indicators movement – as well as the more recent, 'second wave' of the Stiglitz, Sen and Fitoussi commission and wider interest in measuring subjective wellbeing. However, we still feel a long way from a world in which looking at the wellbeing of nations will be more than looking at economic welfare, as measured by GDP, not least because for many nations it is improving economic performance that is paramount.

The second wave is still in play. The High Level Expert Group attached to the OECD that is to continue the work of the Stiglitz *et al.* commission will have a work programme reaching to 2016. There will also be many international discussions over a similar timescale to put in place successors to the Millennium Development Goals, with the aim of measuring wellbeing and sustainable development in all countries, and in support of the core aim of reducing or eliminating poverty.

It is tempting to say that the second wave is a time of experimentation, of consolidation and of placing measures on a more rigorous footing. Many measures of national wellbeing and progress have already been proposed, and we see early moves towards international standards and the sharing of good practice. But, we have not actually found a lot of real experiments, exploring which measures work best and which capture the most relevant information. There has been some evaluation of different subjective wellbeing scales, some testing of specific subjective wellbeing questions, and policy areas that should benefit from the use of subjective wellbeing measurements have also been proposed. Beyond that, however, we are not aware of efforts to assess how measures of national wellbeing and progress are being used, nor how they could be used. And this last is, after all, the ultimate aim. Without this, the entire exercise is rather pointless.

Going beyond GDP in how we assess wellbeing and progress requires a paradigm shift – for governments, businesses and individuals to switch to thinking about wellbeing and progress in terms of the kinds of areas suggested in Chapter 6, rather than just the financial bottom line, GDP and a monetary return on investment. It is not clear how such a shift will be effected: there is no real precedent. We understand that GDP and the national accounts evolved with the need to monitor and affect the economy. Until we have widespread political willingness to take the broader view, it seems to us unlikely that wider measures will gain much traction.

So our second overall conclusion is that processes to explore measures wider than GDP and, crucially, how these will be used, must continue. These processes should be as inclusive as possible. We see the prospect of a new set of development goals, to follow on from the Millennium Development Goals when they expire in 2015, as a good way to advance the measurement of wellbeing, progress and sustainable development within a coherent framework, involving all nations. It would be good to make as much use as possible of existing statistics, as the basis for new system of economic, social and environmental accounts.

At the start of Chapter 1, we listed some of the questions about the measurement of national wellbeing, so that we can all better understand how a country is doing these days, and how sustainable are its current lifestyles. We have found much work going on around the world to help us answer our questions about the meaning of national wellbeing, the motive for measuring it and how it should be measured. However, we have not found full, clear or widely accepted answers. There is much more to be done, and we do not underestimate the hurdles ahead. They are probably best tackled through incremental steps. Here are a few suggestions to start along the way:

- More joining up of GDP and wellbeing measures from national and regional statistical offices. This is needed not only in countries like the United Kingdom, where the Office for National Statistics now publishes on both fronts, but also in countries like Canada, where Statistics Canada publishes GDP while academics publish the Canadian Index of Wellbeing.

- More companies reporting on a wellbeing bottom line, not just on profits made.

- More probing of value for money. When, for example, a business leader says of a major infrastructure investment, 'The case for judging this absolutely has to be value for money. At what point does it cease to be value for money?' then we should ask whether or not this is a judgement solely on the financial cost of the investment and the financial return on that investment. Do things look different if we include the environment and social costs and benefits? 'Value' should be interpreted more broadly than the purely financial.

- Widen the System of National Accounts development programme to become a System of National Wellbeing Accounts programme, all under wing of the UN Statistics Division – working, of course, with the plethora of organisations and developers who already have a stake in all of this.

After all, if we do not come up with better measures for how countries are doing, it is difficult to see how we can understand what progress we are making, and what sort of world we are handing over to future generations.

References

Anderson C. (2006) *The Long Tail: How Endless Choice Is Creating Unlimited Demand*. Random House Business Books, London.

Anderson P., Cooper C., Layard R., Litchfield P. and Jane-Liopis E. (2012) Well-being and Global Success. Report prepared by the World Economic Forum Global Agenda Council on Health and Well-being for the World Economic Forum Annual Meeting, January 2010. World Economic Forum, Switzerland. http://www.weforum.org/reports/well-being-and-global-success (accessed 20 June 2013).

Anderson V. (1991) *Alternative Economic Indicators*. Routledge, London.

Baldwin J. and Macdonald R. (2011) Natural Resources, the Terms of Trade, and Real Income Growth in Canada: 1870 to 2010. Economic Analysis research paper series. No. 079. Statistics Canada catalogue number 11F0027M. Ottawa, Canada. Data in CANSIM Table 383-0027 at http://www5.statcan.gc.ca/cansim/home-accueil?lang=eng&p2=49&MM (accessed 14 August 2013).

Barrett R. (2013) 2011 Census Analysis, 170 Years of Industry. UK Office for National Statistics, http://www.ons.gov.uk/ons/rel/census/2011-census-analysis/170-years-of-industry/index.html (accessed 28 October 2013).

Carr N. (2010) *The Shallows: How the Internet Is Changing the Way We Think, Read and Remember*. Atlantic Books, London.

Chang H. (2004) *Inventing Temperature: Measurement and Scientific Progress*. Oxford University Press, Oxford.

Cukier K. and Mayer-Schöenberger V. (2013) *Big Data: A Revolution That Will Transform How We Live, Work and Think*. Houghton Mifflin Harcourt, New York.

Dorling D. (2013) *Population 10 Billion*. Constable, London.

Easterlin R.A. (2003) Building a better theory of well-being. Discussion Paper No. 742, Institute for the Study of Labour, Bonn.

Gordon R.J. (1999) U.S. economic growth since 1870: one big wave? *The American Economic Review*, **89**(2), 123–128.

Gordon R.J. (2012) Is U.S. Economic Growth Over? Faltering Innovation Confronts the Six Headwinds. NBER Working Paper No. 18315, http://www.nber.org/papers/w18315 (accessed 11 December 2013).

Hand D.J. (2013) Data not dogma: big data, open data, and the opportunities ahead. In Advances in Intelligent Data Analysis, XII, 12th International Symposium, LNCS 8207, Springer, Berlin, pp. 1–12.

Harries J. (2012) Strengthening Science in Wales, Momentum (Research news from Swansea University), Issue 8, December 2012, pp. 6–7.

Hutton W. (2013) Ignore the hype: Britain's 'recovery' is a fantasy that hides our weakness. http://www.guardian.co.uk/commentisfree/2013/jul/21/british-economy-still-in-bad-position (accessed 23 July 2013).

Keynes J.M. (1930/1963) Economic possibilities for our grandchildren. In: J.M. Keynes (ed.) *Essays in Persuasion* (1963 ed.). Norton & Co., New York. http://www.econ.yale.edu/smith/econ116a/keynes1.pdf (accessed 27 June 2013).

Kruskal W. (1981) Statistics in society: problems unsolved and unformulated. *Journal of the American Statistical Association*, **76**, 505–515.

Lyons L. (1964) Cedric Hardwicke Didn't Care That the Sand of Time Ran Out, Lawrence Daily Journal-World.   http://news.google.com/newspapers?nid=2199&dat=19640813&id=FocyAAAAIBAJ&sjid=G-YFAAAAIBAJ&pg=3309,3693400 (accessed 24 May 2013).

Manyika, J., Chui, M., Brown, B. *et al*. (2011) Big data: the next frontier for innovation, competition, and productivity, http://www.mckinsey.com/insights/business technology/big data the next frontier for innovation (accessed 30 December 2013).

Marmot M. (Chair) (2010) Fair Society, Healthy Lives: Strategic Review of Health Inequalities in England post-2010. The Marmot Review, University College London, London. http://www.ucl.ac.uk/whitehallII/pdf/FairSocietyHealthyLives.pdf (accessed 11 December 2013).

Martin J. (2007) *The Meaning of the 21st Century: A Vital Blueprint for Ensuring Our Future*. Riverhead Books, New York.

McMichael P. (2012) *Development and Social Change: A Global Perspective* (5th ed.) SAGE Publications, Thousand Oaks.

O'Donnell G (2013) *Inaugural Lecture: Building a Better Government*. University College, London.

Peston R. (2012) *How Do We Fix This Mess? The Economic Price of Having It All, and the Route to Lasting Prosperity*. Hodder & Stoughton, London.

Royal Academy of Arts (2013) *Richard Rogers RA, Inside Out, Gallery Guide*, Royal Academy of Arts, London.

Royal Society (2012) People and the planet. The Royal Society Science Policy Centre report 01/12, London.

Sainsbury D. (2013) *Progressive Capitalism: How to Achieve Economic Growth, Liberty and Social Justice*. Biteback Publishing, London.

Scott K. (2012) *Measuring Wellbeing: Towards Sustainability*? Routledge, Abingdon.

Shakespeare, S. (2013) Shakespeare Review: An independent review of public sector information, https://www.gov.uk/government/publications/shakespeare-review-of-public-sector-information (accessed 11 December 2013).

Silbereisen R.K. and Chen X. (2010) *Social Change and Human Development: Concept and Results*. SAGE Publications, London.

Stiglitz J.E. (2011) Of the 1%, by the 1%, for the 1%. *Vanity Fair*, May 2011, http://www.vanityfair.com/society/features/2011/05/top-one-percent-201105 (accessed 28 May 2014).

Stiglitz J.E., Sen S. and Fitoussi J-P. (2010) *Mismeasuring Our Lives: Why GDP Doesn't Add Up*. The New Press, New York.

Tainter J.A. (1988) *The Collapse of Complex Societies*. Cambridge, Cambridge University Press.

Wilkinson R. and Pickett K. (2010) *The Spirit Level: Why Equality Is Better for Everyone*. Penguin Books, London.

Zhang J. (2012) Delivering Environmentally Sustainable Economic Growth: The Case of China. On Asia Society website, http://asiasociety.org/policy/environmentally-sustainable-economic-growth-possible-china (accessed 9 May 2013).

Appendix: Sources of methods and measures of wellbeing and progress

In this appendix we provide links to:

- Cross-national measures of wellbeing and progress, such as the UN Human Development Index, OECD's Better Life Index and Gallup's World Poll;

- Cross-national developments and methodologies, including the Stiglitz, Sen and Fitoussi Commission recommendations and work coordinated by Eurostat across the European Union;

- National, regional and local measures of wellbeing and progress, either under development or in regular production.

We are sure we will not have identified every initiative! We have drawn particularly on a list of 75 'indicator projects' around the world compiled by Australian Statistician, Brian Pink, and presented at the OECD World Forum in India in 2012. The Australian Bureau of Statistics also kindly provided a list of a further 55 indicator projects within Australia, at national, state, city and community levels. This leads us to suggest that readers search out initiatives by their own national statistical office, universities and colleges, national, regional and local government and non-governmental and civil society organisations. Do please tell us about initiatives we have not included here (email to p.allin@imperial.ac.uk) or if links need updating – we accessed them all during 2013, mainly between September and December.

Cross-national measures

United Nations Development Programme, Eight Millennium Development Goals for 2015
http://www.undp.org/content/undp/en/home/mdgoverview/

The Wellbeing of Nations: Meaning, Motive and Measurement, First Edition. Paul Allin and David J. Hand.
© 2014 John Wiley & Sons, Ltd. Published 2014 by John Wiley & Sons, Ltd.

MDGInfo 2012 database published by the UN Statistics Division contains the official UN statistics used in monitoring the world's progress towards the Millennium Development Goals http://www.devinfo.org/libraries/aspx/Home.aspx

United Nations Human Development Index and Report http://hdr.undp.org/en/statistics/

World Happiness Report 2013, published by the UN's Sustainable Development Solutions Network, http://unsdsn.org/resources/publications/world-happiness-report-2013/

United Nations Children's Fund (UNICEF) report cards on the wellbeing of children in developed countries http://www.unicef-irc.org/Report-Card-11/

World Development Indicators – World Bank http://data.worldbank.org/data-catalog/world-development-indicators

Doing Business Indicators – World Bank http://www.doingbusiness.org/

Your Better Life Index – OECD http://www.oecdbetterlifeindex.org/

Gallup World Poll http://www.gallup.com/video/106357/introducing-gallup-world-poll.aspx

New Economics Foundation – Happy Planet Index http://www.neweconomics.org/projects/happy-planet-index

Legatum Prosperity Index http://www.prosperity.com/Methodology.aspx

Social Progress Index http://www.socialprogressimperative.org/data/spi/methodology

Global AgeWatch Index of the wellbeing of older people http://www.helpage.org/global-agewatch/about/about-global-agewatch/

Yale University Environmental Performance Index http://epi.yale.edu/epi2012/methodology

Global Peace Index, developed by the Institute for Economics and Peace http://economicsandpeace.org/research/iep-indices-data/global-peace-index

Many sets of common indicators for European countries are published by the European Commission, for example:

- EU Social Indicators http://ec.europa.eu/social/main.jsp?catId=756&langId=en

- The European Common Indicators initiative in the urban environment is focused on monitoring environmental sustainability at the local level http://ec.europa.eu/environment/urban/common_indicators.htm

Latinobarómetro Corporation is an NGO researching the development of democracy, the economy and society in 18 Latin American countries http://www.latinobarometro.org/latino/latinobarometro.jsp

Ibrahim Index of African Governance http://www.moibrahimfoundation.org/iiag/

Fraser Institute Index of Economic Freedom http://www.freetheworld.com/

Cross-national developments and methodologies

UN Fundamental Principles of Official Statistics http://unstats.un.org/unsd/dnss/gp/fundprinciples.aspx

Virtual Statistical System online resource https://www.virtualstatisticalsystem.org/

UN System of National Accounts http://unstats.un.org/unsd/nationalaccount/hsna.asp

See also the short guide to national accounts on ONS website http://www.ons.gov.uk/ons/guide-method/method-quality/specific/economy/national-accounts/articles/uk-national-accounts—a-short-guide-2012.pdf

UN 2012 Conference 'Happiness and Well-being: Defining a New Economic Paradigm' http://www.un.org/apps/news/story.asp?NewsID=41685

System of National Accounts 2008 revision http://unstats.un.org/unsd/nationalaccount/sna2008.asp

European System of National and Regional Accounts http://circa.europa.eu/irc/dsis/nfaccount/info/data/esa95/en/titelen.htm;   http://epp.eurostat.ec.europa.eu/statistics_explained/index.php/Update_of_the_SNA_1993_and_revision_of_ESA95

International Classification of Diseases (ICD): The current version is ICD-10. Development of the 11th revision will conclude in 2015 http://www.who.int/classifications/icd/en/

Millennium Ecosystem Assessment http://www.unep.org/maweb/en/Index.aspx

UN System of Economic and Environmental Accounts (SEEA) http://unstats.un.org/unsd/envaccounting/seea.asp

UN Sustainable Development Knowledge Platform – the Post-2015 process http://sustainabledevelopment.un.org/index.php?menu=1561

OECD Better Life Initiative, global project on measuring well-being and the progress of societies http://www.oecd.org/statistics/betterlifeinitiativemeasuringwellbeingandprogress.htm see also their 'frequently asked questions' page at http://www.oecd.org/site/progresskorea/globalproject/frequentlyaskedquestions.htm

OECD Statistics Working Papers http://www.oecd-ilibrary.org/economics/oecd-statistics-working-papers_18152031?page=1

Wikiprogress http://www.wikiprogress.org/index.php/Main_Page and Wikiprogress's ProgBlog http://theblogprogress.blogspot.co.uk/

Istanbul Declaration on measuring the progress of societies http://www.oecd.org/site/worldforum/49130123.pdf

Commission on the Measurement of Economic Performance and Social Progress http://www.stiglitz-sen-fitoussi.fr/documents/rapport_anglais.pdf

Two years after the Stiglitz-Sen-Fitoussi Report: What well-being and sustainability measures? Conference (12 October 2011) presentations at http://www.oecd.org/site/ssfc2011/

4th OECD World Forum on Statistics, Knowledge and Policy: Measuring Wellbeing for Development and Policy Making, October 2012 http://www.oecd.org/site/worldforumindia/

Busan Action Plan for Statistics (2011), to drive statistical developments in countries receiving international aid http://paris21.org/busan-action-plan

World Health Organisation Study of Quality of Life (WHOQOL) project developed a number of assessment instruments including WHOQOL-BREF for use in large research studies http://www.who.int/substance_abuse/research_tools/whoqolbref/en/

European Commission developments and methodologies include:

- Beyond GDP initiative http://www.beyond-gdp.eu/

- European Statistical System (ESS) work programme to support Beyond GDP http://epp.eurostat.ec.europa.eu/portal/page/portal/gdp_and_beyond/introduction

- First set of quality of life indicators http://epp.eurostat.ec.europa.eu/portal/page/portal/quality_life/introduction

- Europe 2020 strategy for jobs and smart, sustainable and inclusive growth, currently measured by eight headline indicators http://epp.eurostat.ec.europa.eu/portal/page/portal/europe_2020_indicators/headline_indicators

- The e-Frame Project (European Framework for Measuring Progress) is fostering the measurement debate, developing a European network and supporting national measurement initiatives http://www.eframeproject.eu/

- Policy Influence of Indicators (POINT) research project http://theblogprogress.blogspot.co.uk/

- BRAINPOol initiative, helping to bring Beyond GDP indicators into the policy world http://www.brainpoolproject.eu/

- EU Statistics on Income and Living Conditions (EU-SILC) http://epp.eurostat.ec.europa.eu/portal/page/portal/microdata/eu_silc

- European Social Survey measures attitudes, beliefs and behaviour patterns in more than thirty nations http://www.europeansocialsurvey.org/

- European Quality of Life Surveys conducted by Eurofound, the European Foundation for the Improvement of Living and Working Conditions http://www.eurofound.europa.eu/surveys/eqls/2011/index.htm

- Harmonised European Time Use Survey https://www.h2.scb.se/tus/tus/

World Database of Happiness http://worlddatabaseofhappiness.eur.nl

International Association of Research in Income and Wealth (IARIW) http://www.iariw.org/default.php

Human Development and Capability Association http://www.hd-ca.org/index.php

International Society for Quality-of-Life Studies http://www.isqols.org/

World Economic Forum is an independent, international organisation committed to improving the state of the world http://www.weforum.org

C40 Cities Climate Leadership Group is a network of world megacities committed to addressing climate change http://www.c40.org

Global Green Growth Institute aims to put green growth at the heart of economic planning in developing and emerging countries http://gggi.org/

Community Indicators Consortium's website is a resource for individuals and organizations working to improve the use of indicators for better planning, decision-making and communities' quality of life http://www.communityindicators.net/

Oxford Poverty and Human Development Initiative's purpose is to build a multidimensional economic framework for reducing poverty grounded in people's experiences and values http://www.ophi.org.uk/

GESIS, the Leibniz Institute for the Social Sciences, hosts the Social Indicators Research Centre, which is focused on monitoring well-being and general social change http://www.gesis.org/en/institute/competence-centers/social-indicators-research-centre//

John Hall's website contains many links to quality of life and social indicator research from the 1970s onwards http://surveyresearch.weebly.com/

Positive Psychology Centre at the University of Pennsylvania provides information about subjective wellbeing questionnaires http://www.ppc.sas.upenn.edu/ppquestionnaires.htm#top

British Library holdings on Social Welfare Policy http://socialwelfare.bl.uk/

Equality Trust has information and resource material on why more equal societies are happier, more stable and more successful http://www.equalitytrust.org.uk

Chris Farrell's Technology Matters website discusses what innovation does for us http://www.techmatt.com/techmatt/index.htm

Natural Capitalism, the resources and ecosystem services provided by nature, features at http://www.natcap.org

The Cambridge Trust for New Thinking in Economics promotes a number of principles, including that the pursuit of self-interest in economic behaviour can impact adversely on both society and the environment http://www.neweconomicthinking.org/index.htm

Among journals publishing papers about measuring wellbeing and progress are:

- International Journal of Wellbeing http://www.internationaljournalofwellbeing.org/index.php/ijow

- Journal of Happiness Studies http://www.springer.com/social+sciences/wellbeing+%26+quality-of-life/journal/10902

- Social Indicators Research http://www.springer.com/social+sciences/journal/11205

- Survey Research Methods https://ojs.ub.uni-konstanz.de/srm/

- Political Studies http://www.psa.ac.uk/members/membership-benefits/publications/political-studies

- Journal of European Public Policy http://www.tandfonline.com/toc/rjpp20/current

We are aware of a number of online communities with an interest in measuring national wellbeing and progress, including:

- Official Statistics Network on LinkedIn (being used at the time of writing to share experiences of building a wealth index, and of working with SEEA 2012) http://www.linkedin.com/static?key=what_is_linkedin&trk=hb_what

- National Well-being community on the Royal Statistical Society's StatsUserNet http://www.statsusernet.org.uk/StatsUserNet/Home

- Sustainability Research and Policy Network http://www.ssrn.com/srpn/index.html

- Sustainable Development Research Network http://www.sd-research.org.uk/

- Community Indicators Network http://communityindicators.blogspot.co.uk/

- Rethinking Economics Network of students, citizens and academics https://www.facebook.com/rethinkecon

- The Alliance for Useful Evidence champions the use of evidence in social policy and practice http://www.alliance4usefulevidence.org/

National, regional and local measures of wellbeing and progress

Links to the websites of all national statistical offices are held on the UN Statistics Division website at: http://unstats.un.org/unsd/methods/inter-natlinks/sd_natstat.asp. We list here some initiatives particularly about social progress, wellbeing and sustainable development, both in national statistical offices and elsewhere.

Ireland

- Measuring Ireland's Progress http://www.cso.ie/en/releasesandpublications/measuringirelandsprogress/

France

- Implementing the Stiglitz Commission Report: the French national statistical agenda summary http://www.insee.fr/en/publications-et-services/dossiers_web/stiglitz/stiglitz_agenda_anglais_080212.pdf

- Updates: Following up on the Stiglitz Report http://www.insee.fr/en/publications-et-services/default.asp?page=dossiers_web/stiglitz/performance_eco.htm

- 'France, portrait social' http://www.insee.fr/fr/publications-et-services/sommaire.asp?codesage=FPORSOC12

- Forum pour d'autres indicateurs de richesse (FAIR) http://www.idies.org/index.php?category/FAIR

Netherlands

- Life situation reports http://www.scp.nl

Belgium

- Federal sustainable development reports http://www.plan.be/publications/Publication.php?lang=en&TM=41&IS=63

Spain

- The Social Barometer of Spain http://barometrosocial.es/en/que_es_el_barometro

Nordic Countries

- Nordic Statistical Yearbook http://www.dst.dk/en/Statistik/Publikationer/VisPub.aspx?cid=016611

- Sustainable Development Indicators based on National Accounts (found on Statistics Finland's website) http://www.stat.fi/abo2004/foredrag/mulalic.pdf

- Key figures on Norwegian municipal activities http://www.ssb.no/en/offentlig-sektor/kostra

- Sustainable development indicators research in Norway http://www.ssb.no/en/forskning/energi-og-miljookonomi/baerekraftig-utvikling/sustainable-development-indicators-sdi-in-the-context-of-the-precautionary-principle

Germany

- Sustainable development indicators https://www.destatis.de/EN/FactsFigures/Indicators/SustainableDevelopmentIndicators/SustainableDevelopmentIndicators.html

Switzerland

- MONET indicator system, measuring sustainable development http://www.bfs.admin.ch/bfs/portal/en/index/themen/21.html

- Cercle indicateurs is a forum dedicated to the development and use of sustainability indicators for Swiss cities and cantons http://www.bfs.admin.ch/bfs/portal/en/index/themen/21/02/autres.html

Italy

- Territorial Indicators: system of demographic, social, environmental and economic indicators, including sustainable development http://sitis.istat.it/sitis/html/index.htm

- Equitable and Sustainable Wellbeing in Italy http://www.misuredelbenessere.it/fileadmin/upload/Report_on_Equitable_and_Sustainable_Well-being_-_11_Mar_2013_-_Summary.pdf (and the BES programme log Italian media reports of their work at http://www.misuredelbenessere.it/index.php?id=10)

- Istat household survey on aspects of daily life http://siqual.istat.it/SIQual/visualizza.do?id=0058000

Hungary

- Establishing indicators for measuring social progress in Hungary http://www.docstoc.com/docs/49809773/Establishing-Indicators-for-Measuring-Social-Progress-in-Hungary

- Indicators of sustainable development http://www.ksh.hu/apps/shop.kiadvany?p_kiadvany_id=15626

United Kingdom

- Office for National Statistics (ONS) Measuring National Wellbeing Programme http://www.ons.gov.uk/ons/guide-method/user-guidance/well-being/index.html

- ONS and Cabinet Office work on national wellbeing https://www.gov.uk/government/publications/national-wellbeing

- UK Sustainable Development Indicators http://sd.defra.gov.uk/progress/national/

- UK Parliament briefing paper on measuring national wellbeing http://www.parliament.uk/business/publications/research/briefing-papers/POST-PN-421

- Scotland Performs http://www.scotland.gov.uk/About/Performance/scotPerforms

- Scottish Health Survey http://www.healthscotland.com/understanding/population/Measuring-positive-mental-health.aspx

- Carnegie UK Trust 'Measuring What Matters' http://www.carnegieuktrust.org.uk/changing-minds/enterprise-and-society/measuring-progress,-measuring-wellbeing

- Welsh Government, Programme for Government, Environment and Sustainability http://wales.gov.uk/about/programmeforgov/environment/?lang=en

- National Survey for Wales http://wales.gov.uk/statistics-and-research/nationals-survey/?lang=en

- New Economics Foundation Centre for Well-being http://www.neweconomics.org/programmes/well-being

- New Economics Foundation 'Valuing What Matters' programme http://www.neweconomics.org/programmes/valuing-what-matters

- New Economics Foundation guide to measuring children's well-being http://www.neweconomics.org/publications/entry/a-guide-to-measuring-childrens-well-being

- Oxfam Scotland Humankind Index http://policy-practice.oxfam.org.uk/our-work/poverty-in-the-uk/humankind-index

- The Warwick-Edinburgh Mental Well-being Scale (WEMWBS) http://www.hqlo.com/content/5/1/63

- Child Poverty Map of the UK, 2012 http://www.guardian.co.uk/news/datablog/interactive/2013/feb/20/child-poverty-uk-map-2012?zoom=7&lat=52.452521107411414&lng=-4.480839843749997

- ONS Social Capital Project http://www.ons.gov.uk/ons/guide-method/user-guidance/social-capital-guide/index.html

- UK National Ecosystem Assessment http://uknea.unep-wcmc.org/

- Biodiversity Indicators in Your Pocket 2013 http://sd.defra.gov.uk/2013/11/new-biodiversity-indicators/?utm_source=email&dm_i=A78,21X84,9TKNV6,7EFPU,1

- Legatum Institute Commission on Wellbeing Policy http://www.li.com/programmes/commission-on-wellbeing-policy

- Understanding Society, the UK household longitudinal study has been tracking life satisfaction and other wellbeing measures https://www.understandingsociety.ac.uk/

- Economic and Social Research Council evidence briefings http://www.esrc.ac.uk/news-and-events/publications/evidence-briefings/index.aspx

- All Party Parliamentary Group on Wellbeing Economics http://parliamentary wellbeinggroup.org.uk/

- London School of Economics Growth Commission http://www.lse.ac.uk/researchAndExpertise/units/growthCommission/home.aspx

- Young Foundation: Measuring wellbeing, resilience and social progress at the local level http://youngfoundation.org/publications/beyond-gdp-measuring-social-progress-at-the-local-level/

- Lambeth First has produced a handbook 'Measuring Wellbeing in Lambeth' as part of its mental wellbeing programme http://www.lambethfirst.org.uk/whatwedo/mentalwellbeing/measuringwellbeing/

- Well-being Institute, University of Cambridge http://www.wellbeing.group.cam.ac.uk/

- Centre for Comparative Social Surveys, City University London, is host to the European Social Survey http://www.city.ac.uk/arts-social-sciences/sociology/research/centre-for-comparative-social-surveys

- Centre for Health and Wellbeing in Public Policy at the University of Sheffield https://www.shef.ac.uk/cwipp

- Newcastle University Institute for Social Renewal's themes include wellbeing and resilience http://www.ncl.ac.uk/socialrenewal/research/researchthemes/wellbeing/index.htm

- Imperical College London has a number of relevant research areas including the Centre for Environmental Policy http://www3.imperial.ac.uk/environmentalpolicy

- New Philanthropy Capital's measure of the well-being of young people http://www.well-beingmeasure.com/?dm_i=UL9,PP4O,461V4V,22L4U,1

- Action for Happiness is a movement for positive social change http://www.actionforhappiness.org/

- 'Breaking new ground: addressing key challenges in the measurement of national well-being', ONS/ESRC seminar 2012 http://www.ons.gov.uk/ons/guide-method/user-guidance/well-being/about-the-programme/news-and-events/ons-esrc-seminar/index.html

- The Barrett Values Centre provides metrics for leaders to measure and manage the cultures of their organisations http://www.valuescentre.com/

- BBC *Shared Planet* series and website http://www.bbc.co.uk/programmes/b02xf2qg

Israel

- Israel's Progress Index http://www.oecd.org/site/progresskorea/44096120.pdf (and home site, in Hebrew http://www.ecoeco.org.il/)

Turkey

- Sustainable development indicators http://www.turkstat.gov.tr/PreTablo.do?alt_id=1097

Palestine

- National Strategy for the Development of Official Statistics 2014–2018 http://www.pcbs.gov.ps/Portals/_Rainbow/Documents/Strategy2014-2018E.pdf

Africa

- African Conference on Measuring Well-being and Fostering the Progress of Societies http://www.oecd.org/site/devprogress/

- The African Child Policy Forum publishes reports on the wellbeing of children http://www.africanchildforum.org/site/index.php/component/docman/cat_view/68-child-wellbeing.html

- Wikiprogress Africa http://wikiprogressafrica.blogspot.fr/

India

- India Development Indicators http://cdf.ifmr.ac.in/?cdf-site=india-development-indicators and http://www.indiadevelopmentindicators.org/

China

- Hong Kong Quality of Life Index http://www.cuhk.edu.hk/ssc/qol/eng/hkqol.html

Bhutan

- Gross National Happiness http://www.tourism.gov.bt/about-bhutan/Gross-National-Happiness

Vietnam

- Vietnam Development Goals http://vdg.gso.gov.vn/

Thailand

- Societal Progress Indicators (paper on Wikiprogress) http://www.wikiprogress.org/images/SocietalProgressIndicatorsTHAILAND.pdf

- International Research Associates for Happy Societies http://www.happysociety.org/EN/index.php

South Korea

- Statistics Korea's Social Survey http://kostat.go.kr/portal/english/surveyOutlines/3/1/index.static

Philippines

- Social Weather Stations http://www.sws.org.ph/

New Zealand

- Measuring New Zealand's Progress Using a Sustainable Development Approach http://www.stats.govt.nz/browse_for_stats/environment/sustainable_development.aspx

- Quality of Life in New Zealand's Cities http://www.qualityoflifeproject.govt.nz/index.htm

- The Social Report (2010) http://socialreport.msd.govt.nz/

- MARCO (monitoring and reporting community outcomes) indicators of quality of life in the Waikato region http://www.choosingfutures.co.nz/

Australia

- Measures of Australia's Progress – Australian Bureau of Statistics (ABS) http://www.abs.gov.au/ausstats/abs@.nsf/mf/1370.0

- Australian Social Trends - ABS http://www.abs.gov.au/AUSSTATS/abs@.nsf/mf/4102.0?opendocument#from-banner=LN

- State and Territory Indicators - ABS http://www.abs.gov.au/ausstats/abs@.nsf/mf/1367.0

- National Regional Profiles - ABS http://www.ausstats.abs.gov.au/ausstats/nrpmaps.nsf/NEW+GmapPages/national+regional+profile?opendocument

- Australian Unity Wellbeing Index http://www.australianunity.com.au/about-us/Wellbeing/AUWBI and 'What makes us happy?' report http://www.deakin.edu.au/research/acqol/auwbi/survey-reports/survey-018-2-report.pdf

- Council of Australian Governments - National Agreements and performance reporting http://www.federalfinancialrelations.gov.au/content/performance_reporting.aspx

- Measuring the Economic Wellbeing of Australia's Regions – 2008 Bureau of Infrastructure, Transport and Regional Economics staff paper http://www.bitre.gov.au/publications/2009/files/ip_063.doc

- Australian National Development Index http://www.andi.org.au/

- Australian Community Indicators Network http://www.acin.net.au/

- National Growth Areas Alliance http://www.ngaa.org.au/

- MyRegion http://myregion.gov.au/

- Regional Databases - Department of Infrastructure and Regional Development http://www.bitre.gov.au/databases/regional.aspx

- Sustainability Indicators for Australia – Department of the Environment http://www.environment.gov.au/topics/sustainable-communities/measuring-sustainability/sustainability-indicators

- State of Australian Cities - Department of Infrastructure and Regional Development http://www.infrastructure.gov.au/infrastructure/pab/soac/index.aspx

- State of the Environment Reporting – Department of the Environment http://www.environment.gov.au/topics/science-and-research/state-environment-reporting

- Project to measure sustainability of Australian tourism - Institute for Sustainable Futures https://www.uts.edu.au/research-and-teaching/our-research/institute-sustainable-futures/our-research/social-change/news-12

- Global Access Partners Taskforce Report (May 2012) Progess in Society http:// www.globalaccesspartners.org/LiteratureRetrieve.aspx?ID=125567

- Western Australia, State of the Environment reporting http://www.epa.wa.gov.au/AbouttheEPA/SOE/Pages/default.aspx

- Northern Territory 2030 http://newsroom.nt.gov.au/www.newsroom.nt.gov.au/indexd4bb.html?d=5&fuseaction=viewRelease&id=4985

- South Australia's Strategic Plan Progress Report http://saplan.org.au/

- The former EasyData site has been decommissioned. This page lists a number of website on which up-to-date local level data on a range of socio-economic indicators is available: http://www.southaustralia.biz/why_south_australia/easydata

- Economic and Social Indicators - South Australian Centre for Economic Studies http://www.adelaide.edu.au/saces/economy/

- South Australia State of the Environment reports http://www.epa.sa.gov.au/environmental_info/state_of_the_environment_sa_reports

- Queensland Happiness Index (news of work in progress in 2008) http://www.couriermail.com.au/news/queensland/how-happy-are-queenslanders/story-e6freoof-1111117501726

- Towards Q2 - Tomorrow's Queensland http://www.cabinet.qld.gov.au/documents/2008/sep/toward%20q2/attachments/Towards%20Q2_%20Tomorrows%20Queensland.pdf

- Social Wellbeing Listing - Office of Economics and Statistical Research, Queensland http://www.oesr.qld.gov.au/subjects/society/social-wellbeing/index.php

- Community Indicators Queensland (CIQ) – this initiative is featured in the following link, although the CIQ website referred to there is no longer available http://www.abs.gov.au/ausstats/abs@.nsf/Lookup/by%20Subject/1370.0.00.002~2011-12~Main%20Features~Community%20indicator%20initiatives~10018

- Queensland State of the Environment http://www.ehp.qld.gov.au/state-of-the-environment/

- Gladstone and Maranoa Wellbeing Studies http://www.santos.com/Community/Detail.aspx?p=478&id=36

- New South Wales State of the Environment http://www.environment.nsw.gov.au/soe/

- NSW 2021 State Plan http://www.2021.nsw.gov.au/

- Growing Victoria Together http://www.whealth.com.au/documents/health/kwhd_growing_vic_together.pdf

- Indicators of Community Strength (State of Victoria) http://www.dpcd.vic.gov.au/home/publications-and-research/indicators-of-community-strength

- Community Indicators Victoria http://www.communityindicators.net.au/

- Victoria State of the Environment Report http://www.ces.vic.gov.au/publications-and-media-releases/state-of-environment-report

- Australian Capital Territory State of the Environment Report http://www.environmentcommissioner.act.gov.au/publications/soe

- The Canberra Plan http://www.cmd.act.gov.au/policystrategic/canberraplan

- Tasmania Together http://www.tasmaniatogether.tas.gov.au/__data/assets/pdf_file/0003/160554/111706_TasTogether_2011_final.pdf

- Tasmania State of the Environment Reports http://epa.tas.gov.au/epa/state-of-the-environment-reports

- City of Onkaparinga Community Wellbeing Monitor http://www.onkaparingacity.com/monitor/

- Wyndham City Quality Community Plan http://www.wyndham.vic.gov.au/aboutwyndham/planspolicieslocallaws/qcp

- Glenorchy City Community Plan http://www.gcc.tas.gov.au/content/upload/Community_Plan_2009_2029_199.pdf

- Yarra Ranges Community Indicators Report http://www.yarraranges.vic.gov.au/Council/About_the_Region/Community_and_Population

- Greater Dandenong Wellbeing Report http://www.communityindicators.net.au/wellbeing_reports/greater_dandenong

- Mornington Peninsula Health and Wellbeing Plan http://www.mornpen.vic.gov.au/Our_Shire/Publications_Media/Strategies_Plans_Policies/Health_Wellbeing_Plan

- Redland City Community Indicators http://www.redland.qld.gov.au/SiteCollectionDocuments/Plans_Reports/Corporate/CommunityPlan/Community%20Plan%20Indicators.pdf

- Hunter Valley Research Foundation Wellbeing Watch - scorecard and report http://hvrf.com.au/breaking-news/151-wellbeing-scorecard-and-report-released

- Waverley Council Waverley Together 2 http://www.waverley.nsw.gov.au/__data/assets/pdf_file/0014/20291/WaverleyTogether2Summary1.pdf

- Moreland City Council, Moreland community health and wellbeing http://www.moreland.vic.gov.au/health-safety-and-wellbeing/health-moreland.html

- The Brisbane Vision http://www.brisbane.qld.gov.au/about-council/governance-strategy/vision-strategy/Brisbane-Vision/index.htm

- Newcastle 2030 http://www.newcastle.nsw.gov.au/about_newcastle/Newcastle 2030

- City of Sydney Community Wellbeing Indicators http://www.cityofsydney.nsw.gov.au/learn/research-and-statistics/community-indicators

- Hurstville City Council Hurstville Snapshot http://www.hurstville.nsw.gov.au/Hurstville-Snapshot.html

- Options for a Local Government Framework for Measuring Liveability – prepared for Penrith City Council and the Australian Centre of Excellence for Local Government http:// www.acelg.org.au/downloadUpdate.php?docId=155

South Africa

- South African Development Index http://www.sairr.org.za/services/development-projects/SADI/

Brazil

- Portal ODM (Objetivos de Desenvolvimento do Milênio) http://www.portalodm.com.br/

Mexico

- Measuring the Progress of Societies – A Mexican Perspective (Midiendo el Progreso de la Sociedades – Una Perspectiva desde Mexico) http://www.midiendoelprogreso.org/english/index.html

Latin America

- Wikiprogress Latin American http://wikiprogressal.blogspot.com.au/

Canada (National)

- Well-being Measurement Act 2001(Nova Scotia) http://nslegislature.ca/legc/bills/58th_2nd/1st_read/b065.htm

- Canadian Index of Wellbeing http://uwaterloo.ca/canadian-index-wellbeing/

- Canadian Environmental Sustainability Indicators (CESI) http://www.ec.gc.ca/indicateurs-indicators/ (see also this National Round Table on the Environment and the Economy 2003 report http://neia.org/wp-content/uploads/2013/04/sustainable-development-indicators.pdf)

- Statistics Canada http://www.statcan.gc.ca/start-debut-eng.html

Canada (Regional)

- Newfoundland and Labrador Community Accounts http://nl.communityaccounts.ca/

- Genuine Progress Index for Atlantic Canada http://www.gpiatlantic.org/

- British Columbia Atlas of Wellness http://www.geog.uvic.ca/wellness/

- Alberta Measuring Up http://www.finance.alberta.ca/publications/annual_repts/govt/

USA (National)

- The State of the USA http://www.stateoftheusa.org/

- US Government Accountability Office 2011 report on key indicator systems http://www.gao.gov/new.items/d11396.pdf

- Genuine Progress Indicator http://genuineprogress.net/

- Glaser Progress Foundation Measuring Progress Program http://www. glaserfoundation.org/program_areas/measuring_progress.asp

- The Measure of America Project http://www.measureofamerica.org/

- United States Misery Index http://www.miseryindex.us/

USA (Regional)

- Jacksonville Community Council Inc. – Community Indicators http://www.jcci.org/indicators

- The Boston Indicators Project http://www.bostonindicators.org/

- King County AIMs High (Annual Indicators and Measures) http://your.kingcounty.gov/aimshigh/index.asp

- Baltimore Neighborhood Indicators Alliance http://www.bniajfi.org/

- Community Assessment Project of Santa Cruz County http://www.unitedwaysc.org/community-assessment-project

- Central Texas Sustainability Indicators Project http://www.centex-indicators.org/

- Indicators Idaho http://www.indicatorsnorthwest.org/

- Virginia Performs http://vaperforms.virginia.gov/

- Truckee Meadows Tomorrow Quality of Life Indicators http://www. truckeemeadowstomorrow.org/quality-of-life-indicators

- Orange County Community Indicators http://ocgov.com/about/infooc/facts/indicators

- Long Island Index http://www.longislandindex.org/

- Silicon Valley Index http://www.jointventure.org/index.php?option=com_content&view=article&id=157&Itemid=182

- Arizona Indicators http://arizonaindicators.org/

- Maine Development Foundation Measures of Growth in Focus http://www.mdf.org/publications.php

- Oregon Benchmarks http://benchmarks.oregon.gov/

- Sustainable Seattle Indicators http://www.sustainableseattle.org/programs/regional-indicators

- Livable Tuscon Vision Program – see http://cms3.tucsonaz.gov/files/budget/02BOOK-ES.pdf

- Maryland's Genuine Progress Indicator http://www.dnr.maryland.gov/mdgpi/

Mauritius

- First set of indicators on Quality of Life (QoL) and Sustainable Development (SD) http://statsmauritius.gov.mu/English/StatsbySubj/Pages/quality-of-life.aspx

Further reading

Finally, we are aware that there are many books, papers and other material relating to the wellbeing of nations, beyond those that we have referred to in our book. Here is a small, personal selection:

Beckett C. and Taylor H. (2010) *Human Growth and Development*. Sage Publications Ltd., London.

Campbell A. and Converse P.E. (1972) *The Human Meaning of Social Change*. Russell Sage Foundation, New York.

Coyle D. (2014) *GDP: A Brief But Affectionate History*. Princeton University Press, Princeton.

de Mello L. and Dutz D.A. (eds) (2012) *Promoting Inclusive Growth: Challenges and Policies*. OECD Publishing, Paris.

Diamond J. (2012) *The World until Yesterday: What Can We Learn from Traditional Societies?* Allen Lane, London.

Dietz R. and O'Neill D. (2013) *Enough Is Enough: Building a Sustainable Economy in a World of Finite Resources*. Routledge, Abingdon.

Fredericks S.E. (2014) *Measuring and Evaluating Sustainability: Ethics in Sustainability Indexes*. Routledge, London.

Hämäläinen T. and Michaelson J. (eds.) (2014) *Well-Being and Beyond: Broadening the Public and Policy Discourse*. Edward Elgar Publishing Ltd., Cheltenham.

Jackson T. (2009) *Prosperity without Growth: Economics for a Finite Planet*. Earthscan, London.

King S.D. (2013) *When the Money Runs Out: The End of Western Affluence*. Yale University Press, New Haven.

Lamy P. *et al.* (2013) *Now for the Long Term: The Report of the Oxford Martin Commission for Future Generations*. Oxford Martin School, The University of Oxford, Oxford. http://www.oxfordmartin.ox.ac.uk/downloads/commission/Oxford_Martin_Now_for_the_Long_Term.pdf (accessed on 15 January 2014).

Leggett J. (2014) *The Energy of Nations: Risk Blindness and the Road to Renaissance*. Routledge, London.

Lietaer B., Arnsperger C., Goerner S. and Brunnhuber S. (2012) *Money and Sustainability: The Missing Link (A Report from the Club of Rome – EU Chapter)*. Triarchy Press, Axminster.

Morozov E. (2013) *To Save Everything, Click Here: Technology, Solutionism and the Urge to Fix Problems that Don't Exist.* Allen Lane, London.

O'Donnell G., Deaton A., Durand M., Halpern D. and Layard R. (2014) *Wellbeing and Policy.* Legatum Institute, London.

Patel R. (2009) *The Value of Nothing: How to Reshape Market Society and Redefine Democracy.* Picador, New York.

Piketty T. (2014) *Capital in the Twenty-First Century (translated by Arthur Goldhammer).* Belknap Press, Cambridge, Massachusetts.

Pinker S. (2012) *The Better Angels of Our Nature: A History of Violence and Humanity.* Penguin Books, London.

Proto E. and Rustichini A. (2013) A reassessment of the relationship between GDP and life satisfaction. *PLoS One* **8**(11): e79358. http://dx.doi.org/10.1371/journal.pone.0079358 (accessed 2 December 2013).

Rosanvalion P. (2013) *The Society of Equals.* Harvard University Press, Harvard.

Sandel M.J. (2012) *What Money Can't Buy: The Moral Limits of Markets.* Penguin Books, London.

Walport M. (2013) Lecture on climate change, Centre for Science and Policy, University of Cambridge at http://www.csap.cam.ac.uk/news/article-mark-walport-csap-lecture-on-climate-change/.

Wayman E. and Stewart D. (2013) *Monitor of Engagement with the Natural Environment: The National Survey on People and the Natural Environment.* Natural England Commissioned Report NECR129 at http://publications.naturalengland.org.uk/publication/6710511932538880?category=47018 (accessed 28 May 2014).

Weber M. (1905/2012) *The Protestant Ethic and the Spirit of Capitalism.* Renaissance Classics, Provo (accessed 28 May 2014).

Index

The Wellbeing of Nations: Meaning, Motive and Measurement, First Edition. Paul Allin and David J. Hand.
© 2014 John Wiley & Sons, Ltd. Published 2014 by John Wiley & Sons, Ltd.